Migration, Diasporas and Citizenship Series

Series Editors: **Robin Cohen**, Former Director of the International Migration Institute and Professor of Development Studies, University of Oxford, UK and **Zig Layton-Henry**, Professor of Politics, University of Warwick, UK.

Editorial Board: **Rainer Baubock**, European University Institute, Italy; **James F. Hollifield**, Southern Methodist University, USA; **Jan Rath**, University of Amsterdam, The Netherlands

The Migration, Diasporas and Citizenship series covers three important aspects of the migration progress. Firstly, the determinants, dynamics and characteristics of international migration. Secondly, the continuing attachment of many contemporary migrants to their places of origin, signified by the word 'diaspora', and thirdly the attempt, by contrast, to belong and gain acceptance in places of settlement, signified by the word 'citizenship'. The series publishes work that shows engagement with and a lively appreciation of the wider social and political issues that are influenced by international migration.

Also published in Migration Studies by Palgrave Macmillan

Bridget Anderson and Isabel Shutes (*editors*)
MIGRATION AND CARE LABOUR
Theory, Policy and Politics

Rutvica Andrijasevic
MIGRATION, AGENCY AND CITIZENSHIP IN SEX TRAFFICKING

Floya Anthias and Mojca Pajnik (*editors*)
CONTESTING INTEGRATION, ENGENDERING MIGRATION
Theory and Practice

Claudine Attias-Donfut, Joanne Cook, Jaco Hoffman and Louise Waite (*editors*)
CITIZENSHIP, BELONGING AND INTERGENERATIONAL RELATIONS IN AFRICAN MIGRATION

Loretta Bass
AFRICAN IMMIGRANT FAMILIES IN ANOTHER FRANCE

Michaela Benson and Nick Osbaldiston
UNDERSTANDING LIFESTYLE MIGRATION
Theoretical Approaches to Migration and the Quest for a Better Way of Life

Grete Brochmann, Anniken Hagelund (*authors*) with – Karin Borevi, Heidi Vad Jønsson, Klaus Petersen
IMMIGRATION POLICY AND THE SCANDINAVIAN WELFARE STATE 1945–2010

Gideon Calder, Phillip Cole and Jonathan Seglow
CITIZENSHIP ACQUISITION AND NATIONAL BELONGING
Migration, Membership and the Liberal Democratic State

Michael Collyer
EMIGRATION NATIONS
Policies and Ideologies of Emigrant Engagement

Enzo Colombo and Paola Rebughini (*editors*)
CHILDREN OF IMMIGRANTS IN A GLOBALIZED WORLD
A Generational Experience

Saniye Dedeoglu
MIGRANTS, WORK AND SOCIAL INTEGRATION
Women's Labour in the Turkish Ethnic Economy

Huub Dijstelbloem and Albert Meijer (*editors*)
MIGRATION AND THE NEW TECHNOLOGICAL BORDERS OF EUROPE

Thomas Faist and Andreas Ette (*editors*)
THE EUROPEANIZATION OF NATIONAL POLICIES AND POLITICS OF IMMIGRATION
Between Autonomy and the European Union

Thomas Faist and Peter Kivisto (*editors*)
DUAL CITIZENSHIP IN GLOBAL PERSPECTIVE
From Unitary to Multiple Citizenship

Katrine Fangen, Thomas Johansson and Nils Hammarén (*editors*)
YOUNG MIGRANTS
Exclusion and Belonging in Europe

Martin Geiger and Antoine Pécoud (*editors*)
THE POLITICS OF INTERNATIONAL MIGRATION MANAGEMENT

John R. Hinnells (*editor*)
RELIGIOUS RECONSTRUCTION IN THE SOUTH ASIAN DIASPORAS
From One Generation to Another

Ronit Lentin and Elena Moreo (*editors*)
MIGRANT ACTIVISM AND INTEGRATION FROM BELOW IN IRELAND

Catrin Lundström
WHITE MIGRATIONS
Gender, Whiteness and Privilege in Transnational Migration

Ayhan Kaya
ISLAM, MIGRATION AND INTEGRATION
The Age of Securitization

Majella Kilkey, Diane Perrons, Ania Plomien
GENDER, MIGRATION AND DOMESTIC WORK
Masculinities, Male Labour and Fathering in the UK and USA

Amanda Klekowski von Koppenfels
MIGRANTS OR EXPATRIATES?
Americans in Europe

Marie Macy and Alan H. Carling
ETHNIC, RACIAL AND RELIGIOUS INEQUALITIES
The Perils of Subjectivity

George Menz and Alexander Caviedes (*editors*)
LABOUR MIGRATION IN EUROPE

Laura Morales and Marco Giugni (*editors*)
SOCIAL CAPITAL, POLITICAL PARTICIPATION AND MIGRATION IN EUROPE
Making Multicultural Democracy Work?

Eric Morier-Genoud
IMPERIAL MIGRATIONS
Colonial Communities and Diaspora in the Portuguese World

Aspasia Papadopoulou-Kourkoula
TRANSIT MIGRATION
The Missing Link Between Emigration and Settlement

Prodromos Panayiotopoulos
ETHNICITY, MIGRATION AND ENTERPRISE

Dominic Pasura
AFRICAN TRANSNATIONAL DIASPORAS
Fractured Communities and Plural Identities of Zimbabweans in Britain

Ludger Pries and Zeynep Sezgin (*editors*)
CROSS BORDER MIGRANT ORGANIZATIONS IN COMPARATIVE PERSPECTIVE

Helen Schwenken, Sabine Ruß-Sattar
NEW BORDER AND CITIZENSHIP POLITICS

Migration, Diasporas and Citizenship
Series Standing Order ISBN 978–0–230–30078–1   (hardback) and
978–0–230–30079–8   (paperback)
(*outside North America only*)

You can receive future titles in this series as they are published by placing a standing order. Please contact your bookseller or, in case of difficulty, write to us at the address below with your name and address, the title of the series and the ISBN quoted above.

Customer Services Department, Macmillan Distribution Ltd, Houndmills, Basingstoke, Hampshire RG21 6XS, England

Transnational Mobilities in Action Sport Cultures

Holly Thorpe
University of Waikato, New Zealand

palgrave
macmillan

First published 2014 by
PALGRAVE MACMILLAN

Palgrave Macmillan in the UK is an imprint of Macmillan Publishers Limited, registered in England, company number 785998, of Houndmills, Basingstoke, Hampshire RG21 6XS.

Palgrave Macmillan in the US is a division of St Martin's Press LLC, 175 Fifth Avenue, New York, NY 10010.

Palgrave Macmillan is the global academic imprint of the above companies and has companies and representatives throughout the world.

Palgrave® and Macmillan® are registered trademarks in the United States, the United Kingdom, Europe and other countries.

ISBN 978–0–230–39073–7

This book is printed on paper suitable for recycling and made from fully managed and sustained forest sources. Logging, pulping and manufacturing processes are expected to conform to the environmental regulations of the country of origin.

A catalogue record for this book is available from the British Library.

A catalog record for this book is available from the Library of Congress.

Typeset by MPS Limited, Chennai, India.

*This book is dedicated to Joyce Elaine Thorpe (1917–2013),
for her endless love, grace and inspiration.*

Contents

List of Figures

Acknowledgements

This book has had a long gestation, changing many times in shape and size. Thus, there are many individuals and organizations to thank for their contributions over the years. Firstly, for academic inspiration, support and friendship, I am particularly grateful to Professor Douglas Booth, Dr Rebecca Olive, Dr Kirsten Petrie, Dr Robert Rinehart, Dr Belinda Wheaton, and my colleagues in the Department of Sport and Leisure Studies at the University of Waikato. My conversations and collaborations with Bob, Bec, Belinda and Doug have been especially invaluable for my critical understanding of different dimensions of action sport cultures. I am also thankful for the support of the Leverhulme Trust that enabled me to spend nine months at the University of Brighton, UK, in 2010, and the New Zealand Fulbright Foundation that generously supported a six-month Fellowship at Georgetown University, Washington, D.C., in 2012. I am deeply grateful to both of these organizations for the opportunities these Fellowships provided to conduct my fieldwork and for sharing my developing ideas with new audiences. Once again, I am grateful for the patience and support of the editorial staff at Palgrave Macmillan, particularly Naomi Robinson and Richard Bouwman.

To all of those many wonderful individuals who have supported my fieldwork in various ways, thank you for helping me to make contacts and connections within and across local fields. I express my special gratitude to the many participants who so generously offered their time and shared their experiences with me. This book would not have been possible without your stories and voices that weave through every chapter.

Finally, to my incredible family who not only support my academic adventures, but also have always offered the unconditional love that has provided me with the confidence and courage to travel the world in search of new experiences and knowledge. To Kris Thorpe, my mom and best friend, thank you for sharing your passion for words and ideas, and love of action sports with me, and to Geoff and Anna Thorpe, for always being there and supporting me in every way you can. My brothers – Brook, Jack and George – never cease to provide me with fresh inspiration about the role of action sports in the lives of contemporary youth. Finally, thanks to our beautiful Carlos Tui Edward Borrero for keeping me company over the past nine months of writing this book, and José Borrero who has travelled extensively with (and without) me, and with whom I have had the pleasure of discussing and debating many of the topics in this book. As I write these words, I am filled with excitement about the journeys that lie ahead of us.

1
Introduction: Transnational Mobilities and Action Sport Cultures: Conceptual, Theoretical and Methodological Considerations

On October 14, 2012, Austrian skydiver and BASE jumper Felix Baumgartner stepped out onto a platform more than 120,000 feet from earth. After a nervous journey in which he was carried into outer space by a helium-filled balloon, Baumgartner emerges from the capsule in a white space suit covered in logos of energy drink company Red Bull, and stands on the ledge overlooking the speckled earth surface. After brief communications with his mission team located in eastern New Mexico, he then proclaims 'the whole word's watching . . . I'm going home now', before leaning into the fall. After a few moments of free-fall, Baumgartner begins to spin wildly, out of control, his body blurs. Audio from the control room is cut, leaving millions of viewers around the world perching on the edge of their seats, holding their breath in anticipation. It is only upon regaining control of the spin that the audio from Baumgartner's mission team is switched back on, and family members and viewers alike are able to sigh with relief. Landing safely on the dry desert crust, Baumgartner collapses to his knees and looks briefly to the sky, raising his fists in elation. A Red Bull helicopter arrives on cue and the cameramen come running to capture the emotional moment. Indeed, it is a moment worthy of celebration. Baumgartner set an array of world records. Not only did he become the first person to free-fall while breaking the sound barrier, he also achieved the greatest distance travelled and speed reached by a skydiver.

The jump was seven years in the making, with Red Bull's investment ultimately costing more than £9 million. The final budget was three times over the original calculation due primarily to the time required for the scientific development of the capsule. Although a highly risky marketing initiative, Baumgartner's successful jump ultimately became an incredibly valuable media asset for Red Bull. Of course, this was not by happenchance. The jump was a carefully choreographed media event with National Geographic, BBC and the Red Bull Media House detailing every second with more than 20 cameras. The event broke the record of the most watched live streaming event on YouTube with more than eight million people around the world watching the live footage. The previous record for a live online audience was the 2012 London Olympics with 500,000 concurrent streams. It is reported that 7.6 million viewers also tuned in for Discovery Channel's live coverage of the jump. Another 40 television stations showed the jump across 50 countries, with an additional 130 digital outlets. As with all Red Bull events, new media was integral to the choreography of this spectacle. Red Bull's Facebook post-jump photo of Baumgartner gained almost 216,000 likes, 10,000 comments and over 29,000 shares within 40 minutes. Further revealing the digital significance of this event, more than three million tweets were sent about the jump (Clancy, 2012), and half the worldwide trending topics on Twitter were related to the 'Red Bull Stratos' event. The night of the jump, Baumgartner tweeted: 'One small step for man, one giant step for energy drink marketing' (cited in McGiugan, 2012, para. 9).

Clearly, this is a historic media event, not only redefining the role of new media in the production and consumption of global sporting spectacles, but also the role of transnational corporations in producing such mega events. In contrast to previously comparable achievements, such as Sir Edmund Hillary and Tenzing Norgay's successful climb of Mount Everest in 1951 or Neil Armstrong's first steps on the moon in 1969, the event had very few connections to the nation or nationality. Rather than being narrated as a huge achievement for Austria – Baumgartner's home country – or the United States – where the event took place – the successful jump was largely attributed to a transnational company (Red Bull) and a transnational celebrity (Baumgartner). Arguably, this sporting spectacle raises important questions about the changing nature of sport in the 21st century, and particularly the long-standing connection between sport and national identity.

For many, the idea of the nation appears commonsensical. However, most theorists consider the nation to be a modern phenomenon, 'a product of economic, cultural and political developments that occurred over the course of the eighteenth and nineteenth centuries' (Gruneau & Whitson, 1993, p. 250; Edensor, 2002). The role of sport in the construction of the nation as 'imagined community' (Anderson, 1983) has garnered considerable academic attention from both sociologists and historians (for example, Bale, 1986; Edensor, 2002; Hunter, 2003; Jarvie, 1993; Porter & Smith, 2004; Scherer & Jackson, 2012; Tomlinson & Young, 2006). In his book, *Sport, Nationalism and Globalization*, Alan Bairner (2001) reveals both the positive and less than savoury aspects of the relationship between sport and nationalism:

> Sport does provide us with an important arena in which to celebrate national identities. It also forces us at times to consider the precise nature of our own national identity. It provides opportunities for representatives of different nations to engage with each other in honest competition and for their fans to enter into the world of carnival. [But] it is also disfigured

at times by the darker side of nationalism. Competitors cheat and are often officially encouraged to do so in order to promote athletic prowess of the nation. Fans riot in some strange attempt to conduct war by other means. (Bairner, 2001, p. 17)

He concludes by stating that whether 'benign or aggressive, the relationship between sport and nationalism is, nevertheless, inescapable' (p. 17). Since the early 1990s, a number of sport scholars have also debated processes of globalization in sport (for example, Donnelly, 1996; Houlihan, 1994; Maguire, 1994; McKay et al., 2001). In so doing, they have revealed the forces of globalization as contributing to major changes in the production and consumption of sport. However, just as global forces are influencing contemporary sport, it is important to note that sport is also playing a role in the 'intensification of global connectivity and growing social consciousness of the world as a single place' (Robertson, 1992, p. 8). Acknowledging the two-directional flow of such processes, Harvey et al. (1996) explain that while 'globalization transforms sport by inducing trends of homogenization as well as national diversity', sport also 'contributes to globalization in that it is a vehicle for global mass consumption culture' (p. 258). More recently, Giulianotti & Brownell (2012) acknowledge sport as a 'potent catalyst of globalization'. Indeed, events such as the Football World Cup and the Olympics draw 'nations, cities and social groups into transnational contact' and contribute to 'enhancing public imagining and experience of the world' (p. 203). For such global events, however, sport continues to be intimately connected to nationalism: athletes proudly represent their nations, and fans cheer primarily for their national teams and athletes. In this book, I argue that the production and consumption of contemporary action sports, such as B.A.S.E jumping, surfing, snowboarding, skateboarding, BMX, parkour and kite-surfing, differ from traditional sports in their relation to the nation and thus offer a valuable case for exploring new trends in the transnationalism of sport and physical youth culture.

Action sports and the 'global imaginary'

In *The Rise of the Global Imaginary: Political Ideologies from the French Revolution to the Global War on Terror*, Manfred Steger (2008) offers a detailed explanation of the historical transition from the dominance of the nation-state – lasting approximately from the French Revolution through to the end of World War II – to the emergence of a global society shaped by material, informational and cultural networks that transcend national boundaries. According to Steger (2008), it was only after World War II that a global imaginary really began to displace the national imaginary that had dominated social and political consciousness in the 19th century and the first half of the 20th century. Here Steger is not dismissing the nation in the latter, or global processes in the former. Rather, he uses the term 'imaginary' to reveal a shift in consciousness based on various social, economic, political and cultural factors (Kling, 2012). I see the relevance of Steger's framework for understanding differences between traditional and action sports in relation to their connection to the nation.

Many traditional sports (such as rugby, soccer, ice hockey, American football and tennis) developed during periods in which the 'national imaginary' was dominant (Andrews, 1991; Holt, 1989; Pope, 2007; Vamplew & Stoddart, 2008). In contrast, most action sports developed during the 1960s and 1970s, during a period in which, according to Steger (2008), the 'global imaginary' was emerging, and thus it is perhaps not surprising that we see quite different connections between the national and the global emerging in action sport cultures. While there are certainly similar processes of globalization that can be observed across traditional and action sports, here I argue that action sports offer a particularly insightful case for examining new trends in contemporary sport and physical youth cultural formations (also see Wheaton, 2004b, 2013).

The term 'action sports' broadly refers to a wide range of mostly individualized activities, such as BMX, kite-surfing, skateboarding, surfing and snowboarding, that differed – at least in their early phases of development – from traditional rule-bound, competitive, regulated western 'achievement' sport cultures (Booth & Thorpe, 2007; Kusz, 2007a; Wheaton, 2004a, 2010). Various categorizations have been used to describe these activities, including extreme, lifestyle and alternative sports. In this book, however, I use the term action sports, as it is the preferred term used by committed participants, many of whom resent the label 'extreme sports', which they feel was imposed upon them by transnational corporations and media conglomerates during the mid- and late 1990s (see Thorpe & Wheaton, 2011a). Many action sports gained popularity in North America and some parts of Europe during the new leisure trends of the 1960s and 1970s, and increasingly attracted alternative youth who appropriated these activities and infused them with a set of hedonistic and carefree philosophies and subcultural styles (Booth and Thorpe, 2007; Thorpe & Wheaton, 2011a; Wheaton, 2010). While each action sport has its own unique history, identity and development patterns (Wheaton, 2004a), early participants *allegedly* sought risks and thrills, touted anti-establishment and do-it-yourself philosophies, and subscribed to an 'outsider identity relative to the organized sports establishment' (Kusz, 2007b, p. 359). They saw their activities as 'different' to the traditional rule-bound, competitive, regulated western traditional institutionalized sport cultures (Beal, 1995; Humphreys, 1997; Wheaton, 2004a).

Developing during the rise of the 'global imaginary' and in a 'historically unique conjuncture' of transnational mass communications and corporate sponsors, entertainment industries, and a growing affluent and transient young population, action sports have experienced unprecedented growth both in participation and in their increased visibility across public space (see, for example, Booth & Thorpe, 2007; Rinehart, 2000; Thorpe, 2011a; Wheaton, 2004b). During the mid- and late 1990s, television agencies and corporate sponsors began to recognize the huge potential in action sports as a way to tap into the highly lucrative youth market. Mainstream companies quickly began appropriating the 'cool' images of surfers, skateboarders and snowboarders to sell products ranging from energy drinks to credit cards. The global exposure of the X Games and Gravity Games, the inclusion of action sports, such as snowboarding, BMX, mountain biking and freestyle skiing, into the Olympic Games, and the popularity of action sport video games (such as *Tony Hawk Pro Skater*) and movies (such as *Blue Crush, Dogtown and ZBoys*) helped further expose these sports to the masses. Action sport athletes increasingly appeared on mainstream television, including an array of reality shows, on the covers of magazines such as *Rolling Stone, Sports Illustrated* and *FHM*, and featured in advertisements for corporate sponsors such as Nike, Mountain Dew and American Express. As a result, action sport athletes became household names. Indeed, skateboarder Tony Hawk, surfer Kelly Slater and snowboarder Shaun White were identified as being among the top ten most popular athletes among 13–34 year olds in North America ('What is Transworld all about?', 2007).

As a result of mainstream media coverage and the inclusion of action sports into mega sporting events, many action sports experienced exponential growth between the late 1980s and the early 2000s. For example, snowboarding witnessed a 385 per cent increase in participation between 1988 and 2003, reaching an estimated 8.2 million snowboarders in the US and Canada in 2010 (Lewis, 2011a). The number of recreational surfers in the US grew by 49.4 per cent between 1987 and 2001 to an estimated 2.2 million participants. In Australia, there were more than 2.5 million recreational surfers in 2012 (note that this is more than 10 per cent of the Australian population), and according to the International Surfing Association, there are more than 35 million surfers in more than 100 countries (Aguerre, 2013). In 2008, skateboarding was identified as the fastest growing sport in the US with more than 10.1 million participants (NSGA, 2008). Since the economic recession of 2008 and 2009, however, some cultural commentators have observed a slowing in the growth rates of some action sports. For example, *Time* magazine recently suggested that snowboarding 'may have reached its peak' (Tuttle, 2013) and the *New York Times* also asked 'has snowboarding lost its edge?' (Solomon, 2013). Some studies also show a decline in the number of highly committed skateboarders in North America (Wixon, 2013). While growth rates may be slowing, many action sports remain highly popular activities with participation rates ebbing and flowing in response to broader trends in sport and leisure consumption patterns.

Young, white males continue to constitute a dominant force in the core of many action sport cultures (Atencio et al., 2009; Evers, 2010a; Kusz, 2007a,

2007b; Thorpe, 2010a). In the US, for example, approximately 65 per cent of snowboarders are male (Lewis, 2012), more than 75 per cent are 24 or younger (NSGA, 2005a), 42 per cent come from households with an income of more than US$75,000 (AMG, 2007), and approximately only 11 per cent are members of racial/ethnic minority groups (NSGA Newsletter, 2001). Similar trends are observable across other action sports. For example, 86 per cent of committed BMX participants are male; and 88 per cent of core skateboarders are under the age of 25 (SFIA, 2013). Yet these activities have increasingly attracted an influx of participants from around the world, and from different social classes and age groups, as well as females and minority groups (see Anderson 1999; Thorpe, 2009, 2010; Wheaton, 2013). Some cultural commentators have described the 'greying' of action sports such as surfing, skateboarding and snowboarding (Lewis, 2010a; Williams, 2012). In 2010, approximately 60 per cent of US snowboarders and surfers were over 25 years of age, as were 17 per cent of skateboarders (Lewis, 2010a). The female action sport demographic has also grown over the past two decades (Thorpe, 2007). In 2007, there were three million more female skateboarders in the US than in 1995 (AMG, 2007), and by 2003 women made up approximately 34.3 per cent of the US snowboarding population (NSGA, 2005b). As well as targeting the aging action sport demographic and the female niche market, many action sport companies and organizations are also employing an array of strategies to attract more minority customers and patrons (see Lewis, 2010b; Bang et al., 2010).

Recent estimates suggest there are more than 22 million Americans currently participating annually in the four most popular action sports – skateboarding, snowboarding, BMX riding and surfing – with many participating on a regular basis and engaging in an array of other action sports (AMG, 2007). For example, 33 per cent of US snowboarders also skateboard; 39 per cent of BMX riders also skateboard and 16 per cent snowboard; and 33 per cent of surfers are also avid skateboarders and 26 per cent participate in snowboarding (AMG, 2007). Unfortunately, reliable international statistics are scarce, yet similar trends have been observed in many western, and some eastern (China, Japan, South Korea) countries (see Booth & Thorpe, 2007; Thorpe, 2008a; Wheaton, 2004b, 2010). Moreover, it is important to note that participation rates do not account for the broader cultural reach of these activities. According to a recent report by Global Industry Analysts, Inc, the action sport industry, which includes media, events, clothing and equipment, continues to expand, with predictions that the global board sports industry will reach US$20.5 billion by 2017 (Global Boardsports, 2011). Indeed, the rise of transnational action sport media and corporations continues to play a significant role in the spreading of ideas, images, and styles across borders (see Chapters 2 and 3).

In contrast to many traditional sports, action sports have never been closely associated with the nation. Adopting a counter-cultural ideology, many early participants explicitly rejected nationalistic sentiments. For example, Terje Haakonsen, a snowboarder of legendary status, described snowboarding as about making 'fresh tracks and carving powder and being yourself' rather than 'nationalism and politics and big money' (cited in Lidz, 1997, p. 114). While local weather, terrain and socio-cultural factors continue to influence the experiences of action sport participants in different locations around the world, a discourse of transnationalism pervades the global action sport culture. Despite many languages and countries of origin, action sport enthusiasts overwhelmingly describe their experiences using the same jargon and express similar cultural sentiments. Many read the same magazines, watch the same videos and visit the same websites, many of which are owned by transnational corporations. Thus, it is perhaps not surprising that skateboarders in Barcelona (Spain), Auckland (New Zealand), Melbourne (Australia), Washington, D.C. (US) and Vancouver (Canada) embody similar styles of clothing and bodily deportment; surfers in Raglan (New Zealand), Byron Bay (Australia), Los Angeles (US) and Ericeira (Portugal) also sport similar fashions; and snowboarders in Banff (Canada), Wanaka (New Zealand), Saas Fee (Switzerland) and Colorado (US) wear clothing and equipment from many of the same companies, and similar hairstyles and fashions as their favourite snowboarding celebrities.

Approaching these sports from positions of privilege, many action sport participants also travel extensively – locally, nationally, internationally and virtually – in pursuit of new terrain, and social interactions and cultural connections with fellow enthusiasts. According to *Transworld Snowboarding* journalist Jennifer Sherowski (2004),

> when it comes to seeing the world, snowboarders are lucky:
> . . . we belong to a *planet-wide culture* that makes journeying to the remotest places the equivalent of visiting a pack of friends for a day of slashing it. You shred a place, you live it, you know it – you don't just buy the postcard at the airport. (p. 106; emphasis added)

Glossing over local, regional and national differences, as well as the logistical complexities and privileged nature of such travel opportunities, Sherowski (2004) continues to wax lyrical; snowboarding is a 'global culture' that 'transcends borders and language barriers' (p. 106). Such discourses of transnationalism are common in action sport media and everyday dialogue between participants, and as action sport enthusiasts continue to travel to more remote destinations, the global reach of (western) action sports is expanding. Importantly, however, individuals and groups around the world are rejecting, accepting and reappropriating these styles in local contexts, such that we are witnessing processes of both globalization *and* glocalization in operation (see Chapters 2 and 8).

In contrast to traditional sports, early action sport competitions typically celebrated self-expression, with athletes representing themselves and/or their sponsors rather than their nation of origin. However, with the institution-alization of action sports, some have been incorporated into mainstream sporting event structures that expect and/or impose national identifica-tion, thus causing some tensions for action sport participants whose trans-national sporting identity takes precedence over nationality (see Wheaton, 2004b; Thorpe & Wheaton, 2011a). For example, in my work with Belinda Wheaton, we found that many action sport participants resist the discourse of nationalism at the Olympics, seeing it as opposing the transnational friendships they have developed with their fellow competitors, and the cor-porate (rather than nation-based) 'teams' with whom they train and from whom they receive financial support. When Norwegian snowboarder Terje Haakonsen was asked to explain his highly controversial decision not to compete in the 1998 Winter Olympics, for example, his response revealed stronger identification with the global snowboarding culture, and a trans-national action sport company, than his nation:

> How can you have a sponsor for ten years and then you go to the Olympics and you can't even pack your own bags because the nation has sold you as a package? Norway is a great country to live, but it's never supported me like my sponsors. My flag should be Burton not Norway. (cited in Reed, 2005, p. 135)

More recently, action sport journalist Henning Andersen observed a 'funda-mental clash of values' at the Vancouver Winter Olympics, comparing 'the dead-serious contest of nations pitted against each other' as enforced at the Games to the 'transnational, fun concept of snowboarding' celebrated at other international action sport events (Andersen, 2010, para. 4). Similarly, New Zealand windsurfer Barbara Kendall explained that, in contrast to the other sailors who socialize solely with their national teams, the Olympic windsurfers had developed close relationships with athletes from various nationalities over the course of their careers, such that they were 'like a family' (cited in Thorpe & Wheaton, 2011b, p. 194). Indeed, while conduct-ing research at action sport events at the Winter Olympics in Vancouver and then the first European Winter X Games held in Tignes, France, a few months later, I was struck by the 'hot nationalism' (Billig, 1995) in the for-mer and the almost complete absence of any national symbols (such as flags, national anthems or banners supporting athletes from particular nations) at the latter. This juxtaposition between these two mega-sports events prompted me to further consider the broader socio-cultural and historical factors contributing to the difference between traditional and action sports in their national and transnational connections and imaginations.

In contrast to the significance of national identity in many traditional sports, the (almost) irrelevance or irreverence of nationalism in action sport cultures is striking. In this book I build upon the excellent work of Belinda Wheaton

(2004b, 2013) and other action sport and youth cultural scholars to examine how transnational action sport companies and media, the international travel patterns of action sport participants, and the high usage of virtual and social media among enthusiasts, are contributing to the increasingly global scope and scale of the transnational connections operating within and across action sport communities. Emerging during the 'rise of the global imaginary', action sports prompt new questions about transnational flows in sport and physical youth culture in the 21st century. To understand the transnational complexities of action sports in global and local contexts, I draw much inspiration from recent academic developments in the fields of transnationalism and mobilities studies.

Understanding transnationalism

Transnationalism broadly refers to 'multiple ties and interactions linking people or institutions across the borders of nation-states' (Vertovec, 1999, p. 447). Transnationalism is not a new phenomenon, yet it has been argued that technological developments (especially telecommunications) have contributed to the intensification of systems of ties, interactions, exchange and mobility, such that they are spreading throughout the world with increasing speed and efficacy (Vertovec, 1999). According to transnational theorist Ulf Hannerz (1992), 'it must now be more difficult than ever, or at least more unreasonable, to see the world . . . as a cultural mosaic, of separate pieces with hard, well-defined edges. Cultural interconnections increasingly reach across the world' (cited in Crang et al., 2003, p. 439). Indeed, it is now widely accepted that 'social and cultural processes regularly exceed the boundaries of individual nation states, sketching "transnational" cartographies of cultural circulation, identification and action' (Crang et al., 2003, p. 439). In their efforts to understand and explain such global developments, scholars from various disciplines have drawn upon an array of theories, concepts and methods to examine the different social, economic and political characteristics of transnationalism. The result, however, has been 'much conceptual muddling' (Vertovec, 1999, p. 448). Attempting to 'disentangle' the term, Vertovec (1999) identifies six interrelated conceptual premises of work concerned with transnationalism. These include studies of transnationalism as social morphology (or social formations and networks spanning borders), as a type of consciousness, as a mode of cultural reproduction, as an avenue of capital, as a site of political engagement, and as a (re)construction of 'place' or locality.

Transnationalism as social morphology broadly refers to 'social formations spanning borders' (Vertovec, 1999, p. 5). Drawing upon Manuel Castells' (1996, 1997, 1998) analysis of the current Information Age, Vertovec (1999) explains that 'dense and highly active networks spanning vast spaces are transforming many kinds of social, cultural, economic and political relationships' (p. 5). Continuing, he describes 'transnational communities' increasingly being sustained by 'a range of modes of social organization, mobility and communication', and discusses the significance of new technology for connecting complex systems of 'nodes and hubs' (Vertovec, 1999, p. 5). In contrast to traditional understandings of migration as 'a single, discrete event involving movement from one geographically and socially bounded locality to another', scholars are increasingly examining migrants' experiences within transnational communities that 'embody and exchange concerns, relationships, resources and needs immersed in multiple settings' (Gold, 2000, p. 73). In this book I critically examine action sport cultures as transnational communities that maintain links in multiple settings and 'build synthetic networks and outlooks' (Gold, 2000, p. 74). Another related term is 'transnational imaginary' which refers to the 'cognitive sensibility' held by individuals who feel a sense of belonging to groups beyond national borders. In other words, the transnational imagination is a shared outlook, or 'a mode of perception that frames local circumstances within a global historical trajectory and shapes collective desires and actions as a result' (Prestholdt, 2012, p. 509). A transnational imaginary has certainly developed among action sport participants around the world as a result of travel patterns, the marketing efforts of action sport companies, media coverage of global events and celebrities, and the active use of new media by various groups to facilitate inter-social linkages.

Transnationalism as a 'type of consciousness' refers to the dual or multiple identifications experienced by migrants and travellers. Cultural Studies scholars, in particular, have examined the global diasporas of dispersed ethnic groups who demonstrate an 'awareness of de-centered attachments' that contributes to a 'common consciousness or bundle of experiences which bind many people into social forms or networks' (Vertovec, 2009, p. 6). In the words of Vertovec (2009), the 'awareness of multi-locality stimulates the desire to connect oneself to others, both "here" and "there" who share the same "routes" and "roots"' (p. 6). Due to the ethnic understandings implicit in the term diaspora, I do not use this concept in relation to action sport cultures, which continue to be dominated by white, privileged youth. However, many action sport migrants who have dedicated many years to pursuing careers in the transnational action sport industry and working and playing across borders, do develop 'dual or multiple identifications' with the places in which they work and the people they meet during their travels. Many frequent action sport travellers also experience new negotiations of space, place, identity and subjectivity as a result of their highly mobile lifestyles (see Chapter 6).

As Vertovec (2009) and many others have observed, contemporary youth are increasingly exposed to global media and communications that are contributing to the 'flow of cultural phenomena and the transformation of identity' (p. 7). Thus, for many transnational youth their 'primary socialization' is taking place 'within the cross-currents of differing cultural fields', such that they are 'often self-consciously' selecting, syncretizing and elaborating on styles and everyday practices from multiple places (p. 7). Arguably, the styles and fashions of action sport enthusiasts offer a good example of the transnational imagination leading to processes of 'cultural interpretation and blending', or what Vertovec (2009) refers to as the 'production of hybrid cultural phenomena' (p. 7). For example, skateboarders in Tokyo may draw inspiration from videos and magazines covering local skaters in New York, Montreal or Berlin, as well as broader popular and music culture (such as hip hop and/or punk); and kite-surfers in New Zealand may take cues from the personal styles, technological developments and manoeuvres popular among surfers, windsurfers, skateboarders and/or wakeboarders in the US, Australia and/or Europe, combining these to create their own unique, hybrid identity.

The subject of transnationalism as 'avenue of capital' has garnered considerably the most academic attention. Indeed, economists, sociologists and geographers are investigating the role of transnational corporations (TNCs) – 'globe-spanning structures or networks that are presumed to have largely jettisoned their national origins' (Vertovec, 2009, p. 8) – in processes of globalization (Castells, 1996). Reflecting these broader trends, over the past two decades, an array of action sport companies (such as Quiksilver, Billabong, RipCurl, Burton and Volcom) have developed into TNCs such that their systems of supply, production, marketing, investment, information transfer and management are creating paths which define many flows within contemporary action sport cultures (see Chapter 2).

Another key feature of transnationalism is as a 'site of political engagement'. As Ulrich Beck (1998) observed, '[T]here is a new dialectic of global and local questions which do not fit into national politics' and 'only in a transnational framework can they be properly posed, debated and resolved' (p. 29). While local and national politics are still significant in most parts of the world, 'a considerable amount of political activity is now undertaken transnationally' (Vertovec, 2009, p. 10). Since the mid- and late 1990s, action sport participants have established non-profit organizations and movements relating to an array of social issues, including health, education, the environment and anti-violence. While the majority of these organizations are grounded in particular locations, they creatively employ global media and communication to tap into transnational action sport networks, with many also gaining support from action sport-related TNCs who are responding to consumer expectations for greater corporate philanthropy (see Chapter 9).

The final feature of transnationalism identified by Vertovec (2009) is the '(re)construction of place or locality'. According to geographers and migration and tourism scholars, people engaging in transnational 'social fields', either through physical or imaginative travel, and/or participating in 'microelectronic transnationalism' through the Internet and various forms of social media, may be developing new relations with space. Vertovec

(2009) draws upon the work of Appadurai (1995) to explain that, as a result of transnationalism, many people 'face increasing difficulties of relating to, or indeed producing, "locality" (as a structure of feeling, a property of life and an ideology of situated community)' (p. 12). Interestingly, many action sport migrants who have spent many years working between the hemispheres describe experiencing socio-psychological difficulties when they try to 'settle' into a less mobile lifestyle. Yet action sport enthusiasts who continue to pursue their passion for the snow, surf or trails across international borders often proclaim that they find 'belonging in movement' and thus are renegotiating understandings of 'home', place and self through the process of transnationalism, and often in highly mobile places (see Chapters 5 and 6).

With so many different interpretations and applications of the term, it is easy to see how work in transnationalism has led to some 'conceptual muddling'. But for Vertovec (2009), 'transnationalism' provides a 'umbrella concept for some of the most globally transformative processes and developments of our time', and the 'multi-vocality' of the term may 'actually prove to be advantageous' (p. 459). Similarly, Portes (1997) suggests the concept of transnationalism

> may actually perform double duty as part of the theoretical arsenal with which we approach the world system structures, but also as an element in a less developed enterprise, namely the analysis of the everyday networks and patterns of social relationships that emerge in and around those structures. (p. 3)

Yet very few studies of transnationalism have succeeded in revealing both the macro structural features of transnationalism *and* the everyday lived experiences at the local level. Rather, to date, most studies have focused on one, or a select few, of the key dimensions of transnationalism. For practical and analytical purposes, this is understandable. However, such compartmentalization too often artificially separates the macro and micro, and the structural and the agentic, features of this complex phenomenon. Both the global and the local are 'bound together through a dynamic, irreversible relationship, as huge flows of resources are drawn into and move backwards and forwards between the two' (Urry, 2003, p. 15). Setting out to understand the 'transnational imagination' currently operating within contemporary action sport cultures, I realized that each dimension of transnationalism is intimately interconnected to the others, and that the global and local cannot be neatly separated. Thus, in this book, I seek to offer a more holistic understanding of the multiple and dynamic dimensions of transnationalism as they are occurring within contemporary action sport cultures, and how these practices and processes are being experienced and negotiated at both macro and micro scales, and in both global and local contexts. As well as drawing inspiration from the work of transnational scholars such as Vertovec (2009), Castells (1996) and Steger (2008), I also see much potential in what has been termed the 'mobilities paradigm' for examining the movement of people, ideas and objects across borders.

The mobilities turn

According to Rojek & Urry (1997), 'a major reason for the actual and meta-phorical significance of mobility' in the social sciences is because 'cultures travel as well as people' (p. 11). Continuing, they explain that 'knowing a culture involves work, of memory, interpretation and reconstruction', and 'almost always involves travel' (p. 12). In their efforts to 'know' cultures and social groups in the early 21st century, anthropologists, sociologists and human geographers are critically engaging with an array of theoretical approaches to explain some of the profound changes in travel, mobility, migration, flow and displacement. Of particular relevance for this study of action sport social networks, communication across borders, travel, tourism and migration experiences is the recent 'sociology of mobilities' paradigm largely championed by John Urry (2000a):

> Some of the diverse mobilities that are materially transforming the 'social as society' into the 'social as mobility' include imaginative travel, move-ments of images and information, virtual travel, object travel and corpo-real travel. The consequence of such diverse mobilities is to produce what Beck terms the growth of 'inner mobility' for which coming and going, being both here and there at the same time, has become much more globally normal. (p. 185)

According to Urry (2000a), various global 'networks and flows' are 'criss-crossing societal borders in new temporal-spatial patterns' such that 'a novel agenda for sociology' concerned with 'the diverse mobilities of peoples, objects, images, information' and of the 'complex interdepend-encies between, and social consequences of, these diverse mobilities' is required (p. 185). With Büscher, Urry identifies five interdependent 'mobilities' that they believe are producing 'social life organized across distance'; these include: 1) corporeal travel of 'people for work, leisure, family life, pleasure, migration and escape'; 2) physical movement of 'objects to producers, consumers and retailers, and the sending and receiv-ing of presents and souvenirs'; 3) imaginative travel via conversations and consumption of various media; 4) virtual travel in electronic spaces; and 5) communicative travel through 'person-to-person contact via embodied conduct, messages, texts, letters, telegraph, telephone, fax and mobile' (Büscher & Urry, 2009, pp. 101–2). Again, for practical purposes, many mobilities scholars focus their projects on one of these separate mobilities. Yet the mobilities paradigm emphasizes the complex interactions between them and calls for new approaches that can help reveal these interconnections. For Urry (2008), the mobilities paradigm is 'not simply a useful corrective to static notions of social life but is itself transformative of social science' (p. xiv). The 'sociology of mobilities' broadly refers to the project of establishing a 'movement driven social science' in which 'potential movement and blocked movement, as well as voluntary/temporary immobilities, practices of dwelling and "nomadic" place-making are all viewed as constitutive of economic, social and political relations' (Büscher et al., 2011, p. 4). Büscher & Urry (2009) argue that the mobilities paradigm is 'transformative of social science, authorising an alternative theoretical and methodological landscape' (p. 100). Such claims of theoretical revolution, however, appear somewhat premature. Arguably, the mobilities paradigm has yet to provide the proclaimed 'step change in critical social theory' (Büscher et al., 2011, p. 14). According to Favell (2001), despite offering 'a spectacularly ambitious, manifesto-like statement about the demise and rebirth of the discipline', Urry too often 'endorses the deeply mistaken idea that doing social theory is in fact a search for new metaphors' (p. 394). 'Time and again,' Favell (2001) continues to proclaim, 'insightful reflection turns into rhetorical hyperbole, beyond the recall of any operationalizable study' (p. 394). Interestingly, Favell (2001) is equally concerned by the 'top heavy' use of theory in writing on globalization and transnationalism, much of which is 'unable really to operationalize the vast empirical challenges to which such speculation leads' (p. 390). Admittedly, for some time I have been intrigued by the concepts and metaphors (for example, networks, fluids, cyber-spaces, hologram) adapted by Urry and his colleagues. But attempting to use these concepts to help make meaning of the nuances within my empirical data, I came to understand what Favell (2001) refers to as the 'sobering effect' of putting into practice some of the ideas from 'uncontrolled theorizing' (p. 392). While the mobilities paradigm is valuable for thinking about the intersections and the organization of 'networks, mobilities and horizontal fluidities' (Urry, 2000b, p. 3), I found the proposed concepts (which together do not offer a coherent theoretical perspective) to struggle under the weight of the empirical.

Despite theoretical limitations, the new mobilities paradigm continues to gain popularity with research spanning the areas of 'corporeal movement, transportation and communications infrastructures, capitalist spatial restructuring, migration and immigration, citizenship and transnationalism, and tourism and travel' (Hannan et al., 2006, pp. 9–10). The scope of the mobilities paradigm is as broad as studies of transnationalism, and the two fields encompass some similar terrain, including 'an interest in the embodied politics of mobility and immobility, networks and other connections between and within places of origin and settlement', and 'the ways in which migrant mobilities are shaped by, and themselves shape, cultural politics, practices and representations' (Blunt, 2007, p. 8). There are clearly strengths and limitations in studies of transnationalism and the mobilities paradigm, as well as many areas of overlap. In this book I critically engage with recent literature in both fields to inform my analysis of the transnational forces, connections and mobilities within action sport cultures. Before I outline the approach adopted in this project, however, it is first necessary to consider some of the key criticisms levelled at transnational and mobilities studies which inform the structure and focus of this book.

Critiques of transnationalism and mobilities studies

An important challenge in contemporary theorization of transnationalism, and much mobilities scholarship, is 'the question of the appropriate level of analysis and the connection between the scales' (Vertovec, 1999, p. 456). Many studies of globalization and transnationalism have focused upon macro, structural changes, and particularly economic forces that are contributing to new flows of people, objects, resources and ideas. Yet, the effects of these processes on the lives and bodies of people, and their individual and collective acts of agency, negotiation and resistance in local contexts, tend to be empirically revealed in separate projects. Often those focusing on the lived experiences of transnationalism and migration offer only brief analyses of the broader social, cultural and economic structures that enable and constrain such mobilities. Put simply, focusing on either the macro or micro components of transnationalism and mobility can offer only limited understandings of such multidimensional phenomena. As Harney & Baldassar (2007) explain:

> While many researchers use the concept of transnationalism to name or analyse processes, patterns and relations that connect people or projects in different places in the world, its macroscalar associations do have their interpretive limits, obscuring and eliding different scales, networks and manifestations of connections, which, as a result, diminish its clarity as a conceptual tool. (p. 190)

D'Andrea et al. (2011) identify a similar situation in the mobilities paradigm, proclaiming that

> clear-cut micro-macro distinctions are misleading, for, as subjects and objects move across spatial, social and cultural settings, they are not doing so independently of the political and economic structures that shape subjectivity, locality and mobility, but are actually embodying, recoding and updating larger material and symbolic regimes. (p. 158)

For Vertovec (2009), questions of scale are some of the more pressing concerns in studies of transnationalism: 'What are the proper or best scales (such as global/national/urban/local) or levels of analysis (micro-, meso-, micro-) to focus upon in order to gauge processes, their development and their impacts? How can we best conceive of relations between scales and levels?' (p. 20). I concur with D'Andrea and colleagues (2011) who attempt to respond to such concerns by calling for 'a critical reorientation that interfaces experiential and structural dimensions of mobility, while methodologically demonstrating how they are interlinked and how they can be systematically explained' (p. 157). Continuing, they proclaim the need for a 'systematic unbundling and formalization of research protocols, methods and analyses that can integrate macro and micro components, rather than allowing these to continue developing separately' (D'Andrea et al., 2011, p. 156). In contrast to many globalization scholars and those working in the new mobilities paradigm, D'Andrea and colleagues do not proclaim the need for 'new' theories and methods to meet such challenges, but rather see the potential in existing theoretical frameworks, such as Pierre Bourdieu's theory of practice and the later works of Michel Foucault, for revealing how 'structures of power intermingle with processes of subjectivity and identity formation' (p. 157).

The theoretical and methodological approach adopted in this book is a response to recent concerns about the scope and scale of transnationalism and mobilities studies, and the relationship between theory and the empirical. Adopting a multi-method, multi-sited ethnographic approach, it offers an empirically informed account of the pluralism and diversity of the lived experiences of mobilities within contemporary action sport cultures that is informed by a structural analysis of transnational economic, social and cultural processes operating within and across diverse geographical settings. The chapters are broadly organized from the macro, structural features of transnationalism to the everyday lived experiences of individuals and groups in local places, including individuals' and groups' (re)negotiations of subjectivity, identity and belonging, and various forms of politics. Despite the broad macro to micro framework of this book, examples of agency and resistance are evident in the early chapters, just as the power of economic, social and cultural structures and institutions are implicated in the later chapters. In so doing, this book responds to critics who are doubtful whether studies of transnationalism and mobilities are capable of overcoming some of the dualisms that continue to plague much contemporary scholarship, particularly the false dichotomies between structure and agency, the macro and the micro, and the global and the local.

To recognize the 'exceptional levels of global interdependence' and the 'fluidity and malleability' of contemporary social phenomena, 'more mobile theorizing' and greater 'academic mobility' across disciplinary borders is necessary (Urry, 2000a, p. 186). Urry (2000b) encourages the embrace of 'academic mobility across disciplinary borders' because it has the potential to generate 'creative marginality'; 'moving from the centre to the periphery' of one's discipline and then crossing its borders can help scholars 'to produce new productive hybridities in the social sciences' (p. 210). With the aim of developing a more multidimensional understanding of the transnational social formations and mobilities within action sport cultures, I engaged in 'academic migration' across disciplinary borders (that is, youth cultural studies, social and cultural geography, tourism studies, migration studies, and sociology of sport and physical culture), with some chapters drawing more strongly upon some fields than others.

Social theory has always been integral to my research on action sports and physical youth culture (Thorpe, 2011a). However, through the journey of working on this book, I have come to recognize the difficulty of theorizing contemporary global complexities and transnational social formations. In the words of Urry (2003), 'global ordering is so immensely complicated that it cannot be "known" through a single concept or set of processes' (p. 16). While many of the concepts proffered by Urry and others to explain such complexities, such as flows, networks, nodes and scapes, are valuable thinking tools, I found them lacking when I attempted to use them as heuristic devices in dialogue with my highly nuanced, and often contradictory, empirical data. Moreover, these concepts do not offer a coherent analysis of the workings of power. Indeed, I concur with Bærenholdt (2013) who writes, when dealing with issues of power, hegemony and social order, 'mobilities studies are rather vague' (p. 22). Although I was unwilling to settle upon the highly abstracted concepts offered by the mobilities paradigm, I was equally cautious of attempts by some globalization and transnationalism scholars to develop new single overarching theories and frameworks of contemporary social formations. Hannerz (1996), for example, proclaimed:

> If classical social theory was premised on the emerging national-industrial society of the nineteenth and early twentieth centuries, then a renewal of social theory should take as its starting point the global transformation occurring at the dawn of the twenty-first century. (cited in Vertovec, 2009, p. 22)

In the third volume of his magnum opus, *The Sources of Social Power*, however, Mann (2012) expresses his concern over the tendency among many of his peers to embrace the hottest new trends in social theory, describing such social theoretical excesses as 'globaloney'. Favell (2001) also encourages a 'sceptical eye at works on globalization, with their "new" theories for this "new" world' (p. 390).

Thus, rather than grasping for the hottest new theory, I take a cue from Vertovec (2009) who proposes that 'borrowing' conceptual tools from parallel fields 'might provide insights and help to better structure ongoing research, analysis and theory' concerning transnational social formations (p. 32).

Beyond the process of 'conceptual borrowing', however, I seek to work with and extend concepts from a diverse set of literatures to help make meaning of the nuances and complexities within action sport cultures, and the multiple forms of power operating within and across local and global settings. As well as working closely with scholarship in transnationalism and the mobilities paradigm, I selectively draw upon concepts from the fields of sociology, migration studies, tourism studies, cultural and urban geography, history and cultural memory studies, and media and cultural studies. I engage the work of an array of theorists such as Marx, Bourdieu, Foucault and Lefebvre, in dialogue with my empirical evidence. In so doing, I found value in existing theoretical frameworks for helping 'bridge micro and macro components' in my analysis of the complexities of transnationalism and mobilities within and across contemporary action sport cultures (D'Andrea et al. 2011, p. 157). In each chapter, I employ a theoretical perspective and an array of concepts (ranging from network capital, habitus, governmentality to arrhythmia) from commensurate paradigms that are specific to the research questions being posed. While some theoretical concepts are specific to particular chapters, key sociological themes, such as power, structure, agency, politics, the body and space, are woven throughout the book. Of course, it is the application of these concepts and themes in the shaping and 'gathering and analysis of empirical and ethnographic data' that defines their usefulness (Vertovec, 2009, p. 52).

Methods for movement: transnational ethnography

Understanding the diverse, dynamic and multidimensional mobilities operating within and across local spaces requires a 'methodological framework sensitive to complexity' (D'Andrea et al., 2011, p. 158). Some have argued that new methods are needed for understanding transnational social formations and mobilities. For example, Law & Urry (2004) argue that existing methods of research in the social sciences and humanities deal poorly 'with the fleeting . . . with the distributed . . . with the multiple . . . with the non-causal, the chaotic, the complex' (p. 403). In response to such concerns, Büscher and colleagues propose new 'mobile methods' as the potential way forward (Büscher et al., 2011). Others are more hesitant to begin 'ditching the methodological skills' that have been 'so painfully accumulated' and refined over many years, but rather see the value of creatively working with existing methods for new purposes (Latham, 2003, p. 2000). Continuing, Latham (2003) suggests that, when 'pushed in the appropriate direction there is no reason why these methods cannot be made to dance a little' (p. 2000). Similarly, Haldrup (2011) argues:

> As new forms of corporeal, physical, imaginative, virtual and communicative travel (re)configure social and material worlds, researchers in social

and cultural studies have to rethink how to engage in, capture, notate, analyse and (re)present the spatio-temporal rhythms that choreograph leisure and everyday mobilities. . . . 'the mobility turn' may benefit from the rich and heterogeneous heritage of methods and approaches for capturing mobilities in relation to commuting, everyday life, migration and so forth already developed in anthropology, sociology and human geography. (p. 54)

With Latham (2003) and Haldrup (2011), I see the potential in making our existing methods (such as interviews, participant observations, media analysis) 'dance' a little more. I take inspiration from both Michael Burawoy and colleagues' suggestions for global ethnography, and John Urry and colleagues' proposal for mobile methods, to adapt existing methods such that they became 'flexible enough to link everyday life to transnational flows of population, discourse, commodities and power' (Burawoy, 2000, p. ix). It is perhaps less the flexibility of the methods, however, that influences their usefulness, and more the creativity, adaptability and reflexivity of the researcher.

In my efforts to understand the complexities of transnational mobilities in action sport cultures, I developed a methodological approach that was sensitive to 'the nature, centrality and interconnectedness among mobility forms' (D'Andrea et al. 2011, p. 154). Throughout this project, the multidimensionality of mobility was also entwined with my own 'relative positionality before, during and after empirical research' (D'Andrea et. al, 2011, p. 154–5). While the formal data-gathering for this book took place in eleven countries (Australia, Canada, France, Italy, New Zealand, Portugal, Puerto Rico, Spain, Switzerland, Tahiti and the United States) over nine years (2004–2013), the final product is the result of a lifetime of experiences, memories and observations within and across a wide array of action sport cultures both in my 'home' country and around the world. Thus, before I offer a detailed discussion of the ethnography I undertook with the aim of 'eliciting embodiments, affects, practices, meanings, institutions and structures of mobility' (D'Andrea et al., 2011, p. 155) in action sport cultures, I first provide a little background to this study.

I grew up in a small beach town on the east coast of the North Island of New Zealand. My parents were passionate windsurfers, many of my cousins and childhood friends were avid skateboarders and surfers, and I dabbled in each of these sports during my youth before finding snowboarding during my late teens and early twenties. I then proceeded to dedicate the next six years to developing my skills on the snow and became immersed in the snow sport culture. I spent eight consecutive winters working and competing between the Northern and Southern hemispheres, including three winters working as an instructor at a ski resort in Oregon, and then returning to New Zealand to pursue both my studies and a fledgling career as a semi-professional competitive snowboarder. During this period, I also worked as a waitress, a server in Burger King, and for a student exchange visa program to help fund my journeys. I hitchhiked when I couldn't afford a bus ticket from my university town to the mountains, and slept in crowded backpackers' accommodations or on the couches of friends when they generously allowed me to stay for a night or two. During this time, I lived, worked, trained, competed, travelled and socialized with action sport participants of various nationalities across an array of sports. Despite coming from diverse backgrounds and countries of origin, we seemed to 'share a discourse, a kind of global discourse' (Hendry, 2003, p. 499). I was fascinated by the extent to which action sport participants seemed to form a global network, and how these connections were being experienced in and across different locations. As a seasonal 'lifestyle migrant' (Knowles, 2005) chasing the winter between hemispheres, I was embedded in the 'time-space rhythms' and global processes of snow sport culture (Burawoy, 2000, p. 4). But my knowledge and understanding of transnational cultural flows was initially tacit rather than clearly articulated or theoretical. Thus, driven by an innate sense of curiosity in my immediate world, I set out to gain a deeper understanding of the global–local nexus in action sport cultures via a multi-sited global ethnographic study.

Mobile methods

Most traditional ethnographies of physical youth cultures have focused on a particular site in one moment in time (for example, the punk scene in London during the 1970s; a local skateboarding subculture in Southern California in the early 1990s). However, in light of fundamental trans-formations of space, place and time, anthropologists and sociologists are increasingly calling into question traditionally defined ethnography – as an 'intensively-focused-upon single site of ethnographic observation and participation' (Marcus, 1995, p. 96). They urge scholars to embrace more broad-based research strategies, what some variously refer to as 'globalizing methods' (Stoller, 1997), 'mobile ethnography' (Marcus, 1995; Fincham et al., 2010), multi-site 'transnational fieldwork' (Knowles, 1999), and 'global ethnography' (Burawoy, 2000; Hendry, 2003). Of course, anthropologists have long studied nomadic people, travellers and transhumant populations (Hendry, 2003). The recent emergence of 'multi-sited fieldwork' or 'global ethnography', however, is located within 'new spheres of interdisciplinary work', including media studies, science and technology studies, cultural and social geography, and cultural studies broadly (Marcus, 1995, p. 95).

For Marcus (1995), 'tracing a cultural formation across and within multiple sites of activity' can help us 'examine the circulation of cultural meanings, objects, and identities in diffuse time-space' (p. 96). More recently, Burawoy (2000) described the agenda of global ethnography as being to 'replace abstract globalization with a grounded globalization that tries to understand not only the experience of globalization but also how that experience is produced in specific localities and how the productive process is a contested and thus a political accomplishment' (p. 158). Burawoy (2000) identifies external forces, connections and imaginations as the three essential components of global ethnography. Such an approach values both the structural and the experiential, exploring whether people 'experience [sic] globalization as an external force to be resisted or accommodated', 'participate [sic] in the creation and reproduction of connections that stretch [sic] across the world' or 'mobilize and/or contest [sic] imaginations that are [sic] of global dimensions' (Burawoy, 2000, p. 5). Building upon the work of Marcus, Burawoy and others, Büscher et al. (2011) have adopted the term 'mobile methods' to refer to renewed efforts to 'deal systematically with the fleeting, the distributed, the multiple, the non-causal, the sensory, the emotional and the kinaesthetic' (p. 15). They proclaim the value of mobile methods in which researchers seek to 'capture, track, simulate, mimic and shadow the many and interdependent forms of intermittent movement of people, images, information and objects' (p. 7).

Arguably, transnational ethnography and mobile methods provide us with new and revised tools to begin studying the flows of youth cultural commodities, images, discourses, power and populations across local, regional, national and international fields (Canniford, 2005; Muggleton & Weinzierl, 2003, Nayak & Kehily, 2008). According to Nayak & Kehily (2008), 'global ethnographies' have the potential to facilitate new understandings of the 'interconnections between the local and the global, and the ways in which diasporas, migrations and cultural flows permeate' the everyday lived experiences of youth in late modernity, as well as illuminate how young people are negotiating these global transformations in and across local spaces (p. 31). Robin Canniford (2005) was among the first to discuss the possibilities (and problems) associated with doing ethnography and employing mobile methods in the 'touristic global surfing subculture' (p. 214). For Canniford (2005), moving through a 'multi-vocal, iterative, non-linear process' allowed him to select surfing 'voices from both global and local discourses' and ultimately gain a better understanding of surfing as a fluid and 'complex culture to be found between and within other complex cultures' (p. 214). Of course, there is a plethora of ways in which globally sensitive ethnographies of contemporary youth and physical cultures may transpire. To illustrate the potential of such an approach, I offer a description of the global ethnographic methods employed in my research on transnational action sport cultures.

With the goal of further examining the values, practices and interactions of action sport participants in local cultures, as well as regional, national and global flows of people, objects, value systems, information and images within and across these places, this project consisted of two main phases.

The first was conducted between 2004 and early 2010, and included fifteen 'ethnographic visits' – ranging from one week to one month – in an array of mountain resort communities in Canada (Whistler), France (Chamonix), Italy (the Dolomites), New Zealand (Methven, Ohakune, Queenstown, Wanaka), Switzerland (Saas Fee, Zermatt) and the United States (Mt Hood, Oregon; Salt Lake City, Utah; Telluride, Colorado). While the primary focus of these periods of fieldwork was on snowboarding culture (see Thorpe, 2011a), my observations and interactions in these locations, and the places (such as airports and bus and train stations) on my way to these mountain resort destinations, also included travelling, migrant, and local, skiers, climbers, mountain bikers, skateboarders, hang-gliders and kayakers. During this fieldwork, I found that many snowboarders also participated in an array of other action sports and vice versa. Moreover, I observed action sport participants from various sports interacting on a regular basis, whether it was in shared accommodations, virtual spaces, working together in various shops and businesses, or during their leisure time in bars and cafes. While each action sport is unique, with its own travel patterns and social dynamics, I observed many similarities in the transnational imagination and lifestyles being pursued by participants across an array of action sports.

Thus, the second phase of fieldwork between 2010 and 2013 built upon themes that emerged in the first. Following up on new questions about the transnational social formations within and across action sport cultures, I conducted further ethnographic visits ranging from two days to two weeks in an array of destinations, including Australia (the Sunshine and Gold Coasts), France (Chamonix and Tignes), New Zealand (Christchurch, Queenstown and Wanaka), Portugal (Ericeira), Puerto Rico, Spain (Barcelona and Galicia), Tahiti and the United States (Los Angeles, New Orleans and Washington, D.C.). Although I remained open to various observations and interactions during these phases of fieldwork, they tended to be more focused, with specific questions driving my data-gathering. While all the chapters in this book are informed by both phases of my transnational ethnographic investigations, different chapters draw more heavily upon some methods and sites of analysis than others.

Despite my attempts to anticipate and plan for phases of fieldwork, I took care to remain open to the 'usually messy, unpredictable and serendipitous nature of empirical realities' that then helped to 'redefine the terms of research and representation as new questions, threads and insights are closed and opened up along the way' (D'Andrea et al., 2011, p. 154). Each field was unique in its social, cultural, political and natural geography, and offered different insights into the local, regional, national and transnational flows and connections in the global action sport culture. Attempting to understand how the 'global forces, connections and imaginations' (Burawoy et al., 2000) were being experienced in (and across) these local action sport fields, observations were made in an array of locations. In mountain sport destinations (for example, Queenstown, Tignes, Whistler), I conducted observations in lift lines, chairlifts, resort lodges, and ski, snow-board, climbing and mountain biking shops. In coastal sport destinations (for example, Ericeira, the Gold Coast), I spent time observing interactions on the beach, in car parks, camping grounds, surf and kite surf shops and in the ocean itself. In urban locations (for example, Barcelona, Washington, D.C.) I observed skateboarders, inline skaters, BMX riders and parkour prac-titioners in both found and purposefully built spaces, including skateparks, under motorways, plazas, and parkour gyms. In each destination I sought out events that attracted action sport enthusiasts, such as competitions, prize-giving events and video premières, and spent time in various local hangouts such as sport-specific shops, bars and cafes. I also engaged in con-versation with local residents and business owners, as I was interested in understanding their interpretations of the flows of action sport participants through their local communities. As a travelling researcher and action sport participant, I also spent time in bus-shelters, train stations and airports, where I took note of the travelling patterns and practices of action sport migrants, tourists and athletes. During this fieldwork, I observed, listened, engaged in analysis and made mental notes, switching from traveller to action sport participant to researcher depending on the requirements of the situation.

During my transnational fieldwork I observed and jotted notes in vari-ous environments, and in some cases I was also a participant. Thus my fieldwork was a form of 'sensual research' that offered new opportunities for experiencing, observing and sharing the bodily and social pleasures, as well as pains and frustrations, inherent in action sport mobilities (Evers, 2006, p. 239). During phases of participant-observation I further adopted a 'sensory ethnographic' sensitivity by paying particular attention to the unique sights, as well as the sounds, smells, tastes and touch, of various spaces and places. To facilitate more vivid recall of the multi-sensual aspects of the research experience upon returning 'home' from the field, I employed an array of creative strategies using my notebook, camera and Dictaphone during the first phase of data-gathering (Azzarito, 2010), and then my iPhone during the second (Beddall-Hill et al., 2011; Murthy, 2008, 2013).

In the second phase of fieldwork I became more interested in the economic and institutional structures that were intimately involved in producing the transnational imagination within and across action sport communities. Thus, I conducted fieldwork at five international action sport-related events, all of which were sponsored by an array of transnational and national corporations, featured action sport athletes, coaches, judges and journalists from around the world and spectators from many countries, and were instantaneously being globally communicated via an array of print and digital media. In 2010, I attended the first European X Games in Tignes (France), the Tony Hawk and Friends Show in Brighton (UK), the Big Freeze Festival in London

(UK) and the snowboarding events at the Winter Olympics in Vancouver (Canada); in 2011 I spent a week at the Winter Festival in Queenstown and Wanaka (New Zealand). These were intense phases of fieldwork and I found my iPhone to be a particularly valuable research tool in such situations, enabling me to unobtrusively take photos of various sights and record sounds as well as my own initial observations. Using the voice memo application, I was able to capture some of the multi-layered sounds (such as commentators, music, helicopters, crowds), thus freeing me to focus on other social and sensual dimensions of the occasion. I also used the camera and video on my iPhone to record moments of significance, or interactions or sites that I found interesting but was unable to critically unpack or contextualize in the field. It is important to note that as well as being a researcher in such spaces I was occasionally preoccupied with some of the practicalities of such sites, such as trying to find my way around the sporting complexes, queueing for toilets, and navigating throngs of often drunken and rowdy spectators. While highly distracting from my critical observations, such experiences were also important parts of my sensual research and provided embodied understandings of these sporting and entertainment spectacles. However, listening to the various audio recordings and viewing my photos and videos taken upon returning from the event was invaluable for evoking my multidimensional memories of these socially, physically and sensually loaded phases of fieldwork, which I was then able to critically analyse in relation to the literature and key theoretical concepts at a later date.

Each of the locations I visited for this project posed different opportunities *and* challenges (for example, language, localism, cultural access, accommodation, pre-existing contacts in the field, funding) depending on whether I was travelling alone or with others (for example, my Spanish-speaking partner who is also an avid surfer, skateboarder and snowboarder, a female friend, or a family member). According to Stoller (1997), the key to doing research in complex transnational spaces is 'suppleness of imagination' (p. 91). My past experiences as a travelling snowboarder greatly facilitated my ability to respond and adapt flexibly to social circumstances as they arose in the field, and to remain open to a wide variety of different types of relationships and interactions (for example, on chairlifts or in action sport shops). In the instances where I was travelling with my partner, a friend or family member(s), their everyday interactions with others in cafes, restaurants, action sport shops, or on the road while asking directions, also provided valuable insights into the exchanges between travellers and local residents. Different ethnographic methods became more important when conducting research in some spaces and places than in others. For example, language barriers in France, Italy, Portugal, Spain and Switzerland made the communicative and auditory aspects of fieldwork more difficult. While conducting fieldwork in social spaces in these locations, my visual observations became much more important – I paid more attention to signs and symbols and the posturing and interactions of action sport bodies, as well as the tone and inflections of voices. In this way, it was typically the 'circumstance that defined the method rather than the method defining the circumstance' (Amit, 2000, p. 11).

My ethnographic observations were developed in dialogue with 72 participants from an array of countries, including Australia, Brazil, Canada, France, Great Britain, Japan, New Zealand, Palestine, South Africa, Switzerland and the United States. Participants ranged from 18 to 60 years of age, and included snowboarders, skiers, surfers, skateboarders, mountain bikers, climbers, kite-surfers, SUP (Stand Up Paddle Boarders), and traceurs (parkour participants); many of these participants engaged in an array of action sports. I was interested to capture the experiences of a wide variety of action sport participants, and thus conducted interviews with novices, recreational participants, highly committed 'core' participants, professional athletes, instructors and coaches, journalists, photographers, film-makers, magazine editors, company owners, action sport shop employees and owners, and event organizers and judges. While many of my participants had travelled in pursuit of action sport participation, others had not. For the latter, I was interested in their virtual and imagined action sport mobilities, and their experiences within local places that are influenced by the transnational flows of action sport images, people and objects. Some of my participants were no longer 'core' participants who organized their lives around action sports, and we talked about their memories of travelling for sport, work and/or leisure, how their mobilities have changed over time, and their experiences of adopting a less mobile lifestyle. I deeply value the stories, reflections and opinions of my participants and thus their voices are woven through the chapters of this book. While some of the quotes from interviews have been edited for clarity, I have taken care not to lose the essence of participants' voices. All participants have been given pseudonyms, except where they requested otherwise. Throughout this book, quotes from interviews are referenced as 'pc' for personal communication.

(Im)mobile methods

Importantly, as Favell (2001) reminds us, to access 'the extent or nature of movement, or indeed even *see* it sometimes, you have in fact to spend a lot of time studying things that stand still: the borders, institutions and territories of nation states' (p. 391). Thus, I also drew upon an array of less mobile methods that enabled me to understand the structures and institutions enabling and constraining transnational action sport mobilities. It is also important to note that the various phases of trans-local fieldwork discussed above were interspersed within an otherwise typically 'grounded' lifestyle where I have lived (on and off) in the same small beach town and worked at the same university for the past ten years. During these phases of semi-permanence, I embraced methods from cultural and media studies in my attempts to understand how 'some forms of transnationalism are enacted through the circulation of texts, objects and media products' (Wilding, 2007, p. 345). I gathered evidence from cultural sources, such as magazines, films and websites, to help deepen my understanding of cultural complexities of the global–local nexus in action sport cultures. Some of these sources (such as guidebooks, travel stories in magazines and websites, films) also proved useful for my understanding of regions in which action sports are practised but I have yet to visit (for example, Alaska, China, Japan, Hawaii). In conjunction with my multi-sited transnational fieldwork and interviews, this ongoing media analysis enabled me to understand some of the global forces operating within and across action sport spaces, the social and cultural conditions of mobile subjects, as well as representations of the experiences of (im)mobile subjects in particular destinations.

Electronic sources were an integral part of my transnational ethnography of action sport culture. Action sport participants are prolific users of digital and social media that 'blur the boundaries between physical and imaginative mobility' (Jansson, 2007, p. 6) (see Chapter 3). Critically engaging online sources, such as niche sporting websites, blogs and YouTube videos, in conversation with other sources (such as newspapers, television coverage, movies, flyers) and methods (such as interviews, participant observations), helped expand my understanding of the cultural complexities of the global and local flows operating within action sports. This ongoing media interrogation informed all levels of analysis ranging from the macro to the micro scales. For example, seeking to understand the global forces involved in the production and consumption of the transnational imaginary, I accessed previously published interviews with the founders of transnational action sport corporations and critically examined company websites. At the micro level of the analysis, I was able to glean valuable insights into the lived experiences of action sport migration via the blogs of action sport travellers. Indeed, comments posted on public websites, social media sites, blogs and other interactive forums provided access to the thoughts and feelings of individuals and groups on an array of issues, ranging from the collective grief following the death of an action sport celebrity (see Chapter 3), to personal memories and reflections following a recent trip (see Chapter 6).

Given the highly mobile lives of many of my participants, I also found the Internet, and new technologies such as Skype, to be very useful for making contact and communicating with participants either travelling or living overseas. In some cases, I used email and/or Facebook to make contact prior to visiting a destination and to set up appointments, and I also used these modes of communication to continue dialogue with some participants after I returned from the field. But the use of such technologies for research purposes raises some interesting technical and ethical issues (Murthy,

2013; Ess, 2009). As many scholars have pointed out, 'not everyone has the resources necessary to access these infrastructures or to take advantage of their benefits' (Wilding, 2007, p. 340). Indeed, some action sport participants are more privileged than others, and some parts of the world are 'more globalized and some people are more transnational than others' (Wilding, 2007, p. 340). Through the course of this project, however, I came to understand that there are less privileged children and youth around the world who are gaining exposure to action sports via global and digital media, and are adopting and reappropriating these sports in local spaces, with some using cheap technologies to communicate with the transnational action sport community. Digital media enabled me to learn about such activities and to open dialogue with participants in some remote and high-risk destinations.

In Chapter 8, for example, my analysis draws upon personal communications with key members of parkour groups in Kuwait, Egypt and Gaza. Due to my physical distance, I offered to conduct brief conversations via phone, email, Skype or any other electronic medium that suited the participants. Many participants preferred to use the private message board in Facebook to answer questions. Facebook is a familiar space for these young men, many of whom use it on a daily basis to organize training sessions and communicate with fellow parkour practitioners in their local community and abroad. These digital communications were held asynchronously, allowing for time differences, busy lives and, in the case of the participants, unstable Internet connections. After explaining the details of the project and establishing the preferred mode of communication, I then posed a series of questions and encouraged the participants to add to or extend these questions at their leisure.

While most participants willingly accepted my invitations to share their thoughts and reflections, language difficulties led to some misinterpretations of questions and answers. It quickly became apparent that participants were using Google Translator to convert the interview questions into Arabic, and then typing their responses in Arabic before translating back into English. Due to such translation difficulties, further clarification was often sought with follow-up questions. To facilitate my interpretations in this and other chapters, I adopted the method of triangulation; I engaged my electronic interviews in dialogue with media analysis of various print (for example, magazine articles), digital (for example, YouTube clips, websites) and social media (for example, Twitter postings, Facebook) to identify themes across the data. In so doing, I gained rich insights into how youth are engaging social media for entertainment and inspiration, and also for sharing their own experiences with action sport enthusiasts around the world. As this example illustrates, the methods employed in this book were creatively adapted for the overall project, as well as for the critical questions underpinning each chapter.

The (im)mobile researching body

For Burawoy (2000), global ethnographers should become 'the living embodiment' of the processes they are studying by 'continually switching places [and] moving among sites within the field' (p. 4). Indeed, my multi-sited ethnographic approach offered new opportunities for experiencing, observing and sharing the bodily and social pleasures, as well as pains and frustrations, inherent in action sport-related (im)mobilities. Of course, as Amit (2000) points out, the 'melding of personal and professional roles in ethnographic fieldwork' can make for a 'messy qualitative experience', which 'cannot readily or usefully be compartmentalized from other experiences and periods in our lives' (p. 7). Thus, throughout my transnational fieldwork, I self-consciously reflected on my constantly shifting positions as an (increasingly less) active action sport participant and a white, hetero-sexual, middle-class female researcher and academic from New Zealand, and how these roles influenced the theoretical and empirical development of the study (also see Olive & Thorpe, 2011; Thorpe et al., 2011).

Moreover, as Knowles (1999) explains, 'fieldwork offers the transnational researcher the prospect of reconnection with a former life or the prospect of escape; it sustains the possibility of an alternate sense of belonging and self, deftly busied in conceptions of work and intellectual enterprise' (p. 60). While I certainly enjoyed moments of escapism, nostalgia, adrenalin and joy during my fieldwork, the practice of global ethnography should not be romanticized. Transnational ethnography has the potential to be 'humiliating, belittling, at times dull, boring and downright exhausting' (Silk, 2005, p. 75), as well as dangerous. I learned that, while conducting global (and local) fieldwork the researcher – particularly the female researcher – should be prepared for an array of potentially high-risk or threatening situations in which instantaneous decisions may need to be made. In Chapter 5 I offer a short narrative of a night during my fieldwork in Chamonix, France, that is revealing of how I navigated such tenuous situations. Such moments do not only occur in the field, but also on the way to or from such destinations (for example, at bus or train stations). When confronted with situations requiring an almost immediate ethical response, I always tried to draw upon all of my senses and past experiences to interpret the dynamics and complexities of the particular social, cultural and physical environment.

Upon hearing of such transnational research methods, many people may jest, not recognizing that such methods are physically demanding and a lot less glamorous as they may sound. For example, in my attempts to 'follow' the mobilities of various types of action sport traveller, I often stayed in budget backpacker hostels, which meant I was awoken by drunken backpackers stumbling home after a night 'on the town', and their romantic liaisons in the hallways, bathrooms and/or the bunk bed below my own! As I entered my thirties, I found it increasingly difficult to transition from my lifestyle and career as an academic and lecturer into these hedonistic youthful spaces, and thus I also occasionally sought out alternative accommodations that were popular among older, professional action sport tourists and travellers. The diversity of my experiences was, however, essential for this project, as Burawoy (2000) explains:

> In entering the lives of those they study, ethnographers attune themselves to the horizons and rhythms of their subjects' existence. . . . Global ethnographers cannot be outside the global processes they study. . . . They are also embedded in the time-space rhythms . . . we become the living embodiment of the processes we are [sic] studying. (p. 4)

Many young action sport enthusiasts are travelling on shoestring budgets, and thus attuning myself to their 'horizons and rhythms' meant that I was often outside of my new 'comfort zone'; some phases of this work therefore required considerable researcher flexibility and adaptability. Again, my past experiences and embodied memories as a snowboarding migrant facilitated my ability to 'fit in' to some of these locations, interact somewhat 'naturally' with participants, and navigate risky situations.

Importantly, my observations and analyses of transnationalism in action sport cultures combined 'dwelling with traveling' (Burawoy, 2000, p. 4). As any author will know, the act of writing a book requires a considerable amount of immobility, and thus over the past 12 months I have been living a predominantly permanent existence. However, I have continued to immerse myself in the travels of others via friends', family's and acquaintances' use of an array of social media (particularly Facebook and Instagram), as well as the blogs and various other publicly accessible social media of travelling action sport enthusiasts, tourists and athletes. I also live in an internationally renowned surfing and kite-surfing destination, and thus the transnational flows of action sport migrants have washed over and around me throughout this project. Indeed, while writing at the local cafe, visiting the supermarket or attending a friend's barbecue, I regularly overhear the accent-laden stories of travelling action sport enthusiasts, and can not help but observe their interactions with one another and local residents. Put simply, even when my methods were less mobile, my ethnography was 'no less multi-sited' (Burawoy, 2000, p. 4).

As previously mentioned, while the focus of this research is the transnationalism of 'others', my own privileged transnational experiences – as an action sport participant and researcher – have influenced every phase of this study (Knowles, 1999). Much like the authors in *Global Ethnography*, however, I was determined that this project 'not dissolve [sic] into a welter of postmodern fracturing and fragmentation . . . did not become a pastiche of vignettes, and [I] did not become [a] tourist tripping from resort to resort' (Burawoy, 2000, p. 5). Even as I focused on the movements of others, I took care not to lose sight of dwelling. Moreover, critical reflections upon my own immobilities and experiences of imagined and virtual travel have been just as valuable for my rapport with some participants (particularly those who have 'retired' from the transnational action sport lifestyle) as my highly mobile and active participation was with others.

Transnational mobilities in action sport cultures: an overview

This book consists of three parts broadly organized along a series of continua, ranging from macro to micro, structures of transnationalism to the agency of participants, and the global to the local. Part I consists of two chapters in which I examine global economic, cultural and media forces that are contributing to the production of a transnational imagination within and across local spaces. Part II then draws more strongly from the mobilities turn to examine how a high degree of human mobility in action sports is further influencing this transnational imaginary, and how participants' transnational experiences are contributing to 'new subjectivities in the global arena' (Nonini & Ong, 1997). Focusing on the mobilities of various groups, including tourists, athletes and migrants, the three chapters in Part II aim to reveal fresh insights into the lived transnationalism and global migration of contemporary youth facilitated by the global action sport economic and social networks discussed in Part I. Part III further connects the global and the local, with an emphasis on space, place and immobilities, and the significance of action sports in earthquake-damaged and war-torn communities. The final, concluding chapter draws upon elements from each of the chapters to reveal the unique forms of transnational politics that are emerging as a result of such mobilities. In particular, I examine the development of action sport-related non-profit organizations that utilize transnational networks, media and corporations to initiate change in local contexts. Although the chapters are broadly organized from the macro to micro scales of analysis, with an emphasis on economic and social structures in the first part, and agency in the latter parts, these are, however, largely arbitrary dichotomies utilized for the purpose of organizing the messiness of the multiple flows in transnational action sport cultures. It is important to highlight that some micro-level examples of agency, politics, resistance and negotiation, and processes of glocalization, are evident in the early chapters, just as some of the structural economic, cultural and institutional forces influencing action sport communities are revealed in the later chapters.

Woven throughout the three parts and the eight remaining chapters in this book are the multiple forms of power operating within and across action sport cultures. Concerned to understand the global networks and operations of power within transnational action sport communities, the various chapters offer an array of theoretical analyses of 'how power operates in the context of complex international exchanges' (Kien, 2009, p. 6).

Furthermore, site-specific vignettes and case studies are presented in every chapter to help understand 'how power is experienced in everyday "global" situations, inflected with highly nuanced histories, cultural logics, and intensely personal motivations' (Kien, 2009, p. 9). Some of these 'grounded' case studies include the politics involved in the growth and development of action sports in China (Chapter 2), the dynamics between action sport tourists, migrants and locals within three transnational mountain resort destinations, including Whistler, Chamonix and Queenstown (Chapter 5), the arrhythmic experiences of action sport participants living in Christchurch following a series of devastating earthquakes (Chapter 7) and the emergence of parkour in the Palestinian Gaza strip (Chapter 8). Adopting a multi-dimensional approach to transnationalism and mobilities, each chapter aims to reveal fresh insights into the power of specific practices and processes of transnationalism, and how corporeal, virtual and imagined mobilities and connections across borders are influencing how contemporary youth are positioning themselves in society both here and there (Vertovec, 2009). In so doing, it becomes clear that transnational processes and heightened mobilities are influencing not only how youth are practising and consuming sport and physical activity, but also how such processes are informing their sense of space, place, identity and belonging.

Part I
Transnational Action Sport Cultural Networks

2
Producing Transnational Networks: Action Sport Companies, Media and Events

In this book, transnationalism is understood broadly as the 'growing connectivity of individuals, groups and institutions across multiple national contexts' (Giulianotti & Brownell, 2012, p. 199). In the previous chapter we examined the transnational imaginary that exists within contemporary action sport cultures. Many action sport enthusiasts around the world participate predominantly at the local level, yet due to their access and consumption of global sporting events, media, action sport celebrities and products from transnational companies, many feel connected to a broader action sport community. As will be discussed in Chapters 4, 5 and 6, the travel practices of action sport participants further contribute to this transnational imaginary. In this chapter, however, I adopt a macro focus on the broader structural and economic forces that have played a major role in the production of these transnational networks. More specifically, I examine transnational action sport-related companies (Burton, Red Bull) and action sport mega-events (the X Games, Felix Baumgartner's space jump) to illustrate how 'social links, networks and communities are [produced] and maintained across national and transnational layers' (Giulianotti & Brownell, 2012, p. 200).

As with the development of modern sport, action sports are 'bound up with processes of economic and cultural transformation associated with the global diffusion of capitalist forms of consumption' (Smart, 2007, p. 113). This chapter consists of four case studies illustrating the development of transnational networks within the contemporary action sport industry. Firstly, I examine Burton Snowboards as an example of a transnational corporation (TNC) that has grown from a small one-man snowboard production company in Vermont, USA, to a major force in the global action sport industry. Here I discuss some of the strategies employed by this TNC to expand into new markets and respond to changing economic conditions. The second case builds upon the first, focusing particularly on the efforts by transnational action sport companies, such as Burton, to develop a new market in China for their products. Despite the efforts of TNCs and governmental support, the growth of action sports in China has been considerably more complicated than many Western companies anticipated. Moreover, this case reveals how local and global processes are deeply interdependent and highly political. The development of action sports in China offers fresh insights into the complexities of glocalization. In the third case I examine the recent global expansion of the X Games and the politics involved in the production of action sport mega events in international contexts. The final case focuses on global energy drink Red Bull's relationship with action sport athletes and events. In each of these cases, we see how the transnational action sport culture and industry is 'permeated with neo-liberal ideologies and policies' (Giulianotti & Brownell, 2012, p. 202). Put simply, the powerful commercial and political forces operating within and across the action sport community are only made possible in a neo-liberal world that celebrates free-market ideologies and policies.

Some scholars have developed useful typologies for analysing the complex processes involved in the globalization of modern sport. In particular, Giulianotti & Robertson (2012) provide a sociological model of the world football system or, as they term it, the 'global football field'. They examine how 'influences and interconnections of football's multifarious stakeholders – football consumers, elite clubs, businesses linked closely to football (such as sport-driven media companies), football federations and leagues, and associated governmental organizations – serve to construct and shape the global football field' (cited in Giuianotti & Brownell, 2012, p. 200). They argue that this model might usefully be applied to understand the complex processes involved in various other global sporting cultures. While transnational action sport companies, media and events follow many of the strategies inherent in the globalization of more traditional sport, as the cases presented in this chapter reveal, there is much blurring between TNCs, media, events and associated organizations. For analytical purposes, it is tempting to artificially separate TNCs, events and medias to examine the global, commercial and political processes operating within and across national contexts. However, this paints an unrealistic picture of the complex forces operating within the contemporary transnational action sport industry and culture. Thus, rather than adopting or modifying Giulianotti & Robertson's (2012) model, each of the case studies presented here reveals the close interactions and connections between action sport corporations, media and events, in local and international contexts. In so doing, this chapter examines some of the key factors and agents that have contributed to action sports becoming a truly global phenomenon in the late 20th and early 21st centuries.

Transnational action sport corporations: the case of Burton Snowboards

Each action sport culture has its own historical narratives of participants who started experimenting with technologies to create new equipment, clothing or associated products for local enthusiasts, and then continued to grow their companies to become successful international businesses. In surfing, Quiksilver, Billabong, O'Neil and Rip Curl are all examples of garage businesses set up by passionate surfers who started producing surfing specific boardshorts, wetsuits and/or surfboards for local surfers, before exporting internationally, and ultimately becoming TNCs with offices and production sites around the world where they design, produce and distribute a wide array of products for surfers, as well as participants across an array of other action sports (such as snowboarding, skateboarding and kitesurfing) and fashion consumers more broadly (Stranger, 2011). For example, Alan Green and John Law established Quiksilver, Inc. in Torquay, Victoria, Australia, in 1969. The company started exporting their unique boardshorts to Hawaii in 1974, and then to Japan three years later, followed by France in 1978. Quiksilver grew quickly to become one of the world's largest manufacturers of surfwear and other board-sport-related equipment, and in 2004 they became the first boardriding company to break through a billion dollars in sales, with revenue reaching US$1.3 billion. As with many other action sport companies and retailers, however, surfing corporations such as Quiksilver and Billabong have experienced major difficulties in 'the wake of the global financial crisis and an acute downturn in discretionary spending' (Greenblat, 2010, para. 5), such that many transnational action sport companies have undergone various restructuring efforts and acquisitions over the past few years.

In contrast to surfing companies, the number of longstanding TNCs in other action sports has been fewer. Other successful action sport TNCs include Vans, a skateboarding shoe company that opened its first store in Anaheim, California, in 1966; Volcom, a surf, skate and snow-sport clothing brand targeting younger participants established in 1991; and DC, which began producing skateboarding shoes in 1995, before expanding into snowboarding, BMX and motocross markets with an array of clothing and footwear. Despite having their roots primarily in one sporting culture, many transnational action sport corporations have expanded (often through the acquisition of smaller, niche action sport companies) to provide equipment, clothing and accessories across an array of action sports. Of course, not all action sport companies grow to become TNCs. Rather, some of the companies deemed most 'culturally authentic' by core participants tend to be the smaller companies owned and operated by active participants. As the action sport industries continued to grow during the 1990s and early 2000s, mainstream sporting goods corporations also entered the market. In particular, Nike invested strategically in the skateboarding, surfing and snowboarding markets during the late 1990s. To overcome some initial difficulties entering these markets, Nike sponsored key athletes and events to develop their credibility among core participants (many of whom were highly sceptical of such a mainstream corporation entering their terrain). Winning the approval of many core participants, action sports have become a US$390 million business for Nike (see Atencio & Beal, 2011).

It is beyond the scope of this chapter to examine the development of national and international action sport companies, and the involvement of outside sports companies such as Nike. Rather, in this chapter I focus on the processes in which one local action sport company grew to become a successful TNC. While each action sport company has its own unique economic and cultural challenges and successes depending on various factors, ranging from the local labour market to the global economy, the following case of Burton Snowboards provides insight into the development of a grassroots sport-specific company to transnational action sports conglomerate.

Burton Snowboards: from garage industry to TNC

Twenty-three year-old Jake Burton Carpenter established Burton Snowboards in 1977 in Londonderry, Vermont.[1] Having recently graduated from New York University with a degree in economics, and with work experience at a New York business broker company, Burton wanted to start his own business. An avid Snurfer (a rudimentary form of snowboard without bindings) in his teenage years, Burton saw the activity as an untapped opportunity for capital accumulation (Helmich, 2000). Indeed, he confessed that his primary drive was to 'create a successful business' (Burton, 2003, p. 403) and 'make a good living . . . like 100 grand a year or something' (Burton Carpenter & Dumaine, 2002, para. 12). He calculated that by producing 50 boards a day, he could make at least a comfortable living (Burton Carpenter & Dumaine, 2002). Only now does he admit to being 'blindly optimistic' (cited in Helmich, 2000, para. 5): 'I didn't do any market research; I didn't talk to any competitors. I just brought a little saber saw and started making boards in my apartment . . . It was trial and error' (Burton Carpenter & Dumaine, 2002, p. 64). Burton worked mostly alone, relying on some part-time high-school worker help. After making the boards, he became a 'travelling salesman', loading his station wagon and driving to ski and sports stores across the US Eastern States trying to market and sell his product (Bailey, 1998, para. 28). Within the first year the fledgling company had sold 300 boards for US$88 each, although 'everyone said it was too much' (Burton, cited in Howe, 1998, p. 11). Burton responded with a cheaper version, the 'Backyard', which sold (without bindings) for US$45. The following year, 1979, he sold 700 boards but continued to struggle financially. In his own words: 'I started the business as a get-rich-quick scheme, but very soon I had even less money than when I started' (Burton cited in Morris, 2008, para. 5).

By 1981 Burton had spent his $120,000 inheritance and was $130,000 in debt but orders for his boards climbed into the thousands over the next few years. In the early and mid-1980s Burton shifted his focus from selling boards to promoting snowboarding as a physical activity. To create a market, Burton also lobbied local ski resorts to open their slopes to snowboarding. Paul Alden, who worked for Burton Snowboards from 1984 to 1990, recalls that Burton 'spent hundreds of thousands of dollars to put this sport on the map' (cited in Bailey, 1998, para. 32). In 1983, Stratton Mountain (Vermont) became the first major ski field to open its piste to snowboarders. Others quickly followed. Sensing the growing momentum, Burton turned his attention back to his product. With financial backing from his wife's family, he added better bindings, a high-tech base and steel edges to his boards, making them more manoeuvrable. Burton continued to develop snowboarding technologies, and to improve his marketing and distribution practices. In 1984, sales of Burton Snowboards reached US$1 million.

Snowboarding continued to grow in popularity during the 1980s and into the mid-1990s. By the mid-1990s snowboarding had developed a cohesive industry complete with its own media, international events and competitions, trade-shows, fashions, and professional and amateur athletes. Burton Snowboards grew 'on average about 100% per year' during this period (Burton Carpenter & Dumaine, 2002, p. 64). By 1995 it employed 250 workers and was worth well over US$100 million. The potential for growth in overseas markets was considerable during this period and Burton Snowboards started distribution to Europe in 1985, to New Zealand the following year and to Japan in 1994. Due to the success of sales in these regions, Burton established offices in Innsbruck (Austria) in 1986 and Tokyo (Japan) in 1995. Brad Steward, an employee at Sims Snowboards, recalls that everyone thought Burton was 'nuts for going to Europe' (cited in Bailey, 1998, para. 34) but he admitted that Jake 'always had vision' and knew how to 'look at the much bigger picture' (para. 34). Through geographical expansion, Burton Snowboards was able to fulfil Karl Marx's premise of the basic drive of the capitalist mode of production – growth – as it is only through growth that profits can be assured and capital accumulation sustained (see Thorpe, 2011a).

The growth of the sport and industry during this period attracted an influx of new companies, many of which had their roots elsewhere; in surfing (Billabong, Ríp Curl), skateboarding (DC, Etnies, Airwalk) and skiing (Rossignol, Soloman, Voikal). By 1995 the North American snowboard retail industry was worth US$750 million (Randall, 1995). That same year more than 300 companies peddled snowboard equipment, apparel and accessories at the industry trade show, compared with just 90 companies two years earlier. Industry sources predicted that snowboard market sales would double to US$1.5 billion at retail level by the end of the 1990s (Randall,

1995). When Ride Snowboards became the first snowboard company to go public on the NASDAQ stock exchange in 1994, it sold all 500,000 shares in the first two weeks: it then released another 75,000. Within a month the shares had reached US$28 each, six times the release price. Despite massive growth during this fifteen-year period, some warned that consolidation was inevitable. Rodger Madison Jr., chairman of Ride Snowboards, predicted, 'this is a textbook example of an early-stage, fast-growth market. You're going to see a major shakeout. Instead of 100 companies, in five years you might have 12' (cited in Randall, 1995, p. 46). Madison's prophecy proved correct. Sagging sales in Asian countries (particularly Japan) during their post-1997 economic downturn, and overproduction, triggered a 'shakeout' in the late 1990s. Larger companies acquired many smaller snowboarder-owned companies around this time. In 1998 Quiksilver (a surf company) purchased Lib Technologies (snowboard manufacturers), Gnu Snowboards (snowboard manufacturers), Arcane (snowboard boot manufacturers) and Bent Metal (snowboard binding manufacturers). Similarly, K2 (a ski company) acquired Ride Snowboards and Morrow Snowboards. Others downsized. Joyride Snowboards reduced its number of employees from 120 to six. Still others exited the market (for example, Millennium Three [snowboard manufacturer], Belligerent [bindings manufacturer] and Random Snowboards) (Deemer, 2000).

In 2002, following the September 11 terrorist attacks and a poor snow year in North America, Europe and Japan, Burton Snowboards underwent a restructuring and 102 employees were laid off (Snowboard Shocker, 2002, para. 6). More recently, Burton Snowboards responded to the 'challenging global economic situation' in 2009 by cutting staff salaries, cancelling raises and bonuses, and laying off approximately five per cent of their North American staff, including a number of high-profile professional athletes; Jake Burton and his wife, Donna, further demonstrated their commitment to the company by temporarily foregoing their own salaries (*Business Week*, 2009, para. 1). In 2010 Burton underwent further restructuring and it was decided that a number of subsidiary companies acquired in 2004 (Foursquare, Forum and Special Blend) would be faded out. In Burton's own words: 'Burton has experienced several years of income growth since the recession and paid our bonuses to employees over the last two years. That said, the economy has a voice of its own that we will all have to listen to, and the message is clear: do what you do best and focus purely on it' (cited in The big Burton restructure, 2012, para. 5). Not only is the ability to read the market a prerequisite for financial success, at times of economic difficulty and intensifying competition the 'well organized corporation has marked competitive advantages' through its ability 'to make swift decisions' (Harvey, 1989, p. 230).

Despite some difficulties in recent times, Burton Snowboards has been proactive in its response to a changing global marketplace. As such, Burton

Snowboards remains a good example of a successful TNC (Pries, 2001). While there are various definitions of a TNC, here I examine transnational action sport corporations as companies that possess worldwide infrastructures for the production, distribution and marketing of action sport-related commodities (Giulianotti & Robertson, 2004). Burton Snowboards is currently the leading snowboard company in North America, Europe and Japan (Burton, 2008). The company remains privately owned by Jake Burton and his wife, and thus does not release financial information. However, in a recent financial review it was revealed that Burton Snowboards controls approximately 40 to 70 per cent of the multi-billion dollar global market, depending on the specific category of goods (Brooks, 2010); foreign sales account for 60 per cent of volume, with a very profitable Japanese segment (Burton history, 2005). From their offices in Australia, Austria, California and Japan, and headquarters in Burlington (Vermont), Burton Snowboards distributes via independent Burton representatives to authorized specialty retailers in 36 countries, including the United States, Canada, 28 countries in Europe, two countries in South America, and Japan, Korea, Australia and New Zealand (Fact sheet, 2003). In 2009, Burton Snowboards and its subsidiary companies had approximately 370 employees in Vermont and 900 worldwide (Burton reports, 2009).

According to Perlmutter (1972), TNCs can be distinguished along territorial lines. Whereas a home-based HQ controls 'ethnocentric' corporations, 'polycentric' corporations facilitate local self-determination within centrally defined margins, and globally mobile managers control 'geocentric' enterprises (cited in Giulianotti & Robertson, 2004, p. 551). In 2010, Burton transitioned from an ethnocentric corporation to a polycentric transnational enterprise when it closed its manufacturing plant in Vermont with at least 75 per cent of boards now being produced in China, with the high-end boards being produced in Austria. Burton (2010) offered the following rationale in a press release; 'it costs us significantly more to produce a board in Vermont than we are capable of selling it for, and sadly, this is not sustainable in the current economy' (cited in Burton Snowboards closes Vermont plant, 2010, p. 1). With production having moved offshore, and business ongoing in over 35 countries, Burton Snowboards claims to conform to strict ethical global production guidelines (Burton goes global, 2005). Burton Snowboards proclaims to conform to the following ethical global production guidelines: 1) 'Be a good corporate citizen in every country, respecting customs and languages'; 2) 'Give overseas operations your best manufacturing technology'; 3) 'Keep expatriate headcount down and groom local managers to take over'; 4) 'Let plants set their own rules, fine-tuning manufacturing processes to match skills of workers'; 5) 'Develop local R&D to tailor products made'; and 6) 'Encourage competition among overseas outposts with plants back home' (Burton goes global, 2005, p. 15). While it is difficult to know the extent to which Burton achieves these goals, such guidelines suggest that Burton

Snowboards is what Smith et al. (1997) refer to as a 'truly transnational corporation' (TTNC). Burton Snowboards demonstrates the three definitive features that Smith (1997) believes are constitutive of a TTNC: 'it freely undertakes research and development worldwide; recruits elite employees from anywhere; and is acutely flexible in product development and micro-marketing' (p. 39).

Burton products are marketed worldwide and sold in over 4348 stores around the world, 1536 of which are in the US. To further 'create their own "local", deterritorialized communities of global consumers' (Giulianotti & Robertson, 2004, p. 551), Burton Snowboards established the Burton Global Open Series in 2006, which includes some of snowboarding's most prestigious events, including the Burton European Open Snowboarding Championships, the Nissan X-Trail Nippon Open, the Burton US Open, the New Zealand Burton Open and the Burton Australian Snowboarding Open Championships. Although figures for the company's overall investment in these events are unavailable, the total prize-money (US$100,000 each) for the male and female winners of the Burton Global Open Series is indicative of significant economic investment. The company also invests heavily in the highly esteemed Arctic Challenge and in 2004 established the novel Burton Abominable Snow Jam (Mt Hood, Oregon). To facilitate sales in various national contexts, Burton also practises cultural 'glocalization' via creative localized marketing strategies ranging from the sponsorship of local events and athletes, to the development of unique snowboarding facilities. For example, further raising the visibility of the company in local contexts, Burton recently partnered with various ski resorts – Killington Ski Resort (Vermont, US), Northstar (Tahoe, US), Avoriaz (France), The Remarkables (New Zealand) and Flachauwinkel (Austria) – to develop an original series of organic snowboard terrain parks (featuring natural obstacles such as rocks, stumps and logs) known as the 'Burton Stash' series (see www.thestash.com). Burton Snowboards also partners with various national and international media agencies to produce snowboarding films (*The B Movie*), television programming (Burton TV) and interactive web-based media (Burton Studios with iTunes) to further 'showcase Burton's vast history and knowledge to new and expanded audiences' (Press release, 2004). Burton Snowboards' expansion into the production of events, spaces and media is an innovative attempt at, to paraphrase Harvey (1989), mastering or actively intervening in the volatile national and international snowboarding markets by 'saturating the market with images' (p. 287).

Burton Snowboards also invests in other forms of image-building, including sponsorships and direct marketing, which further enable it to 'manipulate taste and opinion' in local contexts (Harvey, 1989, p. 287). Burton Snowboards sponsors 39 professional snowboarders from 10 different countries, including seven from Japan, three from Finland, two from Norway, Slovenia and Switzerland, and one rider each from Sweden, Belgium and

Austria. There are different levels of sponsorship ranging from a 'rookie' sponsorship, where riders receive equipment and/or clothing, occasional travel budgets and other incentives to the Burton's Global Team which in 2013 consisted of 19 snowboarders (including global action sport celebrities Shaun White, Terje Haakonsen and Hannah Teter) who receive full sponsorship, and in some cases six-figure salaries. In this sense, Burton's involvement in the global snowboarding labour market is not radically dissimilar from TNC football clubs that 'practice cultural "glocalization"' by according status to symbolic local or national figures and recruiting 'foreign' players to help 'build global recognition' (Giulianotti & Robertson, 2004). A key difference, however, is that Burton-sponsored riders do not have to migrate to the city where the team is located, but as members of the global Burton team they are expected to represent the company wherever in the world they are training, competing or filming. As will be discussed in Chapter 4, professional snowboarders often have a highly mobile lifestyle and thus become travelling billboards for their sponsors. Burton Snowboards also conducts an annual 'World Tour' marketing campaign, travelling to major cities throughout North America, Europe and Japan with a selection of its elite global athletes, promoting products and building snowboarding celebrity. Burton-sponsored athletes from each of the countries visited also feature in the local events. Burton Snowboards' sponsorship of events and athletes illustrates the company's commitment to snowboarding, and thus does important corporate image work. Burton Snowboards clearly understands that, in a competitive capitalist system, the need to invest in image-building never ceases, and they continue to produce new and innovative global and local advertising and marketing campaigns.

Yet the North American, European and Australasian snowboarding markets have been at 'saturation point' since the early 2000s, with many concerned about dropping participation rates. Moreover, the Japanese market has been steadily shrinking over the past decade. According to Burton Snowboards representative William Avedon, the company has identified China as 'the next step' for market expansion (William Avendon of Burton Snowboards, cited in Thorpe, 2012b, p. 157). Attempting to raise the profile of the sport and their company among Chinese youth, Burton Snowboards is employing an array of innovative marketing strategies. For example, in 2005, Burton Snowboards signed a three-year deal to sponsor the National Snowboard Team of China. According to Bryan Johnston, vice president of global marketing for Burton Snowboards, 'snowboarding's expansion into China presents a huge opportunity in the sport's overall growth . . . and we're extremely pleased to have the chance to work with the National Snowboard Team of China' (cited in Burton Sponsors, 2005, para. 4). Moreover, in 2008 Burton Snowboards became the title sponsor of 'The Burton Quiabo Mellow Park', a new indoor year-round terrain facility in Beijing. In May 2013, in the wake of Jake Burton's recovery from testicular cancer, Burton Snowboards underwent another restructure with John Lacy assuming the role of Chief Product Officer. In so doing, he was tasked with overseeing the company's various 'Global Resort programs' (Learn To Ride [LTR], Riglet Parks [parks designed specifically for very young children] and Stash), and will take on a leadership role in developing Burton's business model in China, which continues to be 'a key initiative for the brand' (Burton Snowboards announces, 2013, para. 2). As I illustrate in the following case, Burton is one of many transnational action sport corporations trying to promote their brand and develop their sport among the rapidly growing Chinese middle-class youth.

China: the new frontier for the action sport industry

Chinese manufacturing firms have been commissioned by foreign companies to produce action sport-related clothing and equipment since the mid-1980s. It is only recently, however, that these foreign companies recognized the potential of the rapidly growing Chinese middle class, and in particular Chinese middle-class youth. In 2003, China's 'middle class' – people earning more than RMB 50,000 (US$6,500 per year) – accounted for an estimated 19 per cent of the country's 1.3 billion population; this class is expected to constitute 40 per cent of the total population by 2020. Indeed, the current cohort of people 13 to 24 years old is the first generation of the one-child rule, and they have a wide range of lifestyle choices. While action sports grew exponentially in some Asian countries (particularly Japan and South Korea) during the late 1980s and 1990s, it is only over the past decade that western-based action sport corporations have honed in on the potential of the Chinese youth market. In so doing, however, they have had to invest heavily in order to raise the profile of these sports, and to work with the Chinese government to organize events that they hoped would help create a market for their products.

In 2003, action sport giant Quiksilver entered a joint venture with Chinese-owned and -operated apparel manufacturer Glorious Sun Enterprises with the goal of opening retail stores in Shanghai, Beijing and Hong Kong, and tapping into the rapidly growing Chinese market. 'We are very excited about this initiative,' said Quiksilver CEO Bob McKnight:

> China is increasingly linked to the global youth culture. Nearly 50 million Chinese households have access to MTV, and the Internet and satellite television are quickly becoming more and more available. While the development of the board-riding culture is still in its infancy in this market, indoor snow-parks and skate-shops are beginning to show up in a number of high-profile locations. We believe the time is right for our lifestyle message, and are confident that it will resonate strongly with young consumers in this strong and fast-growing market . . . We are excited to

begin to capitalize on what we believe is a range of growth opportunities that exist for Quiksilver throughout Southeast Asia and the Pacific Rim. (Quiksilver to enter Chinese market, 2003, para. 3)

Many other, American-based, companies also saw the potential in the Chinese market, and began investing in major events and spectacles to help raise the profile of action sports and their companies, and to promote global action sport athletes/celebrities, among Chinese youth. For example, professional Californian skateboarder Danny Way grabbed headlines around the world when in 2005, with the financial support of his key sponsors Quiksilver and DC shoes, he constructed the largest skateboarding structure ever built (36.58 metres tall, with a gap distance of 27.43 metres) and performed a 360-degree rotation while jumping over the Great Wall of China on his skateboard. In his own words, 'skateboarding has yet to realize its full potential, and by bringing this event to the people of China and the rest of the world, I hope to contribute to the future of skateboarding and the global attention this sport can achieve' (cited in Skateboarder Danny Way, 2005, para. 3). Interestingly, the Chinese government approved this media stunt; even a number of governmental members, including Wang Jianjur, head of the Ministry of Culture, attended the event and presented Way with part of the wall as a special souvenir.

More recently, the US company Oakley partnered with champion snowboarder and skateboarder Shaun White to co-present the 2010 'Air + Style' event in Beijing. Oakley CEO Colin Baden was frank about the company's motives for investing in this event:

China has one of the largest and fastest growing middle class demographics in the world, and Chinese youth are currently experiencing a cultural revolution. All accounts point to these young people moving toward urban culture, music and action sports, and Air + Style delivers on all fronts. We'll bring the excitement of snowboarding to a new frontier, and the industry will likely follow our lead. (cited in Oakley and Shaun White, 2010, para. 2)

White was equally enthusiastic, describing the event as 'an amazing honour' and 'a huge opportunity' to 'share our ever-progressing sport with Beijing and Chinese society as a whole' (cited in Oakley and Shaun White, 2010, para. 4).

Attempting to build the sport of surfing in China, the Association of Surfing Professionals (ASP) and the International Surfing Association (ISA) have hosted an array of international surfing competitions on Hainan Island in the South China Sea, including the 2011 World Women's Longboard Championship. Interestingly, however, some surfers are publicly raising questions about such initiatives. For example, American World Champion

Figure 2.1 The world's largest skateboarding ramp that helped launch Californian skateboarder Danny Way over the Great Wall of China in July 2005

longboarder Cori Schumacher boycotted this event, citing 'deep political and personal reservations with being a part of any sort of benefit to a country that actively engages in human-rights violations, specifically those in violation of women' (cited in Weisberg, 2011, para. 10). She expands upon her reasoning in an online article, explaining: 'My decision to boycott this and other World Longboard Tour events this year is an attempt to use the platform I have to focus attention on the significant movement of the ASP World Tour [and] surf companies' into China (Schumacher, 2011, para. 2). Continuing, she proclaims:

> Admittedly, China's economic growth is stunning, but what is the current cost? This is essentially the question I am posing to the 'foremost governing body of surfing', the surf companies who are currently doing business in China, and those who plan to move there soon. What is the true cost of growing your profit margins within the current socio-political environment of China? I believe that the surf companies doing business within China have a moral duty to conduct business in a manner that benefits society, otherwise they are tacitly assisting the continued infringement of human rights violations. (Schumacher, 2011, para. 10)

Brodie Carr, CEO of the ASP, responded to Schumacher's concerns, encouraging her to participate:

> This event is an opportunity for female longboarders to be ambassadors of goodwill in a land that seldom afforded role models of this kind. In my humble opinion, I believe you can do so much more good by going there and inspiring the people of this country than by protesting. (Cited in Weisberg, 2011)

Yet Schumacher remained adamant, arguing 'what I, and other female longboarders, are being asked here to be are "goodwill ambassadors" of the most naïve kind. The kind that allows business to overlay their desires, branding and business ethics atop their own individuality and ethics' (cited in Weisberg, 2011). Of course, the event went ahead without Schumacher's participation, but she continued to raise critical questions from a distance.

Others have also used the Internet to challenge the model of development being employed by western surf companies who are increasingly hosting competitions in China; these include the International Surfing Association's (ISA) China Cup and the Association of Surfing Professionals' (ASP) World Qualifying Series Hainan Cup. In particular, Clifton Evers, a critical scholar of sport and physical culture, who is an avid surfer and currently working at a university in China, travelled to the sites where the events had been held to find a permanent contest site used only for the annual events, as well as significant trash from the competitions. He makes a strong case that 'surfing companies, organizations and competitors had (and still have) the chance to show how the environment can be managed to benefit tourism, rather than be destroyed because of it, as tends to be the case in China. To date, they haven't done enough' (Evers, 2012). Both Schumacher and Evers' arguments evoked much controversy, with many readers posting strong responses both for and against their online protests.[2] To date, surfing is the only action sport in which athletes and participants have publically questioned the responsibility of western action sport-related companies' participation in China.

Governmental support and building the market

The Chinese government appears to support the development of action sports. According to Wei Xing, chairman of the China Extreme Sports Association, a division of the State General Administration of Sports, 'China is a sporting nation and we support all action and extreme sports. Our office is working hard to create more BMX tracks and skate parks' (World's largest skatepark, 2006, para. 1). In October 2005 the world's largest skate park opened in Shanghai. Three times bigger than the largest skateboard park in the United States and rumoured to have cost more than US$8 million – a price tag allegedly paid by the government (World's largest skatepark, 2006, para. 1) – the park hosts a number of national and international action sport events each year, and was expected to encourage more Chinese youths to take up skateboarding, BMX and inline skating. However, the park has been less successful than hoped in recruiting Chinese action sport enthusiasts. According to Chen Jie, CEO of the SMP Skate Park, over 90 per cent of the 2,000 members are foreigners: 'we're turning into a club catering exclusively to foreigners. Some wealthy Chinese send their kids here to play only because they want their children to be more international, as the children [can] speak English with kids from other countries in the park' (cited in David, 2011a, para. 5).

Despite the support of the Chinese Extreme Sports Association and the aggressive marketing by Chinese and western – particularly US – companies, many Chinese youth and their parents remain tentative about participating in these sports. Guan Mu, founder of the Beijing Kicker Club – an extreme sports club boasting more than 5700 members across China – explains that although action sports 'are on the rise in Beijing, they are developing slowly . . . Parents in China always think their children should avoid these dangerous sports. It is also still expensive for ordinary guys to get top-quality coaching and equipment' (cited in Li, 2005, para. 13). The *Shanghai Star* reports that many Chinese youth are 'under heavy pressure to study' and that some consider action sports 'a waste of time' (Yu, 2002, para. 18). A strong advocate for snowboarding in China, Steve Zdarsky, identifies some of the unique cultural considerations involved in developing the sport: 'Snowboarding is growing a lot in the bigger city centres, especially Beijing. Here, the people have income and can afford to buy gear and go snowboarding . . . [but due to China's one-child policy] all the riders are twenty-plus, [there are] no young kids. You finish university first and then you start to snowboard' (cited in Air China, 2008, para, 8). Drawing upon two studies on Chinese youth culture, US-based research firm Label Networks notes that few parents want their only child to participate in dangerous sports such as snowboarding or skateboarding, and that they still prefer basketball, table tennis and martial arts (China X, 2007, para. 6). Although action sports have spawned a new culture among youth in China, participation tends to be based on the consumption of apparel, footwear, events, and US and Japanese action sport heroes rather than on active participation. Interestingly, while the 'extreme', high-risk, rebellious, countercultural image of action sports has been effective in appealing to youth in many western, and some Eastern, countries, it is hindering participation rates in China (Thorpe, 2008a). The difficulties of connecting with the Chinese youth market prompted some western companies to rethink their strategies for this unique market.

Building action sport infrastructure

Rather than merely opening stores and hosting events, action sport companies recognized the need to actively create a market for their products in China. As such, some action sport companies have established or invested in programs to teach Chinese youth about these sports. For example, Burton Snowboards set up a Chinese version of their 'Learn to Ride' program at ski resorts to teach Chinese how to snowboard. However, in 2008 they had to extend their efforts by also providing training programs for instructors. 'That's how underdeveloped the marketplace is there,' said Craig Smith, Burton's senior international sales director (cited in Mickle, 2008). In 2012, Camp Woodward – a highly successful US company that provides action sport training camps for emerging athletes and passionate youth – opened its first international facility in the Daxing district of Beijing. Built on a four-star resort property, the camp features 410 acres of indoor and outdoor skate parks. The world-class facilities cost more than US$4 million to build, with some sources reporting that the Chinese government supported the initiative with an investment of RMB21.96 million. The opening ceremony was attended by some of the world's most renowned action sport athletes, including skateboarders Tony Hawk and Ryan Sheckler, as well as governmental dignitaries. The facility offers day and overnight programs throughout the year, including skateboarding, BMX freestyle, inline skating, graphic design, video production and digital photography, dry-land snowboarding and skiing, music lessons and a music recording studio, as well as Chinese or English language classes. According to Zhou Qiang, President of China New Media Investment Inc., the 'Woodward Experience' will

provide a great opportunity to introduce Chinese youth, and international students living in China, to new activities that stimulate creative thinking. In addition, we also anticipate that the customer base will grow to include many action sports enthusiasts from all over the Pacific basin, including Japan, Korea, Southeast Asia, Australia and New Zealand. (Cited in Campbell, 2010)

Managing owner and president of Camp Woodward, Gary Ream, offers similarly optimistic rhetoric: 'Woodward Beijing provides an opportunity to inspire many young Chinese to discover the passion of lifestyle sports by bringing world-class athletes and facilities directly to them. We are excited to be a part of helping grow action sports in China . . .' (cited in Campbell, 2010). Clearly, the development and promotion of action sports in China is being driven by both governmental and corporate motives, and intriguing relationships between Chinese and US investors.

Changing perceptions: a top-down approach

Travelling western youth have been practising a variety of action sports in China since the 1980s, and while a few Chinese youth have picked up the activities after witnessing such displays, action sports were typically perceived as odd American activities and a 'waste of time'. However, Liu Qing, the deputy secretary-general of the Chinese Extreme Sports Association, observes a distinct change in public perception during the early 2000s: 'In the beginning, kids on skateboards caused concerns about teenage rebellion. Now, skateboarding and other extreme sports like BMX have become a means for young people to challenge themselves' (cited in Bolin, 2009, para. 17). Integral to this change in public perception has been the government's attitude towards action sports.

The Chinese government's interest in action sports was piqued with the recent inclusion of an array of action sports (snowboarding, freestyle skiing, BMX, mountain biking) into the summer and winter Olympic Games programs. With shorter histories and less developed national infrastructure, the Chinese government has identified action sports as 'soft sports', offering opportunities for developing Olympic medal contenders within a short period and with relatively little economic investment. During the early 2000s, for example, snowboarding and freestyle skiing were identified as offering a unique opportunity for China to find space on the Winter Olympic podium. As Zhao Yinggang, China's director of winter sports, explains: 'We don't have the foundation and the money to have the same number of clubs as in the US. Winter sports are very expensive compared to summer sports. . . . [But] maybe these events [freestyle skiing and snowboarding] give Chinese and Asians an advantage because of our body type, like in gymnastics and diving' (cited in Longman, 2010, para. 14). The Chinese government initiated new programs to foster the development of Olympic-level action sport athletes, recruiting practitioners from young ages. Wei Xing, chairman of the China Extreme Sports Association, a division of the

State General Administration of Sports, has admitted to developing govern-mental strategies to help 'bring up world class action sports athletes from a junior stage' (World's largest skatepark, 2006, para. 2). For example, in 2005 the Chinese National Snowboard Team, consisting of six boys and six girls, selected solely on their athletic (rather than snowboarding) abilities, was established; by 2010, four Chinese female snowboard team members held top 10 World Cup rankings.

Observing the divergent approach to team selection and skill development, and the highly disciplined and regimented training practices employed by the Chinese snowboarders and their foreign coaches at Whistler (Canada), Tom Hutchinson, the head freestyle coach for Canada's national team, notes: 'What China does is they go out and grab athletes. What we do in Canada is wait for the kids to come to us, even if that takes years . . . Now is that good? Who knows . . . You don't want little robots. But it depends on what you define as success' (cited in Mick, 2010, para. 23). Canadian snowboard halfpipe team member, Dominique Vallee, is less open-minded: 'That's not the heart and soul of snowboarding. It's not a boot camp, and it's not [win] at all costs' (cited in Mick, 2010, para. 9). Originating among western youth during the 1960s and 1970s via grassroots participation and do-it-yourself styles, it is understandable that some action sport participants become concerned as youth from other nations adopt and adapt 'their' sports in ways that appear to contradict the original philosophies underpin-ning their development. In contrast to western youth, however, Chinese youth have been exposed to these sports via a top-down approach driven by corporations and the government motivated by the potential for economic growth and lust for gold medals. Thus, as more Chinese youth participate and compete in these activities, it is likely that they will continue to adopt and develop their own unique approaches towards these sports that may or may not be in line with traditionally western styles and philosophies.

China hosts action sport events

With governmental support and investment from both western and Chinese corporate sponsors, China is increasingly hosting large interna-tional extreme sports events (for example, the Shanghai Showdown Gravity Games, the Nanshan Snowboarding Open, the 720 China Surf Open). The Asian X Games – previously staged on Phuket Island, Thailand (1998–2001), Kuala Lumpur, Malaysia (2002–2004) and Seoul, South Korea (2005) – was held for the first time in the People's Republic of China in 2007. Shanghai hosted the three-day event, which attracted more than 200 of the world's top action sport athletes from more than 20 countries and from five con-tinents. Athletes competed in a variety of disciplines, including aggressive inline skating, skateboarding, BMX freestyle, sport climbing and moto-X, for a prize pool of US$100,000. Between 2007 and 2012, the Kia X Games was sanctioned by ESPN, ESPN STAR Sports and the Chinese Extreme Sports

Association and hosted by Shanghai Sports Federation, Yang Pu District Government and KIC Jiang Wan Stadium. Kia Motors, a secondary sponsor of the Asian X Games since 2005, renewed its support with a three-year primary sponsorship to build the event in China as well as to gain valuable product exposure. Indeed, Kia Motors estimated that in 2005 alone, media exposure from the Asian X Games was worth approximately US$12 million to the company. While Chinese and western companies are increasingly identifying the huge potential in action sports as a way to tap into the growing youth market, some complications have arisen as the Chinese Extreme Sports Association imposed rules upon its athletes that ran counter to the philosophy of the American-based X Games.

A situation arose during the 2011 Asian X Games that highlights some of the complex politics and power relations occurring behind the scenes of the development of action sports in China. As noted in Chapter 1, unlike the Olympic Games and many other traditional sporting events, the X Games does not emphasise nationality (Thorpe & Wheaton, 2011a). Adopting a nationalistic approach to the Asian X Games, however, the Chinese Extreme Sports Association (CESA) made the strategic decision to only allow 'national athletes' to compete in the games. This caused difficulties for Shen Jian, one of China's top BMX riders, who had recently signed an exclusive endorsement deal with Vans. The CESA prohibited Jian from competing in the Games unless he wore a jersey emblazoned with the official Chinese sponsor's logo, which would have nullified his contract with Vans. Yet the CESA do not train or finance action sport athletes, and Shen was reliant upon his endorsement deal with Vans for his livelihood. Unwilling to compromise his relationship with Vans, he was thus banned from the competition. American event organizers then offered Shen a 'wild card' entry into the X Games, but when a CESA official saw him warming up for the event, his wild card entry was quickly revoked. According to one action sport journalist observing the event, 'people from the association asked this ESPN guy right before the match to remove all Chinese athletes who [are] not from the national team from the list. If [they] failed to cooperate, the CESA would not give them the permit to host the X Games Asia in China next year' (David, 2011c). The CESA were unapologetic in their decision: 'If they [Chinese action sport athletes] want to represent their country and get exposure, they need us. For them, being selected is an honour because it means they are the best in China,' proclaimed Liu Qing, CESA Deputy Secretary General (cited in Levin, 2011, para. 35). The General Secretary of the CESA also stated: 'It's not the association doesn't want him to compete. We have a set of rules that the athletes need to follow' (Wei Xing, cited in David, 2011c).

Although Chinese athletes are rarely known for questioning authority, Shen was vocal in his frustrations: 'CESA taught me nothing. I don't need to wear their clothing so they can make money and exploit me. We riders created this community, not CESA. The association's only power comes from the Communist Party' (cited in Levin, 2011, para. 36). In another interview, Shen explains: 'A national team athlete gets very little from the association's sponsorship. The CESA has done nothing for us and their sole aim all these years has been making money by using these players [athletes]' (cited in David, 2011, para. 8). While the American organizers of the Asian X Games followed the CESA's orders during the event, when the Vice President at ESPN's events management group was questioned about the incident he did not see this arrangement as consistent with the X Games philosophy:

> The X Games has always been an open playing field and the qualifica-tions is done on ranking systems. We work with the government agency, the Chinese Extreme Sports Association, to make sure we have the best local athletes competing. So if that's the case (Shen and other athletes barred from participating) that's something we need to look into . . . (Harvey Davis, cited in David, 2011c)

It is difficult to know whether the conflict of interest between the CESA and ESPN contributed to the decision not to host another Asian X Games after 2012. However, the lessons learned in working with local governmental groups and organizations in China certainly informed ESPN's approach to developing the global X Games series in 2013.

The X Games: an action sport mega event

At the centre of the rapid global diffusion of action sports sits the American-based cable television network ESPN (Entertainment and Sports Programming Network, owned by ABC, itself a division of the Walt Disney Group). It broadcast the first Summer X Games in mid-1995. Staged at Newport, Providence, and Middletown (Rhode Island), and Mount Snow (Vermont), the inaugural games featured 27 events in nine categories: bungee jumping, eco-challenge, inline skating, skateboarding, skysurfing, sport climbing, street luge, biking and water sports. Twelve months later, X Games II attracted around 200,000 spectators, and early in 1997 ESPN staged the first Winter X Games at Snow Summit Mountain Resort (California). The initial Winter X Games were televised in 198 countries and territories in 21 languages. Backed by a range of transnational corporate sponsors, the X Games – the self-defined 'worldwide leader' in action sports – has played a significant role in the global diffusion and expansion of the action sport industry and culture (Rinehart, 2000).

The emergence of the first few X Games prompted vociferous debate among grassroots practitioners who contested ESPN's co-option of their life-style into television-tailored 'sports' (Rinehart, 2008). Today, however, most action sport athletes recognize mass-mediated events such as the X Games as a core element of action sport in the 21st century, and are embracing the new opportunities for increased media exposure, sponsorship and celebrity

offered (Beal & Wilson, 2004). With the support of many action sport athletes and celebrities, the X Games have become the ultimate forum for setting records and performing ever more technical and creative manoeuvres
for international audiences. Blurring the boundaries between music festival
and sporting event (Rinehart, 2008), the X Games have been hugely successful in capturing the imagination of the lucrative youth market. Indeed, globally, 63 million people watched the 2002 X Games; in contrast to the aging
Olympic viewership, the median age of these viewers was 20 years (Thorpe &
Wheaton, 2011a, p. 833). The X Games have witnessed exponential growth
in terms of participants and television and online audiences in the nearly
two decades since the first games. The 2012 Winter X Games were the most-
watched yet, with an estimated 35.4 million viewers in the United States
tuning in to ESPN, and a digital media audience that was up 147 per cent
from the previous year (Hargrove, 2012). The X Games were instrumental in
launching ESPN2 and helped spawn dozens of licensing deals including an
IMAX movie, X Games skateparks, and X Games DVDs and toys.

The X Games are good examples of action sport 'mega events'. According
to Smart (2007), global sports events such as the FIFA World Cup, the
Rugby World Cup, the Summer and Winter Olympics, Wimbledon and the
Tour de France, 'now take the form of recurring spectacular commercial
media festivals' (p. 130; also see Horne & Manzenreiter, 2006). At these
'consumer cultural events', sports stars, and 'those elevated to an iconic
global celebrity status, represent local and/or national communities. The
celebrities serve as role models, as objects of adulation and identification,
but also increasingly as exemplars of consumer lifestyles to which spectators
and television viewers alike are enticed to aspire' (Smart, 2007, p. 130).
Action sport stars competing at the X Games are certainly celebrities, overtly
and covertly promoting consumer lifestyles. In contrast to most traditional
sport 'mega events', however, action sport athletes are not representing the
nation. Indeed, there are very few signs of nationalism or national identity
at X Games events. While the athlete's nationality is sometimes declared
during an event, spectators do not wave national flags, athletes do not wear
national uniforms, and national anthems are not played as the athletes
stand on the podiums. Rather, as the athletes receive their X Games medals
they typically appear as 'walking corporate billboards' for TNCs ranging
from energy drink brands to credit card companies (Messner, 2002); their
equipment is covered in the stickers of their sponsors, and their bodies are
branded with multiple logos on hats, t-shirts, jackets and pants. Some will
even be seen holding or drinking from the bottles of their soft- or energy
drink sponsors as they receive their medals. In so doing, the athletes are
representing national and global corporations rather than their nations. In
contrast to many contemporary sports mega events which have increasingly
become 'ideal vehicles for corporate sponsors seeking to raise the global
profile of their brands' (Smart, 2007, p. 127), the X Games and action sport

athletes' relationships with commercial sponsors have always been integral to the production and consumption of these sporting spectacles.

The politics of the X Games global expansion

Originally a US-based event, the X Games have been steadily expanding internationally in the pursuit of new markets and sponsors in local contexts. As previously mentioned, the Asian X Games have been held in Phuket, Kuala Lumpur, Seoul and Shanghai. In March 2010, the first European Winter X Games were held in Tignes (France). The event was attended by more than 66,200 spectators, 150 athletes from around the world, 370 international journalists over three days, and was broadcast to 166 countries (live and highlights). The X Games have also organized smaller action sport events, qualifiers and demonstrations in Brazil, Canada, Japan, Korea, Malaysia, Mexico, Singapore, Spain, Taiwan, Philippines and UAE.

In May 2011, ESPN announced that the X Games were expanding globally to include six major events per year, including the Summer and Winter Games in the US, and the European Winter X Games in Tignes; ESPN also invited cities interested in hosting the other three events to enter a formal bidding process. As revealed in the following comment from Scott Guglielmino, Senior Vice President of Programming and the X Games, ESPN recognizes the potential of action sports to expand into international markets:

> Action sports is a collection of activities that we think travels really well around the world. The reality of what we're doing here is we've created this huge stage for action-sport athletes, and we're taking that global now. We're providing an even larger platform for them to participate in and perform at, and grow themselves. (Cited in O'Neil, 2012, para. 2)

In contrast to other American-based sports such as baseball and American football, which have not been widely embraced by local audiences around the world, ESPN identifies action sports as integral 'to our growth around the world . . . driven by local relevance and in building a passionate connection between fans, our brand and our partners' (Russell Wolff, Executive President and Managing Director, ESPN International, cited in Nine cities advance, 2012, para. 3). Integral to the Global X Games series is not only the potential to reach new audiences, but also new sponsors. In the words of ESPN's Executive Vice President for Multimedia Sales, 'Our goal is to get global sponsors involved in particular categories and create opportunities to sell locally based on whatever regions of the world we're in' (cited in Mickle, 2011, para. 13).

Somewhat ironically, the formal bidding process was modelled on the highly political (and often corrupt) approach employed by the International Olympic Committee (see, for example, Bale & Krogh-Christensen, 2004) in which interested cities must first enter an initial bid, before being shortlisted for a more intensive round of reviews as well as visits from the organizing committee. The X Games website touted the opportunity to become a host city as follows:

> It's all about youth, vitality and energy showcased on a world stage for millions to see. As host to the X Games, your venue, your community and your city become part of a dynamic brand – one that captures the unbridled passion and fearlessness of sport. . . . As a host for the X Games, your city will become synonymous with the celebration of youth, life-style, creativity and community that is the X brand. (The Power of Youth, X Games website, 2013)

The language used here is explicit: the X Games is a global brand that host cities would do well to be connected with. With more than 40 initial entries from 21 countries, ESPN was 'thrilled with the response from cities around the world' (Wolff, cited in Nine cities advance, 2012, para. 3). Nearly 20 of these entries then participated in a two-day workshop at the X Games in Los Angeles in August 2011, designed to 'educate qualified applicants on the vision and long term strategy of the X Games' (Nine cities advance, 2012, para. 2). Finally, in December 2011 the three new X Games host cities were announced. Barcelona (Spain), Munich (Germany) and Foz do Iguaçu (Brazil) were selected from a group of nine finalists. 'A lot of our decision on which cities to select was based on their [the host city and nation's] action sport cul-ture and our point of view on how strong it was,' said Guglielmino, adding that the new hosts will also introduce additional sports and cultural elements unique to their regions (cited in O'Neil, 2012, para. 4). ESPN is clear about the importance of glocalization in each of these locations: 'one of the most exciting parts of this expansion' is, according to Wolff, the potential to 'adopt [sic] the local flair of each host country' (cited in Thornton, 2011, para. 5).

While the winning cities were obviously thrilled to be awarded the Games after such an intensive bidding process, some athletes also expressed their excitement. For example, Brazilian skateboarding star and winner of multi-ple X Games medals, Pedro Barros, believes the global expansion of the X Games 'makes it more democratic, giving athletes from other countries the opportunity to compete in their own country. This can be the start of a new era in action sports history' (cited in O'Neil, 2012, para. 5). Yet, it is perhaps the complaints expressed by those from unsuccessful cities that offer the most insights into the politics involved in the bidding process. For example, one journalist reports on the questions being raised by Whistler residents after receiving news that they were unsuccessful in their bid to be a host for the Winter X Games despite submitting a very strong application that had received positive feedback from the committee:

> Although Whistler Blackcomb, Tourism Whistler and the Resort Municipality each came to the table with $250,000 to host the event, it

still wasn't enough to sway ESPN's decision to make the mountain town a host. This is a disappointment for some, although would bringing the X Games to Whistler really benefit the locals? . . . just like hosting the Olympics there would be lots of pros and cons for playing host to such a big event. (Dean, 2012, para. 2)

Not dissimilar from the bidding process for the Olympic Games, the decisions as to which cities would be awarded the X Games were deeply entrenched in broader social, political and economic power relations. In particular, ESPN was interested to enter new markets with strong action sport communities and the potential for significant growth. While Whistler would be an excellent host for such an event, ESPN did not feel that a Canadian X Games would offer a radically new market, as many Canadian youth are already passionate consumers of the US-based Summer and Winter X Games, with many Canadian athletes competing (particularly in the Winter Games) and numerous fans travelling down for the events. Put simply, the opportunity for market growth in Canada was considerably smaller than it was in Brazil, Germany and Spain.

The politics and practicalities of producing X Games in new locations

In order to effectively record and distribute media coverage of the six annual events, ESPN devised a new 'International Broadcast Center' model. The competition coverage is produced at the events, before being integrated through a Digital Center control room at the ESPN Digital Center control room in Bristol (Connecticut, US). According to X Games Vice President, Tori Stevens, this has

> created an unprecedented model in which we will be simultaneously creating a minimum of six unique telecast (sponsored world-feed, sponsor-free world feed, US customized feed, Spain customized feed, Brazil customized feed and a Germany customized feed). The sponsor-free world feed will allow us to reach numerous territories that have previously been unable to carry X Games live due to restrictions in many countries. We have made creative efforts to expand the distribution of this content both on and off of our networks around the world, and these feeds allow us to do that. We distributed content to more than 430 million homes around the world of our [2013] Aspen event. (Stevens, cited in Tobias, 2013, para. 6)

It is anticipated that the six X Games events will produce a total of 130 hours of live TV coverage on ESPN networks in the US and around the world, and will be supplemented by coverage on digital platforms, including those of the host cities and a year-round action sports website hosted by ESPN.

Responsible for staging the events in Los Angeles and Aspen, and managing the local organizing committees (LOCs) to execute the events in Tignes, Foz do Iguaçu, Barcelona and Munich, Stevens is a busy woman. While 'pleasantly surprised by the number of cities and countries from around the world who expressed interest in hosting the X Games', Stevens admits that she and her team 'probably underestimated the complexity and time required to sell local sponsorships in markets that have less familiarity with our brand and event' (cited in Tobias, 2013, para. 5). Juggling meetings in Portuguese, Catalan, Spanish and German, Stevens acknowledged that 'the real challenge is going into a new location where we are working in new venues, with new partners and vendors in different cultures' (cited in Tobias, 2013, para. 4).

Of course, image-management is always of utmost concern to corporations such as ESPN and thus it was rare to find ESPN employees expressing doubts and difficulties with this mammoth undertaking. Interestingly, however, a leaked email from ESPN operations manager Severn Sandt to X Games staff revealed some of the financial and cultural concerns among upper management. In the email, Sandt wrote openly to staff involved in organizing the first of the new X Games events in Foz do Iguaçu:

> I'm going to be completely honest with you: this global X Games series is far from a sure thing long-term. Financially, things are extremely difficult. I have personally banged my head against the budget wall for countless hours, especially on this event. Every negotiation has been exhausting, trying to wring every spare *reais* out of it. (Cited in Koblin, 2013, para. 2)

He encourages staff to cut costs wherever possible at the event, including buying their own water rather than taking water from the hotels, and rounding down rather than up when entering their overtime hours. Continuing, he attempts to prepare the typically young American staff for the cultural differences they are likely to experience while working in Brazil. 'Don't make fun of the people here or the way they do things,' he warns, 'You might find things you see here backward, ludicrous, even stupid. Hold your laughter till you get back home. We need these people to put the event on, so don't insult them' (cited in Koblin, 2013, para. 6). He also asks staff to 'bring your patience' because 'many people in Brazil do not operate at the same pace as most of us do'. He goes on to warn:

> Getting service at the hotel could be slow. Getting a cab could take time. You could be told, 'yeah, a guy will come chain your tripod down in the next half hour', then say it again in a half hour, and again a half hour after than, and then maybe 4 hours later it could actually happen. This is the kind of reality you must handle without losing it. (Sandt, cited in Koblin, 2013, para. 10)

While the language used in this email may seem crude, and the characterization of cultural differences somewhat obnoxious, it is possible that Sandt was writing for his audience of mostly young action sport enthusiasts and media and sports event workers familiar with producing events in the US, but with little awareness of the unique cultural differences they are likely to experience while working abroad. As Giulianotti & Brownell (2012) explain, sport mega events 'provide a political space in which the transnationalization of local issues and the localization of transnational dynamics occur simultaneously' (p. 206). Indeed, at the same time as the local organizing committee in Foz do Iguaçu were dealing with their own internal politics in preparation of hosting hundreds of international visiting officials, competitors and media, and thousands of local spectators, the American-based X Games organizing committee were making plans based on broader economics of the X Games Global Series, as well as local considerations based on cultural differences and sponsorship difficulties, and organizing staff in two locations to co-produce a sporting spectacle for a global audience. As this example illustrates, mega action sport events such as the X Games 'act as transmitters of political processes between the domestic and international domains, facilitating reciprocal influences between the two levels' (Giulianotti & Brownell, 2012, p. 206).

Almost as soon as the names were announced for the three new X Games host cities, ESPN revealed that they were opening a new bidding process for US cities eager to host the 2014 Summer and Winter X Games. After 10 years in LA, the Summer X Games would be moving due to contractual difficulties between the X Games and the Anschutz Entertainment Group (the Los Angeles entertainment giant behind Staples Center and several LA sports franchises). According to a study by the Los Angeles Sports and Entertainment Commission, hosting the games in 2010 had an economic impact of approximately $50 million, attracting as many as 58,000 additional visitor days in Los Angeles (cited in Gardner, 2013, para. 8). Four cities were shortlisted from more than 20 initial bids to host the US-based summer X Games from 2014–2016, including Austin (Texas), Chicago (Illinois), Detroit (Michigan) and Charlotte (North Carolina). While each city approached their applications differently, the Detroit committee consisting of young, technologically savvy action sport enthusiasts, put forward a strong and innovative case that touted the grungy, edgy, youth culture of Detroit as an excellent setting for the games. According to one Detroit journalist, the 'influx of young professionals to the city during the revitalization process' has 'brought a better understanding of technology, including social media, and a new wave of music that goes hand in hand with the X Games' (Katzenstein, 2013, para. 19). The group started a Facebook and Twitter campaign and a website encouraging people to sign up and 'join the movement', and in the final stage of the bidding process released a YouTube video that professionally and creatively demonstrated the variety and skill of action sport participants in grungy, urban settings that reveal some of the essence of Detroit. Indeed, the campaign was unique in that it emphasized the potential of the X Games for contributing to the regeneration of Detroit. Commenting on the appeal of the Detroit proposal, Guglielmino stated that, 'to potentially connect with a city like Detroit, which is clearly on the way back . . . and to be able to support that is a very intriguing proposition to us' (cited in Katzenstein, 2013, para. 5). Despite such potential, Austin, Texas, ultimately won the bid to host the annual US-based Summer X Games from 2014 to 2018.

While the future of X Games events in the US and beyond continues to evolve, with six major events held every year, we can be certain that ESPN and the X Games will continue to play a dominant role in defining the styles of representation, participation and consumption of action sports around the world. The impetus behind the global expansion of the X Games was, according to Guglielmino, the realization that 'action sports travel well. There aren't many sports that travel well' (cited in Thornton, 2011, para. 12). Reading between the lines, what Guglielmino is suggesting here is that action sports offer ESPN an opportunity to enter local markets they would otherwise be unable to access with traditional American sports. Despite efforts to local-ize the events and capitalize upon the unique culture of each of the new host cities, the X Games is firmly controlled and arranged by the American-based media conglomerate ESPN. Yet, the lack of national symbolism associated with the events, and the already global media exposure of the games, have disguised the influence of an American media conglomerate on a global brand that has 'become synonymous with the celebration of youth, lifestyle, creativ-ity and community' (The Power of Youth, X Games website, 2013). The global expansion of the X Games is part of broader processes of Americanization. While ESPN touts the global X Games series as empowering action sport ath-letes, providing them with 'an even larger platform . . . to participate in and perform at, and grow themselves' (Guglelmino, cited in O'Neil, 2012, para. 2), this is merely marketing rhetoric. The motives underpinning such develop-ments are primarily economic, that is to attract new global *and* national spon-sors, and to expand the reach of televisual and online media to previously inaccessible audiences. Over the next few years, as the X Games continue to settle into new locations and/or reopen the bidding process, there will be rich opportunities for examining in more depth the promises, practices and politics of organizing and hosting action sport mega events in local contexts.

Transnational action sport media and marketing

It is increasingly being argued that, with most of the world's leading sport-media companies based in either Europe or America, we are witnessing 'a cultural convergence and homogenization of . . . sports television coverage across the globe' that is contributing to the impression that there is indeed one world of sport (Jarvie, 2006, p. 134; also see Smart, 2007; Sugden & Tomlinson, 1998). Similar processes are occurring in the action sport media complex. In 2013, ESPN dominated the production of televised action sport coverage in the US and internationally, and is continuing to publish ever more material online.

Transworld Media is also a powerful media house. Based in California, Transworld Media produces a wide array of action sport magazines that are distributed throughout the world, including *Transworld Skateboarding*, *Transworld Snowboarding*, *Transworld Surf*, *Transworld Motocross*, *RideBMX*, *Quad* and *Transworld Business*. Each of the magazines has its own website and produces videos, as well as an array of events. Transworld describes itself as a:

> rapidly evolving multimedia and entertainment company with tremendous assets. With seven monthly print magazines, thriving and robust Web properties, industry leading events and ten years of feature-length movies, Transworld can customize any number of multimedia opportunities. With further expansion planned into video-on-demand, linear television partnerships as well as the delivery of customized mobile content, Transworld will be reaching the core action lifestyle enthusiast at every touchpoint. (What is Transworld, 2008, p. 7)

Indeed, with more than four million magazine readers per month, 200,000 movie viewers per year, and 21.5 million online page views per month, the Transworld media network has a total yearly audience of over 25 million (What is Transworld, 2008). With 87 per cent of these viewers being male, with a median age range of 14–28 years, the media house is proficient at selling space to advertisers eager to reach the young male consumer. Indeed, advertisers range from the US military to deodorant companies. For example, in 2004 *Transworld Snowboarding* had an international monthly circulation of 207,000, featured a total of 1333 pages of advertisements, and generated US$21.9 million in revenue, up from US$14.9 million in 2000 (Stableford, 2005, para. 7).

Another US-based action sport media agency is GrindMedia, which owns various globally distributed magazines (including *Surfer, Surfing, Snowboarder, Skateboarder, Powder, Biker, SUP-Standup Paddler, Dirt rider, ATV Rider* and *Paved*) as well as various media websites (GrindTV.com, Newschoolers.com, Motocross.com). In so doing, GrindMedia magazines and websites reach more than 22 million active sport enthusiasts per year.

While many of the journalists, photographers and editors of specific magazines, websites or films for Transworld Media and GrindMedia are active participants in these sports themselves, both media companies are owned by transnational media conglomerates. During the early 2000s, Transworld was owned by Time4Media, a subsidiary of Time Warner Inc, but in 2007 was purchased by the Bonnier Group – a 200-year-old Swedish media and entertainment company with businesses in 20 countries – for US$200 million. In May 2013, however, GrindMedia – a division of Source

Interlink Media (a 'premier source of special interest media in the United States' with more than 75 publications, 100 Web sites, 800 branded products, more than 50 events, and TV and radio programs) – acquired the Transworld action sport brands from Bonnier Corporation. The combined business of Transworld and GrindMedia reaches an average monthly audience of more than 30 million action sport enthusiasts. With small, national action sport magazines and websites continuing to be acquired by larger media companies that are then purchased by transnational media conglomerates, we are witnessing an increasing cultural convergence and homogenization of media coverage of action sports around the world.

Much of the imagery and texts surrounding action sports is controlled by just a few transnational media conglomerates. Yet this does not mean the market is completely closed to alternative media approaches. A particularly noteworthy example is the energy drink company, Red Bull, that has been redefining the production of action sport media and marketing since the late 1990s. Thus, I conclude this chapter with a case study revealing Red Bull's innovative use of action sports and mega events for building brand recognition and consumer commitment.

Red Bull redefines the action sport media event

Red Bull is much more than an energy drink containing water, sugar, caffeine (equivalent to that in a cup of coffee) and taurine (an amino acid). It is a transnational brand closely associated with youth culture and the action sport lifestyle. Largely as a result of its innovative marketing strategies, Red Bull currently has an estimated 70 per cent share of the US$1.6 trillion global energy drink market (Johnson, 2012; McGiugan, 2012). With 200 staff at the Austrian headquarters and another 1800 staff worldwide, more than 4.6 billion cans per year are produced and distributed to 162 countries, with most being purchased by men between the ages of 18 and 35. According to one journalist, young men are 'voracious endorsers of the brand, and that's because with the beverage, Mateschitz [Red Bull's co-founder] commandeered – if not created – a new, high octane lifestyle category' (O'Brien, 2012). As the following case illustrates, Red Bull developed an innovative approach to connect the product with the action sport lifestyle. Red Bull does not merely pay to advertise in the transnational action sport magazines or sponsor mega sports events such as the X Games, but rather produces their own events, media and action sport celebrities. In so doing, Red Bull is blurring previously conceived divisions between media, events, corporations and celebrity.

Red Bull was co-founded in 1987 by Austrian toothpaste salesman Dietrich Mateschitz after he stumbled across Krating Daeng – a local energy drink popular among truck drivers – during his travels in Thailand in the early 1980s. Mateschitz had been eager to start his own business for some time, and he recognized the potential in this relatively obscure, unpatented energy drink for creating a new beverage category. He spent the next few years refining the recipe, developing a brand name and logo, and seeking approval from health authorities. Despite some initial resistance, the product gained popularity in Austria. Recognizing the need for market expansion, Mateschitz started selling Red Bull in neighbouring Hungary in 1993, before focusing his energies on 'conquering the German market', and then doing the same in England (Gschwandtner, 2004, p. 4). In 1997, Red Bull entered the US market, where it quickly became one of the most popular mixers with alcoholic spirits, particularly among university students and young, hip, urban professionals.

As the first energy drink on the market, with Red Bull Mateschitz was very aware of the need to build awareness and demand for the new concept of the energy drink, stating 'If we don't create the market, it doesn't exist' (cited in Gschwandtner, 2004, p. 1). Rather than spending millions on advertising, Mateschitz employed 'buzz marketing' to raise product awareness and stimulate sales. A popular strategy was to hire young (typically beautiful) students to drive Minis with a big Red Bull can strapped on top, delivering free samples to campuses and parties. But as sales in Europe and America continued to soar, numerous other energy drink companies continued to enter the market. In response to increasing competition, Mateschitz began to invest even more heavily in building the brand. In contrast to Coca-Cola, which spends 9 per cent of its revenue on marketing, Red Bull spends as much as 35 per cent of its budget on marketing (Clancy, 2012), much of this on action sport-related events and spectacles.

Of course, numerous other food and soft drink companies (for example, Mountain Dew) recognized the potential of action sports for tapping into the difficult consumer group of men aged 15 to 35, and have been advertising in action sport magazines and sponsoring events since the early 1990s. But Red Bull adopted a unique approach that gave the company credibility among even the most extreme action sport athletes and firmly established the connection between the energy drink and the action sport lifestyle. Rather than being one of many sponsors supporting an action sport event, Red Bull creates its own events. Indeed, Red Bull is involved in the creation and organization of more than 90 individually branded action sport events around the world (examples include Red Bull Road Rage, Red Bull Air Race World Championships and Red Bull X-Fighters). Such events take place in Australia, Asia, Africa, New Zealand, North America, South America, Russia, and throughout Europe. The pre- and post-event parties include professional DJs, appetizers, photogenic men and women and plenty of Red Bull. Some events, such as Red Bull's Flugtag – an annual event held in over 35 cities around the world in which participants create their own flying apparatuses and then launch off a jetty with their jumps being judged in three categories – distance, creativity and showmanship – draw crowds of 50,000 people or more. In contrast to the Red Bull Flugtag, in which anyone is able to participate, most events are designed for daring action sport athletes willing to participate in creative, risky and spectacular stunts or competitions. The Red Bull Crashed Ice event is a prime example. Launched in 2001 in Sweden, this event features four ice skaters racing one another down a 535-metre urban ice track with jumps, turns and berms. The event now has five instalments in an annual 'World Championship', with each event providing spectacular wipeouts, large crowds and, as with all Red Bull events, great after-parties.

Through the organization of events and spectacles, Red Bull is adopting an approach known as 'content marketing' in which the brand gives something valuable (in this case, spectacular action sport events for audiences and exciting opportunities for athletes) to get something valuable in return (consumer commitment). According to Rebecca Lieb, a marketing analyst:

> Red Bull has introduced its content marketing around and about the product, but it is never directly correlated to the drink itself. Nobody is going to go to a website and spend 45 minutes looking at a video about a drink. But Red Bull has aligned its brand unequivocally and consistently with extreme sports and action. They are number one at creating content so engaging consumers will spend hours with it, or at least significant minutes. (Cited in O'Brien, 2012)

In an interview with the *Financial Times*, Mateschitz supported such statements, confirming, 'Our media philosophy is as simple as it is correct: the onus is on the media to create content, not on us to provide it. If our results, achievements and activities are worth reporting, you will read about them' (cited in McGiugan, 2012, paras. 6–7).

As well as creating a plethora of spectacular events, Red Bull also sponsors more than 500 action sport athletes around the world and supports them in pursuing the most courageous and daring stunts they can imagine. For example, in the lead-up to the much anticipated 2010 Vancouver Winter Olympics, Red Bull paid more than US$500,000 to build snowboarder Shaun White a private super-pipe in the Colorado backcountry, accessed only by helicopter, and with a specially designed soft foam pit built into one wall. With exclusive use of this world-class training facility, White was able to invent, practice and perfect an array of new highly technical and creative manoeuvres. Rumors regarding the Red Bull 'Project X' quickly spread around the global snowboarding community, with White confirming many of his peers' fears when he unleashed his never done-before 'double cork' manoeuvre at a competition in New Zealand just months before the Olympic Games. He then repeated this manoeuvre during his gold medal run in Vancouver.

By supporting the most progressive action sport athletes in achieving their dreams, Red Bull demonstrates its commitment to the slogan that Red Bull 'gives you wings'. More importantly, however, Red Bull receives extensive media coverage from its investment in such events and spectacles. Shaun White and Project X, for example, were featured on various news programs across the US, as well as transnational snowboard magazines and websites. Of course, all of the footage of White training in this facility featured large Red Bull logos on the helicopter, on the snowmobiles, White's board and helmet, and in the snow alongside the halfpipe.

From its humble beginnings as an energy drink company, Red Bull has evolved to become a publishing empire. All of the athlete projects and events created and supported by Red Bull have been captured by some of the world's best photographers and cinematographers. In the words of Red Bull Media House managing director Werner Brell, 'everything has more or less been put on film. We have been creating media assets from the beginning' (cited in Jessop, 2012, para. 2). The Red Bull Media House (RBMH) was founded in 2007 as an umbrella for Red Bull's massive print, television, online and feature film production. With offices in Austria and Santa Monica (California), RBMH employs over 135 people who are involved in the production and distribution of an extensive array of action sport events and content, including videos (such as the snowboarding film, *The Art of Flight*, that cost US$2 million to create but quickly became the hottest property on iTunes), websites, web-videos, documentaries, Facebook (with more than 32 million fans) and the *Red Bulletin*, an action sport magazine with a global circulation of 4.8 million. The RBMH library consists of more than 5000 videos and 50,000 photos, a portion of which is provided to users free of charge. Much of this content is of such high quality that it regularly shows up on the news, from MSNBC to ESPN, and in speciality markets such as Halogen TV. RBMH is also involved in the development of videogames, including the recently launched Red Bull Crashed Ice game for Xbox 360. In 2012, RBMH announced a television contract with NBC Sports Group to air 35 hours of Red Bull action sport programming throughout the year on the new Red Bull Signature Series. Exploring other avenues of youth culture, RMBH also owns an in-house music label (O'Brien, 2012).

RMBH is also expert at producing 'media events'—'live broadcasts of historic occasions that engage a committed or worldwide audience, which does not merely watch the event, but celebrates it' (Dayan & Katz, 1992, pp. 1–24, cited in Giulianotti & Brownell, 2012, p. 204). Austrian skydiver and B.A.S.E jumper Felix Baumgartner has been instrumental in working with Red Bull to create sporting media events that promote both the Red Bull brand and create a transnational celebrity for Baumgartner. In 2003, he became the first man to fly the English Channel (22 miles) from Dover, England, to Calais, France, with a special six-foot delta-wing made of carbon fibre strapped to his back. Television footage of Baumgartner's world record, and the Red Bull logo plastered across his outfit and flying rig, were seen by more than 200 million people around the world. With Baumgartner landing safely in

France, the achievement was particularly sweet for Mateschitz who, despite his best efforts, had yet to gain permission from French authorities to sell Red Bull in France. Of course, the most significant Red Bull media event to date was Baumgartner's world record free fall jump from more than 120,000 feet in space in October 2012 (see Chapter 1).

According to Emmy Cortes, director of communications for Red Bull, many of Red Bull's extreme events (such as cliff diving in Hawaii, skateboarding the hills in San Francisco) are primarily for the athletes, designed 'to support a community of athletes and to bring credibility to the sports they compete in' (cited in Rodgers, 2001). Yet Red Bull's motives for organizing such events and so generously supporting action sport athletes are not as altruistic as such claims suggest. An important factor in Red Bull's dominance in the action sport media is its policy of ownership of all media assets resulting from action sport events and athletic achievements in which it has been involved. Not only does RBMH own media assets from such events, but also the copyright. According to RBMH managing director Wrenner Brell:

> In content, everything has to do with rights ownership. If you don't own the rights, it's a little more expensive to do things in media. The advantage we have is we own the life cycle from beginning to end. It puts us at an advantage from creation, production and distribution . . . With the media house now in place and creating our own media channels, we have greater leverage and opportunities to bring our events to life and to the audiences we want to reach. (cited in Jessop, 2012, para. 4)

Such ownership rights, however, raise critical questions about athletes' rights. While most action sport athletes, including Baumgartner, embrace the opportunities presented by Red Bull and often benefit from the publicity resulting from media events made possible by the generous sponsorship of Red Bull, they do not own the media produced from their efforts. The athletes are in a labour relationship in which they are (often freely) producing media assets for Red Bull who then proceeds to make money from both the media products and, ultimately, the sales of energy drinks.

It is also worth noting that not all action sport athletes survive Red Bull-sponsored events. For example, world-renowned American extreme skier and B.A.S.E jumper Shane McConkey died in the Dolomites (Italy) while completing a highly technical skiing B.A.S.E. jump for Red Bull. The RMBH owns all media of this event, including footage of McConkey plummeting to his death when the parachute did not open correctly. Thus, it is no surprise that, in contrast to the phenomenal Red Bull-produced media coverage of Baumgartner's successful jump from outer space, Red Bull's response to this tragedy was one of relative silence. Carefully managing the post-event media coverage, the incident was largely interpreted as McConkey's

individual choice to pursue such risky activities rather than that of a corporation encouraging him to strive for ever more spectacular feats. Although
such cases are rare, they raise important questions regarding action sport
athletes' agency and rights in this new context of mega corporations, transnational media and ever more extreme sporting spectacles.

Yet action sport athletes and enthusiasts are not necessarily duped by the
power of transnational corporations, events and media. As will be illustrated
in the following chapters, the production and consumption of action sport
media and events are not solely top-down processes. Rather, athletes, participants and fans are increasingly using social and digital media for their
own ends, and some are using new modes of communication to critically
challenge the dominance of transnational corporations, media and events
for defining action sports in local contexts around the world.

3
Digital Media and the Transnational Imaginary: Virtual Memorialization of Global Action Sport Stars

Three sun bronzed young men – George (11), Jack (14) and Kelly (14) – gather around the large iMac screen in the kitchen. With his hand on the mouse, Jack controls the activity; their faces, just inches from the screen, light up as he clicks play on the YouTube clip. The music begins as a group of teenaged long boarders are seen carving through the busy urban streets of Miami, Florida, narrowly missing collisions with cars and one another. The action is captured by one of the skaters riding with a GoPro digital camera installed on his/her helmet. The identity of the skater is unknown; we see everything through the eyes of the skater. In essence, the viewer is the skater. As he/she skateboards through a red stoplight, George gasps out loud. The GoPro has affectively transplanted him into this time and place – it is as if he is the one running a red light and his body responds to the possibility of serious consequence. George tucks into himself, as if trying to optimize the speed of the skateboarder on the screen through this subtle bodily adjustment. As the cars stop just in time and the skateboarder makes it safely through the intersection, Jack elbows his little brother in the ribs. The three boys chat and laugh together as the short video comes to an end. Kelly then points to the screen and prompts Jack to click on another video, then another, and another. Almost 45 minutes has passed when the boys tire of watching the videos online. A group decision is made and they scurry off to their bedroom, returning with three helmets, gloves with pads on the palms, and their own GoPro camera. It looks as if they have stepped out of a longboarding magazine. As Jack installs his camera onto his helmet, Kelly is busy texting his friends to join them for a skate session on 'the hill'.

Three hours later, the boys regather in the kitchen, sweat drips down their foreheads and George's shorts are stained with blood from a fall that badly scraped layers of skin from his knee. After gulping a few glasses of juice and almost swallowing a sandwich whole, they regather at the computer. Jack connects the GoPro to the computer and they begin downloading their videos. The boys oooh and aaah over the various clips – analysing their own and each other's style, laughing at near collisions, and replaying George's fall. The remainder of the afternoon and evening is spent editing their footage, and debating the clips to be included/excluded in the video, the first skater to appear in the video, the music,

68

Figure 3.1 Three young skateboarders consuming YouTube videos before uploading their own video

the title of the video, and the font style. Largely oblivious to the adult activities in the kitchen, the boys negotiate and decide upon these various features amongst themselves. Finally, happy with their product, they upload the video through their personal YouTube account. As the boys wait for their video to upload, they watch a few more videos online, check out the latest Californian-produced longboarder magazine website, and then post a note on their individual Facebook pages to remind their 'friends' to check out their latest production. Weary after a long day in front of the screen and on 'the hill', the boys head to bed, eagerly awaiting any comments their local friends or other international viewers may post on their video while they are sleeping.

Action sport participants have always been actively involved in the consumption *and* production of niche and micro media. For example, during the 1950s and 1960s, Californian surfers (such as Taylor Steele and Bruce Brown) were filming their peers and producing low-grade black-and-white videos (see Chapter 4 for a discussion of the significance of Bruce Brown's *Endless Summer* for inspiring future generations of travelling surfers), and skateboarders were creating their own do-it-yourself style zines (Borden, 2003). Action sport participants produced these relatively low-circulating media with their peers as the intended audience. During the 1980s, action sport films and magazines increasingly became commercial ventures with established national and international distribution channels. Yet many participants continued to produce their own forms of relatively low-budget and locally distributed niche and micro media. Often regarded as the most 'authentic' types of media among highly committed participants (Wheaton & Beal, 2003; Thorpe, 2008b), these videos and magazines continue to play an integral role in sharing new styles and ideas across local action sport cultures. Some of these cultural products travelled to action sport communities around the world via the backpacks of travelling surfers, skateboarders, climbers, snowboarders or BMX riders, yet the conversations about such media tended to remain between participants in local settings (such as at the local surf shop, or a popular skate spot).

In the contemporary context, however, new digital technologies and networks have made the recording and dissemination of homemade videos, photos and stories much more accessible. Whereas the early cameras used by surf cinematographers were large and expensive, and often required high levels of photographic knowledge and expertise, new technologies such as the GoPro 'Hero' – a very small, waterproof, high-definition, low weight, digital camera – are relatively affordable and easy to use. For those without access to a GoPro, recording on digital phones and lightweight digital cameras are also popular activities (see Chapter 8). Recording, editing and publishing one's peers 'in action' is no longer an activity enjoyed solely by the most proficient and/or wealthy action sport participants, but is part of the everyday experiences of many groups of committed (yet often not highly competent) action sport enthusiasts. The interactions within these groups as they record themselves, and make decisions about the production and publication of their own media, have the potential to offer fresh insights into the dynamics within contemporary youth social formations. The focus in this chapter, however, is how the highly interactive consumption and production of new social and digital media have opened new channels for communication beyond the local, and are expanding the boundaries of action sport communities.

In contrast to earlier generations, contemporary action sport participants are actively consuming and producing media that, while produced in local contexts, is almost instantly disseminated across the global action sport community via new social media and networking platforms such as YouTube and Facebook. In so doing, the conversations about such media are no longer locally based, but rather involve dialogue with action sport enthusiasts around the world. Paul du Gay (1994) makes a similar observation in relation to recent developments in media and communications technologies:

> . . . the new electronic media not only allow the stretching of social relations across time and space, they also deepen this global interconnectedness by annihilating the distance between people and places, throwing them into intense and immediate contact with one another in a perpetual 'present', where what is happening anywhere can be happening wherever

Figures 3.2 & 3.3   A GoPro camera installed on the nose of a surfboard

we are . . . This doesn't mean that people no longer lead a local life – that they are no longer situated contextually in time and space. What it does mean is that local life is inherently dislocated – that the local does not have an 'objective' identity outside of its relationship with the global. (cited in Hall, 1997, p. 210)

Arguably, recent technological developments have facilitated the production of a transnational imaginary in action sport cultures by creating spaces for trans-local interactions with participants within and across local settings around the world (Thorpe, 2012b).

The remainder of this chapter consists of two parts. Firstly, I provide a brief overview of these latest developments, arguing that popular media theories such as the 'circuit of culture' (du Gay, et al., 1997) need to be reconsidered in this 'participatory media moment' (Jarrett, 2010, p. 330). Put simply, the division between media producers and consumers has long dissolved. Although transnational corporations and media conglomerates continue to hold a great deal of power in defining the dominant ideas and value systems across local action sport cultures (see Chapter 2), the new 'user-driven' social media and networking platforms provide new opportunities for sharing alternative media, and for cultural discussion and debate. Second, to illustrate the role of new media platforms in contributing to the transnational imaginary in action sport cultures, I focus on the cultural responses to the deaths of two global action sport heroes – Andy Irons and Sarah Burke – in both virtual and physical spaces. Through these case studies, we see that social and digital media provide new sites for the global action sports community to actively participate in the production of cultural meaning surrounding death and memorialization. Yet, while such platforms seem to provide a more open and democratic approach to the production of dominant cultural narratives, they are certainly not free of cultural politics. Action sport participants frequently regulate their peers within these mediums. Moreover, transnational corporations are not absent from these virtual spaces, and continue to play a powerful (yet often far from transparent) role in defining dominant cultural meanings in transnational action sport communities.

Action sports and Web 2.0: rethinking the 'circuit of culture'

The Internet has a relatively short history. In November of 1969, the Internet's predecessor, the Arpanet, consisted of just two specifically designed communications computers located in Los Angeles and Palo Alto, California. Its initial users were scientists and technicians, particularly those with Defense Department connections (Hafner & Lyon, 1996; Hauben & Hauben, 1997; Rosenzweig, 1998). But in the 1980s and 1990s the Internet rapidly became a broadly accessed medium that, according to the *Washington Post*, began to rival the telephone and post office in importance (cited in O'Malley & Rosenzweig, 1997). In 1993 there were only 130 websites in the world; today, there are more than 644 million active websites on the Internet. Recent estimates suggested there were more than three billion Internet users in the world in March of 2012 – 45 percent of whom were under the age of twenty-five years (Bennett, 2012). In 2013, Facebook boasted more than 1.06 billion monthly active users, and more than 50 million pages, with major growth in India, Brazil and the Middle East (Abudheen, 2013); Twitter hosted 225 million accounts; and there had been more than one trillion video playbacks on YouTube by this date, with more than four billion views per day (Bennett, 2012). Clearly, the Internet and new social media have become an integral part of the personal and professional lives of many around the globe.

The recent development and phenomenal popularity of highly interactive, user-driven platforms such as YouTube, MySpace, Facebook and Twitter have been termed Web 2.0. In contrast to earlier websites and platform designs, technologies coming under the umbrella term 'Web 2.0' are 'driven by social connections and user participation' (Song, 2010, p. 249). According to Jarrett (2010), the significance of highly interactive sites, such as YouTube, lie not in their production and accessibility of a plethora of video texts, but rather in the 'use of these videos within the culture(s) of a community' of video producers and consumers (p. 328). Many of the newer digital information portals, such as Wikipedia, are co-produced by the readers who can add and change information with very little accountability. According to Song (2010), Web 2.0 technologies can be distinguished by a 'participatory habitus', which separate them from earlier versions of web-based culture. Similarly, Cover (2006), believes new interactive and user-focused media technologies have 'fostered a greater capacity and a greater interest by audiences to change, alter and manipulate a text or textual narrative, to seek co-participation in authorship, and to thus redefine the traditional author-text-audience relationship' (p. 140). Reflecting such changes in social and online media engagement, some scholars are using the term 'prosumption' (Ritzer & Jurgenson, 2010; Woermann, 2012) as a 'sensitizing concept' that points to the 'rather banal observation' that various Web 2.0 social media are facilitating the 'increasing participation of people in formation of media content' (Beer & Burrows, 2013, p. 49).

Moreover, the development of highly mobile technologies, such as smartphones, enables users to connect to these interactive platforms and access information while on the move. Simply, a smartphone is distinguished from a mobile phone by its ability to connect to online applications and services via 3G, 4G and/or Wi-Fi networks, giving the owner potential to individualize their online consumption/usage. In their book, *Studying Mobile Media*, Hjorth et al. (2012) identify the iPhone as representing

> a distinctive moment, both in the very short history of mobile media and in the much longer history of cultural technologies. Like the Walkman three decades earlier, it marks a historical conjuncture in which notions about identity, individualism, lifestyle, and sociality – and their relationships to technology and media practice – require rearticulation. (p. 1)

Similarly, Watkins and colleagues (2012) proclaim: 'through their amplification of many questions around the changing nature of media and communication practices, smartphones have become a poignant symbol for rethinking cultural and media studies today' (p. 665).

Some scholars argue that new communication technologies are facilitating new understandings of time, such that we are now operating in a 'new all-encompassing temporal spectrum that extends from nanoseconds to millennia' (Adam, 2006, p. 119) Barbara Adam (2006), for example, proclaims that 'cause, sequence, linearity and predictability have been swept away in [this] quest for the ultimate compression of time' (pp. 124–5). Ben Agger (2011) offers another interesting perspective, arguing that new social media and communication devices are creating a kind of 'iTime' that 'challenges the pre-Internet boundaries between public and private, day and night, work and leisure, space and time' (p. 120). He describes iTime as 'mobile time, time that is portable as well as elastic. [. . .] Mobile iTime feels infinite, never to be bracketed by beginnings and endings' (p. 124).[1] Within this context of new and rapidly evolving Internet-based and mobile communication practices, other technologies such as Twitter offer further 'evidence of an accelerated information order' in which 'telepresence – "keeping in touch" without literally being in touch – is a pervasive feature' (Hutchins, 2011, p. 237).

Cultural sociologist John Tomlinson (2007) uses the term 'telemediatization' to describe the 'proliferation of communication technologies and media systems within the quotidian rhythms of social life', a phenomenon that he believes has 'altered the "everyday flow of experience"' (p. 94). Drawing upon Tomlinson's (2007) work, Paul Hutchins (2011) proclaims that tele-, meaning 'at a distance', is the 'pivotal prefix here':

> opening the possibility of real-time 'presence at a distance' as a readily available method of interaction for social actors who form and maintain meaningful relationships in and through media systems, including websites, bulletin boards, social networking services, chat rooms, and online games and spaces. (p. 241)

Indeed, these types of virtual interaction 'weave relations between people known to each other through online interaction, offline contact, and more traditional forms of media representation and celebrity' (p. 241). While new media and technologies have supplemented rather than replaced 'old' media forms, they are radically impacting on modes of communication and embodied experience in physical and digital spaces. The constantly connected, always available communications environment is 'transforming relations of time, space, transmission and reception, giving rise to an accelerated information order in which immediacy, instantaneity and immanence are constitutive of social experience' (Hutchins, 2011, p. 241; also see Redhead, 2007).

Of particular significance for this chapter, new media technologies are impacting upon contemporary youth's cultural allegiances and identities in local and trans-local contexts:

> offering instant communication across the world, new media technologies may have accelerated the dissolution of barriers of time and space, redefining notions of the global and local and offering possibilities for the development of new communities based on affinities of interest, politics or any form of cultural identity. (Osgerby, 2004, p. 193)

In this chapter I focus less on the *new* communities enabled by online technologies, and more on how action sport participants who already identify with their sporting community via active participation (and consumption) in local and/or international contexts are using social and digital media to further 'establish, cultivate and maintain their social relationships' (Osgerby, 2004, p. 208) within local communities and across the global action sport culture.

Various critics and theorists have sought to understand 'not only new forms of media delivery, but also new convergencies between media technologies and the new ways in which people use, and interact with, media texts' (Osgerby, 2004, p. 193). In so doing, some have drawn upon du Gay et al.'s (1997) 'circuit of culture' to explain the production of meaning in a context of interactive, multimedia and hyper-textual format of communication. Du Gay et. al., (1997) devised the 'circuit of culture' based on Stuart Hall's (1981) famous four-stage heuristic of the moments of Production, Circulation, Use and Reproduction. In their revision, the cultural circuit included the spheres of Representation, Identity, Production, Consumption and Regulation, all of which were interconnected (du Gay et al., 1997). This model has enabled media scholars to identify 'interrelated "moments" in which the meanings of cultural products are determined, negotiated, and subverted in interaction between producers and audiences' (Taylor et al., 2002, p. 607). They illustrated this model brilliantly via the case of the Sony Walkman. Technologies have obviously changed significantly since Sony first released the Walkman in Japan in 1979, and the 'Soundabout' in the US and many other countries in 1980. Some have attempted to revise and extend the model in relation to more recent technological developments in the context of the contemporary capitalist political economy. For example, Taylor et al. (2002) examined the Internet music-exchange service, Napster, arguing that despite some similarities between old and new media, the 'cultural circuit model must be modified to accommodate the emerging media of cyber-culture' (p. 607). Despite the richness of this heuristic, recent attempts to modify the 'cultural circuit' have fallen short of realizing the interactivity and convergences of social and digital media in the context of Web 2.0 (Taylor et al., 2002).

The model devised by du Gay and colleagues focuses largely on the role of commercial media and products in the production, consumption and negotiation of cultural meaning in the context of capitalist society. However, the lines between commercial and non-commercial media, and (paid, paying and volunteer) producers and consumers, have become increasingly blurred. As the vignette at the head of this chapter illustrates, even children are active consumers *and* producers – or 'prosumers' – of new digital and social media. In so doing, they are often critical consumers of mass media products, and enjoy the social activities of responding to existing cultural products, as well as co-producing their own. It is typically one's peers (in local and international contexts) who regulate each other's practices via the comments, 'like' buttons, and various other 'linking' or 'liking' options. Put simply, the production and consumption of media in the context of Web

2.0 can no longer be understood as a circuit with clear roles, processes and effects. The interactions within and across the various forms of media and social groupings are complex and non-linear, such that new approaches are needed (Bolter & Grusin, 2000; Leonard, 2009).

Despite such concerns, I believe it is important to continue to work towards Hall's (1981) original aim of locating the production of cultural meaning – via the production, consumption and regulation of both commercial and non-commercial cultural artifacts – within the power relations of the local context and the broader capitalist economy. As will be illustrated in this chapter, despite recent claims that new technologies are creating more democratic and accessible spaces for individual and community participation and critique, some groups and individuals continue to have more power to access, contribute, define and control the flow of information than others, both on- and off-line.

The emerging field of cybercultural studies is making a valuable contribution to understanding and explaining such complexities. Simply put, cyberculture is the

> electronic environment where various technologies and media forms converge and cross over: video games, the internet and email, personal homepages, online chats, personal communications technologies (such as the cell phone), mobile entertainment and information technologies, bioinformatics, and biomedical technologies. (Nayar, 2010, p. 1)

Cybercultural studies extends the work of cultural criticism and cultural studies by locating cybercultures within the context of global flows of people and finance, recognizing that cybercultures are 'both the driving force behind and the consequence of globalization where information technology enables the swift, constant and unlimited movement of data' (Nayar, 2010, p. 2). Cybercultural studies also recognize that 'all media is crossover media, adapting, borrowing from, or echoing another format' (p. 2). As well as recognizing the complexities of contemporary media convergence, there is also an acknowledgement that media products are always a process rather than an object. Contemporary media products are the result of 'a series of actions, negotiations, and interactions in dynamic relations' (p. 3). Such processes cannot be separated from everyday life and our everyday interactions and embodied experiences in the material world. Cybercultures are 'at various points, and in different ways, attached to and connected with real-life material conditions' which they can replicate, extend, augment and, in some cases, challenge (p. 2).

Despite some claims of the liberatory aspects of cyberculture, these spaces are not always democratic. Racial and class inequalities exist in terms of access to and use of digital resources, and, just like any culture, cybercultures are 'prone to power struggles, inequalities, subversion and appropriation'

(Nayar, 2010, p. 3). Drawing inspiration from cultural studies and new media and ICT (Digital Information and Communications Technologies) studies, cybercultural studies explores

> the impact, consequence, context and manifestations of computer technology and ICTs on the social, cultural, economic, and material (i.e., fleshy) conditions of real bodies. It explores the shifts in the nature of living for material bodies via ICTs and new media (p. 4).

In the remainder of this chapter I draw inspiration from cybercultural studies to understand the shifts in the experiences of sporting bodies, focusing particularly on how new technologies are changing the meaning of death and the processes of cultural memorialization in global, local and virtual action sport communities.

Sporting communities in the age of Web 2.0

The Internet and new media are an integral part of contemporary sport and physical cultures. Indeed, a recent study showed approximately 85 million Americans visited sporting websites (for example, ESPN Digital Network; FoxSports.com) during March 2012 alone (Top online brands and sports websites, 2012). In response to such trends, sport sociologists are increasingly examining the 'shift in the media sport content economy' in terms of the production, distribution and consumption of digital content (Hutchins & Rowe, 2009, p. 354; Hutchins & Rowe, 2012; Wilson, 2007). In 2009, the *Sociology of Sport Journal* featured a special issue titled 'New Media and Global Sporting Cultures'. Edited by David Leonard, this issue included articles on topics ranging from blogging the FIFA World Cup finals to the growing popularity of sport video games, fantasy sports and digital activism for sport and youth development. More recently, Brett Hutchings and David Rowe (2012) published *Sport beyond Television: The Internet, Digital Media and the Rise of Networked Media Sport*. A few sport scholars are also considering how new social media are affecting sport consumers' sense of space, place, and time (see, for example, Hutchins, 2011).

As suggested in the vignette at the head of this chapter, the Internet and new media and communication technologies (iPhones, GoPro) are playing an ever more important role in sharing information across borders and facilitating trans-local communication within and across action sport communities (Gilchrist & Wheaton, In Press; Kidder, 2012; Woermann, 2012). For example, the surfing website www.surfline.com attracts more than 1.5 million visitors each month. According to *Transworld Business* (2007) magazine, action sport participants spend an average of two hours every day playing a video game system, and at least ten hours per week online. The European snowboarding magazine, *Onboard*, surveyed its readers (a total monthly audience of over 170,000) to find that 96 per cent have access to the Internet, 93 per cent use the Internet to catch up with snowboarding news and snow conditions, and 80 per cent buy clothes and snowboard equipment online (OnBoard Media, 2012). Action sport companies, media and athletes are actively utilizing virtual and social media to connect with consumers, audiences and fans, such that a leading French marketing analyst proclaims: leading action sport brands (Billabong, Quiksilver, Rip Curl) 'have a much larger social media presence than global sports brands' and their creative online marketing strategies 'should be a source of inspiration for other brands', helping them to 'strengthen their relationships with their different audience circles or tap into an emerging community' (Chovet, no date). Transnational action sport print media are also effectively utilizing new technologies to connect with their highly mobile audiences. The websites for *Transworld -Surfing*, *-Snowboarding*, and *-Wakeboarding* magazines have 300,000, 440,000, and 448,000 visitors per month, respectively. As well as featuring an array of videos and print articles, and an array of interactive forums, these websites also have thousands of Twitter followers. Action sport participants rarely purchase such digital media. Offering (mostly) free access to a regular stream of videos, images and stories, these sites attract thousands of visitors that are then 'sold' to advertisers. In so doing, many action sport websites are essentially platforms for a multitude of advertisements.

As with many traditional sports (see Hutchins & Rowe, 2012), action-sport-related events are increasingly being designed and choreographed for online audiences. The 2011 Vans Triple Crown surfing contest series, for example, set a new record for the action sport industry with more than 10.4 million online viewers during the event; 25 to 30 per cent of these watched the event online via competition applications (apps) designed specifically for iPhone, iPad and iPod Touch (Lewis, 2011). Nearly 10 per cent (or 1.1 million) of these viewers streamed the event via their iPhones. Some action sport events, such as the XGames, have specifically designed Apps for iPhone, iPad, Android mobile and Android tablet. The latest X Games app features instant results, news, schedules, athlete bios and live music from the summer and winter events, and guest information (such as venues, parking). The app touts the 'Hypemeter' as its newest feature, a 'built-in game that lets you contribute to the overall excitement around X Games via tweets, Facebook posts or device interaction (shaking your phone or tapping your tablet)' (Foss, 2013). As a result of such new technologies, the 2012 Winter X Games were the most-watched yet, with an estimated 35.4 million viewers in the United States tuning in to ESPN, and a digital media audience that was up 147 per cent from the previous year's X Games (Hargrove, 2012).

The Fantasy Action Sports League is also growing in popularity, with various leagues including Fantasy-Supercross, -Snowboarding, -Surfing, -Skateboarding, and -BMX. Not dissimilar from other Fantasy Sports leagues (see, for example, Billings & Ruihley, 2013; Bowman et al., 2012; Davis & Duncan, 2006), players choose a 'dream team' of athletes who they predict to do well throughout the sport-specific competition series, with prizes ranging from US$10,000 (winner of the 2012 Street League Fantasy Skateboarding series) to an all-expenses paid trip to Hawaii (2012 winner of Fantasy Surfer). For many participants, Fantasy action sports leagues are time-intensive pursuits requiring considerable research into the social (for example, relationship status; tendency to engage in partying pre/post competitions; current sponsorship status) and performance (for example, injury, pre-season training) aspects of their athletes, as well as knowledge of upcoming events and details surrounding competition locations and draws. Hosted by *Surfer* magazine, Fantasy Surfer has been touted as 'one of the largest growing fantasy sports in the world' with more than 90,000 participants (Minsberg, 2013; Reilly, 2010).

Professional surfers, skateboarders, snowboarders, BMX-riders, climbers and mountain bikers are also embracing new media to connect with their fans around the world, and promote their personal brand. For example, more than 30 professional skateboarders have Twitter accounts, with global skateboarding icons Tony Hawk, Rob Dyredrek and Ryan Sheckler having more than 3.4 million, 3 million and 2.4 million followers, respectively. Most also have their own websites and/or Facebook pages which are often managed by their agents. Indeed, many action sport fans, and Fantasy Sport players seeking the latest information about 'their' athletes, visit these sites frequently.

Many recreational and committed action sport enthusiasts are heavy consumers of the social and virtual media of the companies, events and athletes. According to one skateboarding journalist:

> we are being fed so much amazing skateboarding on a daily basis that... we are getting desensitized. Even when we come across a section we actually enjoy, we don't even bother downloading it anymore. We'll watch it once or twice, click on another link, passively stare at the clip even if it sucks, click on another link and so on, until everything we've just witnessed fades into a blur of wallies, yo flips [skateboarding manoeuvres] and high fives. (Top 5, 2013, para. 1)

As well as passively consuming online videos and event coverage, action sport participants are also actively employing an array of new social media, such as Twitter, Facebook, YouTube and Instagram, to share information and images, organize events and discuss and debate issues ranging from the quality of the waves at a local beach to the effects of global warming on the snow-sport industry. Some participants have set up interactive platforms that become important spaces for the sharing of information and communication across local and national fields. One of the earliest examples of an interactive digital action sport community was alt.surfing, which was established in (or around) 1990 prior to the development of the World Wide Web. Participants were mostly passionate surfers with the technological skills necessary to access and contribute to the dialogue. The site has been described as a surfing 'newsgroup' with a 'distributed, worldwide system with somewhat transient information' (Altsurfing.org history, no date), and it was revolutionary in its use of new technologies for transnational communication among surfers. In contrast to easily accessible and user-friendly websites, blogs and forums common today, alt.surfing required participants to have access to networked computers which were not readily available outside of the high-tech business or university environment. Participants from around the world wrote informative, evocative and/or humorous stories of their local and international surfing experiences, with a high amount of banter between members. Many members of the original altsurfing.org global community continue to stay connected via a private Facebook group page.

During the early 2000s, www.snowboard.com (now defunct) was the world's largest snowboarding website, hosting 550,000 registered members – 313,000 from the USA, 98,000 from Canada and 144,000 from other countries around the world. While the majority of members were males (70 per cent) aged between 13 and 25 years, the website also hosted specific forums for older and female participants (Media Man, no date) where they shared stories of their previous and recent local, national and international journeys and adventures, reflected upon past and present lifestyle constraints and opportunities, and debated local and global cultural issues and controversies. This website also included virtual spaces representing real locations within popular snowboarding locations (for example, famous nightclubs in Whistler, Canada) where members could choose an alias and then interact with other members in this space, including live chats which were a relatively recent development. Similarly, www.theskateboardersjournal.com website encourages members to 'share your skateboarding life with skateboarders from all around the world, contribute to the culture, lifestyle and sport of skateboarding'. While most of the early online action sport community platforms were not moneymaking ventures, today the majority of interactive action sport websites are riddled with a wide variety of advertisements ranging from vehicles to energy drinks.

With many (though certainly not all) action sport participants coming from privileged backgrounds, iPhones and other smartphones are common accessories. The European snowboarding magazine, *Onboard*, found that 95 per cent of its readers owns a mobile phone (OnBoard Media Pack, 2012). Such technologies have allowed participants to communicate with their peers, organizing times to gather for a skate, surf or climbing session, and access relevant information about conditions, products and events while on the move. Each action sport has its own preferred iPhone apps, including games, news, forecasting and event coverage. For example, surfers can access more than 150 apps via iTunes designed specifically for their needs. According to *Surfers Village*, however, '99% are rubbish' (Best of the best, no date). Snowboarders can also download a plethora of apps that calculate their on-snow statistics during a day of riding, and provide detailed, up-to-date information on resort facilities. Transnational action sport media and events (such as the X Games) have designed many of these apps, thus offering their audiences/consumers yet another platform to connect to their products. Targeting a particularly high-end demographic, *Transworld Wakeboarding* produced 13 custom apps in 2012 alone.

Based on my observations of contemporary action sport participants online and new media usage, I concur with Williams & Copes (2005) who argue: '[E]xpressing subcultural identities online is part of the identity work individuals perform in their everyday lives,' yet 'identity online is not separate from the face-to-face world . . . rather [it] complements and supplements it' (p. 73). Certainly, for many athletes, coaches, fans and recreational participants, their on- and off-line sporting experiences are increasingly blurred, complementing and supplementing the other, and contributing to a transnational imaginary in which many feel a sense of belonging to a larger community beyond their immediate social groupings.

Of course, care needs to be taken not to exaggerate the extent of these new media. Access to and ownership of such technologies requires some level of expendable income. Indeed, the group of young men described in the vignette at the head of this chapter, and many of their local and international action sport peers and heroes, are from privileged backgrounds. They have access to computers and mobile devices (cellphones, iPads) at home and in their classrooms or workplaces. However, such resources and access are not available to all. For example, after being invited to join a group of local American-Mexican skateboarders on a private skateboarding session in a 'secret spot' in El Paso, Texas, I asked whether anyone had an email address to which I could send them copies of the photos I had taken. Despite their enthusiasm to see the photos, none of the eight young men (ranging from 10 to 22 years old) had an email address. Admittedly, this surprised me at first; I had assumed local schools would be providing American youth with at least some access to computer technologies. In contrast, however, I was equally surprised to learn of the high levels of access and use of social and digital media among young male parkour participants in the war-torn region of Gaza. As discussed in Chapter 8, young men in the Middle East are creatively engaging social media (YouTube, Facebook, Twitter) to gain inspiration from the transnational parkour community, and also for opening new dialogue and establishing informal cultural exchanges with parkour enthusiasts around the world. The key point here is that access to the Internet and digital technologies is far from universal, and we should not assume clear distinctions in terms of access between the developed and developing world. In contrast to my observations among some groups of youth in parts of the United States, individuals and groups in some of the remotest and least privileged spaces in the world (such as Gaza) do have access to electronic communications, and in so doing, are contributing to shifts in their own and others' understandings of space and place.

In the previous chapter we examined the involvement of transnational corporations and media conglomerates in the production of transnational imaginaries in action sport cultures. These corporate-driven events and media utilize social and digital media (often very successfully) to disseminate ideas and advertise products and people to their key niche groups, and also to (create the appearance of) open(ing) a dialogue with their consumers. In this chapter, however, I focus on action sport cultural participants' (rather than companies') active use of new technologies. More specifically, I examine how their everyday use of digital media contributes to the production and consumption of the transnational imaginary in action sport cultures, focusing specifically on the virtual practices and politics involved in the production of transnational cultural memory. I bring these issues to light via an investigation into how the transnational action sport community grieves and memorializes fallen athletes in both virtual and local spaces. Throughout the following chapters, however, various other examples of the use of ICTs by action sport participants are discussed (for example, to organize travel, to maintain connections with those met during travel, personal and commercial dissemination of travel stories).

Trans-local action sports communities and Web 2.0: two cases of virtual memorialization of fallen heroes[2]

With the global mediatisation of action sports competitions and events (for example, the X Games) and transnational campaigns employed by sport-related and mainstream companies (see Chapter 2), the most skilful, successful and marketable action sport athletes have become celebrities within their respective sports culture, and in some cases, mainstream society. Some well-known examples include Tony Hawk in skateboarding, Shawn White and Torah Bright in snowboarding, and Kelly Slater, Laird Hamilton and Bethany Hamilton in surfing. Indeed, Hawk, Slater and White were identified as being among the top ten most popular athletes among 13 to 34-year-olds in North America, and White was identified as the 'most popular' and 'recognizable athlete' attending the 2010 Winter Olympic Games in Vancouver (Ebner, 2009). The global production and consumption of such athletes mirror many of the patterns discussed by David Andrews & Steve Jackson (2001) in *Sport Stars: The Cultural Politics of Sporting Celebrity*. Some of these athletes earn seven-figure salaries from competitions, endorsements from transnational sport-specific sponsors and mainstream companies, and an array of other entrepreneurial endeavours (such as clothing and product lines, videogames, films, books and events). With their sporting successes and larger-than-life personalities, these athletes become iconic within the global action sport communities; they hold the highest position within their respective sporting cultures. Their influence tends to be strongest on young action sport enthusiasts who often idolize their 'heroes', closely following their achievements and lifestyles via niche magazines, videos, websites and other social media (such as Facebook and blogs), and attempting to imitate their skill and style in the waves, on the mountains, or in the skate park. While action sport stars may appear to be flexible transnational citizens with opportunities to travel and work in countries around the world, it is important to keep in mind that they are always located within wider 'power geometries of globalisation' (Knowles, 2005, p. 90; see also Maguire & Bale, 1994; Stead & Maguire, 2000; also see Chapter 4). As Bruce & Wheaton (2009) have explained, the 'emergence and ongoing expansion of internationally mobile transnational sporting "celebrities" . . . is an important characteristic of the global flow of sport capital', and can 'provide insights into the wider processes of cultural globalisation' (p. 586). In the remainder of this chapter I consider the function of the Internet and social media in the memorialization of transnational action sport heroes within the 'complex and fluid articulations of power' (Bruce & Wheaton, 2009, p. 586) operating within the global action sport culture and industry, and across local communities.

Action sports have long been labelled 'risky' and 'extreme' by the mainstream media and general public. While there is an element of risk involved in all activities labelled extreme, in most cases risk is a subjective calculation that individuals make in the context of their ability (see Booth & Thorpe, 2007). Yet, serious injury and death do occur as a result of sporting accidents (Booth & Thorpe, 2007; Laurendeau, 2006) as do lifestyle-related incidents (Thorpe, 2012b). Action sport participants grieve privately and collectively for their lost friends and colleagues. As will be discussed later in this chapter, some action sport cultures have developed unique mourning rituals that draw upon symbols and cultural practices from the sports past or present, and in locations of significance (such as paddle-outs among surfers). In his discussion of death in local skydiving communities, Laurendeau (2006) explained that, while fellow jumpers grieve such losses personally, rarely do such deaths prompt others to question or change their own risk-taking practices. Rather, skydivers tended to explain the accident as caused by avoidable human error, such that it saves them from having to reflect on their own mortality, thus freeing them to continue enjoying their high-risk pursuits.

The recent deaths of some top action sport athletes, however, sent 'shockwaves of grief' through the respective sporting communities. For example, when an avalanche tragically killed four-time World Champion snowboarder Craig Kelly in 2003, one journalist likened the loss to snowboarding to 'the passing of a Pope or the untimely death of Princess Diana' (Reed, 2005, p. 61). Similarly, the deaths of legendary Hawaiian big-wave surfer Eddie Aikau, extreme skier and B.A.S.E. jumper Shane McConkey, and free-style motocross (FMX) rider Jeremy Lusk, evoked deeply affective responses within the global surfing, skiing and FMX cultures, respectively. As with most other elite action sport athletes, the niche media had worked to create mythic status for these individuals – not only did they 'live the dream' of travelling to remote and exotic locations where they conquered enormous waves or mountains (of snow or dirt), they also seemed to cheat death on numerous occasions. The deaths of action sport athletes then are particu-larly shocking to many of their peers and fans because they disrupt the narrative repeated across magazines, websites and films that they possess seemingly superhuman qualities. Of course, the cultural responses to such deaths vary depending on the individual's past and present sporting suc-cesses and contribution to the progression and development of the sport, and their media profile at the time of death.

In the past, the action sport industries and media responded to such losses with local memorial events, in-depth editorial features in print magazines, and/or segments in videos. Some athletes are further memorialized in documentaries, sporting museums and the organization of events and foundations in their names (for example, the 'Quiksilver in Memory of Eddie Aikau' big wave event). While such memorial products might appear to be honourable acknowledgements of the deceased athletes' contributions to their sport, it is important to keep in mind that they are often produced with the support of action sport companies seeking to capitalize on the mythic status of the athlete and their connections to the legend.

In the increasingly networked and digital world, journalists, family members, friends and fans around the world are also using the Internet to communicate with others, to share their condolences, and to memorialize deceased athletes in highly creative, interactive and dynamic ways. In the remainder of this chapter I adopt a critical interdisciplinary approach to examine action sport participants' use of the Internet to mourn and memorialize US surfer Andy Irons and Canadian freestyle skier Sarah Burke, in both virtual and local contexts. In so doing, I am less interested in the historical 'facts' of Irons' or Burke's sporting achievements, or the details surrounding their deaths, and more concerned with the dynamic transnational cultural politics involved in the collective memorialization of action sport athletes in 'an age of high mobility, greater technological access, and virtual social connectivity' (Kern et al., 2013, p. 8).

Cultural memorialization in the digital age

In his widely cited book, *Theatres of Memory*, Raphael Samuel (1994) pointed to the function of memory keeping and presentation as being 'increasingly assigned to the electronic media' (p. 25). A few years later, John Urry (1996) proposed that the 'electronification' of memory might provide another twist in understanding how societies and cultures remember the past within an extraordinarily changing present. More recently, a growing number of historians and cultural studies and media scholars recognize that the processes of remembering (and forgetting) are 'transforming under the impact of the digital revolution' (Brockmeier, 2010, p. 14). Digital culture is, according to Jose van Dijck (2007), 'revamping our very concepts of memory and experience, of individuality and collectivity,' and 'unsettling the boundaries between private and public culture in the process' (p. 52). Analysing how a community's collective memory was acquired, digitized and stored in the online Living Memory project, Casalegno (2004) also observed the emergence of a new 'social aesthetic' where everybody contributes to and shares the collective – and what he terms 'connective' – memory. This form of online

> expressing and sharing of sensations and information shapes the communal and living memory of the community we belong to, and it allows in the last place to give meaning to our existence: to create associations, and share common and shared emotions. If sharing a memory is one of the sine qua non conditions for the creation of a community, the ways in which this process takes place evolve together with the transformation of those means in which memory settles in. (Caselegno, 2004, p. 323)

Of course, various power relations influence the production and consumption of particular cultural memories in both on- and off-line spaces. As a result of the recursive linkage between real and cyberspaces, the latter are 'as open to control and regulation as any space' (Nayar, 2010, p. 77). In this chapter I build upon and extend the growing body of literature on the digitalization of personal and cultural memory by examining how contemporary action sport cultures are using the Internet to *collectively* remember and memorialize their recently fallen sporting heroes.[3]

Death is a universal experience marked differently by individual cultures around the world. Since the late 1950s, anthropologists, historians and sociologists have studied the unique mourning rituals in cultures and communities across a wide array of local and foreign contexts (for example, Corkill & Moore, 2012; Faron, 1967; Kong, 2012; Malinowski, 1958; Mandelbaum, 1959; Reilly, 2012; Wigoder, 1966). As illustrated in such studies, mourning rituals are often 'elaborate, lengthy affairs, where those connected to the deceased commune in celebration, in silences, in viewing, in feast, or in some form of communal gathering' (Kern et al., 2012, p. 2). Mourning and memorialization practices are typically processes of memory-making in which individuals and/or groups privately or collectively remember the life of the deceased. According to Becker and Knudson (2003), mourning is a responsibility, a 'heroic act' (p. 713), a need to 'carry on memories of the life of the person, particularly if that life affected the mourner in a positive or meaningful way' (Kern et al., 2012, p. 2). Of course, such memorialization practices are temporary acts; they are cultural performances with a duration defined by both the grieving processes of the mourner(s), and by the broader society.

Despite the general 'privatization of death', mourning often involves public practices, social rituals and cultural performances. As Gibson (2007a) explains, this is especially observable in cases of deaths from wars, political assassinations and natural disasters, which have long been 'a means of rallying National unity and collective forms of identification, mourning and memorialization' (p. 420). Some scholars have explored similar themes in relation to historical sporting events, teams, and personalities (for example, Corkill & Moore, 2012; Huggins, 2011; Radford & Bloch, 2012). In a new context of global media culture, however, the deaths of famous or newsworthy people have evoked cultural mourning beyond the nation-state (Gibson, 2007a; Wark, 1999). Not all public figures are capable of amassing large-scale, transnational collective emotive responses, but some certainly are. Consider, for example, the millions around the world who mourned the deaths of John F. Kennedy, John Lennon, Kurt Cobain, Princess Diana and, more recently, Michael Jackson, Steve Irwin and Amy Winehouse, almost as if they were a personal loss (Bennett, 2010; Gibson, 2007a, 2007b; Sanderson & Hope Cheong, 2010; Thomas, 2008).

Such public figures and celebrities are rarely known personally to the bulk of their fans through face-to-face relationships, but their frequent presence and visibility in the global media created them as 'people who are familiar' such that their deaths had a profound affect on many peoples' psyches (Gibson, 2007a). For Kern et al. (2012) the notion of 'para-social interaction' (Horton & Wohl, 1956) helps explain this 'sense of intimate, unidirectional connection' that many media consumers establish with certain celebrities and public figures (p. 3). Gibson (2007a) argues that when public figures and celebrities die, what is lost is 'the link between collective myths and ideals, and their embodiment in real flesh and blood people':

> This is partly why people respond so powerfully to such deaths because what seemed so fantastic, so beyond the fray of ordinary existence – the elevated, romantic life of a princess or the fearless wildlife warrior – turns out to be mortal after all. That fantasy or rather the spell that is cast by all fantasies is broken in death and this is partly what is mourned rather than simply the person-in-themselves who died. (p. 420)

Celebrity deaths resonate in the lives of some individuals because they 'belie simple distinctions between real and fictional, myth and reality, public and private' (Gibson, 2007a, p. 418).

Celebrity deaths are increasingly events through which collective and public forms of mourning are becoming ritualized (Gibson, 2007a). Spontaneous shrines are often created at places of significance (either during their life or death) to the public figure. For example, thousands visited Kensington Palace to leave flowers and personal notes following Princess Diana's death (Thomas, 2008); mourners decorated the entrance to the Australia Zoo, in Queensland, in tribute to Australian wildlife personality Steve Irwin (Gibson, 2007b), and following the death of NASCAR race driver Dale Earnhardt, Sr, hundreds of fans flocked to the auto dealership bearing his name in western North Carolina; many others turned their personal cars, or rooms in their houses, into shrines for their NASCAR hero (Radford & Bloch, 2012). The bodies of some mourners also become living shrines through the wearing of clothing symbolic of the celebrity (such as khaki shirts worn by Irwin, or the black No. 3 hats and 'The Intimidator' jackets worn by Earnhardt), or other more permanent markers of mourning (such as tattoos) (Connerton, 2011; Gibson, 2007b; Radford & Bloch, 2012). Through creating their own memorial objects (such as art and craft items, letters), visiting particular sites and wearing memorabilia, individual fans identify themselves as belonging to a larger group, a transnational community of mourners.

Perhaps not surprisingly, when large groups of people are affected by catastrophic death or tragedy, the media plays an integral role in the processes of public mourning and memorialization. While many researchers interested in death and memorialization have emphasised how various forms of media (newspapers, radio, telephones, television) contribute to rituals and mourning practices, the role of digital technologies in this process is only beginning to garner critical scholarly attention. According to Hutchings (2012), online networks and digital media are increasingly being 'integrated into contemporary processes of dying, grieving and memorialization', which is 'changing the social context in which dying takes place' and 'establishing new electronic spaces for the communication of grief' (p. 43). Indeed, the World Wide Web now hosts a vast archive of virtual cemeteries, grief chat rooms, grief blogs and condolence messages. Web-based memorials, cybershrines and virtual funerals are gaining popularity (Arthur, 2008; Foot et al., 2006; Grider, 2001; Roberts, 2004, 2006), and social media sites, such as Facebook, have developed an array of options for friends and family members to memorialize lost loved ones and participate in virtual 'communities of mourning' (Kear & Steinberg, 1999, p. 6; deGroot, 2009; Garde-Hansen, 2009; Kern et al., 2012; Vealey, 2011).

The 'Diana event' triggered renewed academic interest in the role of media in representing and producing public mourning (see, for example, Kear & Steinberg, 1999; Pantti & Sumiala, 2009; Re.Public, 1997), but it was the passing of Michael Jackson (Hutchings, 2012) and fall of the Twin Towers on September 11, 2001 (Vealey, 2011) that prompted scholars to explore in greater depth the role of digital media for cultural memorialization. According to Hutchings (2012), online media is 'actually changing the way death is experienced and shared' (p. 47). In his analysis of the global, public response to Michael Jackson's death, Hutchings (2012) identifies Twitter and Facebook as 'key to the vortextual storm of feedback loops and mutual references' that contributed to what is now known as the 'Michael Jackson effect' – a viral response so wide-reaching and immediate that it significantly slows existing systems (p. 47). More recently, Radford and Bloch (2012) note that Twitter traffic reached near record levels following the death of Apple Inc. co-founder and CEO, Steve Jobs. Such digital media work in conjunction with other 'media of memory' (Kansteiner, 2002) to contribute to the production and consumption of cultural memories of particular public figures and key events.

In times of trauma, crisis, grief and mourning, digital media can contribute to a 'comfort culture' (Sturken, 2007, p. 6), giving 'immediate access to sites of memory, national identity, community and consumerism' (Garde-Hansen et al., 2009, p. 6). This was certainly the case in the immediate aftermath of the attacks on the Twin Towers, where web-based memorial sites and cyber-shrines 'made it possible for a worldwide, bereaved community to participate in the pathos of the event' (Foot et al., 2006, p. 92). Offering an alternative analysis, Vealey (2011) draws upon Judith Butler's (2004) work in *Precarious Life: The Powers of Mourning and Violence* to explain the appeal of social networking sites, such as Facebook, following the attacks. He argues that these sites 'act implicitly as a type of national and cultural mourning, operating through the urge to "exchange one object for another"(Butler, 2004, p. 20), replacing the vulnerable, biological "skinbag" with that of a digital (and therefore enduring) distributed body' (Vealey, 2011, para. 2). Continuing, Vealey (2011) proclaims it 'a curious thing' that, in a 'post-9/11 effort to pre-emptively secure our bodily/national borders, the cultural response comes in the form of social networking – literally, a digital tethering of bodies to other bodies' (para. 14). For Vealey (2011), the value of social networking sites, such as Facebook, is that they provide a 'rhetorical space for the articulations of grief and mourning', and thus 'public and networked feelings' (para. 2).[4]

The key point here is that web-based memorials and social media are contributing to the formation of cultural memory in new ways. During the late nineteenth and early twentieth centuries, public memorialization for public figures or significant events tended toward 'controlled, official, carefully planned forms of expression' (Foot et al., 2006, p. 75). As Foot et al. (2006) explain, the architects of such public memorials sought to 'frame the significance and meaning of the precipitating event for everyone' (p. 75). Official public memorials continue to be developed to commemorate public figures (such as Princess Diana) or tragic events (such as the September 11 attacks on the US; the Japan tsunami). While such memorials continue to attract visitors, mourners are increasingly visiting virtual spaces to connect with the deceased and/or other grievers. According to Foot et al. (2006), memorial websites not only offer greater accessibility, but also create space for a wider array of voices and the co-production of cultural memory. In particular, they describe post-9/11 memorial websites as enabling 'government employees, private citizens, and volunteers to contribute to corporate understanding and interpretation of events' (Foot et al., 2006, p. 92). For Bodnar (1992), such 'collective expression' made it possible for participants and witnesses to tell the story in terms of 'heroism and valor rather than of uncertainty and death' (p. 247).

Such observations have led some to suggest that the Internet offers potentially more democratic and interactive spaces for dynamic, fluid and creative memory construction and public and private mourning practices (Foot et al., 2006). Roberts (2004) concurs, arguing that cyberspace bereavement communities do more than serve as a poor substitute for traditional bereavement activities; 'web memorialization is a valuable addition, allowing the bereaved to enhance their relationship with the dead and to increase and deepen their connections with others who have suffered a loss' (p. 57). For grieving individuals, web-based memorials and social media give immediate access to highly interactive, dynamic, affective (and affecting) sites of 'communities of mourning'. It is important to note, however, that while some participants offer critical perspectives and challenge others' selective remembering, most sites eventually work to produce a dominant narrative of the event, and/or the individual's life and legacy. Thus, as a record of the multiple, contested and changing emotional responses over time, these sites also become valuable archives of the public affective responses to cultural trauma. Arguably, these sites can provide researchers with fresh insight into the production, consumption and contestation of cultural memory in various groups, including contemporary sport and physical cultures.

Drawing upon research in cultural memory, death, mourning, memorialization, ritual and media studies (Connerton, 2011; Gibson, 2007a; Hallam & Hockey, 2001; Hewer & Roberts, 2012; Hutchings, 2012; Kern et al., 2012; Krapp, 2004; Nathan, 2003; Pantti & Sumiala, 2009; Thorpe, 2010b), I examine the practices and politics of local and virtual mourning and cultural memory production following the deaths of two action sport stars, US surfer Andy Irons and Canadian freestyle skier Sarah Burke. As Kansteiner (2002) reminds us, 'all media of memory, especially electronic media, neither simply reflect nor determine collective memory but are inextricably involved in its *construction and evolution*' (p. 195). As illustrated via these two case studies, virtual memorialization practices are important because they contribute to the ways 'current and future generations remember (or forget) historical figures' (Parsons & Stern, 2012, p. 66) in transnational action sport cultures. While action sport participants' use of virtual media for memorialization and cultural memory construction is the focus of this chapter, it is important to keep in mind that cultural memory is always a 'collection of practices and material artefacts' (Klein, 2011, p. 124). The Internet is, of course, just one of many 'media of memory' that contributes to the 'dialectics of remembering and forgetting' in contemporary sporting cultures (Brockmeier, 2002; Klein, 2000).

Virtual memorialization of action sport stars: Andy Irons and Sarah Burke

On November 2, 2010, three-time World Champion surfer Andy Irons was found dead in a hotel room in Dallas, Texas. He was en-route to his pregnant wife in Hawaii after withdrawing from a World Tour surfing competition in Puerto Rico citing ill-health. Most initial media reports suggested complications from dengue fever as the primary cause of death. But the details surrounding the illness and subsequent death of 32-year-old Irons were blurry, with conflicting reports appearing in the mass and niche media. While the mass media delved into Irons' past, digging up details about his previous battles with bipolarism, alcohol abuse and drug dependency, the niche surfing media 'closed rank, refusing to discuss the circumstances of his death' (Higgins, 2011, para. 12), preferring instead to focus on his achievements and contribution to the sport of surfing. The family delayed the findings from the autopsy report for many months citing the need to protect his heavily pregnant wife from further stress. Ultimately, the report revealed that Irons had succumbed to a 'combination of a heart attack and drugs in his system' (Higgins, 2011, para. 11). As noted above, it is not my intent to reveal the 'true' cause of Irons' tragic death. Rather, I am interested in the response from the global surfing community and the use of virtual and social media to communicate and contribute to the memorialization of this fallen hero.

Highly photogenic with a dynamic and charismatic personality and 19 World Tour victories, Irons had achieved legend status within the global surfing community. Following the discovery of his body, the Association of Surfing Professionals issued the following statement: 'The world of surfing mourns an incredibly sad loss today with the news that Hawaii's Andy Irons has died. Andy was a beloved husband, and a true champion.' Indeed, news of Irons' unexpected death shocked family, friends and fans around the world. Many of Irons' peers and supporters engaged in highly creative rituals and memorialization practices both in local and virtual spaces in their attempts to pay their respects to the fallen surfing star and reaffirm his significant role in the history of surfing. Further revealing his broader social celebrity, the Governor of Hawaii declared February 13 forever 'Andy Irons Day'.

Twenty-nine-year-old world champion Canadian freestyle skier Sarah Burke died in Salt Lake City hospital on January 19, 2012, as a result of a vertebral artery tear sustained nine days earlier from a fall while training at Park City Mountain Resort (Utah, USA). A world champion freestyle skier, winner of five World Cup championships, and four-time X Games gold medallist, Burke was the darling of the global freestyle ski culture. Shortly after the accident, Canadian Freestyle CEO Peter Judge made the following statement: 'Sarah is the top female half-pipe athlete in the world. She was instrumental in launching the sport and has continued to be a leader moving towards the sport's Olympic debut in 2014' (Statement regarding Sarah Burke, 2012). In June 2012, the late Burke was inducted into the 2012 Canadian Olympic Hall of Fame for her contributions to the sport and her successful efforts to include freestyle skiing in the Winter Olympic programme in Sochi, Russia.

Combining physical prowess, a daredevil attitude, humour and humility, and a 'flirtatious smile and beach-blond hair', Burke gained eminence in the broader North American popular culture (Saslow, 2012). In 2006, *FHM* readers voted her one of the 100 sexiest women; the following year she received the ESPN Female Action Sport Athlete of the Year award. Burke's death devastated the global freestyle snow sport community, many of whom responded immediately to calls from her agent to contribute to an online fund to help pay the estimated US$200,000 hospital bill not covered by her insurance policy. Less than a week after Burke's death, the site had raised more than $300,000 with donations coming from 22 countries and tributes left in English, French, German, Italian and Japanese (Saslow, 2012). The donations and tributes posted on the website are revealing of her status as both a transnational action sport celebrity and her broader cultural impact, with offerings coming from NBA players, NASCAR drivers, television personalities, snowboarders, skiers, and various other sporting celebrities, including Billy Jean King, who posted:

> I'm saddened by the passing of @sarah_j_burke. She was a great friend to all of us and gave so much of her time to the @WomensSportsFdn [Women's Sports Foundation] and helping young people. She was a champion on and off the slopes and will be greatly missed. [. . .] We will keep her spirit and memory alive! (cited in Donaldson, 2012, para. 7)

The financial and sentimental tributes continued to flow from many directions for many weeks.

Irons and Burke are not the first (or last) action sport stars to die unexpectedly, and thus it is worth considering why these individuals evoked such strong responses from the action sport communities and broader popular culture at this particular historical moment. Drawing upon the work of Nora (1989), Parsons & Stern (2012) explain that, 'in order for a person, group or event to be remembered, there must be a "will" (expressed by a select group) to keep the memory of the person, group or event alive' (p. 66). As such, our understanding of 'important people or events from the past can vary with power shifts among different social groups or may be disproportionately influenced by individuals or groups with relatively high levels of social power' (Parsons & Stern, 2012, p. 66). Irons and Burke had been deeply invested in the surfing and freestyle skiing industries, respectively, for many years; they both had multiple major sponsorships with sport-specific companies, and close relationships with many members of the niche media (including journalists, photographers and editors). With stakes in how Irons and Burke would be remembered, some of these individuals and companies became what Fine (1996) refers to as 'reputational entrepreneurs' (p. 1159). Their role in memorializing these athletes was not simply a matter of presenting stories and images, and creating spaces for others to share their own memories of them. Rather the careful selection and presentation of particular photos, videos and voices contributed to the creative construction of (some) cultural memories (over others).

Cultural memories are passed on to us in various cultural practices, routines, institutions, artifacts and media (such as magazines, videos, books, newspapers, television), and they are always political and often contested. For example, in a highly controversial article titled 'Last Drop' published in *Outside* magazine two weeks after Irons' death, surfing journalist Brad Melekian (2010) exposed the selective silences in the surfing industry and media regarding the less-than-savoury dimensions of Irons' lifestyle that led to his death. As a result, he was 'threatened by numerous people within the surf industry and accused of spitting on Irons's grave' (Melekian, 2011, para. 3). In the remainder of this chapter I build upon this discussion of the politics involved in cultural memory construction by focusing on the production and consumption of virtual memorial websites, as well as the creative uses of Facebook, and the virtual representation of memorial events, by family, friends and action sport participants, seeking to mourn and memorialize Irons and Burke. The virtual memorialization practices discussed in this chapter are, to paraphrase Misztal (2003), culturally significant because they 'enact and give substance' to the 'group identity' of surfers or freestyle skiers, their 'present conditions' and 'vision of the future' (p. 7).

Instant memorialization on the Internet

Within moments of the news of Irons' and Burke's deaths, friends, peers and fans of the athletes took to using an array of new social media (including Twitter, Facebook, Skype, text messaging) to confirm, discuss and debate the news among their social networks. The following comments posted immediately after the news of Irons' death on the *Surfer* magazine message board (at 2.50pm) reveal the initial disbelief and shock within the virtual surf community: 'if this is a joke you should be hung by your nutsack' (2.52pm); 'man, please tell us this is not true' (2.54pm); 'Sh1t. I can't fvcking believe it' (2.56pm); 'Is there any source on this other than Surfermag blog? Someone could have hacked an account and put up a bogus story' (3.02pm); 'Horrifying news. Just in the middle of his comeback too. I'm devastated' (3.03pm); 'poop, it's already on Wiki . . . Andy Irons July 24,1978 -- November 2, 2010' (3.10pm). Analysing the media response to Michael Jackson's death, Garde-Hansen (2010) observed a similar 'lack of coherence and consensus' in the early Twitter and forum discussions; these postings spoke in a 'variety of voices, modes, tones, styles and registers before the rules of traditional media have encoded a response' (p. 234). One day after Jackson's death, however, 'once the mediated memorials on and offline have formed a collective memory', social networks such as Twitter 'produced an extensive iteration and reiteration of grief, trauma, sadness and loss, with few detracting voices' (p. 234). Similar temporal patterns can be observed in the narrative constructions of Irons' and Burke's deaths.

Many friends and fans embraced social media to express their personal grief experiences. For days following Irons' death, a new Tweet was being posted almost every minute from friends and fans around the world. One such example was from fellow professional surfer Joel Parkinson who Tweeted: 'I think I feel worse today than I did yesterday. I woke up this morning and just bawled because it was real now. I'm never going to see him again' (cited in David, 2010, para. 11). The global freestyle skiing community responded similarly. For example, British half-pipe champion Katie Summerhayes wrote on Twitter: 'RIP Sarah Burke. Can't believe I was training with her last month. Such sad news. I honestly cannot speak right now' (cited in Winter Sports, 2012, para. 2). Such 'comments' instantly connect the message sender to the deceased, identifying them as a member of the quickly growing transnational community of Irons or Burke mourners.

The memorialization of Irons and Burke commenced almost as soon as their deaths had been confirmed. Within hours of the news, video montages of Irons' and Burke's sporting achievements had been uploaded on YouTube and Vimeo and were being viewed and commented on by thousands from across the world. For example, a video montage created by a 14-year-old fan of Burke garnered more than 106,000 views within 13 hours of being posted on the *Powder* magazine website. Others uploaded their own creative memorial offerings, including a rudimentary 'Andy Irons Dead – RIP – tribute song' posted on YouTube by an overzealous fan. Friends and fans wrote emotional eulogies on their personal blogs, and some set up memorial websites featuring photos and videos of Irons and Burke. Others posted their (favourite) personal memories of Irons and Burke on existing websites, forums and blogs (for example, Celebrate Sarah, 2012; Surfer remembers, 2010). Such memories range from deeply personal, extended familial relationships or friendships, to fans' brief encounters with their sporting heroes. Most individuals who post statements or share their memories on such forums are friends or fans of the deceased, and thus tend to wax lyrical about the athlete's contributions to the sport or how the athlete inspired their own (or others') sporting participation. The comments posted on such forums vary across the five responses to grief – denial, anger, bargaining, depression and acceptance (Kübler-Ross, 1969) – with an array of communication styles employed to express these emotions.

Of course, some websites and forums carry more credibility than others depending on the authenticity of the producers and the quality of the memory product. Forums on popular websites, such as Surfermag.com, Surfline.com, Transworldsurf.com and Freeskier.com, featured hundreds of posts ranging from condolence messages to the families, expressions of grief and memories of (sometimes one-off) personal interactions with, or viewings of, the athlete, to statements of admiration and respect. Some examples of comments posted on such sites include:

> Still can't believe it and just so thankful to have ever been in the presence of such an amazing person. You [Sarah] lit my candle and I'm going to try and make it burn brighter every day :) ('Kelly', California)

> Skiing has lost one of its greats . . . but she'll never be forgotten. May her legacy live on in all the women (and men) she inspired. I'll be counted among those ('Brandon', Alaska)

> As a person and as a surfer there will never be another Andy Irons. He was like an older brother to me. Somebody I looked up to, somebody I counted on to inspire me and to show me what was possible in this life. [. . .] For the rest of my life I will feel like something really important is missing, something that can't be replaced (professional surfer Keala Kennelly, 2011)

> RIP my bruddah! I hope they have constant perfect sets where you are. If there are, I know you're in the fold getting shacked all day like no ones business!! Aloha to the whole Irons tribe, my thoughts and prayers are with you all ('Chris', www.surfermag.com/features/tribute-to-andy/)

In so doing, these sites contributed to the development of global 'communities of grief'; they offer a 'place to mourn collectively, where there is a potential for dialog and constant evolution of memory' (Kern et al., 2012, p. 3).

As well as providing space for friends and fans to express their grief and communicate with other mourners, some forums feature debates among members regarding the politics surrounding the death or memorialization of the athletes, or the appropriate social etiquette for speaking of the recently departed. For example, Californian writer Chas Smith advocated for the need for self-censorship in surfing on *Surfing* magazine's website:

> We are a family. The outside world will bellow that an evil conspiracy is afoot. They will insist they have a right to the truth and they will angrily

denounce the way our family takes care of its business. They can go to hell. (cited in Pawle, 2011, para. 17)

Others used these spaces to question the involvement of corporate 'reputational entrepreneurs'. For example, on the Billabong forum dedicated to the memory of Andy Irons, 'Mike' posed the following critical questions:

One of the first alerts of this terrible tragedy that I read was by Billabong. Dengue fever, hospitals and IV drips . . . Turns out there were no hospitals [or] IV drips. Why is a clothing company 'managing' a death? (retrieved from www.Billabong.com)

Occasionally, heated discussions take place in these virtual forums. Indeed, in response to a two-page tribute to Irons by eleven-time world champion surfer and long-time rival Kelly Slater (2011), comments ranged from those waxing lyrical about Slater's 'sincerity', 'honesty' and surfing prowess, to more critical arguments such as the following by 'Frank': 'Kelly is the ultimate politician. [. . .] This was a political speech that sounds as carefully scripted as anything you'll hear from any other bullshit artist in politics. Stop blindly bobbing your heads to essentially a bunch of words that said NOTHING.' 'Frank's' comment gained eight 'Likes' from other thread-followers, some of whom supported his arguments: 'So true . . . It's not cool to seek the truth in the surf world. The athletes are nothing more than pawns on the chessboard, and a bunch of self-narcissists to boot' ('honesty'); 'In the surf biz, truth is what Billabong says it is' ('ASP_Guru'). Many other posters, however, balked at these comments: 'This is a eulogy. Your comments are better served in a proper context . . . Grow up' ('Al Baydough'); '[This is] the wrong context . . . respect for Andy's closest family and friends would be appreciated' ('Dandaman'). Although virtual forums provide space for critical comments and questioning, these disquieting voices tend to be heavily policed and regulated by other posters and, in some cases, the website producers. Indeed, this dialogue has since been erased from the Billabong website. Thus, as time passes, most of these virtual forums settle on a dominant narrative of Irons and Burke as action sport heroes without peer. This is a narrative largely (re)produced by corporations which, although they may express genuine emotion toward the loss of their athlete, also have much to gain from the commodification of their memory.

There appear to be at least two dominant forms of cultural memory construction operating on such websites. Firstly, the extensive discussions and debates about what 'really happened' to the athlete, who is accountable, and what lessons must be learned for the culture more broadly (for example, the importance of health insurance for athletes training abroad; the dangers involved in high-level freestyle skiing; the silences in the surfing sport and industry surrounding drug and alcohol usage among some professional athletes), work to create a dominant historical narrative that will likely be repeated across an array of future memory products (such as books, videos, events) (Thorpe, 2010b). Secondly, various agents contribute to the production of Irons' and Burke's mythologies by selectively remembering their sporting lives, particularly their vivacious personalities and contributions to the surfing or freestyle skiing cultures. While Burke seemed to be adored by the freestyle skiing community prior to her death, the surfing culture had been divided in their opinions about Irons' behaviour in and out of the water. Following his death, however, the global surfing culture seemed (almost) united in their grief for this fallen hero. Of course, selective remembering (and forgetting) is not a new phenomenon. As Hutchings (2012) observed in his analysis of the public response to Michael Jackson's death: 'the passing of Michael Jackson led to a striking reappraisal of his life and work, which suddenly returned to popularity and critical approval, and found new audiences after many years of social unacceptability' (p. 46). The same could also be said for Irons' legacy. In sum, while the Internet and new social media may be transforming some of the practices of mourning, the web is not free from the politics of cultural memory construction, memorialization and commodification.

Facebook memories

Facebook has become the most popular social networking site for people to connect and share their everyday lived experiences, and engage in discussion with online communities (Ahn, 2012; Chayko, 2002; Manago, Tamara & Greenfield, 2012; Miegel & Olsson, 2012). But what happens when a Facebook member dies? How do Facebook members use this medium for the purposes of grieving and memorialization? The Facebook memorial policy offers bereaved family and friends at least two options. Firstly, when a Facebook member dies, friends and family can apply to have their profile page converted into a digital memorial. The privacy settings are readjusted and communication functions reduced, but all existing 'Friends' of the member can continue to write on their wall. The deceased member's profile remains unchanged – previously uploaded photos, posts and dialogues remain for all existing 'Friends' to see. The 'Official Sarah Burke Fan Page' established in January 2009 by Burke (or her agent) was converted to a memorial page following her death with the addition of the following statement: 'this is a memorial page for Sarah. Please do not use it for your political, social or other beliefs. It is for condolences only. Her loved ones are reading this page for comfort.' More than six months after her death, the site had more than 60,000 members from around the world, many of whom wrote personal statements to Sarah, or 'commented', 'liked', 'linked' or uploaded new photos, videos and news-clips. For example, an image of the road sign 'Sarah Burke Way' – a tribute by her home town in Midland, Ontario, Canada – garnered almost 5000 'likes', 108 'comments' and was 'linked' by 580 other users.

The second option allows family or friends to set up a 'memorial page' that does not require visitors to be Facebook members or previously listed 'Friends' of the deceased, and thus operates as a public space for the 'articulation of grief and remembrance' (Vealey, 2011, para. 4). Within days of his death, the 'RIP Andy Irons' Facebook memorial page had 114,000 fans, and by July 2012 had more than 218,000 'likes'. The site includes photos and videos of Irons' surfing, as well as photos of his young son, comments and tributes from friends and fans (for example, a photo of a friend's leg featuring a new 'AI Forever' tattoo; a song written by a well-known musician), links to other media coverage, and other surfing-related posts. Multiple memorial pages were set up as tributes to Irons and Burke, some by family and friends, others by fans or opportunistic groups seeking to capitalize on the 'traffic' to the page. Yet Facebook pages that are maintained by loved ones, or at least those with access to their personal archives (such as agents), have more cultural credibility and thus popularity among friends and fans. However, some of the latter are also capitalizing on the transnational 'community of grief' facilitated via such networks. For example, the managers of the 'RIP Andy Irons' Facebook page 'wanted to do something beneficial with this large, amazing community we've developed around Andy Irons', and thus produced memorial t-shirts with profits being donated to the Surfrider Foundation. As Radford & Bloch (2012) observed in the cultural response to the death of Dale Earnhardt, some fans turn to celebrity-related products as 'remedies for feelings of loss' (p. 137) and to 'immortalize the celebrity' (p. 151). Arguably, the consumption and display of memorial objects (an AI t-shirt, or a 'Celebrate Sarah' sticker) are also practices of distinction in that they clearly identify cultural insiders as belonging to a group of mourners.

In the remainder of this section I offer five key insights into the use of Facebook for the processes of memorialization: 1) Facebook is a unique space to commune with the dead; 2) Facebook offers individual mourners opportunities to participate in a transnational community of living others; 3) Facebook is a digital archive of affect; 4) the dead remain in 'dialogical limbo' in such virtual spaces; and 5) Facebook memorial pages have unique etiquette for speaking of, and representing, the dead.

As is common with most Facebook memorial pages (see DeGroot, 2009; Roberts, 2004; Vealey, 2011), many of the comments posted on Irons' and Burke's memorial walls are addressed directly to the deceased athletes (for example, 'RIP Andy. You were the king in the sport of Kings'; 'No matter how the weather is, you will always be our snow-angel Sarah'). According to Kern et al. (2012), such direct communications with the deceased suggest that, for many posters, 'Facebook is a place to commune with the dead in a space where the communication may actually be "received". The dead live in a virtual cloud . . .' (p. 8). Drawing upon the work of Butler (2004), Vealey (2011) examines the appeal of writing on Facebook memorial sites, asking 'what are the rhetorical and performative implications of [such] discursive practices?' (para. 14). He concludes that Facebook offers a unique 'space for articulation', one wherein individuals are not 'forced to inscribe', but rather 'the openness, the possibility of articulation . . . compels inscription, thus rhetorically constructing a community that articulates these affects publically' (Vealey, 2011, para. 18). This sense of community is important here. While many come to memorial Facebook pages with the intent to 'communicate with the dead', in the process of doing so, they 'come into community with living others'; their seemingly private posts are in fact 'public intimacies' (Vealey, 2011, para. 21). Put simply, posting on such websites is a form of cultural performance; the writer posts their comment with the implicit understanding that other group members will observe their expression of grief. Similar to gravesites in the offline world, Facebook memorial pages provide 'a place to visit with dead loved ones' or, in these cases, fallen sporting heroes. But, unlike the former, 'these online places of remembrance provide a platform where individual conversations with the dead are permanently recorded and publicly displayed' (Kern et al., 2012, p. 7). Facebook memorial pages are thus 'digital archives of affect', offering a record of both private and public processes of mourning and memory construction (Vealey, 2011).

Vealey (2011) raises pertinent questions about the digital remains once the haptic body has gone – 'what kind of electronic life persists? How are we to grieve the absence of a body when a digital form of that body remains?' (para 2). Within virtual spaces such as Facebook, it seems 'the dead never really die' but rather 'perpetually remain in a digital state of dialogic limbo' (Kern et al., 2012, p. 1). Indeed, Burke's husband, Rory Bushfield, admits to keeping her two iPhones close: 'it sounds weird, but it feels comforting to know those old text messages and pictures are still right there. It's like part of her still exists' (cited in Saslow, 2012, para. 28). As Clark (2003), Munster (2006), Vealey (2011) and others point out, new communication technologies and devices, such as iPhones, are increasingly 'cognitive and affective extensions of our own bodies' (Vealey, 2011, para. 7). If, as Clark (2003) suggests, the mobile phone is 'both something you use (as you use your hands to write) and something that is part of you' (p. 9), Bushfield's comments above suggest a need to rethink the relationship between death, new media and the (corporeal and virtual) body. For those who are grieving, 'the digitalized body (as a memorialized account) allows one lost love-object to be replaced by another', suggests Veale (2011). Continuing, he clarifies:

> This is not say, as Butler surmises from Freud, that a digitized message board can take the place of a warm body. Rather, it is to say that affective attention – one that was directed toward a physical (and perhaps digitalized) body is now turned toward a completely digitalized entity, one that persists as a static, unresponsive digital signified. (para. 9)

The ongoing digital presence of deceased individuals such as Irons and Burke may contribute to both personal and communal efforts at 'experiencing and overcoming the process of mourning' (Vealey, 2011, para. 21).

Facebook memorial pages are said to 'aid in the bereavement of the deceased' by offering a 'continuing space to engage with the deceased in a mediated, virtual and spiritual space' (Kern et al., 2012, p. 9). The more extensive the memorial and the greater its permanence, 'the more the deceased remain with the living' (p. 9). Certainly, Irons and Burke continue to have a visible virtual presence on Facebook; the managers of these pages regularly update their memorial pages with new photos, news and links, and visitors continue to post messages (although with less frequency as time passes). It may be suggested, however, that as with most memorial objects and artefacts, the lifespan of these websites (and thus the 'digital life' of the deceased) depends on the mourning processes of the producers (family and friends) and consumers (friends and fans).

As with attending a wake or visiting a tomb, Facebook memorial pages have developed their own unique etiquette that is carefully policed and regulated by family, friends, some fans and, occasionally, Facebook employees. Blurring boundaries between the private and public, mourning and memorial sites on the Internet and social networking sites such as Facebook open up a number of potentially 'contentious issues' (Gibson, 2007a, p. 423), including the hacking of personal and highly sensitive materials, or disrespectful comments from indignant 'others' or, in some cases, strangers. For example, the 'RIP Sarah Burke' memorial page has had some questionable visitors; the page is now closely monitored and features the following warning: 'Due to some inappropriate photos that have been added, we will from now on moderate this site. This site is a memorial site for Sarah Burke and should be only used as a memorial site. Rest in peace Sarah!' Just as a gravesite can be vandalized, digital memorials can also be subjected to sacrilegious practices.

Transnational mourning: local and virtual rituals and events

Importantly, the processes of virtual mourning for Irons and Burke discussed above cannot be separated from the memorial rituals and events held in local spaces. Revealing Irons' transnational celebrity, memorial 'paddle-outs' were held in Australia (Snapper Rocks, Gold Coast), Bali (Kuta Beach), California (Huntington Beach, and El Porto, Manhattan Beach, Los Angeles), Florida (Jacksonville Pier), New Zealand (Christchurch), Puerto Rico (Middles Beach, Porta Del Sol), South Africa (New Pier, Durban), and in Irons' home country of Hawaii. Memorial paddle-outs are a relatively recent surfing 'tradition' in which a group of surfers meet at a specific beach at a designated time and then paddle out to a calm spot where they form a circular formation. Sitting atop of their boards, often holding hands, friends and family engage in an array of ritualistic practices (such as chants, speeches, moments of silence, song, stories, shouting, arms raised, water splashing) to collectively mourn the recently deceased surfer. The Andy Irons memorial paddle-out held at his home beach of Hanalei Bay, Hawaii, on November 14, 2010, was supposedly the largest paddle-out to date. More than 5000 friends, family and well-wishers travelled from within Hawaii and the United States, and across the world, to attend the memorial. This event featured an array of cultural performances, rituals and symbols from surfing and the Hawaiian culture (including Polynesian dancers, Hawaiian priests, the Hawaiian flag), and members of the local community decorated the town with creative surfing-inspired shrines (such as surfboards painted with memorial tributes to Andy).

Similar memorial rituals have developed in the snow-sport culture. For example, skiers and snowboarders will often gather at the top of a favourite mountain or slope where they share speeches and memories of a friend or family member who has recently died, before collectively riding down the slope together. Due to the scope of the network affected by Sarah Burke's death, her husband devised an alternative memorial service. Family and hundreds of friends from the local community and the global freestyle snow-sport culture attended a memorial event held for Burke in the Whistler Village (British Columba, Canada) on April 19, 2012. The event included speeches and readings, video and photo montages, and drew upon symbols from skiing culture and the mountain environment (such as snowflakes) to create an emotional candlelit ceremonial event.

As Durkheim (1915/2001) suggested almost a century ago, groups use tradition and ceremony to keep the past alive, create social bonds and instil a sense of community in participants (see Fowler, 1997; Parsons & Stern, 2012). Memorial events such as the paddle-outs for Irons and the Whistler tribute for Burke are 'moments of gathering, the forming of community however disparate' which work to 'create a collectivity of memorializing' (Kern et al., 2012, p. 3). At such memorial events, the group – in this case, surfers and skiers – 'highlight that which is most important, writing (or rewriting) a socio-cultural history of the individual' (Kern et al., 2012, p. 3). The selective recalling of particular individual memories of Irons or Burke at such events helps to support the production of a dominant cultural memory that is simultaneously emerging across an array of other media and memory products. According to Kern et al. (2012), such 'moments of gathering' are important because they satisfy 'a need for both the individual and the collective in the remembrance process' (p. 3).

The memorial events for Irons and Burke were choreographed for both local and global audiences. Virtual media played an important role in organizing, broadcasting and reporting on these 'moments of gathering' to international audiences. Indeed, the four-minute video of the Andy Irons memorial paddle-out in Hawaii was of superior cinematographic quality. Featuring aerial footage from a helicopter showing hundreds of surfers floating in a circular lattice formation, and underwater footage of Irons' ashes dispersing through the crystal clear waters, it seems little expense was spared in the production of this highly affective memorial object. The official memorial video was viewed more than half a million times before being removed from YouTube for reasons unknown. Versions of this video – varying in quality and length – are still available for viewing on YouTube, Vimeo and an array of surfing magazine and company websites. Another video of a memorial paddle-out held at the 2010 Rip Curl Pro Search Puerto Rico event and attended by more than 100 professional surfers has also received more than 108,000 views on YouTube.

Just as the athletes at the Rip Curl Pro paid tribute to Irons by postponing the event for two days and having a memorial paddle-out, the 2012 Winter X Games program commenced with a memorial tribute to Burke who had died just one week before the event at which she had long been a crowd favourite. The live tribute commenced with a video of Burke and a short announcement by Winter X Games emcee Sal Masekela acknowledging her sporting achievements and commitment to the development of freestyle snow sports, this was followed with a slow procession of X Games skiers and snowboarders walking solemnly down the darkened super-pipe carrying candles toward Burke's family and the X Games crowd waiting in silence at the bottom of the half-pipe. Shortly after the tribute aired on national television and once the competition was underway, Burke's name was briefly the second-hottest trending topic on Twitter (Huffington Post, 2012); almost 200,000 others watched this video on YouTube. Revealing the affective power of the video, one YouTube viewer commented: 'I was crying at 1.41[minutes].' The key point here is that virtual media coverage of these memorial events alters how ritual is performed, and perhaps also how those in attendance, or consuming it via the Internet and social media, can experience it.

Reflecting again on a Durkheimian model of group ceremonial behaviour and memory construction, it might be argued that memorial events for Irons and Burke not only contribute to the maintenance of a trans-local community, but also work to reaffirm the existing hierarchies within surfing and freestyle skiing cultures. As Dayan and Katz (1992) observe in their analysis of the mediatization of 'ceremonial' and 'traumatic' memorials, such events work to 'spotlight some central value of some aspect of collective memory' (p. xi). Memorial events often 'portray an idealized version of society, reminding society what it aspires to be rather than what it is' (p. xi). Interestingly, the memorial events for Irons and Burke emphasized the supportive, familial-type bonds between participants based on shared understanding of what it means to *be* a surfer or a skier. This is, of course, a romantic notion that overlooks the ruthless competition, individualism and cultural fragmentation that is emerging as action sports become increasingly institutionalized and commodified (Thorpe & Wheaton, 2013), and the less than savoury dimensions of these sporting cultures, such as the aggressive localism, celebration of hyper-masculinity, and social and physical risk-taking, homophobia and sexism evident among some core groups (Booth, 2002; Evers, 2010; Frohlick, 2005; Henderson, 2001; Kay & Laberge, 2003; Olive & Thorpe, 2011). The video of the memorial paddle-out held at the 2010 Rip Curl Pro Search Puerto Rico features interviews with fellow professional surfers, including two-time World Champion Australian surfer Mick Fanning, who proclaims an idealistic version of surfing culture as all-inclusive: 'We're a *surfing family*. We all look out for each other. Just for us to paddle out and show our respects to Andy, to his family, to all his friends on Kauai and Hawaii – it's good' (Cote, 2010, para. 3). A comment posted on an online surfing magazine forum by an individual attempting to organize 'the biggest [simultaneous] paddle out ever' evokes similar rhetoric: 'just paddle out (at your sunset wherever you are) with all your friends to celebrate the life of Andy Irons! Pass the word and show the world how surfers respect their family . . .' The X Games memorial to Sarah Burke also included the following statement: 'The action sports family recently lost a very cherished member, freeskier Sarah Burke . . . tonight, Sarah's X Games family would like to pay tribute to her in their own special way . . .' In sum, to paraphrase Dayan and Katz (1992), memorial events for Irons and Burke, and the virtual representation of these 'moments of gathering', worked to portray an idealized version of surfing and skiing cultures, reminding the transnational action sport communities what they (should) aspire to be, that is a global 'family' united by a shared value system and cultural practices and rituals.

Final thoughts: death, mourning, community and the digital body

In this chapter I have examined the contributions of the Internet and social media to the production of cultural knowledge within and across trans-local action sport communities. More specifically, I revealed the uses of virtual media for engaging in cultural mourning and memorialization via two cases studies of recently deceased action sport stars – surfer Andy Irons, and freestyle skier Sarah Burke. While the Internet and social media offer new spaces for personal and collective mourning and cultural memory construction, I am cautious of recent arguments that the Internet offers 'a more open, democratic, free-market space' (Gibson, 2007a, p. 423) for 'communities of mourning' (Kear & Steinberg, 1999, p. 6). Through the cases of Irons and Burke, I suggest that, in a way not dissimilar from more traditional objects and media of memory, certain individuals and groups continue to 'have more power than others to create cultural memories' in virtual spaces (Parsons & Stern, 2012, p. 69).

In conjunction with print media and other memorial events, commemorative practices in virtual media and online spaces work to stabilize particular cultural memories that reinforce the established cultural order within action sports such as surfing and freestyle skiing. New social and digital media platforms and networks may appear to provide open and accessible spaces for the voices of action sport participants to contribute to the global action sport community via the sharing of memories and emotions. Yet the power relations operating within the broader action sport culture and industry determine whose voices are heard in these virtual spaces. In the case of Irons and Burke, everyday participants used virtual spaces to express their thoughts and feelings and connect with other mourners in local and trans-local contexts, yet within hours a dominant narrative had emerged that was quickly repeated across various media (such as Twitter, Facebook, blogs, online magazines) such that these narratives became accepted as cultural truths across the global action sport communities; participants quickly censored the few voices that questioned these narratives. Perhaps not surprisingly, the transnational corporations who sponsored these athletes during their careers also continued to play a significant role in defining the production and consumption of their memories. Virtual memorial spaces are not free from the power dynamics and politics within the broader action sport culture and industry. The key argument in this chapter is that, while digital technologies and social media are creating new spaces for a wider array of voices and the co-production of cultural memory, such spaces are always infused with relations of power.

In sum, future studies of the use of Internet and social media for cultural memorialization, communication and politics should also consider the broader context within which these practices and performances cannot be separated. Indeed, while the new media and communication technologies have been an important factor in the promotion of trans-local cultural dialogue and fusion, equally crucial have been patterns of population movement with 'new cultural forms and identities shaped at the juncture of different peoples' histories and experiences' (Osgerby, 2004, p. 166). In the second part of this book I examine how the travel experiences of action sport participants further contribute to the transnational imaginary within and across national borders. In the first of three chapters in this section, I focus specifically on how existing transnational networks are facilitating the corporeal mobilities of action sport athletes, tourists and migrants as they travel the world in pursuit of new social, cultural and physical experiences.

Part II
Action Sport Migration and Transnational Mobilities

4
Corporeal Mobilities in Action Sport Cultures: Tourists, Professionals and Seasonal Migrants

Action sport participants are avid travellers. Travelling regionally and internationally in pursuit of uncrowded waves (surfers), fresh snow (skiers and snowboarders), new routes (climbers) and trails (mountain bikers), or consistent wind and warm water (kite-surfers and windsurfers), is considered an integral part of many action sport cultures. This is particularly the case for those action sports in which the natural environment – oceans, beaches, mountains, and rivers – is central to participation.[1] The release of Bruce Brown's film *The Endless Summer* in 1964 was pivotal in creating the transnational imaginary among action sport enthusiasts. According to some sources, Brown was encouraged by a travel agent friend to create a film that captured the essence of the 'surfari' experience. The film follows two young American surfers, Mike Hynson and Robert August, on their journeys to Australia, New Zealand, South Africa, Tahiti and Hawaii, with various other locations along the way. Rather unexpectedly, the amateurish film grossed US$20 million and quickly became a cult classic. The surfing historian Drew Kampion identified the 'search for the perfect wave' as epitomized in this film as a symbol that 'ignited the explosion of surf travel that would shape the sport for the rest of the millennium' (p. 2). Adopting a more critical analysis of the impact of this film, surf journalist Steve Barilotti observed Hynson and August adopting a friendly but condescending tone with local communities in Africa and South Africa, thus 'set[ting] the paradigm early of surfers as goofball neo-colonialists' (Barilotti, 2002, p. 36; also see Ponting, 2007).

The film not only inspired surfers around the world to set off on their own neo-colonialist journeys in search of 'the perfect wave', but committed participants in an array of other action sports (such as climbing, skiing, and later sports such as windsurfing, snowboarding, kite-surfing and mountain-biking) also went searching for new, unique terrain in both developed and developing nations. The highly evocative narratives and images from many such adventures were widely distributed across an array of niche media (such as magazines or films). Many action sport corporations also recognized the allure of such adventurous travel to exotic and remote locations, and started incorporating such imagery into their campaigns, which further fuelled the desires of others to seek out such destinations and experiences. As more and more youth went in search of new terrain, or to experience for themselves the places they had seen in magazines or films, local and foreign individuals and groups began setting up businesses and organizations to capitalize upon the new action sport mobilities. The early facilities were often rudimentary, but as the flows of action sport tourists continued to grow, the options proliferated ranging from budget backpackers and home-stays in local villages to luxury charter boat surf trips and private heli-snowboarding trips. Action sport tourism has become an important feature of the local, regional, and even national, economy of many communities around the world. The broader effects of such action sport tourist mobilities on local communities cannot be ignored, and will be discussed later in this chapter, and expanded upon further in the following two chapters.

The key point here is that travel – corporeal, imaginative and virtual – has become integral to the action sport experience. In the words of one surf journalist:

> As surfers, we are pulled towards adventure, where others might push away. [. . .] There is something that pulls a certain type of person to the unknown. Whether it be going toe-to-toe with the powerful elements in the ocean, or traveling around the world. With surfers... there is a strong correlation of that daring adventure into the ocean and the adventure to new places. (How Surf . . . , no date, para. 3)

The writer concludes by warning the reader that 'surf-traveling may change your life': 'Once your trip is over, be prepared for endless mind-surfing at your desk, searching for new unexplored destinations, and yearning for new adventures. Even as I write this, I've got the surf report open for Japan' (How Surf . . . , no date, para. 19). As this quote suggests, while corporeal travel might be limited by time and finances, imaginative and virtual travel are part of many committed action sport enthusiasts everyday experiences.

Drawing upon broader travel discourses, many action sport participants proclaim their travel practices as having a positive impact on their psychological well-being (such as stress release), as well as personal growth and development. For example, a professional snowboard photographer waxes lyrical about his travel experiences:

> Travelling is an integral part of snowboarding for me. Stepping off the beaten track and leaving familiarity behind can add an entirely different dimension to a snowboard trip. Experiencing new environments and different ways of living brings rewards all of its own. The most important thing that snowboarding has given me has been the opportunity to expand my horizons. It's hard to forget the feeling of cranking a turn in bottomless powder, but

when I'm too old to strap in anymore, the memories that I'll hold tightest will be the places I've been and the people I've met along the way. (James McPhail, snowboard photographer, cited in Barr et al., 2006, p. 92).

Such narratives are common across the action sport cultures, and feed back into the justifications individuals offer themselves and others for their privileged and hedonistic travel practices.

Most of the early action sport journeys were pursued by small groups of highly committed, proficient, young, white, male surfers, climbers, skiers and riders. Occasionally, a girlfriend would be invited to join the group. The demographics of contemporary action sports, however, have changed significantly over the past five decades. Today, action sport cultures are highly fragmented – participants include male and female professional athletes, devoted or 'lifestyle' participants (Wheaton, 2000), less committed newcomers and novices, marginal participants (such as 'poseurs' or 'weekend warriors') and various subgroups. With such cultural diversity, it is not surprising that the travel patterns facilitated by the action sport economy vary considerably. In this chapter, I build upon existing research on lifestyle or action sports (for example, Booth & Thorpe, 2007; Evers, 2004, 2010; Ford & Brown, 2006; Ponting et al., 2005; Ponting, 2007; Rinehart & Sydnor, 2003; Wheaton, 2004a, 2004b), sports migration (for example, Carter, 2011; Maguire & Falcous, 2010) and youth and travel more broadly (for example, Deforges, 1997; Skelton & Valentine, 1998; Vogt, 1976; Wearing et al., 2010), to offer a discussion of the corporeal mobilities and migratory practices of action sport professionals, tourists (ranging from backpackers to high-end travellers) and action sport migrants, respectively.

While the travel practices and patterns vary considerably among these three groups, it is important to keep in mind that action sport participants have traditionally shared a white, middle-upper-class habitus (Bourdieu, 1992). Thus, for many action sport participants, travel – real, virtual and imagined – is a highly valued, yet often taken-for-granted, part of their social location. Put simply, action sport participants are often able to consider possibilities, freedoms and opportunities for sport- and leisure-related travel or action sport migration unavailable to those from less-privileged social fields. Many of the early action sport travellers were not particularly wealthy and travelled on very tight budgets, but they had the privilege to imagine the world as a place for them to play. While they made many sacrifices to do so, they grew up in countries and/or families where they had the luxury of imagining and realizing time free from responsibilities (such as putting food on the table for a starving family) and international travel in pursuit of their own individualistic desires. These are a privileged group indeed! It is also important to keep in mind that the various corporeal mobilities examined in this chapter cannot be separated from the global action sport economy discussed in the first part of this book. Thus, both in this chapter and the following two chapters, I will also examine some of the various ways that broader structural powers enable and constrain the mobilities of action sport enthusiasts, as well as the everyday lives of local communities.

While this chapter focuses on 'corporeal mobilities', action sport participants' experiences of transnationalism cannot be separated from 'imaginative mobilities' and 'object mobilities' (Bærenholdt et al., 2004). Here the term imaginative mobilities refers to representations of transnational action sport travel circulating in the global flows of cultural objects and artefacts such as photographs, brochures, videos and magazine articles, and technologies such as the Internet and television. Object mobilities refer to items such as action sport equipment (board bags carrying surfboards and wetsuits, or snowboards and boots, or bike boxes, and so on), which are often transnational in both their production and usage. For example, a snowboard may have been designed in the United States, manufactured in and transported from China, purchased in Australia, packed into a bag designed specifically for the sport (or makeshift travel packaging often involving cardboard boxes, tape and towels or clothing to protect the equipment) and then dragged, lifted, carried, thrown and dropped from planes, trains, buses, taxis, chairlifts and gondolas, within and across many other nations; in so doing, action sport bags and equipment often mark the action sport body with chaffing, bruises and strained muscles. Interestingly, action sport-related luggage (board bags, bicycle boxes) are a site of distinction, often garnering the attention of fellow participants or intrigued travellers in places of transit such as airports, train and bus stations. Such equipment distinguishes the body of the action sport enthusiast from all other travellers in such spaces. Yet, luggage lost and damaged by airlines and other modes of transport can have major implications for the participant's experiences upon arrival. Experienced action sport travellers tend to give much consideration to their luggage and to appropriate modes of transport (for example, the pre-hire of a rental vehicle that will fit board bags as well as the required number of travellers). The increased costs for additional luggage imposed by many airlines and other modes of travel (such as buses/coaches and trains) have also impacted action sport travellers, prompting many to take less equipment or hire it upon arrival in their destinations. Put simply, corporeal, imaginative and object mobilities are intimately connected to action sport travel, tourism and career migration.

The hyper-mobilities of professional action sport athletes

The life of the contemporary professional action sport athlete (for example, surfer, snowboarder, freestyle skier, mountain bike rider, climber) is a particularly privileged one, typically consisting of extensive national and international travel for competitions and events. Like professional golfers or tennis players, competitive action sport athletes often follow international competition circuits. For example, the 34 professional male surfers on the ASP World Championship Tour compete in 10 events in Australia, Brazil, Fiji, France,

Figure 4.1   A group of snowboarders are marked by their luggage as they wait at an airport

Hawaii, Indonesia, Portugal, Tahiti and the US, and the top 17 female surfers compete in eight events in Australia, Brazil, France, New Zealand, Portugal and the US. During the four to six weeks between events, many of these surfers are chasing swells and doing promotional photo shoots in countries ranging from the well-known surf destinations of Indonesia, Fiji, Tahiti, and Costa Rica, to more remote locations, such as Namibia, Madagascar and Iceland.

Similarly, a competitive snowboarder following the International Ski Federation (FIS) Snowboard World Cup circuit will compete at ski resorts in various countries, including Argentina, Austria, Canada, France, Germany, Italy, Japan, Korea, New Zealand, Russia, Spain, Sweden, Switzerland and the US. As a competitive snowboarder on the World Cup tour during the mid- and late 1990s, Pamela reflects upon her hyper-mobility as follows:

> I can't remember all the places I have travelled to for snowboarding . [. . .] Japan, Canada, USA, Italy, Switzerland, Austria, Germany, France. [. . .] Obviously some places are not so memorable – but each is connected by that sense of newness, adventure and trepidation. But travelling for competitions is pretty nerve-wracking, so you don't get much of a chance to soak up the place and *be a tourist* – you are preoccupied and focused on the competition preparation and trying to have an optimal competition experience. (personal communication [pc], July 2008; emphasis added)

In another interview, Pamela described a particularly low moment during her travels when she had broken her ankle, missed some important competitions, and was feeling 'incredibly home sick': 'I remember being really discouraged and . . . calling my dad and being quite upset and saying "look I have no idea what I'm doing here". He told me to just go out and *be a tourist*, be glad that you're on the other side of the world, look around, walk the streets, sit in the cafes . . . and that took a lot of pressure off' (pc, September 2005; emphasis added). Interestingly, in both of these quotes Pamela distinguishes between the pleasures of travelling as a 'tourist' and more stressful 'athletic' mobilities.

Not all professional action sport athletes, however, follow a strict international competition circuit. Some make a living from sponsorships from companies who pay salaries based primarily on niche media coverage (for example, interviews and photos in action sport magazines and websites, segments in niche videos), as well as self-promotional media (for example, athlete blogs, webisodes – short online videos). Some of these athletes are paid to travel to exotic and remote locations to pioneer new spaces and places. For example, in 2011, Red Bull-sponsored big-wave surfer, Ian Walsh, flew from Hawaii to Africa for a month of chasing swells 'from the sharky waters of Cape Town to the remote sand spits of Namibia', before heading to New York City for a Red Bull snowboarding film première, followed immediately by a road-trip chasing a hurricane swell hitting Rhode Island. Following his quick US visit, he then flew to Bulgaria to begin working on a documentary based on searching for surf in the Caspian Sea. His year also included two surfing trips to Indonesia, two to Fiji and three to Mexico, none of which were for competitions. On each of these trips, Walsh (as with most professional surfers) is travelling with a quiver of between four and ten surfboards of varying shapes and sizes for different conditions, as well as an array of media technologies (camera, video, laptop) to document his expeditions for his sponsors, magazines and surf companies. As with many professional action sport athletes, Walsh shares his adventures on his personal blog (see www.weekwithwalshy.com).[2]

The international journeys of professional action sport athletes are covered in an array of niche magazines, films and websites, as well as some mainstream documentaries and television programs. The dominant representations of male and (typically fewer) female action sport athletes' travels, however, focus on their idyllic transnational lifestyles (travel to exotic and remote destinations, financial independence, apparent lack of commitment, partying). Sporting companies, media and corporate sponsors carefully choreograph such images and narratives to create a compelling mythology for the millions of recreational participants around the world (also see Frohlick, 2005; Kay & Laberge, 2003). In an interesting analysis of the relationship between the surf media and tourism, Ponting (2009) describes surfing magazines featuring 'heavily illustrated articles about professional surfers on trips organized by the surfer's corporate sponsor', that led to a heightened 'demand for surfing tourism . . . based on four symbolic elements:

perfect waves, uncrowded conditions, soft adventure, and an exotic, pristine environment' (p. 182). He offers the example of the Mentawai Islands in Indonesia, which became a 'focal point for surfing culture' during the 1990s, after 'featuring in hundreds of advertisements and scores of videos and travel articles'. By 2009, the Mentawai Islands hosted the world's largest surf charter fleet with more than 50 live-aboard yachts and six upmarket resorts in operation (most of which are foreign-owned and -operated), with several more in various stages of planning and construction (Ponting, 2009, p. 177).

Evocative imagery of professional snowboarders during the same period had a similar effect on the desires of recreational snowboarders. According to Chris Sanders, CEO of Avalanche Snowboards,

> The dream is basically what the kids see when they look in the magazines and see Damian [Sanders] or Terje [Haakonsen]. They are great lifestyle icons. They have it great. It looks like their lives are 24-hour-a-day adventure. You get handed these plane tickets, you hang out with cool photographers, dye your hair however you want to, and you're making money so your parents have no say in your life. It's all sex, action, and glamour. To an 18-year-old snowboarder, this is the dream. (cited in Howe, 1998, p. 68)

Action sport companies and media continue to invest heavily in the transnational hypermobility of professional athletes because it enhances global connections, and promotes youth cultural consumption of discourses, images, product and travel.

Not all professional action sport athletes, however, receive the same levels of support from their sponsors; some struggle for many years to subsidize their own transnational careers and lifestyles. For example, Alex Johnson, a professional US female climber, explains:

> . . . climbing isn't the richest sport out there, but my sponsors definitely help me out a lot with my trips. [But] I still try to budget my trips accordingly, and that's why I've been sleeping in my van for the past four months instead of staying in hotels. I struggled a lot financially in Europe last summer because I was spending so much more than I was making traveling to World Cup competitions. (cited in DPM, 2012, para. 5)

Professional snowboarder and editor of *New Zealand Snowboarder* magazine, Dylan Butt (2005), also offers readers a sobering perspective:

> Becoming a professional 'Extreme Athlete' has gotta be the best career in the world. Getting paid huge amounts of money to do what you enjoy, living the 'rock star' lifestyle, rolling around in pimped-out wagons, groupies hangin' off each arm, non-stop parties and travelling the world to the most luxurious of destinations . . . You better pinch yourself

because you're dreaming . . . Any true snowboarder will tell you that what it's all about [is] living in the mountains and snowboarding as much as possible, working your ass off to make enough money to go overseas so you can do it all over again while everybody else is back home lying on the beach. (p. 88)

Similarly, Mick Hannah, a professional mountain biker who has been on the world tour for more than a decade, reveals: 'as with many things, people tend to fantasize [the life of the professional mountain bike rider] too much. This is still a real full time job. There are lots of challenges and stresses associated . . . it can be very tiring traveling from country to country and trying to stay healthy and in good shape for racing' (Interview with . . . , no date, para. 16). Continuing, Hannah explains that while he 'just love[s] traveling and racing', he has two young sons such that 'it's really hard to be away so much' (Interview with . . . , no date, para. 7). Indeed, the highly mobile lifestyles of the professional action sport athlete can become more difficult as some athletes establish commitments and obligations (such as long-term relationships or family) in one location. The relatively fickle nature of the industry and high costs of travelling for competitions can also put pressures on those not consistently at the top of their game.

When contextualizing the relationship between what action sport athletes receive (free travel to exotic locations, financial incentives) and what they produce (highly evocative images used by editors to sell magazines, and in global advertising campaigns for transnational corporations), it becomes apparent that action sport athletes are not free agents but rather workers in the capitalist system (see Beamish, 2002; Rigauer, 1981; Thorpe, 2011a). Although action sport athletes have some agency to control the direction of their careers, and often work with companies to produce events and footage that they deem to be personally rewarding and culturally authentic, their highly mobile lifestyles are based on explicit expectations for them to place in competitions and/or produce magazine-worthy shots and stories, which can put action sport athletes in vulnerable positions. In a highly competitive industry with throngs of up-and-coming stars, action sport athletes' positions of status and cultural privilege are never guaranteed. If an athlete ceases to produce results at competitions, or media-worthy images and narratives, their sponsors will readily replace them. Thus, knowing that their careers can be short-lived, most action sport athletes embrace all opportunities to travel, and 'work' hard to produce the results and images desired by their sponsors.

Writing about the highly mobile lives of professional surfers for a mainstream travel blog, one travel writer reminds his (assumedly privileged) readers of the risks endured by such athletes:

. . . next time you're riding business class lamenting the fact that you've been on the road for the last two weeks, consider the fact that there's some surfer out there trying to stuff a big silver board bag into a decrepit Nicaraguan taxi who's chasing a swell he spotted while camping out somewhere in Sri Lanka. He's sleep-deprived, heavily vaccinated, and willing to throw himself over a 20-foot ledge onto a jagged coral reef all for a chance to chase the dream we call the cover of a magazine. (Ellison, 2011, para. 13)

Early professional snowboarder Mike Basich further reveals the frustrations and dangers associated with his highly mobile career:

A lot of people say I'm lucky for what I do for a living. Sure, maybe that's true. I get to travel the world and not have to work a nine-to-five job. But when I get to work, my worries are not about giving a report to my boss or something. I worry about making it through the day without break-ing a bone or getting stuck in an avalanche (knock, knock). You're body takes a beating. You're never home. Lots of lag time at airports. (cited in Baccigaluppi et al., 2001, p. 95)

Two further examples of the risks facing action sport athletes while training or competing overseas were offered in Chapter 3. Top freestyle skier Sarah Burke suffered a critical brain injury while training in the United States. Sadly, as a Canadian citizen without adequate travel insurance, Burke's fam-ily faced hundreds of thousands of dollars of hospital fees following her death. Also, when triple world champion surfer Andy Irons fell ill during a competition in Puerto Rico, he faced a long journey home, ultimately dying in a hotel room in Dallas.

There are inherent risks involved in action sport athletes' highly mobile careers, yet the action sport media and companies work hard to (re)create the 'dream' of the transnational action sport lifestyle via extensive coverage and sponsorship of travelling professionals. Despite the saturation of such images across action sport media, it is important to keep in mind that, in reality, such opportunities are afforded only to a select few. In pursuit of this 'dream' lifestyle, however, many others (tourists, committed enthusiasts, aspiring athletes) invest heavily (financially, physically, temporally) in their own journeys, and in so doing support the global action sport economy.

Action sport tourism: backpackers, surfaris and heli-ski holidays

For many years, international action sport travel was an activity enjoyed primarily by competitive athletes, hard-core participants (who would do almost anything to enable their travels) and the wealthy. Recent changes in international travel and action sport tourism, however, have contributed to shifts in the social demographics of action sport tourists. While each action sport has its own unique tourism mobilities, here I focus on surf and snow sport tourism to illustrate these changes.

Surf tourism

Since the late 1960s, the surf tourism industry has grown from a few hundred young, white, highly committed male surfers searching the globe for 'the perfect wave' into 'a highly commodified industry in which more than two hundred and fifty specialized agencies sell thousands of tours to hundreds of thousands of surfing tourists and turn over hundreds of millions of US dollars each year' (Ponting, 2007, p. 1). The commercial surf tourism industry began during the 1970s with rudimentary surf camps catering to low-budget surfers. The first official 'surf camp' was established in 1977 in relatively remote Garajagan, East Java. The camp offered very basic services with a capacity of 10 surfers per day. Over the next decade, more low-cost surf camps emerged in a range of developing countries such as Fiji, Costa Rica, Indonesia and Mexico (Ponting, 2007). As surfing continued to gain popularity around the world and well-known surf breaks became increasingly crowded, more and more recreational and committed surfers set out on journeys ranging from a few days to many months to find new, or at least less crowded, surf breaks. Responding to such trends, an array of surfing tour operators and surf travel agencies were established to provide surfers with package deals suited specifically to their budget, timetable and desires. During the early 1980s, live-aboard surf charters emerged as an exclusive form of surf travel. As a result of the explosion of media coverage of professional surfers travelling via boat to exotic and pristine destinations such as the Mentawai Islands, this became the most desired form of surf travel. For many, a live-aboard surf charter holiday is an unrealistic dream. An 11-night trip with Seabourn Surf Charters in the Mentawai Islands, for example, costs approximately US$24,500 for seven people, not including flights, ground transport or travel insurance. Despite the cost of such trips, they remain highly popular, particularly among groups of male friends who justify it as 'a trip of a lifetime'.

Since the 1980s, the surfing tourism market has witnessed considerable demographic and socio-economic changes. As an article in the *Sydney Morning Herald* (2000) accurately observes: 'The time-rich, cash poor travellers of the 1960s and 1970s were replaced by wave hunters with more disposable income who wanted to get there quickly and get as many waves as possible during their annual holiday' (cited in Ponting, 2007, p. 3). Similarly, the author of an online article about surfing in Nicaragua explains:

> . . . in the current crush of global surf tourism . . . most two-weeks-of-vacation-a-year people just want uncrowded good waves . . . They want to go home exhausted and sunburned with aching shoulders and a kaleidoscope of saltwatery memories, which is exactly what Nicaragua

offers. Although Nicaragua isn't a surfing nirvana, it should suffice for the majority of surf tourists who are happy to leave world class surf to the magazines and the ferals. (Nicaragua: Pacific Side Introduction, no date, para. 3)

Here an important contrast is made between the 'two-weeks-of-vacation-a-year' surfers and 'the ferals'; the latter are renowned for travelling and living on a very tight budget, often setting up camp (with few luxuries) in surf destinations for many months.

Catering to the increasingly bourgeois desires of modern surfers, however, the surf tourism industry now features an array of national and international businesses set up to capitalize on this trend. For example, Wavehunters Surf Travel, Inc., is 'a full-service travel and tour agency selling land and sea-based surfing vacations and flights' (www.wavehunters.com). Nomad Surfers, another surf tourism business, also offers an array of surf camps for adults and children, as well as surf charters, surfaris, surf accommodation, surf resorts, and kitesurf, windsurf and SUP (stand-up paddle boarding) camps (www.nomadsurfers.com). The Nomad Surfers website encourages surf travellers to book with them because 'we have already committed ... the mistakes ourselves for you':

If you only have one or two weeks' holiday, you don't want to be taking any risks and running around blindfolded. [. . .] We have already tried and selected the best accommodations, surf camps and boat charters worldwide for you . . . Someone will be at the airport to meet you, regardless of what time you arrive. Your beds will be ready. Your food will be ready. Clean rooms, proper toilets! The best local surf guides in the area will advise you where to go surf and when. What tides, what winds, where to go in and out of the water, etc. They will take you to that magical place that you would never in the world find on your own or would take ages to do so, wasting your precious time!

As well as saving 'precious time', the website warns travellers of potentially negative experiences that can be avoided by using their service:

Sometimes you arrive to [sic] a country you have never been before and when leaving the arrivals terminal at the airport, you are literally assaulted by 50 persons yelling at you in an unknown language, harassing you to get a taxi or take you to a hostel . . . These situations are very chaotic . . .

After some intense and stressful moments, you eventually get money from the ATM and jump into a taxi. All you know is the name of the surf place you want to go to . . . the problem is that this taxi driver rips you off and charges twice as much as you should pay. Not only this, but he takes you to a hostel of his family or where he gets commission. You don't like the place too much, it smells, dirty sheets, dirty floor, dirty bathroom, but it is too late . . .

This narrative aims to evoke fear in the traveller, and particularly fear of the locals. Other services, such as Girls Gone Surfing, target specific niche markets, often utilizing girl power rhetoric in their marketing materials. Indeed, female surf, yoga and health camps have grown in popularity over the past decade (Comer, 2010). As with most action sport enthusiasts, travelling surfers also use surf websites and/or online magazine forums to discuss their travel plans, and share their stories and experiences. For example, the *Surfer* magazine travel forum features hundreds of posts under topics such as 'Northern Baja advice?', 'Surf travel bag recommendations', 'Kauai in October: Surfaction veiled as honeymoon', 'Wanna go to Oz', 'Nicaragua in May', and 'Boards to take to Bocas Del Toros, Panama'. Some posts foster much discussion and debate, with others recording in excess of 35,000 views.

As a result of the rapidly expanding niche for tourism entrepreneurs targeting 'cash-rich, time-poor' travellers, surfers now have a plethora of travel options available to them, ranging from budget flights into a country, hiring a van and camping at a variety of surf spots, to new 'business class' packaged surf holidays including 'direct flights, prompt and comfortable transfers, relatively luxurious surf charter yachts and resorts and, in some cases, exclusive access to world-class breaks' (Ponting, 2009, p. 177). As Ponting (2009) highlights, whether it is for one week or many months, the international travel of most surfers is driven by the quest for the 'four symbolic elements' reinforced in the surfing media: perfect waves, uncrowded conditions, soft adventure and an exotic, pristine environment. As for many action sport travellers, the opportunities for interacting with like-minded travellers (either friends or strangers) is also important, with some surfers compromising some elements of the above criteria in order to be in places with good music, cafes and/or nightlife.

Some salient flows among travelling surfers include the longstanding exodus of American surfers to the North Shore of Hawaii for the North Pacific winter swells, and more recently, to Mexico and Costa Rica for warmer waves; surfers living on the East Coast of the US to Puerto Rico and the Caribbean; the gradual migration of European surfers (often travelling in their own or rented vans) travelling south through Spain, France and Portugal to North Africa to escape the European winter; and Australian and New Zealand surfers to Indonesia (particularly Bali) during the southern hemisphere winter months. Yet, the flows of travelling surfers are in flux, constantly shifting with exchange rates, the political situation within and between countries, and the media exposure of particular destinations.

Snow-sport tourism

In contrast to the early surf travellers who tended to travel to less developed nations on very tight budgets, snow sport tourism has traditionally been dominated by upper-class travellers who tended to seek out highly developed ski resort destinations in Europe and North America. The consumption of skiing holidays in exclusive mountain resort destinations, such Chamonix (France), Zermatt (Switzerland) and Aspen (Colorado), has long been a practice of distinction among the upper classes (Bourdieu, 1984). During the 1990s, however, many ski-fields and mountain resort destinations in North America, Europe and Australasia could no longer rely solely on their traditionally elite clientele for continued economic growth. With the popularity of snowboarding, many resorts recognized the potential in the middle-class youth market for ongoing economic prosperity. Attempting to further attract regional, national and international snowboarding and skiing patrons, many (not all) resort destinations began offering cheaper travel and accommodation options for the typically younger and less affluent (though still privileged) snowboarder, as well as developing unique events for niche groups (such as snowboarding competitions for university students, women's snowboarding clinics, coaching camps, and gay ski and snowboard weeks). Some airlines also re-tooled to better service the influx of snow-sport tourists. For example, in 2007 low-cost carrier Ryanair announced a new winter schedule 'designed with skiers and snowboarders in mind' (cited in Ski Tourism, 2007, p. 5).

Many travel companies also realized the economic potential in middle-class snow-sport tourism and began offering a wider range of snow-sport travel options (for example, budget or backpacker specials, long-weekend student deals, and all-inclusive family packages). For example, in 2009, Ski New Zealand (a tourism agency) offered Australian snow-sport enthusiasts an array of all-inclusive packages ranging from 'luxury holidays' to 'backpacker specials' (the latter comprising five nights' accommodation in a multi-share room in a hostel in Queenstown, a four-day lift pass, and rental equipment for NZ$595). Indeed, during the three peak months of the 2009 winter season (June, July and August), Queenstown hosted more than 250,000 Australian visitors (Stats Confirm, 2009, para. 4). Similarly, British snow sport tourists can choose from a variety of all-inclusive packages to resorts across Europe (for example, Andorra, Austria, Bulgaria, Finland, France, Italy and Switzerland). During the winter season of 2008–09 a three-day trip to Courchevel, France, including flights, lift passes, chalet board, rental, flights and three days' packed lunch cost just £465. Attracting 37.5 per cent of the 1.22 million British ski and snowboard holidaymakers, the French Alps continue to be the most popular destination for British snow-sport tourists (UK Ski Market, 2008).

Yet, while international snow-related travel has become more accessible to (some) middle-class families, younger participants and budget travellers, other experiences (such as helicopter-accessed skiing and snowboarding) and locations (such as Aspen [Colorado] and St Moritz [Switzerland]) remain remote, costly and exclusive. Indeed, lift-pass prices at some resorts have sky-rocketed in recent years. During the 2013 winter season, one-day lift passes at Treble Cone (Wanaka, New Zealand) and Vail (Colorado, USA) cost NZ$97.00 and US$114.00, respectively. During the same year, five helicopter-accessed runs in the Southern Alps (New Zealand) cost NZ$1080.00 per person, and a week of helicopter-accessed snowboarding in Valdez (Alaska) costs US$9895 per person (including accommodation and food). An even more exclusive weeklong 'private package' for eight snow-sport enthusiasts in Valdez costs over US$88,970!

A critical analysis of action sport tourism

Just as surfers, skiers and snowboarders now have a plethora of travel options, similar tourism industries have been established around most other action sports (exceptions include the urban, and typically less privileged activities, of skateboarding, BMX and parkour). For example, mountain bikers are exploring new trails and package deals in destinations ranging from Utah to Morocco. Hut-to-hut mountain biking trips are also gaining popularity in countries such as the US and New Zealand, particularly in areas where winter sport and/or hiking accommodations can be used for summer mountain biking trips. Typically white, privileged kite-surfers are also travelling to locations with warm water and consistent winds, such as Brazil, Egypt, Greece, Honduras, Mexico, Morocco, Portugal and Turkey. As well as hundreds of action sport travel websites, a plethora of action sport travel books are now available to help individuals and groups plan their next adventure, and most action sport magazines include travel features on a regular basis.

As a result of the increased flows of action sport tourists, however, many previously remote and semi-exclusive action sport destinations have become crowded, thus prompting more committed enthusiasts to seek out even more remote locations. The authors of *Snowboarding the World*, an extensive guidebook written by two ex-professional snowboarders and a snowboarding journalist, recognize the increasingly diverse demands of travelling snowboarders:

> Fifteen years ago people were just happy to go riding where they could. As resorts became more crowded, the travelling habits of snowboarders correspondingly became more sophisticated as people began to look further afield for something new. [. . .] As snowboarding broadens its horizons, new areas are gradually opening up as intrepid riders seek to escape the mainstream. [. . .] Bulgaria, Iran, Poland and Russia . . . As snowboarding destinations, each offers something slightly different to the essentially homogenized riding experience that is snowboarding in Europe or North America. [. . .] Underdeveloped towns and antiquated

Figure 4.2 Heli-skiing and snowboarding for a privileged few in the Southern Alps of New Zealand. (Photo used with permission of photographer, José Borrero)

lift systems – things that in the past would have seemed like massive failings in any resort – just add to the experience. (Barr et al., 2006, p. 91)

In so doing, we are seeing more snowboarders and other action sport enthusiasts embodying a neo-colonialist approach not dissimilar to that of early surf travellers (Barilotti, 2002). Few snowboarders, surfers or other action sport travellers see their tourist mobilities to remote destinations in developing nations as problematic. Yet action sport tourist mobilities are intimately connected to the 'economic and political relations of power in the contemporary global (dis)order' (Bianchi, 2009, p. 484), and the flows of tourists – not separate from the flow of capital and resources – are supported by inequitable power relations and exploitative practices and politics. Working within the critical tourist studies framework helps us understand contemporary action sport tourism as 'a set of complex, negotiated, contingent, blurred and incomplete practices and ideas' that have real impacts on local communities (Hannan & Knox, 2010, p. 4).

Of course, the interactions between travelling action sport enthusiasts and local peoples in developing nations can offer positive experiences for both parties. For example, Benjamin, a 21-year-old Liberian fisherman, recalls seeing foreign surfers in his village for the first time in 2005: 'When I first saw this guy surfing, it was like magic to me.' The early surfers in the region of Robertsport were relief workers on their weekend breaks, some of who took time to teach intrigued locals such as Benjamin. Under the tutelage of a Scottish ecologist and aid worker, Benjamin stood up on his fourth attempt. In his own words, 'I felt like I was on a motorcycle. I was so happy. I didn't know you could do this'. According to the author of a *New York Times* article about the growth of surf tourism in Liberia, 'Benjamin, along with a growing – but still small – number of Liberian surfers, and a much-faster-growing number of world-class surfers always on the lookout for the next big wave, are slowly carving out this country's embryonic surfing scene' (Cooper, 2010, para. 17). According to the Liberian-born author, the development of surf tourism in this developing nation is the result of both local surfers and business-minded residents, and surfing tourists. Shayne McIntire, a professional surfer who spent 17 days filming an 'On Surfari' episode for National Geographic television, waxes lyrical about the cultural experience of surfing in Liberia:

The whole experience in Robertsport felt like living inside a classic book about an African adventure. We were staying on the water in wood-decked safari tents, watching fishermen dodge absolutely perfect waves while pulling in their catch from hand-carved dugout canoes, while ladies with their children wrapped to their backs in beautiful print clothes crossed the sand. And behind us an immensely thick, impenetrable jungle rich with the sounds of singing birds and dew dripping on the leaves. (cited in Cooper, 2010, para. 18)

While articles, documentaries and programs, such as those from the *New York Times* and National Geographic mentioned above, reveal the positive relationships and cultural exchanges between travelling action sport partici-pants and locals, the less savoury aspects (such as travelling male surfers' rela-tions with local women, or their participation in local sex or drug trades; the environmental impact of foreign surfers camping for long periods of time) of the global diffusion of action sport tourism have received less attention.

Surfing scholar Jess Ponting, however, is a noteworthy exception. In his critical analysis of surf tourism, Ponting (2009) questions the implications of a tourism industry 'that continues to develop in remote, less-developed regions as an ad hoc response to demand fuelled by media imagery of com-mercially created symbols designed to sell fashion items and consumer goods' (p. 175). He explains that much surf tourism traffic has 'involved wealthy Western surfers travelling to less developed destinations and with-out forethought, planning or consultation, triggering a new tourism indus-try often with significant deleterious environmental and cultural impacts' (Ponting, 2007, p. 1). For Ponting, the commercially produced imagery associated with surfing in these destinations has contributed to the prob-lem. Rarely do commercial images of these locations show anything beyond high-performance surfers riding perfect waves. Local residents and culture are typically invisible. Thus, when tourists travel to these locations they are not looking for local residents, they are often unaware of what is going on beyond the shoreline, and the charter industry also tends to ignore them. According to Ponting (2007), this type of 'unregulated free-market develop-ment relegates local people to a relatively powerless position, usually last to benefit from the exploitation of their resources' (p. 4). Yet some surfers and tourist businesses are working with local communities to develop more sustainable and equitable enterprises. Ponting compares the problematic developments in the Mentawai Islands with management models from the Pacific (particularly surf camps in Fiji and Papua New Guinea) that better 'respect the traditional ownership of reef, sea and land resources and priori-tise the needs of local communities' (Ponting, 2007, p. 1).

In the case above, Ponting (2007) points to the surfing companies and media, and foreign investors, for the exploitative tourist industry that has developed in some regions of the world. Yet action sport travellers can also directly and indirectly insult or harm local residents. This is particularly the case for groups of young, predominantly male, travellers who are too often oblivious to local, regional and national differences. For example, an article in *Australian/New Zealand Snowboarding* magazine titled 'Aussies behaving badly: Global thugs?' vilifies the behaviour of young male Australians while overseas:

A mob of Aussies overseas can be heavy. When one swallows you, you truly feel like part of a team. A team on a mission to spread Australianness.

Indestructible. [. . .] From the days of yore, Australians have bravely used alcohol to increase their Australianness. [But] when the smoke clears, and all the local women have been hit on, and the local men beaten and affronted, and the cranky Australasian mob tear off to the next town, there is only one thing that the locals can be sure of – that another wave is not far away . . . (Costios, 2005, p. 15)

To further illustrate this point, the article offers the following narrative to reveal the dangers imposed on the local professional and volunteer mountain rescue team by a group of inexperienced snowboarders:

Recently, a story came to our attention; a tale of Auzzie can-do, mateship, [and] larrikinism . . . It's the story of some blokes who decided to take themselves on an impromptu tour through the backcountry of the Zillertal Mountains in Tirol, Austria. Ill-prepared and ill-equipped, the lads trekked boldly through a deadly environment . . . Deciding unanimously that radios and provisions are for chicks – it was therefore up to the local rescue teams to locate and save their sorry hides when foul weather set in and the lads became lost. After a night in the cold, they were found the next day. [The Australians were taken to safety] but two members of the Austrian rescue team were forced to wait behind . . . Cue avalanche. Both men were harnessed and roped together, with one anchoring the other. The latter fell off a ledge, the rope becoming taut, and so took the full force of the avalanche on his body with the harness breaking his back. (Cotsios, 2005, p. 15)

As a fellow travelling snowboarder, the male Australian magazine editor publicly condemns the reckless actions of his countrymen.

Over the past few years, as a result of more critical journalism in the action sport media and broader discourses about social responsibility (particularly evident among the middle classes), there has been a growing awareness among some groups of travelling action sport enthusiasts of the social, cultural and economic impacts of their mobilities on local communities, and that they have the option to not only be more culturally respectful travellers, but also more conscious consumers of action sport tourism places and packages that adopt more ethical and moral approaches. For example, a surf journalist commenting on the extensive media coverage of surf travel in Nicaragua, proclaimed:

while there are a few expats who will bemoan its popularity and subsequent crowds, it is up to those who visit Nicaragua in the next few years to create a sustainable surf environment with respect given to the locals and an eye for the future. There are enough surf ghettos in the world, and we have a chance to keep this place beautiful, one surf trip at a time. (Nicaragua: Pacific Side Introduction, no date, para. 13)

Of course, among the difficulties facing the development of sustainable action sport tourism models that respect local ownership and prioritize the needs of local communities is that many action sport tourists are from privileged, western backgrounds and have embodied assumptions that, if they work hard enough and can afford it, then it is their 'right' to be able travel to wherever they want in the world, whether it is for work, play or a combination of the two. This neo-colonial approach to action sport travel is highly problematic for many local communities in developing regions around the world. While travelling action sport enthusiasts may adopt friendly and culturally respectful approaches in their interactions with locals, for many, their consumption of foreign places and experiences are typically underpinned by individualistic, hedonistic and short-term ways of thinking. In so doing, their travel practices support the global action sport economy, but typically overlook both the immediate and long-term effects on local communities.

Action sport migration: working to play

In contrast to professional athletes who are paid to travel to destinations for competitions or media events, or tourists who go on action sport vacations, there is another group of action sport travellers whose mobilities combine both work and leisure. Here I use the term 'action sport migrants' to refer broadly to those action sport enthusiasts who travel internationally to work for a short period in an area that offers rich opportunities to participate in their chosen activity, as well as social interactions with likeminded action sport enthusiasts. Importantly, however, action sport migrants are not a homogenous group. Some consume a summer or winter working abroad much like an OE (Overseas Experience) or 'gap year', before returning to their studies or in search of a 'real job'. Others develop long-term careers working in the action sport industry (for example, as instructors or resort managers) and invest a lot of time and energy into developing the skills, qualifications and international connections necessary for working across two or more countries on a seasonal basis. Many of the latter group commence their transnational careers much like the former group, but enjoy the lifestyle and/or work so much that they continue to chase the snow, waves, sun and/or wind across continents for many years. In the remainder of this chapter I draw upon a growing number of case studies of specific forms of transnational youth migration, including student mobility (Collins, 2008; Findlay et al., 2006), volunteer tourism (Raymond & Hall, 2008), lifestyle migration (Korpela, 2009), and the working holiday (Duncan, 2012; Mason,

2002; Wilson et al., 2009; Frändberg, 2013, p. 4), to examine the experiences of those who combine their passion for action sports with a working holiday.

From regional migration to the 'Big OE'

The cultural demographics of action sport tourists are shifting, yet young, white, privileged men and women continue to constitute a dominant force at the core of most action sport cultures. In their late teens and twenties, many core participants have yet to take on adult responsibilities (marriage, children, mortgages, long-term employment, and so on), and their commitment to their preferred action sport is such that it organizes their whole lives (at least for a few years) (see Wheaton & Tomlinson, 1998). Action sport journalist Jennifer Sherowski (2005) observes varying levels of commitment, identification, and associated mobilities, in the snowboarding culture:

> Not everyone who rides a snowboard is a snowboarder but for those who do bear this illustrious title, it's an undeniable *way of life*. High school ends, and the road starts calling – off to mountain towns and the assimilation into weird, transient tribes full of people who work night jobs cleaning toilets or handing you your coffee in the early mornings, all so they can shove a fistful of tips in their pocket and ride, their real motives betrayed by goggle tans or chins scuffed by Gore-Tex. In this world, people don't ask what you 'do,' they ask you where you work – knowing that what you do is snowboard, just like them, and any job you might have is simply a means for it. (p. 160)

Many core action sport participants, as suggested in the quote above, are nomadic, travelling nationally and internationally to experience new terrain, meet new people, or 'live the dream' of the endless winter or summer. Moreover, the places travelled and the number of years dedicated to pursuing one's preferred activity are important symbols of commitment within action sport cultures, which offer participants access to symbolic capital from their peers.

Often at the end of high school or tertiary education (or during a leave of absence from education or the workforce), many committed action sport participants migrate to mountain or beach towns where they find accommodation and employment, and spend several months to many years practising, playing and performing in the various physical (mountains, waves, beaches, rivers) and social (bars, cafes, shops) spaces and places (see Chapter 5). Core action sport participants typically begin their lifestyle migration by moving to destinations with good quality snow, surf, wind, routes or trails in their country of origin. For example, many surfers living on the east coast of the United States move to California or Hawaii. Similarly, Canadian skiers and snowboarders living on the east coast relocate to larger resorts in Alberta (such as Banff) and British Columbia (such as Whistler). In New Zealand, passionate action sport enthusiasts living in the North Island often move to mountain towns in the South Island (Queenstown, Wanaka) which host thriving international snowboarding and skiing scenes during the winter months, and mountain biking and climbing once the snow has melted (see Chapter 5).

For some action sport enthusiasts, it is not an option to move to a surf or mountain town to focus solely on their athletic pursuits. But for those pursuing higher education, access to good quality mountains, surf breaks or trails can be critical in their choice of college or university. Catering to their student readers, *Transworld Snowboarding* magazine included a 10-page feature covering the best colleges in the US for passionate snowboarders. The article offers readers the following advice:

> . . . what are you seeking? If it's just riding, then go! Ride. Explore. Be a bum! Then go to school later, when you're serious about it. If you have the parental and scholarship backing, then milk it, and go where school meets snow. Take on both and go get a shr-education. (Gavelda, 2010, no page)

Mountain Bike Action Magazine also provides a list of the top 10 colleges for mountain bikers (America's Top 10, 2013). Alternatively (or additionally), many tertiary students pursue a 'working holiday' – also known as a gap year in the UK or an Overseas Experience (OE) in Australia and New Zealand – that incorporates their passion for action sports with their desire to travel overseas before, during or after their studies.

Broadly, the 'working holiday' refers to 'the discretionary movement of young adults – often able and well-educated and mostly from Anglophone countries such as the UK, Canada, Australia and New Zealand – to other parts of the world to temporarily experience life and work elsewhere' (Haverig, 2011, p. 103). The working holiday is an opportunity typically afforded to youth between the ages of 18 and 30 years whose governments have granted them the right to temporarily live and work for a finite period in participating countries before returning to their home countries. While 'the intention to return is often considered as a choice young people make', Haverig (2011) reminds us that it is in fact 'consistent with the regulatory framework of the working holiday' (Haverig, 2011, p. 105). The availability of temporary youth work visas among the Commonwealth countries facilitates the mobility of young Australian, British, Canadian and New Zealand action sport enthusiasts, and J1 Visas enable tertiary students from an array of countries to spend five months working in the US during their university holidays; many of these choose to work at ski resorts or beach destinations. A plethora of commercial services have been established to facilitate (and profit from) the growing number of middle-class students wanting to experience an international 'working holiday' at a ski resort, summer camp or beach resort (for example, STA Travel; Out Break Adventure Recruitment; Work USA, Work Canada; see Duncan, 2008).

As well as offering opportunities for international work and travel, the gap year and the OE in the UK and New Zealand, respectively, have been constructed as 'a time of freedom, fun and cultural experiences' (Haverig, 2011, p. 105). Yet it is not only about pleasure and exploring other countries; 'personal transformation is a highly visible aspiration of those wishing to embark on an OE' (Haverig, 2011, p. 105). Critically examining common representations of the OE in New Zealand media and popular discourse in conjunction with interviews with those heading off on their 'Big OE', Haverig (2011) describes travelling youth as aspiring to 'the notions of maturity, deliberate personal challenge, and self exploration' (p. 105). While similar aspirations underpin the 'working holidays' of many action sport enthusiasts, there are also some unique distinctions, as suggested in the following quote:

> As a snowboarder the 'Big OE' is a bit different from your good old traditional 'going to London and getting a job at a pub' or 'backpacking around Europe on the smell of any oily rag'. It's more a pilgrimage, a mission of intent to ride as much as possible, to experience previously unknown depths of snow, and conquer the peaks and parks that you've seen so many times in DVDs and magazines. (Westcot, 2006, p. 63)

Indeed, privileged action sport enthusiasts who meet the criteria set by their governments make the most of existing infrastructure and the common discourses surrounding the gap year or the OE, and use the opportunity to travel to destinations culturally renowned for their action sport facilities.

While some youth use the OE as an opportunity to gain valuable international work experience, this tends to be low on the priorities for action sport enthusiasts on a working holiday. According to a co-owner of an employment agency in a New Zealand ski resort town that helps hundreds of travelling youth find jobs every winter, many are happy to settle for low-skilled and/or low-paying jobs:

> A lot of the backpackers here for the winter, well, they're not really concerned about the long term. They're just here for a few months and don't mind working crappy jobs with little pay. They just need enough money to go out [party at night]. (pc, 2011)

Indeed, for many action sport enthusiasts on a one-season 'working holiday', the party lifestyle is just as important (if not more so) than action sport participation during the day. As a manager of snow-sport instructors at a New Zealand resort told me: 'Some of these younger traveller guys that work here, they're doing a pub crawl, and just trying to go out and drink as much as possible, on any given night' (Cesar, pc, 2011). The privileged habitus of many action sport participants and their tendency to embrace the 'party lifestyle' while overseas often contributes to the working holiday being a hedonistic celebration of physical youth culture and a temporary escape from the pressures and expectations of adulthood (see Chapter 6).

Living the dream: pursuing back-to-back seasons

Rather than returning to university or to find 'a real job' after their 'Big OE', some of the more fervent action sport participants follow their preferred season between hemispheres, thus becoming what Maguire (1996) termed 'nomadic cosmopolitans' (p. 339), or what I have previously referred to as 'seasonal lifestyle sport migrants' (Thorpe, 2012b). Duncan (2012), however, makes an important distinction that further clarifies the differences between those action sport enthusiasts who spend one or two seasons overseas and those who pursue a career working between the hemispheres. She explains, 'whereas migration can be seen to involve a point of arrival and a point of departure, transnationalism allows for the ongoing movement between two or more places' (Duncan, 2012, p. 116). The remainder of this chapter focuses on the *transnational* practices and experiences of action sport workers (see also Chapter 6).

To facilitate (and prolong) their transnational lifestyles, many action sport migrants pursue further training and education to obtain skilled employ-ment in their action sport industry (as, for example, instructor, coach, journalist, photographer, judge). Chris Stevens is an example of an action sport enthusiast who commenced his travels with 'a gap year to Oz' after which he returned to the UK to save money and complete his surf coaching qualification. Eager to continue travelling, he promptly 'started job hunt-ing' and 'landed a job surf coaching in Ecuador', which has enabled him to 'bounce a few [more] seasons surf coaching' (cited in Levitz, 2013, para. 4). In so doing, action sport participants such as Chris lead a 'peripatetic lifestyle', shifting between two or more countries for the duration of the winter or summer season. It has been suggested that this form of mobility might be more accurately described as 'circulation' as opposed to migration (Williams & Hall, 2000).

It is important to reiterate that, despite the highly skilled nature of many of these jobs, the majority are not high-paying; they tend to be held by passionate action sport participants committed to the lifestyle rather than the economic rewards. Polish kite-surfer Zuza describes her lifestyle as an instructor in Egypt on her blog: 'My instructor life here has been . . . the usual routine – work, ride, eat, sleep, check the tides, forget what day it is. It's just so easy to sink into the life here' (Czaplinska, 2013). Chris, the

British surf instructor working in Ecuador mentioned above, also describes his lifestyle as 'epic':

> surf in the morning, coaching the afternoon, surf in the evening and then party hard all night! It keeps me in shape, keeps the tan topped up, and it has pimped [enhanced] my sex life something crazy. (cited in Turner, 2012, para. 7)

Continuing, he reveals the economic sacrifices he is willing to make for this lifestyle:

> When it comes to the money, I won't lie . . . you're not doing it to make big bucks. In the UK, you may make £30–40 per day, depending on where you work, but it's also very seasonal. When it comes to working abroad, most places tend to offer you free accommodation and meals alongside a small wage. For example, in Ecuador it was $100 a month – which was enough to live on there. I do it to live abroad and surf heaps and enjoy life rather than slave away in an office. I'd happily take little pay over a shit job! (cited in Turner, 2012, para. 5)

David, a Chinese kite-surf instructor who worked for 12 years on the stock market before giving it all up to travel, learn to kite-surf, and eventually start his own kite-surf instructing business on a beach in Xiamen (China), also waxes lyrical about the lifestyle: 'I think you can feel real happiness in kiting. You can travel to different beaches, different countries, different waves. I think it's the best life . . . sunshine, the beach, just waiting for the wind, and when it comes, you kitesurf' (cited in Groom, 2010, para. 11). Yet David also reveals the economic difficulties associated with his chosen lifestyle: 'it cost me a lot to start the business and run it for the first year . . . next year I hope will be better' (cited in Groom, 2010, para. 13).

While many seasonal action sport migrants are from privileged backgrounds, it would be remiss to ignore the considerable social, financial and emotional investments they make in pursuit of the transnational lifestyle. As *New Zealand Snowboarder* magazine editor, Dylan Butt (2006) explains:

> The effort that goes into organizing an overseas mission is pretty huge. The long hours of work to save enough money . . . The calls, emails and random hook-ups through friends of friends . . . Dragging bags off planes onto trains and buses, through cities, small towns and villages . . . (p. 16)

For many transnational action sport migrants, the next season overseas requires careful saving and extensive social networking and organizational skills. As Pamela, a competitive skier and snowboarder during the 1990s, explains:

> If you really enjoy something and work really hard at it, you will find a way to financially survive . . . I've learnt heaps of really good skills about saving and living cheaply. I've learnt lots of things from different snowboarders and skiers over the years, because there is quite a creative, 'scamming element', about how to get by in [expensive ski towns]. Living in Whistler, Paul and Tony [early New Zealand snowboarding migrants] would live in a van, and Tony would wake up with a frozen beard, and all their peanut butter would be frozen. They'd collect aluminium cans and cash them in to get a Subway for dinner. (pc, September 2005)

As Pamela suggests, many contemporary action sport migrants develop highly creative and entrepreneurial skills and strategies to support their lifestyles.

While conducting research in Zermatt (the Swiss town located at the base of the Matterhorn), I spoke with two young Swiss women, Nadja and Johanna, about their passion for travel, surfing, skiing and snowboarding, and their entrepreneurial efforts to support their lifestyle via the establishment of their fledgling enterprise, NAJO, a home-made beanie company. They described meeting over five years ago in Engelberg, an infamous Swiss free-riding resort, where they had both recently migrated for the winter. Here they explored the mountains together during the day, worked at the local bar in the evenings, and crocheted beanies in their spare time; these they would later gift or sell to friends and other local residents. With the support and encouragement of a male colleague, they designed a company logo, developed an interactive website from which purchases could be made, and began distributing their product to select stores in neighbouring mountain towns. To facilitate the mobility and visibility of their product, and support their hyper-mobile lifestyle, they brought an old Mercedes-Benz bus, which they renovated and branded with their company logo. During our conversation, they raved about their transnational lifestyle, which consists of spending their winters skiing, snowboarding and making beanies, and their summers travelling across Europe surfing, climbing, and selling their headwear. In their own words:

> Nadja: We spent a couple of winters just making custom beanies for our friends. Then a guy we worked with at the bar encouraged us to think about doing something with this. So we brought a bus and developed a logo and started selling them on our road trips around Europe. Since then we have knitted our beanies in the Philippines, Thailand, Spain, France, Sweden, Norway, China, and Central America . . . We love our lives. We really love it, just travelling and following the lifestyle, and we don't see our summer road-trips to the coast of Europe and winters in the Alps coming to an end anytime soon.

Johanna: Everyone always asks me, when are you going to get a 'real job'? But I just love my life right now. I read a lot and try to keep track of what's happening in the world. I like learning and knowing, and might go to university one day. But I would miss the skiing, surfing and partying. I guess the 'real job' can come later. Right now, though, I am having so much fun. (pc, December 2007)

For many action sport migrants, the pursuit of the transnational lifestyle can encourage the development of highly creative, entrepreneurial, financial and organizational skills, which in some cases transfer into social fields beyond their sporting cultures (see Chapter 6).

The ebbs and flows of action sport migration

While youth on action sport-related gap years and OEs, and committed action sport migrants, are travelling within and across many Western – and some Eastern (such as China, Japan, Taiwan, and South Korea) – countries, the transnational flows of youth cultural participants are stronger in some directions than others. For example, popular flows among seasonal snow-sport migrants include Australian, British, New Zealand and Japanese youth to Canada – particularly Alberta (Banff) and British Columbia (Whistler) – and the United States – particularly California (Mammoth), Colorado (Breckenridge) and Utah (Salt Lake City); American, Australian, British, Canadian, European and Japanese skiers and snowboarders to New Zealand (Queenstown, Wanaka); and British youth to France (Chamonix). Those working in the action sport industry, or in businesses associated with travelling youth, observe changes in the flows as a result of economic factors in the countries of travellers and visa availability (see Chapter 6). For example, Kim, a co-owner of an employment agency in Queenstown, New Zealand, explains:

Back in the 1990s, when I used to work up the mountain, it was only Kiwis and Australians, and then they [the New Zealand government] released a whole bunch of English work visas and we had a lot of English travellers here for years later. But over the last seven years, we have seen a massive influx of Brazilians, Argentinians, and a lot of French people this year. Most of them have degrees and are generally in their 20s. (pc, 2011)

A long-time ski instructor migrant and resort manager, Rose, also observes changes in the flows of ski and snowboarding migrants to a popular ski town in the south island of New Zealand:

. . . about 8 to 10 years ago, there was a massive amount of Japanese people here, and a lot of young Japanese here for the whole season and it would be like they would just go absolutely crazy. All of a sudden the rules of society were not in place and they would always go crazy . . . crazy hair, crazy

Figures 4.3 and 4.4 Passionate surfers, skateboarders, skiers and snowboarders, Nadja and Johanna travel through Europe selling their crocheted beanies, often living in their van and sharing their experiences with other travellers met along the way. Images used with permission of Johanna Fridheim and Nadja Güntensperger (www.NAJO.ch)

fashion. It was awesome. We don't see that as much anymore. I'm assuming it's an economic thing, or maybe something or somewhere else has come to take its place. Now, we are still seeing a lot of Australians and a lot of backpackers, a lot of Irish, a lot of British people coming through. (pc, 2011)

A snowboarding migrant of more than 13 back-to-back winters between New Zealand and Canada, the US and Japan, Gary also observed a decrease in Japanese action sport migrants, adding 'now we have lots of French here, and lots of Italians and Norwegians as well' (pc, 2011). Of course, such mobilities are affected by changing variables such as exchange rates and visa availability, yet some destinations remain popular among action sport migrants due to the opportunities for employment, accommodation and, most importantly, social interaction and sporting participation with their peers (see Chapter 5).

For most action sport enthusiasts, following the summer or winter around the globe sounds rather dreamy. But developing and sustaining a long-term transnational career in the action sport industry typically carries many challenges. Social and economic pressures and constraints are such that most action sport migrants pursue a few back-to-back summers or winters before adopting a less mobile lifestyle. The manager of the snow-sport centre at a New Zealand ski resort, which hosts a number of season-long ski and snowboard instructor-training programs, observes these trends among their graduates who are typically in their late teens and early twenties:

> the majority of them go overseas for a winter, usually on a J1 visa, and a majority of that percentage then come back to New Zealand. I would say about a quarter of them go back and do another season. From all the graduates from the polytech[nic] courses, I would say about a quarter of them go and do maybe 4–5 seasons, and then they'll move on, maybe go to university or look for a more permanent job somewhere. (Rose, pc, 2011)

Indeed, many of the action sport migrants interviewed for this project described experiencing social pressures from family and peers after a few years of their seasonal migration patterns, encouraging them to 'settle down a bit' and 'get a real job'. According to a long-time American snow-sport migrant:

> It definitely seems hard to sustain, and lots of people seem to do it just because they want to be untied from things. They enjoy this for a while, then they realise that they almost want something to be tied to, maybe a job or a relationship or a house. (Keith, pc, 2011)

For the majority of action sport migrants, the transnational career is short-lived, but for others it becomes a lifestyle and occupation they pursue for many years, and in so doing develop meaningful connections within multiple contexts and networks across countries that contribute to their transnational sense of belonging. As will be discussed in depth in Chapter 6, sustained mobilities in the action sport industry are often the result of many years of hard work, compromises, creativity and negotiation.

Moving on

In this chapter I provided a typology of the various corporeal mobilities in contemporary action sport cultures, particularly professional athletes, tourists and action sport migrants. While it was beyond the scope of the chapter to discuss all of the 'push' and 'pull' factors contributing to the decisions of participants to pursue an action sport-related working holiday, or a career as a seasonal action sport migrant, it is important to note that the opportunities and motivations for action sport enthusiasts to travel internationally in pursuit of a lifestyle and employment in the action sport industry vary considerably and are influenced by an array of personal factors (nationality, class, parental support, sex, age and so on), as well as events and contingencies in the broader social, cultural, political and economic context. The following chapter builds upon this discussion of the various corporeal mobilities in action sport culture, focusing particularly on the importance of place in the travel experiences and lived mobilities of action sport enthusiasts. Acknowledging the importance of place in global flows and networks, the following chapter examines some of complex relationships and networks of power within transnational action sport destinations.

5
Pleasure, Play and Everyday Politics in Transnational Action Sport Destinations

In recent years there has been a growing recognition that research on transnational migration and mobilities needs to encompass *both* the 'large scale movement of people, objects, capital, and information across the world', *and* 'the more local processes of daily transportation, movement through public space, and the travel of material things within everyday life' (cited in Burns & Novelli, 2008, p. xxi). According to Levitt & Glick Schiller (2004), our analytical lens must 'broaden *and* deepen' because migrants are 'often embedded in multi-layered, multi-sited transnational social fields, encompassing those who move and those who stay behind' (p. 1003; emphasis added). Put simply, calls are being made for the 'geographical "grounding" of transnational discourse' (Crang et al., 2003, p. 440; Gieryn, 2000; Jackson et al., 2004). Scholars interested in understanding transnational flows, networks and connections 'from below' (Mahler, 1998), are increasingly exploring the interactions of 'people from various backgrounds' *within* 'complex, multi-dimensional and multiply inhabited' transnational social spaces and places (Jackson et al., 2004, p. 3). Thus, acknowledging the importance of place in transnational flows and networks, this chapter 'grounds' my previous analysis of action sport corporeal mobilities within the physical geographies of transnational action sport destinations. In so doing, I reveal some of complex relationships and networks of power within local spaces and places, as well as some of the wider cultural connections in the global action sports field.

As discussed in Chapter 4, action sport enthusiasts travel regionally, nationally and internationally in pursuit of new opportunities to practise their skills, experience new terrain, and share their activity with friends, family and/or fellow travellers. Each action sport has a list of destinations that have become culturally renowned through media coverage such as films, magazines and websites, as well as the stories told by past and present travellers. While such lists change over time, some destinations remain highly desirable among action sport enthusiasts. For example, surfers around the world dream of surfing the infamously challenging North Shore (Hawaii), the exotic Mentawai Islands (Indonesia), and the heaving waves of Teahupoo (Tahiti); committed mountain bikers seek out the stunning trails in the French Alps, Whistler (Canada), Utah (USA) and Rotorua (New Zealand); skiers and snowboarders imagine carving through fresh powder in Japan and the Canadian Rockies, the challenging terrain of the French Alps, and the perfectly maintained terrain parks at various Californian resorts; climbers desire the challenging routes and spectacular scenery in destinations such as the Yosemite National Park (USA), the Matterhorn, Zermatt (Switzerland) and the Dolomites (Italy); wake-boarders are drawn to the warm weather, smooth waters, and thriving wake culture in places with natural and artificial wake-parks such as Stoney Park (New South Wales, Australia) and Florida (USA); and kite-surfers dream about the consistent winds and warm waters in La Ventana (Baja California), Nabq (Egypt), Tarifa (Spain), Cumbuco (Brazil) and Maui (Hawaii). Strongly influenced by the highly evocative media coverage of such destinations, many action sport enthusiasts create 'bucket lists' of the places they hope to visit during their sporting lives. Of course, many such journeys offer physically stimulating and socially rewarding experiences but, more importantly, the stories that an action sport traveller can tell about their adventures and the number of places they have travelled in pursuit of their sport are important statements of commitment, and thus a valuable source of status and respect – or symbolic capital – among their peer groups (see Humphreys, 2011, for similar observations among golfers). Indeed, travel stories feature strongly in action sport communities both online and in everyday conversations.

In this chapter I am particularly interested in those destinations that attract action sport enthusiasts from an array of sports and nationalities, and the interactions between individuals and groups in these unique places. Every year hundreds of thousands of (typically) young men and women make the pilgrimage to key locations where they proceed to 'play' in the mountains (for example, Whistler, Canada; Queenstown, New Zealand; Chamonix, France), or on the beaches and in the waves (for example, Byron Bay, Australia; Hawaii, USA; Kuta Beach, Bali; Raglan, New Zealand) for days, weeks, months and, sometimes, many years. These locations host a steady flow of action sport enthusiasts from around the world, such that I have termed them 'transnational physical cultural hot spots' (Thorpe, 2011b). Action sport participants of varying levels of skill and commitment (professional, migrant, tourist, novice) travel to these spaces with many different motives, goals and intentions. While many are drawn to these sites by the desire to experience new, more challenging, or culturally infamous, terrain, others are attracted by the opportunities for social interactions with like-minded youth and cultural participants. As passionate snowboarder and mountain-biker, Gary, explains:

> You go to these places where you meet people that are from all around the world that are there for the same reason. You spend the season with them, and share some really intense experiences. Some of them become your lifelong friends. As opposed to just going somewhere and having a

holiday, you're going to these places with the purpose to live as much as you can, as fully as possible. (pc, 2011)

Importantly, participants from various countries and sports cultures (such as snowboarding, skiing, mountain biking, skateboarding, climbing, surfing, kite-surfing, kayaking), and positions within these action sport cultures, interact in various natural (waves and beaches, or mountains) and social (car parks, gas stations, bus stops, cafes, bars, sport-specific shops, sports events) sites in these transnational destinations.

This chapter reveals some of the complexities of the lived experiences of transnational action sport migrants, and illustrates how migrants and residents establish notions of self and the group, and a sense of belonging, and demarcate who belongs and who is excluded in these 'transnational social fields' (Horak, 2003; Huq, 2003; Knowles, 1999; Wiles, 2008). While the focus of this chapter is on the interactions, tensions and everyday politics within transnational mountain-based action sport destinations, similar observations can be made in surf-towns around the world, including Byron Bay (Australia), North Shore (Hawaii), Puerto Escondido (Mexico) and Raglan (New Zealand).

The politics and pleasures in mountain resort destinations

With the diversity of mobilities in contemporary action sport cultures, ski resorts and mountain destinations – once the exclusive domain of upper-class skiers and climbers – are increasingly being shared by action sport participants across an array of activities from the middle *and* upper classes, and various nationalities and age groups. Not only do action sport migrants come into interaction with those from different positions within these action cultures (for example, professional athletes, seasonal migrants, tourists), they also interact with local residents. As a result, the interactions between individuals and groups in action sport destinations are becoming increasingly complex. This is particularly true for some key locations such as Chamonix (France), Queenstown (New Zealand) and Whistler (Canada), which host strong flows of action sport enthusiasts (skiers, snowboarders, climbers, mountain-bikers, kayakers, skateboarders, sky-divers, hang-gliders) from around the world, such that they are excellent exemplars of transnational action sport destinations. According to cultural commentator Rob Reed (2005), such transnational mountain towns are not only 'fantastic resort destinations', they are also snow-sports' 'great cathedrals . . . places of pilgrimage, where likeminded devotees from all over the world congregate during the holy season of winter' (p. 184).

Chamonix, France

Chamonix is a mountain community in south-eastern France situated at the base of the spectacular Mont Blanc. The highest mountain in the European Alps (4810m/15,780ft), Mont Blanc is the third most visited natural site in the world. While the infamous mountain has long held a special allure for climbers and sightseers, the massive peaks of the Aiguilles Rouges surrounding Chamonix also serve as an optimal playground for a growing number of other outdoor activities, particularly in their more extreme variants (such as ice climbing, rock climbing, extreme skiing and snowboarding, paragliding, rafting, mountain biking). The physical geography of the Chamonix backcountry offers experienced participants bountiful opportunities for physical adventure, exploring new terrain, learning new skills and developing new techniques in unchartered terrain. For those less willing (or able) to engage in such high-risk pursuits, the Chamonix valley also offers 12 separate ski areas with 49 lifts, 145 marked ski runs and access to 308 hectares of skiable terrain. Chamonix also boasts the world's biggest lift-serviced skiable vertical drop of 2807 meters (9209 ft); one of the world's longest ski runs through the Vallée Blanche at 22 km (13.7 miles); and the highest gondola in Europe, which transports passengers to an elevation of 12,605 feet and offers views spanning three countries – France, Italy and Switzerland.

During the winter months, thousands of passionate skiers and snowboarders are drawn to Chamonix by the promise of fresh snow and challenging terrain. American big-mountain snowboarder Karleen Jeffery, for example, moved to Chamonix because she 'wanted bigger mountains, steeper terrain, unlimited access to all the goods. I wanted to be able to go wherever I want' (Jeffery, 2000, para. 13). In so doing, however, she quickly recognized the need to educate herself of the risks involved in the French backcountry:

> In Europe . . . there are no rules and you watch your own back. Chamonix is a huge valley developed on three sides – all ski resorts. You can go up a lift, ride down into Switzerland and take a train back. You can go down into Italy and take a gondola over. It's just so vast and extensive, and all the resorts are no more than a five- to ten-minute drive from the centre of town . . . [but] you have to have some knowledge or else there is such danger – you're putting yourself at really high risk. It's more like a personal quest for self-preservation. (Jeffery, 2000, para. 15)

The authors of *Snowboarding the World* (2006) also warn action sport travellers of the risks inherent in skiing and snowboarding in Chamonix:

> Will I die in Chamonix? Well, it's a good question, and one to which the most obvious answer is 'maybe'. [. . .] it's a very scary place up there in the high mountains and people disappear off cliffs and crevasses all the time . . . you never know when you might need your rope, harness and belay to pull some poor random rider out of a crevasse. (Barr et al., 2006, p. 119)

The gendarmes of the Chamonix Mountain Rescue perform more than 1300 operations per year. With an annual average of 60 deaths on the slopes, the description of Chamonix as 'the death sport capital of the world' (Krakauer, 1997) clearly holds some truth.

The mythology of alpine risk and adventure has long been part of the appeal of Chamonix, and has contributed to an influx of action sport migrants over the years. When Chamonix hosted the first Winter Olympic Games in 1924, it had a resident population of 5000, most of whom were French locals. Today, Chamonix has a resident population of approximately 10,000 of more than 40 different nationalities, 15 per cent of residents are English-speaking, and another 15 per cent speak Swedish. Chamonix hosts approximately five million visitors per year, with the number of visitors fluctuating enormously during the tourist seasons, with 100,000 and 60,000 visitors per day in summer and winter, respectively.

Queenstown and Wanaka, New Zealand

Surrounded by the magnificent Southern Alps and nestled by the shores of Lake Wakatipu, Queenstown is 'New Zealand's premier four season lake and alpine resort' (Queenstown New Zealand, 2013). Two ski resorts, Coronet Peak and The Remarkables Ski Area – both owned by Southern Alpine Recreation Limited – are located within a short drive of the Queenstown township. Wanaka, located 120km (75 miles) northwest of Queenstown, hosts another three ski resorts – Cardrona Alpine Resort, Treble Cone Ski Area and Snow Park. During the winter months, the Central Otago region boasts a thriving international ski and snowboard scene with each resort hosting a number of highly esteemed snowboarding and skiing competitions and events throughout the season. A notable example is the annual Winter Games. Held in 2011, the second annual Winter Games attracted 887 athletes (and an additional 333 management personnel) from 36 countries, and almost 200 accredited media from 14 countries (Winter Games, 2011). The surrounding Alps also offer ample opportunities for heli-skiing and heli-snowboarding. For many passionate snow-sport participants from the northern hemisphere, travelling to the Southern Alps of New Zealand offers exciting opportunities to explore new terrain and pursue the dream of the 'endless winter'; professional skiers and snowboarders often travel to Queenstown, and the neighboring town of Wanaka, for competitions, photo-shoots, and to train for the upcoming competitive season in the northern hemisphere.

A particularly popular destination for highly committed freestyle snowboarders and skiers travelling to New Zealand is Snow Park – the southern hemisphere's first 'freestyle resort'. Established in 2003 by Sam Lee, a passionate young skier and entrepreneur with longstanding family connections with the local region and skiing culture, Snow Park caters specifically to young, core snowboarders and skiers. The resort offers one chairlift that provides access to an extensive array of well-maintained artificial freestyle features, including a super-pipe, a quarter-pipe, and numerous jumps and rails, and regularly hosts live DJs who deliver music over the entire terrain-park via a 5000-watt sound system. Described as 'more like a skate park than a snowboarding resort', and offering a 'video-game-like spectacle', Snow Park attracts freestyle snowboarders and skiers from around the world (Barr et al., 2006, p. 231). In the words of professional snowboarder Tim Warwood, 'this one lift freestyle hotspot is the dream of every snowboard park monkey worldwide . . . jumps, rails and the best pipe in the southern hemisphere. It's perfect!' (cited in Barr et al., 2006, p. 230). As well as host-ing numerous high-calibre international freestyle snowboarding and ski-ing events during the winter (such as the Burton NZ Open, the Billabong Slopestyle Jam and the Volcom Peanut Butter Rail Jam), the resort is also fre-quently hired for the exclusive use of snowboarding and skiing companies and filming agencies seeking to capture high-quality images and footage of their sponsored athletes performing on specifically designed obstacles. With images of professional skiers and snowboarders performing on innovative and expertly shaped jumps, half-pipes and rails gaining extensive coverage in many North American and European-produced magazines and videos, Snow Park has become a key destination for travelling freestyle skiers and snowboarders.

During the summer months in Queenstown and Wanaka, mountain biking, climbing, whitewater rafting and kayaking are popular activities among local, regional, national and international action sport enthusi-asts. Following international trends, Skyline Queenstown commenced a trial season for mountain biking by opening New Zealand's first Gondola-assisted bike lift in January 2011. The gondola offered access to 500 vertical metres (1640 feet) of mountain bike trails at the newly formed Queenstown Bike Park. A passionate snowboarder and mountain biker, Gary, recalls opening day:

> The gondola is awesome! It's definitely a positive thing that's going to attract a lot more people in the future. On opening day it was just like opening day up the hill on a powder day. Everyone's just steering their bikes going 'yeah man', it was that same feeling. (pc, 2011)

Widely embraced by the national and international mountain biking com-munity, Skyline Queenstown continues to invest in developing new terrain. Destination Queenstown chief executive Graham Budd reveals the eco-nomic motives behind such investments:

> Resort destinations around the world are striving to assume leadership as to the 'go to' destination for adventure sports, so Queenstown cannot be complacent when it comes to staying ahead of the curve. For many bikers in Queenstown, New Zealand and even Australia, we're the location of choice, so we're really pleased we can increase the number and range of

trails we offer and provide these riders with more thrills. (cited in Bryant, 2013, paras. 5 & 6)

Queenstown also offers visitors a wide array of consumable 'extreme pursuits' requiring little or no skill, such as bungee jumping, jet boating, canyon swinging and tandem skydiving, paraponting and hang-gliding; adventure tourism has thus become a 'cultural foundation' in the region, and for New Zealand more broadly (Kane, 2010, p. 27; Cloke & Perkins, 1998)

Queenstown has a permanent population of approximately 10,000, but visitors can outnumber locals by as many as three to one at the height of the winter and summer seasons. Hosting an estimated 900,000 international visitors and another 500,000 domestic visitors each year, the Queenstown economy is fuelled by tourism. High numbers of domestic and international transient workers are employed in the hospitality and tourism industries (Duncan, 2009); flows of action sport migrants from Australia, Canada and the UK to Queenstown and neighboring regions are particularly strong. International language schools in the Queenstown region also flourished during the late 1990s and early 2000s with the influx of young Japanese and Korean skiers and snowboarders seeking to simultaneously learn English and develop their skills on the snow. A wide range of outdoor- and adventure-sport instructor programs were also established during this period to offer domestic and international action sport enthusiasts the opportunity to gain a qualification while temporarily residing in Queenstown.

Whistler, British Columbia, Canada

Located less than two hours north of Vancouver, Whistler Village is home to some of the world's best skiing, snowboarding and mountain biking terrain. Two mountains, Whistler and Blackcomb, rise up a mile out of the valley (5280 feet) offering access to over 8000 acres of ski-able terrain. The average annual snowfall is 30 feet (or 9.14 metres), and with a total of 33 lifts, skiers and boarders choose from over 200 marked runs. Whistler and Blackcomb also provide freestyle skiers and snowboarders with access to five immaculately groomed terrain parks, with some jumps exceeding 100 feet, as well as three perfectly shaped half-pipes. The resorts are also infamous for their natural terrain, the preferred playground of free-ride skiers and snowboarders.

The snow-sport culture thrives in Whistler. Indeed, the Whistler/Blackcomb resorts are so popular among snowboarders that they win the *Transworld Snowboarding* 'Resort Poll' year after year because they offer 'the complete snowboarding experience on-hill and off – from the perfect corduroy cruisers; long, challenging tree runs; sheer cliffs; and quality of snow, to the epic kickers, rails, and Super-pipe, as well as the restaurants, hotels and night-life in Whistler Village' (Fast, 2005, p. 24). During the summer months, skiers and snowboarders continue to flock to the culturally renowned free-style camps, held in terrain parks and half-pipes built on the high-alpine

(7600 feet) glaciated snow on Blackcomb Mountain. The Whistler Mountain Bike Park – the world's largest and longest running lift-access Bike Park – also attracts mountain bike enthusiasts from around the world during the summer months.

But terrain is not the only thing Whistler has in large quantity and variety; 'this town likes to party'. This is particularly obvious during the 10-day annual World Ski and Snowboard Festival, self-defined as 'the biggest annual gathering of winter sports, music, arts and culture in North America' (World ski and snowboard, 2013). According to the event website, the event combines 'Canada's largest outdoor concert series with an eclectic mix of snow sport contests and anti-contests, fashion shows, film screenings, [and] photography showdowns', concluding: 'Take heed the festival motto: Party in April, sleep in May' (World ski and snowboard, 2013). The legendary big-air event, featuring many of the world's best snowboarders and skiers competing for hundreds of thousands in cash and prizes, is held in the village and draws huge, highly festive crowds. Further illustrating the international calibre of this resort destination, Whistler, with Vancouver, hosted the 2010 Winter Olympic Games, at which action sport participants – as athletes and supporters – were a particularly visible feature.

Whistler has a permanent population of approximately 10,000. During the winter season, however, visitors and seasonal populations contribute to the total daily winter population of 3.3 times this number. Whistler typically hosts more than two million national and international skier and snowboarder visits per year, and during the summer season the world-renowned Bike Park can attract more than 90,000 visits (Whistler2020, 2009). Many more visitors come to sightsee, socialize and enjoy other sporting and leisure activities such as hiking, climbing, golf and fishing. To cater for these visitors, Whistler employs young people from all over the world (with particularly strong contingents from Australia and Europe). Indeed, Whistler hosts a large, rotating transient population of young action sport migrants; recent estimates suggest that there are on average 2362 'seasonal residents' living in Whistler throughout the year. The median age of Whistler residents is 32 years (nine years younger than the provincial median age); almost 60 per cent of the population are aged between 20 and 44 years (compared to 34 per cent for the province); and 57 per cent are characterized as single (compared to 32 per cent for the province) (Whistler2020, 2009). With such a youthful, international and transient population, and ample opportunities for physical and social play, it is perhaps not surprising that Whistler is commonly described as a 'big kid's Disneyland'.

Arguably, what distinguishes these transnational mountain destinations from other nationally renowned and regional ski resorts is that each offers a unique combination of social (quality restaurants, cafes and nightlife) *and* physical geographies (snow conditions, weather and mountain terrain), as well as established infrastructure (relatively easy accessibility via international airports and regional transport, varied accommodation, user-friendly village design and so on). Importantly, these destinations also tend to be places of *privileged* play, pleasure and performance (Bærenholdt et al., 2004; Sheller & Urry, 2004). Compared to the population averages of their respective countries, the resident populations of Whistler, Chamonix and Queenstown are more highly educated, white, young and male, with higher household incomes. The majority of those travelling to, and temporarily residing in, these transnational action sport destinations also come from positions of social privilege. Of course, the global and local flows of tourists, and action sport enthusiasts, are unique to each transnational social space, facilitated (and constrained) by various factors, including weather and snow quality, availability of transport and accommodation, exchange rates, media coverage of the destination, work and travel visas, language barriers, global and national economic conditions ad so on. However, many migrants interviewed for this project saw commonalities across these places. For example, Gary proclaimed:

> Queenstown is catching up to what Whistler was about ten years ago. Just like Whistler, the whole mountain biking scene is huge in Queenstown in summer with gondola access up the Skyline. And, there are lots of drunken Aussies in both [Queenstown and Whistler]. (pc, 2011)

Indeed, many action sport migrants travel to various transnational action sport destinations and, despite many differences, feel 'at home' in these places where they are surrounded by hundreds, even thousands, of fellow action sport enthusiasts from around the world, and immersed in the constant flows of tourists and migrants.

Transnational spaces – and by implication atmospheres – are 'practiced or performed; they are continuously brought into being through a variety of processes that involve dynamic and changing constellations of people, technical artefacts, buildings, symbols, rules, etc' (Ettema & Schwanen, 2012, p. 177). Examining the mobilities of backpackers within 'global Sydney', Allon et al. (2008), explain that 'multiple interacting systems and networks of mobility are appearing, and groups as diverse as backpackers and students, migrants and cosmopolitan professionals are more likely than ever to merge and intersect in various ways, shaping, changing and impacting on "local communities"' (p. 73). As Duncan et al. (2013) observe, 'it is not just individuals who develop through transnational opportunities but the relations within and between wider social networks also become more mobile, complex and fluid through transnational practices and experiences' (p. 8). Indeed, the flows of action sport migrants and tourists through transnational action sport destinations and their interactions with locals and one another in an array of spaces have certainly contributed to the 'remaking of place' (Chang, 2012). Those who have lived in these places for many years have observed radical changes as a result of such action sport mobilities:

> These days Queenstown is becoming so well known, it's become a really popular place to come and do a winter season, so that has changed. New Zealand is giving out so many more work visas, so that it is easier for internationals to come here and work for a winter. Since I've been here, the town has probably quadrupled in size. There wasn't even a supermarket when I first got here and there were just two bars. Now we have five supermarkets and ten bars on every street. New suburbs just keep popping up. It's not even remotely the same place that I first came to back in 1994, but then I don't know if I'd still be here if it was. (pc, Kim, Australian citizen living in Queenstown for two decades, 2011)

> Since first coming to Chamonix in 1962, yes, I've seen massive change. Look around you, the whole place is booming isn't it? During the winter, the Brits are our number one visitor, with the Dutch and the Belgians number two. There's now a lot of Russians coming, which is good news for the [ski and snowboard] shop. They have lots of money and they like to spend it. There are a lot of Australians, then New Zealanders, Americans, and South Africans, in that order . . . colonialists let's call them. So the local economy is not what it was 30 years ago. Thirty years ago you had cows and local peasants so to speak, and now . . . we have skiers, snowboarders, climbers and tourists. (pc, Martin, British citizen living in Chamonix for almost four decades, 2010)

When asked if he viewed these changes in a positive light, Martin responded: 'Well, that's a very difficult question to answer. It's good for my business, but is it good when you make a concrete jungle out of a lovely alpine valley?' (pc, 2010). Indeed, a body of literature has explored the environmental impact of such tourist mobilities (Clifford, 2002; Holden & Fennell, 2013; Pickering & Barros, 2013). A particularly notable example is Mark Stoddart's (2012) *Making Meaning of Mountains* in which he carefully examines the political ecology of the skiing industry in British Columbia, Canada. Despite an increasing environmental awareness among ski resorts over the past decades, similar observations can still be made in many transnational mountain resort destinations such as Whistler, Queenstown and Chamonix.

While some local and permanent residents are critical of the social and environmental impact of the influx of travelling youth, many business owners have embraced the financial opportunities that such mobilities offer. Some also celebrate the vibrancy that action sport migrants bring to the towns. For example, a business owner in Queenstown proclaims: 'I think the backpacker culture is a real positive. I think it adds a real buzz and a vibe to the town [Queenstown]. I don't think this town would be anything without it in my opinion. Definitely. I feel like that *is* the town', before offering the following example:

> In the summer it's awesome actually, the travellers from all around the world have added some colour to the area. Like along that so-called beach area, they have made it actually like a beach. In the summer now they're all there in their bikinis, DJs going, drinking and lots of cool buskers. It's awesome. (pc, Kane, 2011)

Action sport destinations such as Queenstown, Chamonix and Whistler have become hubs of 'innumerable cultural flows' (Osgerby, 2004, p. 167). The increasing movement of action sport migrants between countries, and particularly their migration to particular destinations, is contributing to the introduction of 'new cultural forms and identities into the fabric of local environments' (Osgerby, 2004, p. 167).

Importantly, Whistler, Chamonix and Queenstown have not always been transnational action sport destinations. This is a relatively new development that has emerged alongside changes in international and youth travel (see Chapter 4). While the meanings of these places have always been contested, new groups of action sport tourists and migrants are defining and marking out the localities in terms of their own cultures and collective identities, and thus contributing to the remaking of place. In so doing, migrant and tourist interactions with each other and local residents in an array of local spaces are also contributing to the production of new meanings of place, often over-writing local histories and marginalizing long-time local residents. Yet, as will be illustrated below, not all local residents passively accept the changing social dynamics, and some actively resist the flows of transnational action sport migrants and their attempts to define and mark out the locality.

The multiple mobilities within these transnational mountain destinations raise some common questions: Whose place is this? Who has access to social and physical resources? Who has the power to define place? How do different individuals and groups negotiate space in these fields? How do individuals elaborate or conceal some markers (such as nationality, gender, race, class) within these spaces in attempts to preserve or create status within the local transnational community? Tensions regularly develop between individuals and groups as they struggle for territory and eminence. In the remainder of this chapter I explore some of these symbolic and physical struggles to negotiate space and define place in these 'porous places'. First, however, I explain the enculturation of migrants into the complex networks of power operating within transnational action sport destinations.

Enculturation into transnational hot spots

Many action sport migrants move to transnational action sport destinations with a romantic vision of days spent surfing, kite-surfing, snowboarding, skiing, mountain biking and/or climbing, and nights partying with like-minded peers from around the world. The action sport media (magazines, films, websites) and images and stories shared by travelling action sport migrants via an array of social media (Facebook, personal blogs, Instragram) contribute to the production and distribution of such fantasies. As Urry (2002) explains in *The Tourist Gaze*, the media is integral in creating the anticipation of 'intense pleasures' from tourism and travel experiences (p. 3). Such images and narratives not only influence the flows and anticipations of action sport migrants, but also their interpretations upon arrival, and indeed, their own narrative recordings and dissemination. This is what Urry (1990a, 1990b) has termed the 'hermeneutic circle' in which media influences the motives and expectations of tourists, as well as their experiences upon arrival, and then ultimately their own media production which then feeds back into the circle by recreating common images from tourism media of this destination and being shared among social networks.

Most media and narratives of transnational action sport destinations focus on the remarkable features of the natural environment and its suitability for action sport participation, with some comments about the quality of the nightlife. In contrast to many other forms of tourism media, however, most action sport media and stories from travellers themselves do not gloss over the practicalities and difficulties of living in these unique action sport destinations. Often an integral feature of stories of action sport migration is the low-budget style of living, such that most migrants anticipate the need to be flexible in accommodation and work arrangements, often accepting situations outside their usual living conditions as just 'part of' the overall experience. Indeed, the sacrifices made for this lifestyle make for even better storytelling and as further evidence of migrants' commitment to their action sport. Drawing upon their own lived experiences and observations, the authors of *Snowboarding the World* discuss some of the logistical considerations for those seeking 'careers' as snow-sport migrants:

> Jobs in resorts tend to be incredibly low paid – more often than not, way below national pay barriers. They can often be hard to find, and most likely will have no safety net should you fall ill or become unavailable to work. [. . .] many people have a great time working in resorts . . . But working in a resort throws up several problems, not least of which is: what if your job keeps you off the mountain during the day? Because of this, many riders find it more appropriate to save up during the summer and then live throughout the winter on a strict budget, thus earning the dubious accolade of 'bums'. (Barr et al., 2006, p. 78)

Continuing, Barr et al. offer snow-sport migrants the following sage advice for sourcing affordable accommodation in high-rent destination ski-towns: 'fin[d] an apartment or chalet (the Internet can help, but nothing beats visiting your chosen resort in late summer to check the local agencies and supermarket corkboards), then fill it with double the amount of people it was intended for and hav[e] the time of your lives' (2006, p. 78). Recalling the difficulties of finding (and affording) accommodation during his first season in Queenstown, Thomas explained:

> I was sleeping in my snowboard bag beside a guy's bed. I barely knew the guy but for $40 a week I could sleep there. [. . . I think I lasted about six days and then a friend helped me out. It was in a basement and it was known as 'the dungeon' but it was paradise compared to where I was. It didn't bother me that it was cold; I just slept in a beanie. On a different occasion I remember not having a bed. Instead I had a deck chair. Actually, when I think about it, that season I was one hell of a moocher . . . bounding from couch to couch, thumbing rides, squeezing every penny. (pc, 2008)

Kim, a co-owner of an employment agency in Queenstown, describes housing as 'a major problem' for the hundreds of action sport migrants who in the first few weeks of the winter are desperate to find affordable accommodation; there are 'massive line-ups for the weekly paper, people sleeping in their cars. Stories of people sleeping in ice caves. It can be an absolute nightmare' (pc, Kim, 2011).

Action sport migrants on their first (and perhaps only) season in an action sport destination are often surprised to find themselves competing with hundreds of fellow migrants for limited employment opportunities. As Kim explains, some young migrants are unable to find suitable employment and either have to shift their expectations or consider alternative destinations:

> Over the winter, it's always really busy with people coming and they want to stay for the whole ski season. They'll start coming at the end of April, but there won't really be any jobs going until the beginning of July, so that's a really tough time. A couple of months ago we had over 100 people coming here in just one day. There are not enough jobs for all of them. A lot of them end up leaving.

> The other problem is that they all want the same thing. They all want to work in the evenings so they can ski or snowboard in the day, but that's obviously a problem because there's a lot more of them than there are jobs.

Although many of the action sport migrants coming through Kim's agency have undergraduate degrees, most end up working 'casual jobs . . . mainly in hospitality . . . kitchen-handing, waitressing, cooking, cleaning and then we'll get some labouring and office admin as well' (pc, 2011). Continuing,

Figure 5.1 A noticeboard in Queenstown advertises accommodation, equipment, vehicles and employment opportunities

Figure 5.2 The latest job postings at an employment agency in Queenstown

she acknowledges that some action sport migrants have more difficulties than others:

> We now have a lot of Argentineans and Brazilians coming for the winter season . . . But if their English is lacking, then it's not really an option for

us to send them into a temp situation where the client needs someone to be switched on right from the beginning. (pc, Kim, 2011)

As an employer of many action sport migrants, Kim has come to understand, and even anticipate, their typically short-term approach to employment while abroad:

> A lot of the backpackers here for winter, they're not really concerned about the long term. They're just here for a few months and don't mind working crappy jobs with little pay. They just need enough money to go out. A massive problem for us, though, is people not turning up to work because they've been out the night before. That's a nightmare, a really big problem in this town.
>
> We have pretty much a zero tolerance policy. If someone doesn't show up to a job that they said they were going to do, well that's it. They'll never hear from us again, but a lot of them don't care if they never hear from us again, they don't feel like they owe you anything, there's no sense of loyalty.
>
> I think a person might not be like that in their hometown and they come across that way in the interview, but while they're away, they do things that aren't generally in their personality to do. They don't feel like there are any real consequences for them here. But it's all part of how it is, and most local businesses understand that. (pc, 2011)

While many action sport migrants prioritize fun over responsibility, and don't take their employment seriously (see also Boon, 2006), it is important to keep in mind that local businesses are also hiring and firing employees based on their seasonal needs. However, such a transient population, the workplace in transnational action sport destinations is constantly in flux, such that finding and keeping a select few long-term employees becomes invaluable to business owners. Some businesses understand the motives of action sport migrants better than others and adopt various strategies to encourage greater staff retention. For example, the owner of a highly popular snowboard, ski and mountain bike shop in Chamonix takes into consideration the employees' sporting commitments: 'Everyone wants to get a job here. Once they get a job here, seldom do they leave. We close for three hours at lunchtime everyday so they can go and do sport, winter and summer. It's the best place to work in town'; continuing, he adds, 'It's relaxed, I don't get too upset when they go on Facebook during the day', and with sarcasm in his voice, 'I only lose my temper once a week, so it's pretty good' (pc, Martin, 2010)

Action sport migrants arriving in a transnational action sport destination for their first season will typically be at the bottom of the 'pecking order' in terms of available accommodation and employment, and perhaps access to other limited resources, such as the best quality waves and/or powder runs. Similar hierarchies are practised and reinforced in the international workplace of the ski resort. Stuart, a ski instructor who has spent many years working for the same resorts in New Zealand and California, is very aware of the hierarchical system that gives preference to 'experience, qualifications, time working for a particular resort', which then influence the amount and quality of the work allocated to each employee (pc, 2011). But, due to the transient nature of most action sport destinations and businesses, opportunities for employment and accommodation typically expand with each consecutive season. Those migrants who stay for the off season, or return for subsequent seasons, gain cultural and social capital within the local community and thus access to the more desirable, and highly sought-after, forms of accommodation (that is, affordable, close to facilities) and employment (more flexible work hours, higher wages).

Whereas many action sport migrants stay for one winter (or summer), others return for multiple seasons. A few settle in transnational action sport destinations, establishing their own businesses or taking up management positions, with some entering long-term relationships with a resident or fellow traveller. Observing the multiple 'layers' within action sport destinations such as Queenstown, Cesar explains:

> There's definitely a lot of young people who are just here for a season and adopt the attitude of 'I'm going to party it out, and I'll do a little bit of work to cover my costs'. Then there's the next tier that have been coming for a few years, they're still having a good time, but they have at least some real relationships with people across the community. Then you've got the final tier, which is the real local crowd with families, houses and maybe a business. (pc, 2011)

Others observe the increasing transnationalism of such destinations, as more action sport migrants become permanent residents. For example, Martin has observed changes in the local school in Chamonix:

> A lot of Brits [British people] have settled here, and there are a fair number of Scandies [Scandinavian people] that have settled too. It's got to the point where 50 per cent of the children at the local school have parents of mixed nationalities. Lots of trilingual kids at school – they speak Swedish, English, just because one of their parents is English, and of course, they speak French, so it's become a big melting pot. (pc, 2010)

Indeed, with the steady flow of action sport tourists, travellers and migrants, destinations such as Chamonix, Queenstown and Whistler have become 'complex, multi-dimensional and multiply inhabited' (Jackson et al., 2004, p. 3) transnational spaces.

The transition from '*seasonnaire*' to resident, however, raises lots of cultural, financial and legal issues that 'one-season wonders' do not encounter in the same way. For example, Martin first came to Chamonix in 1963 as a 16-year-old, and then returned in his mid-twenties after a short career in Britain: 'I came here for my first season as a ski bum and I stayed. I was teaching skiing back then, but when snowboarding came along, that all changed.' When asked why he chose Chamonix, he proclaimed, 'well it's "the" place. I'm a British national, so it had to be in the European Union, and this place has a big social scene, it's very international and it has a reputation of being so extreme'. Martin has been selling snowboards for over 20 years in Chamonix and in so doing, was careful to adopt a culturally sensitive approach, particularly during a time when many British people where buying property and migrating to Chamonix, thus causing concern among French residents:

> I heard before I even came here that if you tried to open a shop they would break your knees. [But] I'm European and so I have the right to be here. I run a French company, pay French taxes and, of the ten people who work here, eight are French, so I'm providing employment for locals. In the 20 years in this business, I've always tried to make sure I have locals working here. I speak the language, abide by the customs, so there's no reason for anyone to reject us. We are known as *chez les anglais*, as the English people, but this shop is as French as anywhere in town. (pc, 2010)

After many years of international snow-sport migration, Belinda has settled in Wanaka, but recognizes the difficulties of making such destinations one's 'home':

> I love living here, it's just so beautiful, we're so lucky. The only thing is . . . if I wasn't in the ski industry, I don't know how people survive. I think it's really hard to survive in this town without money first. It's expensive. The supermarket is really expensive. And the rent . . . it costs so much to live here. There aren't many jobs, so I think lots of people struggle along on quite low salaries and high expenses. Actually, you see lots of families leaving town because of that. Pete and I have two kids and we both work two jobs each to survive. (pc, 2011)

Kim first travelled to Queenstown from Australia with two girlfriends in 1994. Almost two decades later, she is still there. During our interview, she described the various difficulties she experienced as an action sport migrant and, more recently, as a mother and businesswoman living in this transnational place:

> I remember we struggled to get work over May. We got to the point where we were like, 'oh, we're just going to write this off as a good holiday', and in that week all three of us got jobs. Both of my girlfriends ended up going back to Aussie. One went back after the first winter, and the other one and I, we both really loved it. She stayed on for another year, and

then eventually went back. I met somebody after I'd only been here for 3–4 months, and now we're married with kids. Most of my girlfriends now are here in similar situations. Because my partner had a business here, it just made sense to stay rather than drag him back to Australia. But it's so expensive to live here. I think people come here knowing that the wages are going to be low, but whether they can put up with that long term is another thing. (pc, Kim, 2011)

As these examples illustrate, as highly privileged spaces, it is very difficult to create a sustainable lifestyle in a transnational action sport destination unless one comes from considerable wealth or adopts an entrepreneurial approach and is willing to work various jobs. In essence, the exorbitant cost of living encourages a fluid population.

For those few who are able to permanently migrate and develop a sustainable lifestyle in a transnational action sport destination, it is likely that their position in the field changes over time, and they find new pleasures in alternative activities from those that initially drew them to this place. For example, as a mother and business owner, Kim now struggles to find time to get onto the slopes, but she knows this will change as her children get a little older and she can share the mountain experience with them. For Kim, Queenstown is no longer a place to 'ski hard and party harder', but rather a family-friendly environment:

You have that constant coming and going, and your friends are constantly leaving. This was hard for the first few years. But since having kids, that has all changed quite a lot, and Queenstown takes on a new appeal. It's really outdoorsy, and most of the kids your kids play with, you probably know their parents because you have either worked with them, or seen them on the mountain, or something like that. (pc, Kim, 2011)

Martin has also experienced changes that have kept him off the slopes and influenced his enjoyment of living in Chamonix:

This is the first time in 50 years that I haven't been up the mountain, and I'm not going up. They're going to give me a new essential part you need for snowboarding, called a new hip, in the spring. So, after that, I'll be bionic again, so hopefully I'll be back up there next winter. I tried going up a few times last year, but it was not a lot of fun. I don't enjoy it very much this winter in the sense of getting my time on the snow, but then there's lots of work going on, business is booming, so that's keeping me busy. (pc, Martin, 2010).

As Kim and Martin illustrate, the experiences of action sport migrants change over time, and their motivations for living in action sport destinations become more about the people, the physical geography and/ or the economic opportunities, rather than the high-risk sports and hedonistic lifestyles they enjoyed in their younger years. Importantly, however, Kim and Martin both recall fondly their transition into Queenstown and Chamonix, respectively, and thus understand the lifestyles of the many youth flowing into and through the towns they now call 'home'.

Transnational action sport destinations as liminal spaces[1]

Tourist scholarship has increasingly examined the sensory encounters experienced by travellers. As Gibson (2012) explains, 'tourism is visceral, and frequently relies on hedonism: sun-baking, dancing, drinking, taking drugs, pursuing sexual encounters' (p. 58). This is certainly the case in action sport tourism. In this chapter I build upon scholarship on the sensual encounters of tourism (Gibson, 2012; Pritchard et al., 2007; Ryan, 2002), and experts on space and sexuality (for example, Waitt et al., 2008) to examine transnational action sport destinations as 'liminal spaces', offering tourists, migrants, and even locals, 'brief moments of freedom and an escape from the daily grind of social responsibilities' (Preston-Whyte, 2004, p. 350). In a similar way that the beach has been described as a liminal place 'in between, neither land nor sea, where the normal social conventions need not apply', and the seaside resort has been identified as a 'ludic and unconventional site' shaped by 'discourses of hedonism, anonymity and adventure' (Jaimangal-Jones et al., 2009, p. 263; Pritchard & Morgan, 2010), action sport destinations also have their own rule systems and the après sport culture offers many migrants and tourists a liminal space outside of the norms of everyday life and seemingly beyond 'real' consequences. Some local residents are also able to share in these liminal experiences via their interactions with travellers.

As well as demonstrating physical prowess, commitment and courage on the mountain or in the waves, committed male, and increasingly female, action sport participants are also often expected to 'rage equally hard at bars and parties' (Richards, 2003, p. 98). Transnational action sport destinations offer a plethora of opportunities for hedonistic social experiences in various cafes, bars, nightclubs, as well as other social spaces (such as action sport-related events, competitions, shared houses, hotels, youth hostels or backpackers' accommodation). A professional Canadian snowboarder is candid in his observations of the action sport lifestyle:

> Snowboarders party, that's a fact. When you think about it, it's composed of a counter culture of alternative people who tend to resist social norms. At certain snowboarding events and contests, all these people are grouped together and the wheels fall off. [. . .] Sometimes things get broken, sometimes you forget to sleep, and sometimes you're forced to sleep in jail. (pc, Eric, 2008)

Similarly, an English professional snowboarder has witnessed the tendency for many snow-sport tourists to embrace the sense of freedom, escapism and temporality in liminal 'places like Whistler':

> For many people, [snow sports are] associated with letting your hair down, going away to the mountains, to a foreign country, and trying something new. [Skiers and] boarders often get drunk and naked and then climb trees in places like Whistler. I've seen people running around naked, trying to see how many hot tubs they can get into without getting busted. (Jenny Jones, British Olympic snowboarder, cited in Thompson, 2006, para. 25)

The après action sport culture is central to the action sport lifestyle of many young core participants; it is also an integral part of a surf trip or a winter ski holiday experience for many less committed participants (such as tourists or weekend warriors). For example, a recent study of UK snow-sport tourists revealed that '45 per cent planned to drink every night' during their winter sport holiday (Bradley, 2010). Similarly, an Australian study found 56 per cent of the 1084 young adult snowfield resort visitors surveyed had consumed 11 or more standard alcoholic drinks on the previous night; 65 per cent reported having less than four hours' sleep; and 77 per cent had used psycho-stimulants in the previous 24 hours (Sherker et al., 2006). While the après action sport culture in transnational action sport destinations offers participants many opportunities for hedonistic social interactions and experiences, it also carries risks (criminal charges, serious injury, even death), which can have serious consequences for action sport tourists, migrants and professional athletes alike.

The boundaries between spaces of action sport participation (slopes, trails, waves) and the hedonistic lifestyle are often blurred, with some action sport participants drinking alcohol or consuming recreational drugs before or during their sporting participation. This is particularly the case for snow-sport tourists. A recent poll conducted by the 'More Than' travel insurance company found that British winter sports enthusiasts have on average seven units of alcohol in their blood when they arrive on the slopes in the morning (this is the equivalent of being almost twice over the legal drink-drive limit in the UK) (Bradley, 2010). Commenting on this trend, an online snowboarding journalist writes: 'Whether it's whiskey from a hip flask, smoking green in the gondola, or snorting lines of white powder, snowboarders and skiers have been known to dabble whilst on the slopes' (Baldwin, 2006, para. 1). For one male Canadian snowboard instructor: 'Smoking a bowl [of marijuana] before riding puts me in the zone and I like the sensation of cruising when I'm stoned. I feel more confident, spin smoother and it just feels good' (cited in Baldwin, 2006, para. 9). Others, however, recognize that skiing or snowboarding under the influence of marijuana compromises both safety and the overall psycho-physical experi-ence: 'I've tried snowboarding after smoking weed, but I prefer to ride with a clear head. I like to be totally aware of my surroundings and weed makes me feel blinkered. The last time I smoked a joint on a chair lift I ended up sitting in the snow outside a lodge and falling asleep' (Core Australian male snowboarder, cited in Baldwin, 2006, para. 13). Numerous studies show a direct correlation between alcohol and recreational drug consumption and skiing and snowboarding injuries. In 2008, more than 30 Britons died in alpine accidents, half of whom were under 25 – many died because they underestimated the risk of drinking at high altitude (Reuters, 2009). For many tourists, there is an implicit assumption that there can be no serious consequences in the liminal spaces of transnational action sport destina-tions. Unfortunately, this is far from true, with tourist injuries, and even arrests, common in such destinations.

As discussed in Chapter 4, action sport enthusiasts have been travelling to remote and exotic locations in pursuit of uncrowded surf and/or slopes, and good quality environmental conditions, for many decades. Drinking, drug-taking and partying have often been integral to such travel experiences. However, the influx of young action sport travellers and migrants to action sport destinations has increased the visibility of such practices. Indeed, the excessive alcohol and drug consumption of snowboarders and skiers is increasingly garnering the attention of local councils, national agencies, ski resort organizations and the mass media, as well as insurance compa-nies. For example, a study by the UK Foreign Office estimated that at least one third of skiers and snowboarders under the age of 25 had 'experienced problems abroad linked to a mixture of altitude, adrenaline, and alcohol' (Bradley, 2010, para. 10). In response to such studies, and an increasing number of accidents (both on and off the mountain) involving skiers and snowboarders under the 'strong influence of alcohol', the Foreign Office launched an information campaign during the 2009–2010 winter seasons in an array of snow-resort destinations in France, Italy and Switzerland. According to Sir Peter Westmacott, Britain's Ambassador to France, the cam-paign was a coordinated attempt by local and UK authorities to discourage the 'let's get pissed on the piste' attitude (cited in Davies, 2009, para. 8). With posters displayed in airports and hotels, the aim of the campaign was to educate 'young British nationals who perhaps are not fully aware of the effects of low temperatures and how the body reacts to alcohol at altitude' (Bradley, 2010, para. 5). The message on the posters is clear: 'Alcohol can affect you more quickly at high altitude and limit your awareness of danger and cold. Your reactions are slower, reckless behaviour can lead to crime. Alcohol abuse can simply ruin your holiday'. Similar campaigns are being launched internationally.

The intoxicated, boisterous and disorderly practices of (particularly young) snow-sport tourists and migrants on the mountain and in ski resort destinations have also caused some concern among local authorities and residents. For example, a long-time Whistler local proclaims:

> I've worked in Whistler long enough to know that people who live in Whistler eventually move to Squamish, Brackendale, Blacktusk, Pemberton, etc. The problem with actually living in Whistler is the tourists in your backyard everyday. It's not as expensive as everyone thinks, as you get local discounts off most stuff. It's just the constant party, drunk tourists that eventually weigh on you. Living in Squamish and surrounding areas gives you all the benefits of outdoor living without the drunken hooliganism. (SnoDragon, 2011, para. 3)

Similarly, Queenstown police, judges and the local Mayor are reported to have 'had a "gutsful" of overseas tourists behaving badly in Queenstown' (Queenstown's growing problem, 2010, para. 1). For example, following separate trials with two French action sport tourists for alcohol related crimes including theft and urinating in public places, the Queenstown judge proclaimed: 'You are the type of tourist or overseas workers we do not need. You blame the alcohol for your dishonesty instead of yourself. In reality, if I could, I would be directing my comments to immigration to have you removed from New Zealand' (cited in Crosbie, 2012, para. 6). In a subsequent newspaper report, a number of local residents supported the judge's arguments, with the owners of a local backpacker hostel and McDonald's franchise claiming that local alcohol-related crime and disorder had become a serious problem in the town with the current legal diversion process offering few real consequences for international tourists and migrants committing such offenses (Taylor, 2012).

Importantly, alcohol-fuelled festivities are not a new phenomenon in ski resort destinations; skiers have long enjoyed engaging in hedonistic and socially deviant practices on and off the slopes. But, as snow-sport destinations have become more 'complex, multi-dimensional and multiply inhabited' fields (Jackson et al., 2004, p. 3) where skiers and snowboarders from various classes, nationalities and age-groups share the same social spaces (car parks, slopes, cafes and restaurants, bars and nightclubs), they have increasingly become sites of tension in which individuals and groups struggle for territory and eminence. As Bourdieu (1984) has explained, it is typically those who possess large amounts of economic or cultural capital (or both) who occupy 'dominant' positions in a particular social field and will seek to impose a hierarchy of taste on those with less capital. In some ski resort destinations, local (and national) authorities are seeking to control and regulate the tastes of young middle-class snow-sport tourists, and particularly where, when and how young snowboarders and skiers participate in the après snow scene. While some groups certainly have more space to define and redefine cultural meanings pertaining to legitimate (and legal) taste practices within the après snow culture, the rules structuring mountain resort destinations are not fixed but inherently contested by those within local fields (Thorpe, 2012b).

Hyper-heterosexuality is widely celebrated and enforced within many action sport cultures (see Evers, 2010; Laurendeau, 2004; Thorpe, 2012b; Wheaton, 2003a). Bars and nightclubs in transnational action sport destinations are often highly sensuous and hypersexual spaces where action sport tourists, migrants and residents seek short-term social and physical pleasure. The constant flow of tourists and action sport migrants through these spaces further contributes to the sense of anonymity, temporality, and thus liminality. A core New Zealand male snowboarder describes particular bars and nightclubs as 'meat-markets' where locals and tourists go to 'get some loving' (pc, 2008). For a Canadian male snowboarder, 'casual sex and snowboarding go together like tea and crumpets . . . Whistler is nick-named "Club Bed" and Banff is the "STD capital of Canada"'. Continuing, he acknowledges the risks inherent in such interactions: 'I lived up in Whistler for a few seasons and did a season in Banff. [. . .] Most of my hook-ups were alcohol-induced, but luckily I was smart enough to wrap it up [wear a condom], but some of my friends caught the clap [Chlamydia]' (Bakesale, 2008).

While transnational action sport destinations have traditionally been hyper-heterosexual spaces, gay ski weeks have grown in popularity over the past decade. During my fieldwork, I observed gay ski weeks in Queenstown, Whistler and Telluride (Colorado, US). Many European ski resorts, including Chamonix, also host an annual gay ski week. During these carnivalesque-style events, gay, lesbian and queer tourists are being warmly welcomed by businesses organizing special events and packages to cater for this niche market, and many local residents celebrate the novelty of the week. In her study of the 2010 Gay Ski Week (GSW) in Queenstown, tourism and geography scholar Lynda Johnston (2013) found that most of her 18 interviewees 'felt welcome in Queenstown and drew on discourses of "holiday town" openness' (p. 56) both on the slopes and in the town. While the majority proclaimed feeling 'very relaxed about their sexed subjectivities and embodied performances during GSW' (p. 56), others experienced 'traces of social and sexual conservatism' despite Queenstown being a cosmopolitan tourist town (p. 56). I concur with Johnston's (2013) conclusion that such events challenge the heteronormativity of mountain resort destinations, 'their camped-up performances transform both the ski resort town of Queenstown, plus the ski slopes', such that Queenstown and the surrounding ski fields 'become reconfigured spaces during GSW' (p. 56). But, as Johnston (2013) implies, the challenge posed by such events to the heteronormativity of these spaces is short-term. In the words of one of my interviewees, 'once the circus leaves town, everything goes back to normal' (pc, Queenstown male resident, 2010). Put slightly differently, with the exception of one hedonistic, hyper-consumptive, gay ski week per year, transnational action sport destinations remain resolutely heterosexual spaces.

A number of participants involved in this project acknowledged the relationship between sporting prowess and risk-taking and (hetero)sexual desirability. A Canadian male skier interviewed in a British-owned backpacker lodge in Chamonix explained that female skiers and snowboarders who demonstrate skill and courage on the mountain gain 'extra hot points' (pc, 2007). A committed New Zealand male snowboarder interviewed in Queenstown also stated, 'I think a woman who can ride a snowboard well is very sexy . . . It's something about the courage, focus, and disregard for safety . . . and I just love the way women look in snow gear' (pc, 2008). Interestingly, some of the female action sport migrants interviewed for this project, confident in both their sexuality and physical prowess, also described gaining pleasure from being both voyeurs and (active) objects of the male gaze. As a professional female snowboarder from New Zealand put it, 'guys are always checking out girls on the hill, and I like checking out the boys' (pc, Abby, 2006).

The uneven gender ratio of many transnational action sport destinations has prompted some to jokingly refer to them as 'male-dominated sausage parties' (Riding with your spouse, 2013, para. 2). Focusing specifically on mountainous spaces, Stoddart (2010) has explained how gendered embodiment, power and ski resorts are intimately linked. Drawing upon his empirical work in British Columbia, Canada, he discusses the backcountry as a highly masculine space and masculinizing experience. Yet, as I have explained elsewhere, committed female action sport participants are able to negotiate space in such masculine spaces by demonstrating physical prowess and commitment to their sports and the action sport lifestyle (Thorpe, 2009, 2011).

Many women also recognize that they possess their own forms of *feminine* capital in such destinations. According to Skeggs (1997), femininity, as cultural capital, is 'the discursive position available through gender relations that women are encouraged to inhabit and use. Its use will be informed by the network of social positions of class, gender, sexuality, region, age and race which ensure that it will be taken up (and resisted) in different ways' (p. 10). Building upon earlier feminist work, Huppatz (2009) distinguishes between *female* capital – the gender advantage derived from being perceived to have a female (but not necessarily feminine) body – and *feminine* capital – the gender advantage derived from a disposition or skill set learned via socialization, or simply when members of a particular field recognize one's body as feminine – and described women capitalizing on their femaleness and femininity within particular occupations (for example, paid caring work) to gain an income. In male-dominated action sport fields, some female action sport participants capitalize on both their female and feminine capital. Whereas some women embrace a novelty position as 'one of the boys' and thus gain access to opportunities that may not otherwise be available (such as going into the backcountry and building a jump for filming), others embrace their feminine capital to initiate relationships with male action sport participants that may lead to pleasurable experiences, and/or enhance their positioning in the local field. Whereas some less-committed female action sport migrants or tourists embrace this latter strategy, committed female action sport enthusiasts tend to privilege their symbolic capital over their feminine capital.

Indeed, many committed female action sport enthusiasts refuse to accept gender boundaries on the sports field, demonstrating risk-taking, courage and ignoring pain and injury (Thorpe, 2011a). Some of the same women also embrace traditionally masculine hedonistic behaviour off the sporting field (such as alcohol and drug consumption, and/or regular sexual interactions with different partners), with the aim of 'keeping up with the boys' (pc, Mel, 2009). While the majority of female participants in this project asserted that they made informed decisions regarding their risk-taking and pleasure-seeking behaviours, my observations reveal that their actions are never completely free but always constrained and enabled by the structural and ideological situation within the male-dominated action sport field (see also Laurendeau, 2004; Wheaton & Tomlinson, 1998). For example, while completing fieldwork in each of these destinations I was privy to scandalous conversations between groups of core male snow sport enthusiasts, which reduced female action sport tourists and migrants to sexual objects.

Some women – also known as 'pro-hos' – enter the action sport field seeking sexual relations with professional male athletes rather than active participation. According to a committed New Zealand male snowboarder, 'pro-hos just hang around trying to sleep with pro riders because they think it will make them cool-by-association and help them get into the good parties . . . most of them don't even snowboard. All a pro-ho is good for is a suck off [oral sex]' (pc, 2004). The circulation of rumours regarding the sexuality of female action sport tourists and migrants and the use of degrading language that reduces women to sexual objects are examples of 'symbolic violence' that work to remove any threat women's sexual agency (or athletic prowess) may pose to the male-dominated hierarchical structure of the action sport field (Krais, 1993). Clearly, in many social fields, including the action sport culture, young women's 'sexual agency' operates as a form of regulation (Gill, 2008; Harris, 2005; Tolman, 2002; Ussher, 2005). Regardless of changes within the action sport field and society more broadly, young women's bodies, and their sexual and social pleasure-seeking practices, continue to be policed and monitored via an array of subtle and explicit practices and strategies employed by dominant groups (Hutton, 2004). Further research is needed that not only 'attempts to theorize gender and tourism' but also addresses 'the cultural construction of places and people as gendered [and sexualized] sites and sights' (Aitchison, 2001, p. 134).

Of course, those living permanently (or semi-permanently) in action sport destinations have different understandings of these locations – as 'home' rather than a holiday destination for hedonistic pursuits – which can

Figure 5.3 A road sign for Whistler has a handmade poster added that reveals how female action sport migrants' sexuality and pleasure-seeking practices are policed within male-dominated transnational action sport destinations. The sign reads 'Whistler Aussie Slut Factor' with the arrow on 'moderate', with options ranging from 'low' to 'instant S.T.I' (sexually transmitted infection). Here the particular group under attack are female Australian action sport migrants

prompt some conflict between groups (for example, tourists, local residents, seasonal migrants; see Duncan, 2008, 2009; Thorpe, 2011b). I explore some of these tensions in the following section. Here, however, it is necessary to note that it is not only action sport tourists and migrants who are embracing the hypersexual and hedonistic lifestyle offered within transnational action sport destinations. While many residents complain about various aspects of the flows of youth within and through local spaces, some local residents, particularly young men, embrace opportunities for short-term relationships with travelling women. For example, in the transnational surf town of Raglan, New Zealand, where I currently live, local male surfers are often very aware of the flows of tourist buses into the town, particularly companies transporting youth travellers (for example, Stray), as such arrivals often mean the local pub over the next few nights will be brimming with young female travellers. Some of the men trade on their positioning as the 'exotic other', and what might be termed their 'local capital', offering to teach the young women to surf or take them to local places of significance. Such interactions appear to have few real consequences for the local men as the young women often only stay for a few days. Similar observations of young Balinese male surfers and beach boys are the focus of the documentary *Cowboys in Paradise* (2010; see www.cowboysinparadise.com). However, an important distinction needs to be made; whereas the local men in most action sport destinations are seeking short-term sexual relationships with female travellers, the Balinese Cowboys are paid for their services.

Commenting on such trends in tourist spaces more broadly, Franklin & Crang (2001) suggest that the romantic relations between tourists and locals offer evidence that the flows of tourism are not one way; rather the 'constant flows of young tourists through a town may profoundly alter the local pattern of courtship and sexuality such that locals seek a romantic encounter with tourists and not just the other way around' (Franklin & Crang, 2001, p. 9). In other words, the relationship of power in such encounters cannot be understood as 'uni-directional or exclusively associated with the tourist' (Bianchi, 2012, p. 489). Rather, as Miller (2000) argues, the power dynamics in such encounters must be understood in myriad 'localized settings' with consideration given to those situations in which the tourists themselves become 'targets' (p. 376). As these examples illustrate, the 'anatomy of power in the spaces of tourism encounter – whether planned or "serendipitous"' is complex, ranging from 'how trust operates in the micro-spaces of encounter' to the 'intimate mechanics of discrimination' based on 'collisions of class, gender, race and identity' (Gibson, 2012, p. 59).

Trouble in paradise: Tensions between groups

While some locals may embrace opportunities for romantic relations with tourists, they are often more cautious about the influx of action sport migrants who flood their town each season, particularly when they start crowding sporting spaces and competing for other limited resources such as jobs and accommodation. However, in transnational action sport destinations such as Queenstown, Whistler and Chamonix, the 'blurring between work, leisure and travel becomes increasingly complex' (Duncan, 2012, p. 117). Indeed, hosts (often working tourists and migrants) and guests (tourists) often share similar socio-economic backgrounds and experiences of mobility. Despite such similarities, many action sport migrants work to distinguish themselves from tourists, seeking to connect with local residents, or at least perform similar routines and practices to those of locals. Yet local residents (many of whom have been action sport migrants or tourists at various stages of their own lives) work to create symbolic boundaries between themselves and 'blow-ins' or 'transplants', and to protect their 'rights' of access and ownership as local residents. As such, the 'local' identifier becomes highly contested, and strongly protected by those who consider themselves 'real' locals, prompting some long-term action sport migrants to question: 'how long must one live here before they are considered a *real* local?' The key issue here, of course, is who has the power to define a 'local' or a 'blow-in'? In most transnational action sport destinations it is typically the long-time residents who have the power to include and exclude members of such exclusive groups.

Traditionally, tourism studies have focused on the images tourists have of the locals and how these affect their behaviour and attitudes towards their hosts. Yet Maoz (2006) is interested to examine the ways 'guests and hosts view, grasp, conceptualize, understand, imagine and construct each other' (p. 222). According to Maoz, everyone gazes at each other in transnational spaces, and she uses the term 'the mutual gaze' to examine 'not only how "we" see "them", but also how "they" see "us"' (2006, p. 222). The notion of the 'mutual gaze' is relevant in transnational action sport destinations, where tourists, migrants and residents are always 'affecting and feeding each other' (Urry & Larsen, 2012, p. 205). Transnational action sport destinations are thus places of 'enfolded mobility' (Frändberg, 2013, p. 5) in which each individual's 'feelings of insideness or out-of-placeness' (Ettema & Schwanen, 2012, p. 177) are influenced by their interactions with others.

According to Gibson (2012), analysis of tourism encounters needs to move beyond descriptions of 'how bodies and materials interact in fluid, complicated ways – and the spaces in which these encounters take place' (p. 59), with greater attention paid to how power is exercised in such spaces and encounters. Indeed, place formation 'is subject to the workings of power' with 'some agents being able to create conditions of belonging for some people and of exclusion for others' (Ettema & Schwanen, 2012, p. 177; Cresswell, 2004; Wiles, 2005). Here I offer three brief examples that illustrate how the 'mutual gaze' between individuals and groups within transnational action sport destinations is implicated in such workings of power. Furthermore, these examples reveal how the tensions and power relations between groups are place-specific and influenced by various factors, including the socio-cultural-political-historical relations between nations, as well as local migratory politics.

The first example illustrates the tensions between British action sport migrants and some local residents in Queenstown. The attitude expressed by Adam, a New Zealand snowboarder, skateboarder and surfer who has 'lived and worked in Queenstown for three seasons', was common among many New Zealand action sport migrants living in Queenstown:

> I love it here. I don't mind all of the tourists. I mean, they can be annoying, but in the end, if they weren't here, I wouldn't have a job, so I shouldn't complain. But . . . I can't stand all of the Poms [English] that come here for the winter and spend the whole time complaining. They come in hoards and take up all the accommodation and all of the jobs. Lots of them are rich kids on their Gap years with mommy and daddy sending them money throughout the winter. Half way through the season their accents really start to drive me crazy, you just can't seem to escape them. (pc, Adam, 2006)

A key division in Chamonix is between local French residents and English migrants. In the early 2000s local newspapers reported on the 'English Invasion', explaining that, with British buying two-thirds of the local property, French residents could no longer afford to live there. According to the Director of the Chamonix Tourist Board, Bernard Prud'homme, 'It's making everyone jealous and developing tensions between locals and foreigners' (cited in Packard, 2006, para. 4). A long-time Chamonix resident of British origin also explained: 'Some of the Brits come here and throw their money around. They have been buying up all the housing, so there is a real anti-English thing going on these days. On the odd occasion, Brits have had glue put in the locks of their cars' (pc, March 2010).

The third example points to some of the tensions between local Whistler residents and Australian action sport migrants that come to the fore on February 26, Australia Day. The following comments from an Australian action sport migrant's personal blog are revealing:

> Still blind drunk from the night before, the beers started cracking again at 6am on Australia Day. All the Aussie gear came out . . . surf lifesavers, kangaroos, mullets, zinc, vegemite moustaches, cork hats . . . and everyone was getting ready for the Longhorns pub opening at 9am at the base of the ski run. The atmosphere [in the Longhorns pub] was unreal; they imported VB (crap I know but better than Canadian beer) and meat pies . . . Everyone was dressed up . . . At one stage, full of drinks and bullet proof,

I head up the hill with my Aussie flag as a cape and started to tackle the skiers as they came down the hill . . . admittedly, this probably wasn't the brightest idea I've had. The Aussies completely took over Whistler and there weren't many Canadians out at all. Most of the Canadians I work with say it's the craziest day of the year, so they all stay home. (The Aussies take over Whistler, 2009, para. 1).

Of particular interest here is the authors' awareness of the inappropriateness of his own aggressive and drunken behaviour, and his Canadian colleagues' disapproval of Australian action sport migrants' celebrations. Similar celebrations take place in Chamonix, as illustrated in the poster below (Figure 5.4). Arguably, in their celebration of this national holiday, Australian migrants in action sport destinations around the world are creating what Tweed (1999) calls 'trans-temporal and trans-locative space'. The embrace of nationalism on this day and in this space, enable some migrants to recover or recreate a sense of national identity and imaginary transnational connections while away from home. In so doing, however, they often dominate local spaces, imposing their cultural practices on others in ways that frustrate many local residents, thus reinforcing social divisions.

With various groups occupying transnational action sport destinations, symbolic and physical spatial divisions have been developed to minimize conflict between groups, and to allow individuals within various groups to gain a sense of belonging among like-minded peers. As the following comment from Bruce suggests,

Like Queenstown, Wanaka is a totally different town during the winter and summer. Between seasons, it's almost like a ghost town. Fifteen years ago the town was a third of the size. I think lots of the old locals tend to keep to themselves now, and don't frequent the bars and restaurants where all the 'new' locals are hanging out. There are a few bars that are almost exclusively for the old timers.

But, there are people that have been here 15 years that still wouldn't consider themselves local . . . they know that the 'real' locals are the old farmer guys and their families who have lived here for decades. They are careful not to tread on their toes, or stomp on their turf too much. (pc, 2011)

Similarly, British action sport migrants in Chamonix gather at particular bars and avoid other typically French-owned places where they don't feel particularly welcome. The following narrative is an adapted excerpt from my previous ethnographic fieldwork in Chamonix (see Thorpe, 2011a). I include it here because it highlights how some places become 'gathering' points for travellers and residents with a similar habitus. Moreover, it also illustrates

Figure 5.4   A poster advertises Australia Day at Vert Hotel bar in Chamonix

the tensions that can emerge as groups collide with others with different understandings of place markers and boundaries:

> *5:00pm, December 2007: I find my bunk bed, unload my backpack and board-bag, and say a quick 'hello' to my roommate – a female English climber in her mid-20s here on a work trip for a climbing equipment company. Interested to observe the interactions in this British-owned backpacker hostel in this infamous French mountain resort destination, I wander downstairs and take a seat in the bar. A Canadian guy in his early 30s enters a few minutes after me, pulls up a seat, and promptly introduces himself as 'Chris'. He then proceeds to rave about the snow conditions. Chris is travelling home from Dubai where he has been working for over six months; he describes his 'unbearable*

frustration' of knowing it was 'dumping' on his home mountain in British Columbia while being 'trapped in the desert'. He tells me he is in France 'just to warm my legs up' before heading home for a week of backcountry riding with a group of old high-school buddies. During our conversation I notice a steady flow of British expats entering the bar; some appear to have come straight from the mountain – their hair is tousled and their snow-proof pants scuff loudly along the floor – others wear overalls and hard-capped work boots, so I assume the latter have come directly from work at a local construction site. They order pints and relax into what appear to be their 'usual' seats, all the while chatting animatedly in their native language about the day-to-day goings on in the village. In contrast to Chris and I, they seem to know each other well.

A young British guy wearing a stained t-shirt from a climbing company and a beanie pulled down over his dirty blonde hair joins our conversation. A passionate snowboarder, para-glider, mountain bike rider, climber and website designer, 'Tom' has lived here for five years but is going 'home' tomorrow to live with his dad and save some money before returning in spring. 'I love snowboarding, but I am first and foremost a climber, so spring and summer are my preferred seasons,' he confirms. I witness Tom's cheeks become progressively rosier over the next hour as a steady stream of friends approach him to say their farewells – slapping him on the back, exchanging complicated handshakes, and sharing a few quick hugs – all insist on buying him a beer to wish him well. 'I can't really say no, can I? I just hope I don't get so drunk I miss my 6:30am train,' he laughs, eyes glistening as his tightly muscled forearm raises his beer to his sun-scoured and wind-chapped lips.

Outside the bar, dusk has descended into darkness – the snow-capped mountains, luminous in the moonlight, mark the physical boundaries of this mountain village. Inside, the temperature steadily climbs as the bar continues to fill with English-speaking migrants – mostly British, but also a number of Australians – seeking the warmth of familiar faces, accents and stories. A live football (soccer) game is now playing on a large television screen and an open fire roars in the corner. A bell rings loudly and the group of snowboarders, skiers, and climbers gathered behind me seems to surge spontaneously in the direction of the bar eager for a final drink. As I scan the room I see others are sculling the last of their pints, pulling their jackets from the hooks, replacing their beanies, and wrapping their scarves in preparation for the cold walk home. I overhear some of my fellow backpackers debating their next move. I am invited to join a motley crew – an Australian (Sam), a couple of English guys (James and Steve), Chris the Canadian, a South African (Garth) and a Greek guy (Jimmy) supposedly straight out of the army – to 'Brazil Night' at an infamous local bar. It was a few blocks out of town, but James had read about it in a snowboarding magazine and was convinced this was a good place for us to visit.

After a brisk walk, we arrive at our destination. Pushing open the heavy wooden door, I step into a warm, smoky, dimly lit bar. Groups of youth dressed in the latest snowboarding attire sit around tables, lean against the grimy walls, and gather at the bar. A DJ is mixing records, blending layers of Brazilian-style beats and electro-pop. A few young women dressed casually in jeans, skate-shoes, colourful fitted t-shirts, and beanies lean into conversations with a group of nonchalant young men holding the majority of the stools at the bar. A snowboarding video plays on a screen next to the colourful wall of liquor bottles. Our group attempts to navigate space among the throng at the bar. Garth reaches the front first and orders a round of drinks in English with a few French words tossed in. I cringe as I notice steely glares from the group of guys sitting at the bar; the French bartender offers merely a grunt in our vague direction. Feeling a little uneasy, our group retreats to a pool table at the back of the room.

An hour or so has passed when our third game of pool is abruptly interrupted. The music has stopped and the French DJ is yelling violently at us from his booth. I feel a room of unfriendly eyes upon us. Unable to understand the French tirade, I quickly make my way for the door. As I step out onto the snowy street I turn immediately to Chris, desperate for his translation. Before he has a chance to respond, we witness four of the guys stumbling out the door, and Steve being thrown forcefully into the street. Picking himself up from the cobbled pavement and brushing the stones and ice from his jeans, I see rage in his eyes. Luckily, I am not the only one to notice this and two of the guys grab his shoulders and start walking him away from the door. 'What was all of that about?' I inquire. 'The dude was telling us to fuck off. He was angry because we were speaking English. This is a local bar and we should be speaking the local language, but he said it was OK for the girl to stay,' explains Chris. I'm confused by the last statement. 'Why did he say it was OK for me to stay?' I query. Chris laughs, 'Haven't you noticed? This town is a total sausage-party. So any girl, even an English-speaking one, is OK. More "meat" on the barbie, as you Kiwis might say.' I don't have time to respond. The group seems to have forgotten the scuffle already and is now egging each other on in their efforts to slide as far as possible along the icy street. Within minutes, the attention shifts again, an icy rock becomes a makeshift puck in a game of street hockey. By the time we stumble across our final destination my toes are throbbing and I have lost all feeling in most of my fingers.

As we approach the nightclub I notice condensation streaking the windows. Inside throngs of intoxicated tourists sway, twist and bend on the dance floor. The top-of-the-pops style music rattles through my chest cavity. Here it doesn't matter what language or accent you have, the music is so loud that conversation is impossible; the bouncing, grinding, sweating, groping bodies seem to be speaking an infra-language of their own. Within minutes, Chris and Garth are dancing with a group of young women wearing short skirts, sparkly tank-tops, and glittery lips. Desperate to avoid this situation, I make my way to the bathroom where I find water-logged toilet-rolls littering the floor and doors covered in scribbled graffiti. Two young women in tight black leggings and high-heeled shoes lean into the mirror, reapplying eyeliner, mascara and lipstick. Their conversations fast, high-pitched, and in an unidentifiable foreign language. On my way out, I notice two small plastic zip-lock bags strewn near the rubbish bin, on the other side of the doorway a condom dispenser glows on the wall. I decide it is time to leave, and instead of saying my goodbyes, I make a beeline for the door through a maze of stumbling bodies. The bouncers step aside and I gasp at the fresh mountain air.

As I begin my weary walk home, I will the cold darkness to wash me clean of the spilt beer, the clammy hands and the drunken slurs. As I look skyward, I am excited to see heavy clouds hugging the surrounding mountaintops; the forecasted front has arrived. Sensing snow, my body begins to ache in anticipation for a powder filled morning. I pick up my pace.

Passing a dark alley, I hear muffled murmurs and turn to see two shadowy figures entwined in a moment of drunken passion. I extend my stride further across the cobbled pavement. I cross a bridge and through an intersection, and feel my chilled quadriceps stretching inside my frozen jeans. Over the babble of the mountain stream, I hear stifled laughter and catch a waft of a distinctly aromatic smoke. Glancing down the side street, I see a beanie- and baggy-jacket-clad group huddled under an awning, passing a glowing ember; as one draws the light to his lips, the others converse in hushed tones.

As I approach the backpacker hostel, I am smiling to myself. Despite being miles from home, the sights, smells, sounds, tastes and textures of this nightscape are so familiar. As I tiptoe up the dark stairs of the backpackers, my sensual knowledge and embodied memories of mountain towns from other times and places comfort me, temporarily. However, my smile quickly disappears when, upon opening the door to my bunkroom, I am overwhelmed by the pungent smell of drying snowboard boots and sweaty gloves. As I shift uncomfortably on the thin slat-bed, kept awake by a chorus of snoring strangers, I rehearse the few French phases I know in anticipation of using them tomorrow.

The group of young travellers I accompanied in this narrative were all new to Chamonix and largely unaware of divisions of space and existing tensions between particular groups of locals, migrants and tourists. While I quickly sensed our 'out-of-placeness' in the French 'hipster' bar, it wasn't until they were literally thrown from the bar that some of my male peers gained some understanding of the tensions brewing under the surface. Interestingly, they did not dwell long on the reasons for this altercation. While this group of travellers seemed to enjoy the welcoming atmosphere of the British bar, they appeared most comfortable surrounded by fellow tourists in the nightclub. It should be added here that the long-term British residents at the British-owned bar were not willing to join us at the local French bar, thus suggesting a tacit understanding of such symbolic boundaries. Similarly, many action sport migrants who have spent many years living in Whistler and Queenstown actively avoid bars that are popular among the tourist and

Figure 5.5   Après ski culture at a local bar in Chamonix

backpacker crowds. The longer an action sport migrant spends in a particular destination, the more knowledge they acquire as to the places in which they feel most welcome – that is, attended by others like them – and those places where they might prefer to avoid.

Everyday politics in transnational action sport fields

Cultural hierarchies are contested, negotiated and reinforced in various social and physical spaces and places (for example, buses, bars, sports stores, supermarkets, cafes) in transnational action sport destinations. Many local residents develop a tacit understanding of the subtle (and not-so subtle) 'rules' structuring the social and physical spaces within the local transnational action sport field. It is typically through the process of enculturation into the local field that the practical transmission of local physical cultural knowledge via peers' comments and stories, observation and local media become embodied. During this socialization process, participants learn the 'rules' of the local field, and the 'consequences' of breaking these rules (physical or verbal confrontations, rumours, ridicule or social exclusion) as well as the identities of individuals or groups who reinforce the valuation system and cultural hierarchy (Bourdieu, 1984). In the final part of this chapter I briefly examine how individuals and groups in transnational action sport destinations 'experience multiple loci and layers of power and are shaped by them' or 'act back upon them' (Levitt & Glick Schiller, 2004, p. 1013). In so doing, I point to some of the embodied practices and symbolic strategies employed by (permanent and temporary) residents and action sport migrants as they simultaneously maintain and shed cultural repertoires and identities, and interact in transnational action sport destinations within unique socio-cultural, economic, political and temporal contexts (Levitt & Glick Schiller, 2004).

As previously mentioned, distinctions between 'local' and 'tourist' are often blurred within popular mountain resort destinations. Thus, local residents, tourists and lifestyle sport migrants employ an array of embodied practices to establish notions of self and the group, and a sense of belonging, and demarcate who belongs and who is excluded from particular spaces within these unique mountain resort destinations. Transnational action sport destinations are unique 'fields' with distinctive social 'norms' and 'rules' for accessing terrain and facilities (see Thorpe, 2007, 2012). While some rules are well known across the global action sport field (for example, don't 'drop in' on someone already riding a wave or half-pipe), all transnational action sport destinations have distinctive histories, social and natural geographies, and development patterns, and thus cultural hierarchies.

The concept of capital sits at the center of Bourdieu's (1985) construction of social space: 'The structure of the social world is defined at every moment by the structure and distribution of the capital and profits characteristic of the different particular fields' (p. 734) and it is important to work out the correct hierarchy 'of the different forms of capital' (p. 737). Some of the forms of capital structuring local action sport fields include: *social capital* (personal contacts in the local field, and the more connections with long-time locals the better), *cultural capital* ('local' or 'outsider' status, cultural commitment to the activity in either the global or local field); *physical capital* (demonstrations of courage, skill and physical prowess), *symbolic capital* (wearing clothing, using equipment or displaying other cultural symbols that subtly demonstrate cultural knowledge and insider status); *gender capital* (demonstrations of masculine- or feminine-appropriate bodily practices); and *national capital* (historical relations between the action sport migrant's country of origin and country of travel; historical relations and interactions between travellers from various countries and local residents in transnational 'hot spots') (see also Corner, 2008). The cultural value system within local fields is important because it determines who gets access and priority when natural (such as waves) and socio-economic (such as accommodation, jobs) resources are limited. In contrast to tourists, action sport migrants become keenly aware of subtle (and not-so subtle) local differences in the value given to various forms of capital in particular fields.

Despite local differences across each of the transnational action sport destinations visited for this project, some commonalities can be observed. This is perhaps not surprising giving the high levels of mobility of tourists, migrants and even residents within and across such action sport destinations. The most valued forms of capital tend to be social and cultural, and physical. For example, even if an individual is no longer the most proficient skier or snowboarder on the mountain, or surfer in the waves, if they have lived in the town for many years and demonstrated their commitment to the lifestyle and the community, it is likely they will have more status among their local peers than a highly proficient, young athlete only in town for a few weeks. However, it is typically those who can combine social, cultural *and* physical capital who have the most status and respect, and thus access to limited social and physical resources, as well as power to define the 'rules' of the local field.

The body is an important symbol of status and a site of distinctions in these transnational action sport destinations. Local residents and committed action sport participants often become highly efficient at reading the body and all its national, cultural and gender symbols. For example, having observed new participants in the early stages of socialization into the Whistler action sport culture, Marie commented that:

> There are lots of guys here for their first season; they are wearing Volcom hats for the first time. You can see it in their faces . . . they are so pumped. They are spending, spending, spending, to buy all the gear. They get on the bus with a new board, boots . . . and they have an Aussie accent, then they start talking so big, about all the jumps they are going to hit and all the videos they have watched. I don't think they realize how hard it actually is and how many years of practice and hard work that it requires. They come here and spend thousands of dollars on gear, they will learn to ski or snowboard but they will never learn how to make it a part of their life. (pc, November 2005)

Continuing, she identifies various female participants in Whistler:

> It's pretty easy to tell the local girls from the tourists and 'mall girls'. You can tell the local girls, because they are wearing the labels, the brand names, they are sometimes going for a more masculine look. They are not dressed as feminine as the girls that have come in from Vancouver for a weekend; the local girls are wearing the ball-caps, and baggy pants . . .
>
> But the girls that are more 'in-your-face' in Whistler are the young girls that are here just to party every night. Overall, this place is a party town. There are lots of girls that don't ski or snowboard. They plan to be here for one year and doing the party thing, and these sports just happen to be a means of being social and meeting guys and having the whole 'look'. I don't necessarily think that's wrong, but I think there are lots of girls that have bought into the whole thing.
>
> But the girls you don't really see in the town are the ones that have been here for a couple of seasons and are really passionate about snowboarding, or skiing, or mountain biking. These chicks really don't give a crap about what they look like. You don't see these girls drooling all

over the guys in the cafes and in the bars. But you do see them up on the mountain, and they are ripping. (pc, November 2005)

For snow-sport journalist Jennifer Sherowski (2005), local Whistler residents and committed snow-sport participants can be distinguished from tourists by their 'goggle tans and chins scuffed by Gore-Tex' (p. 160). According to another journalist, the 'archetypal' figure in Chamonix is the 'hard-core mountain man' typically 'under 30 [years old] and kitted out in such a way that you immediately know he's an aggressive backcountry animal who'll snarl if you mess with his powder' (Murphy, 2006, para. 6):

> The helmet, the Gore-Tex clothing, the ice-axe, harness and transceiver all have a double role. On the mountain, they may save his life; in the bars they announce his toughness to impressed intermediates who wish to God they were like him. (Murphy, 2006, para. 7)

The key point here is that action sport participants 'gaze' upon others' bodies, reading them for all of their cultural symbols, and then consciously practice and perform their own bodies in an attempt to offer a particular presentation of self that best situates them in the field.

While clothing and equipment constitute important symbolic markers of group membership in most action sport destinations, other cultural practices and embodied symbols also help distinguish the bodies of 'local' and committed residents from tourists. A local Queenstown resident, for example, described the symbolic significance of material objects:

> Driving up the mountain or around town, I can look at people's cars and instantly know if they are locals or tourists . . . I can tell a lot by the stickers . . . [including] the sex and age of the owner, how long they have been skiing or snowboarding for, and where they have come from. I can also usually tell how committed the owner is by the state of their car – the tires, the dust, the mud. (pc, July 2006)

Action sport bodies are performed and read differently by individuals and groups from various positions within transnational action sport destinations. Of course, key to reading these symbols and practices, and making meaning of action sport bodies and material objects within local fields, is the tacit knowledge – or 'nexus of competences' (Amin & Cohendet, 1999) – embodied by the resident, migrant or tourist during their past or present local and/ or transnational experiences.

Importantly, not all tourists are oblivious to these nuanced cultural performances, and not all action sport participants are seeking to gain capital and 'negotiate' space within these transnational fields. As the following comments from an action sport tourist visiting Whistler for a one-week holiday illustrate, some are critical of the interactions and dynamics within these places of hedonism and privileged play:

> If I had come here a few years ago, I would have absolutely loved it. I'm only in my late 20s, but everyone here seems so much younger than me. They are just here to party, party, party and play in the mountains; I have responsibilities back home . . . I'm not interested in getting wasted every night and trying to chat up the cutest snowboarder boys . . . It looks like they are having heaps of fun, but it all just seems very superficial, almost high schoolish. (pc, December 2006)

As this comment suggests, the 'gaze' is always relative to one's social positioning and lived experience. Whereas some action sport migrants living in Whistler for a season or two might dismiss this young woman as 'just another tourist' uncommitted to action sports or the lifestyle, she reads their performances as 'very superficial' and not a lifestyle she desires. The distinctions between tourist and host, migrant and locals, are blurred, with each group 'gazing' upon the other from their own position in the transnational action sport field, as well as fields beyond these dynamic, highly international and hierarchical places.

As illustrated in the following comments from Emily, an Australian core snowboarder, physical and national capital are also important. Having spent many frustrating months trying to negotiate space in an infamously busy terrain-park at a Californian ski resort, Emily learned the importance of a good 'first run' (physical capital) to 'gain respect' from her (mostly male) peers, otherwise 'you are forced to drop-in on people and piss them off all day just trying to get a turn' (pc, August 2004). Continuing, Emily explained that, while working as a snowboard instructor at the same resort during the late 1990s, her 'Aussie accent' occasionally worked as an advantage among the local snowboarders, her employers and some customers, who 'probably saw me as a bit of a cute novelty'. Emily noted that after returning to this resort for three consecutive winters, each year she was more warmly embraced by the local community who finally came to consider her 'one of them and not just another "one season wonder"'. In contrast, during her subsequent travels to Whistler, Emily witnessed 'a kind of racism against Australians . . . probably because too many young, drunk, obnoxious Australian skiers and snowboarders have pissed off the locals on too many occasions' (pc, August 2004). As an experienced transnational action sport migrant, Emily had become adept at reading embodied performances and interactions in social situations, and navigating space within different contexts based on her tacit understandings of the social and cultural dynamics. During her time in Whistler, Emily's 'transnational consciousness' prompted her to engage in various 'transnational acts' in attempts to disassociate from her national identity and integrate into the local culture. In her own words: 'I tried to hide my Aussie accent as much as possible, and would try to keep my voice down in public places'; she also 'made a conscious choice to live with a group of Canadians rather than in staff accom[modation] where it was about 90 per cent Aussies, and the rest were Kiwis [New Zealanders] and Poms [British]' (pc, August 2004). Continuing, she explains:

> If I wanted to live and ride with Australians, I would have stayed in Oz. I wanted to feel a part of the Whistler community, so I kind of made an effort to prove to my Canadian friends that, like them, I was a snowboarder first, and an Aussie second. [. . .] Sure, we come from different countries, but we share the same passion for snowboarding. We became like family during my time in Whistler, but first I had to prove that I was not like most of the other Aussies here. (pc, 2006)

The key point here is that for Emily to develop a sense of belonging in the transnational space of Whistler, she took to selectively revealing only some aspects of her Australian identity based on her understanding of the rules and valuation system within and across local 'fields' (that is, a small Californian resort in contrast to Whistler).

Transnational action sport destinations are hierarchical spaces with everyday interactions, practices and performances embedded within complex webs of power relations. But, as Gibson (2012) suggests, 'surely there is something in the unexpected surprises and comforts of strangers . . . that enables community and communality to be remade in unlikely ways' (p. 60). Indeed, it would be remiss to overlook the shared experiences and sense of community that develops in many transnational action sport destinations. It is important to reiterate that, despite some tensions between groups, those attracted to action sport destinations often share a similar habitus. They are often from privileged backgrounds that enable them to find the time and space in their lives to enjoy physical play in the natural environment. Moreover, they pursue a common lifestyle, and are similarly affected by weather conditions and seasonal chances. As a migrant to Wanaka explained:

> I feel that everybody that lives here has a common bond. You know, people live in Wanaka for one reason. We all like the outdoors and we like the environment. You feel that you have something in common with everybody from the beginning. (Cited in Thulemark, 2011, p. 44)

In sharing (or at least understanding) the pleasures of skiing or snowboarding on a powder day, lining up for first chair on the lift at the opening of the mountain bike season, or the exhausted satisfaction from a day in perfect surf, these transnational communities certainly have more in common than many other multi-cultural societies around the world. As discussed in Chapter 3, these communities (and the virtual communities of travellers that remain connected to them following their departure) often grieve together during times of loss and sadness, and rally together to support those residents (including migrants) experiencing times of difficulty. Put simply, the divisions and tensions within transnational action sport destinations are predominantly symbolic struggles over privileged resources, rather than the life-threatening concerns, such as disaster, poverty and war, that continue to plague many less privileged places in the world (see Chapters 7 and 8).

In sum, it is not enough to examine the corporeal mobilities of action sport tourists, migrants and athletes across borders. Focusing on the everyday interactions among a variety of actors within transnational action sport destinations can also shed light on the 'complexity and multiple inhabitation' (Crang et al., 2003, p. 449) and unequal 'power geometries' (Massey, 1994) that characterize these transnational social spaces. In this and the previous chapter, I focused on the different scales of action sport mobilities, from the motivation to travel to particular destinations to the 'smaller, more local movements that impact on how individuals are accepted and absorbed into local communities' (Duncan, 2012, p. 118). However, it is also important to consider the affective and emotional consequences of these international and local mobilities. As Conradson and Latham (2007) explain, 'geographic mobility may be a route to different modalities of feeling. Because migration inevitably involves an encounter with new ecologies of place, the possibility for new affective and emotional dynamics is present' (p. 237). The following chapter builds upon this and the previous chapter to examine how action sport participants' transnational experiences influence their emotional connections to place and understandings of 'home', including their sense of national, gender and cultural identity.

6
Transnational Action Sport Career Migration: Reflections From Home and Away

For the majority of action sport travellers and migrants, the transnational lifestyle is short-lived, a working holiday after university or between 'real' jobs. But for some, it becomes a career they pursue for many years. In so doing, committed action sport migrants develop meaningful connections within multiple contexts and networks across countries that contribute to their transnational sense of identity and belonging. Sustained mobilities in the action sport industry are often the result of many years of hard work, compromises, creativity and negotiations. This chapter consists of two parts, both of which draw upon interviews with long-time action sport migrants conducted either during their travels or upon adopting a less mobile lifestyle. To make meaning of their reflections, I adopt an interdisciplinary approach that engages selectively with literature and key concepts from the fields of sociology, cultural geography, and transnational and migration studies. In the first part I examine the opportunities, constraints and negotiations of career action sport migrants, focusing particularly on the experiences of those working in the ski industry. Here I also draw upon Foucault's notion of circulation to examine the role of governments and the nation-state in enabling and constraining action sport mobilities via visa regulations. In the second part of this chapter I draw upon Conradson & McKay's (2007) notion of 'translocal subjectivities' to examine the 'dynamics of mobile subjectivities' and describe the 'multiply-located senses of self' amongst action sport migrants who inhabit transnational social fields (p. 168). More specifically, I reveal action sport migrants' attachments to places, sense of belonging in movement, emotional consequences of 'dwelling and movement through places' (Conradson & McKay, 2007, p. 169), and the potential for reflexivity initiated by such mobilities.

Sustained transnationalism: living back-to-back winters

Here I draw upon in-depth interviews with six long-term snow-sport migrants all living and working in New Zealand during the 2011 winter season. Interviews were conducted during a weeklong ethnographic visit to Queenstown and Wanaka in August 2011. This case reveals some of the lived pleasures and difficulties experienced, and compromises and negotiations made, by those pursuing transnational careers in the action sports industry.

Belinda is a New Zealand ski instructor and an ex-extreme skiing competitor in her early 40s who started travelling between New Zealand and the US in 1991. She continued instructing and competing for many years, and quickly climbed the ranks into management positions at ski resorts both overseas and at home. While Belinda continues to operate in a management role at a ski resort in New Zealand, she no longer pursues the back-to-back lifestyle due to recently starting a family with her ski instructor husband. Another seasoned ski instructor, *Cesar*, was born in Brazil and then migrated as a child to Australia. At the age of 22, he travelled to the US with a group of university friends on a working holiday. With little skiing experience, he assumed they would 'work at a bar and ski all day', but his friend 'was really keen to be a ski instructor and, with a somewhat misleading application as far as skiing ability, he got us both jobs'. At the time of our interview, Cesar had just completed his 23rd consecutive winter season and was now managing the snow-sport centre at a major New Zealand ski resort. He was careful to note that his enculturation into this lifestyle was 'somewhat by accident' and his primary motivation was for travel rather than skiing or instructing:

> I'm in a different boat to most instructors, because I didn't start to ski until I started instructing. Growing up in Brazil, there's not a lot of skiing, and moving to Australia we could never afford to ski. Travelling always was my first passion, so instructing was initially a means to an end for me.

In contrast, *Rose*, an English-born skier brought up in Scotland who has completed more than 40 consecutive winter seasons working as a ski instructor and manager between New Zealand and the US, proclaims her love for teaching as driving her longstanding career:

> I do it because I love that interaction with people. It's really a teaching thing for me. If you were just passionate about skiing or riding, you honestly would be better getting a high-paying job somewhere and taking two weeks off, because there are lots of times it is blue sky and beautiful snow and you're on the beginner hill. You know, I come from a long line of teachers. This is my classroom really.

Keith is an American snowboard instructor in his mid-30s who has spent the past 16 years working between ski resorts in the United States and France, Austria and New Zealand. Keith shares the transnational lifestyle with his British girlfriend, but prefers to travel alone 'because sometimes travelling can be stressful, and I think it's best if you're the only person you have to deal with'.

Gary, a passionate snowboarder in his early 40s, started snowboarding in 1993 when he first moved to Queenstown. In 1998, after finally saving enough money, he did his first northern hemisphere winter in Whistler, Canada. He recalls: 'I sort of fell on my feet and got a job teaching and trail guiding for Whistler, which was super cool.' After four years travelling between Whistler and Queenstown, he then spent another five winters working for a ski resort in Northern California. During his 13-year career as a transnational action sport migrant, Gary also spent time working in Australia as a member of the snow-park maintenance and design team, and in Japan setting up a snowboard shop and school, and doing some coaching and 'bits and pieces'.

Like many action sport migrants, Belinda, Cesar, Rose, Keith and Gary all commenced their transnational careers during their late teens and early twenties. In contrast, *Stuart* became a ski instructor later in life after something of an epiphany:

> I was in the corporate world . . . My career was taking me into that crowd of people that I really can't stand, and from a personal point of view, they were horrible people, from the way that they have to interact to get where they're going, and how they treat other people in that process. This just wasn't part of my mindset, so I asked myself: what would I like to do, what am I into? But the catalyst was being made redundant and then being reemployed by the same company. I realized there is no job security; it just doesn't exist, so that was a part of my big decision.

In 1996, he left his job in downtown Auckland and moved to a ski-town in the South Island of New Zealand where he began working nights in a ski-rental shop as a ski technician. He spent the days on the mountain:

> I started training at Treble Cone and trying to just become a better skier. Part of that training was getting certification levels and instructor training, but mostly it was about my skiing and getting better, because to be honest, I was a really horrible skier.

In 2002, Stuart got his New Zealand instructor certification, and then a work visa that enabled him to gain employment as an instructor at Mammoth Resort in California. He has since developed a longstanding relationship with the resort and his clients, and spent the past decade following the winter between New Zealand and the US. Although he continues to work 12-hour days, for Stuart it's worth the effort: 'it's normal corporate hours, but it's a much more fun environment to do it.'

As with most of the other snow-sport migrants interviewed, Stuart continues to face questions from family and friends, such as 'how long are you going to do this?' and 'when are you going to get a real job?' But he interprets such concerns as merely 'a bit of envy' from those who have yet to 'figure out a way to release themselves from their situation'. Cesar also experienced 'some pressure to go to a normal traditional type career' from family and friends, but admits that most of them are 'now very supportive. They understand that it is a career, and I think the fact that I have an office now makes everyone a bit happier'. Belinda's parents also continue to refer to her as a 40-year-old 'ski bum', which she finds amusing given her achievements and responsibilities in the sport and industry over the past 20 years.

While the action sport lifestyle is still highly valued by these participants, many have been proactive in seeking out opportunities to improve their potential earnings and sustain their careers in an industry that requires ongoing economic investment (for example, high rents, flights, visas) on the part of the workers:

> From my point of view, I mean it's an awesome lifestyle and if you work your way through the system you can get paid beyond existence wages. But, unless you're prepared to come and explore several avenues you're not going to make it, and you'll give up on it because it just ends up costing you too much. (Stuart, 2011, Cardrona)

Many long-term snow-sport migrants adopt highly creative approaches in their work and accommodation arrangements. For example, Stuart continues to top up his income as an instructor by driving the employee bus and sharing budget accommodations with several of his colleagues.

For some, the economic motives have become integral to their decisions in where to go, and whether or not to continue pursuing this expensive transnational lifestyle. For example, Gary admits that after being headhunted for a job in Australia, he accepted the position: 'I didn't go there for the snow. I went for the money really, they were paying twice what they were in New Zealand.' Keith also admits to financial incentives:

> As much as I love this job – and I do – but if I stayed at home, I mean there's also a monetary thing as well, I make more money doing this job than I would doing any job in the States, because I'm qualified in this field. In other fields, I'm not nearly as qualified so I make a lot less money, so you have to weigh that up with the cost of the travel, which seems to be going up every season.

Spending most days out on the snow with clients, snow-sport instructing is also 'hard on your body'; thus it becomes particularly important for those pursuing a career in this industry to 'maximise what we earn by getting more qualified' (Rose). With further qualifications, many of the snow-sport migrants interviewed have become instructor trainers or examiners, positions that offer better wages and ultimately less pressures on the body.

Furthermore, while each of the participants enjoyed the party lifestyle common in ski resort destinations (see Chapter 5) during their youth, they have each come to recognize it as not financially or physically sustainable for a long-term career in this industry:

> Back in the early 90s, it was me running amok, doing nothing but riding and partying. So I remember what it's like, but I am so far from that these days. I might go out once every few weeks, but just to catch up with friends. It's just not what I'm into anymore, but I still wake up on a sunny morning and feel that 'stoke' of going up the hill, I just don't want to be doing this with a hangover. (Gary)

> As we've gotten older, you back off the hard partying because your body can't handle it. And, to tell you the truth, you're just not that interested in it anymore. You might go out once a week and have a few drinks, but it's not like my first season here when I was going out three to four nights a week. (Keith)

> Partying every night is just not sustainable. It is a very expensive lifestyle, and it's also not sustainable from the point of view that the way to sustain a career in this industry is to have a deep connection with your guests who then come back and hire you year after year. Nobody wants to spend $100 on an hour lesson with someone who smells like booze and is unshaven. (Cesar)

Thus, as snow-sport migrants transition from their more youthful, short-term approach to a more longer-term, financially and physically sustainable career in the ski industry, their motives and strategies for participation often change.

Many of the snow-sport migrants also discussed the need for highly creative, flexible and tenacious approaches to maintain their transnational careers. 'We tend to be the type of people that roll with the punches,' proclaimed Keith, 'you have to . . . if you went over[seas] and all of a sudden someone rented out the house you're supposed to be staying in, you just don't stress about it, and just get on with trying to find somewhere else.' Belinda also emphasized the importance of hard work and perseverance:

> I think the only people that survive are people that work unbelievably hard. You have to work so hard to make enough money. There are so many people that want to make money easily and quickly, and this is not the right place to do that. You have to work long hours. You have to work really hard, cold, double jobs. As a first-time instructor, you start out at the bottom of the ladder, and it can take years at the same resort and the best qualifications and customer rapport to build up your credibility and to get into a position where you get the hours you need and are paid enough to survive.

Keith also describes the importance of careful financial planning through-out the season to cover upcoming flights, visas and seasonal set-up costs such as bonds for rental accommodations. During our conversation he dis-cussed the financial discipline required during the 'in-between' times, that is, after one season finishes and before the next begins:

> There's always a bit of twiddling the thumbs during the month or so between seasons. That can definitely be a bit of a downer, and you've got to manage your money really carefully during that time. Maybe you have some money sitting in your account at the end of the season, and you might sit at the computer and go, 'oh, I'll buy this or that', but you have to remind yourself that you just don't have money for throwing away, it always costs quite a bit to get set up on the other side of the world and you need money in your account to cover you before your next paycheck which could be months away.

Others described the importance of trying to create variation in their roles across the seasons in order to 'keep things interesting'. In contrast to the other snow-sport migrants interviewed, Gary found the back-to-back career as an instructor and a snow park manager as 'somewhat mind numbing', and thus returned to New Zealand to complete a diploma in graphic design which enabled him to have more flexibility in when and where he worked, as well as greater work and lifestyle satisfaction: 'I had my laptop and was sitting in the States doing work, then I was riding powder, and then working afterwards and just emailing it back to New Zealand', adding, 'that probably prolonged the existence I was leading' as a transnational snow-sport migrant.

In my previous research I have discussed some of the difficulties expe-rienced by female snowboarding migrants trying to maintain a career in the male-dominated industry (Thorpe, 2011a). Despite the newfound opportunities for young (typically privileged) women seeking international travel and professional careers in the snow-sport industry, I observed that many female snowboarding migrants 'retire' earlier from the 'back-to-back' lifestyle than their male peers. A conversation with Erin, Kim and Lisa – three highly esteemed New Zealand snowboard instructors who have been doing consecutive winters between New Zealand and North America since the early 2000s – about the dearth of elite-level female instructors and examiners in the international snowboarding industry, was revealing here. Observing the tendency for 'even the most hard core' female participants to 'drop out in their late twenties' while male snowboarders 'can keep going well into their thirties', they offered the following comments:

> It is quite hard to stay in the industry for a long time, whether it's because you're sick of travelling, or sick of being broke, or you're ready to settle down. While doing back-to-back winters is awesome, it can take a lot out

of you; you are always living out of a bag . . . you definitely can't have 15 pairs of shoes like city girls [laughing]. (pc, Erin, 2008)

To get your riding skills up to the level where you can pass the higher instructor qualifications, you need to do back-to-back seasons, but it's so expensive. You're always struggling with money, and travel, and finding a good place to work . . . It also takes a lot of confidence to take the higher level instructor exams, and I think some female instructors struggle with this, whereas the male instructors, well, don't [laughing]. [. . .] I also think that my success in the industry is partly due to the fact that I've never had a boyfriend that I wanted to stop what I was doing for. Snowboarding is my priority right now, not boys. But I've seen lots of very talented female instructors stop doing back-to-backs when they fall in love, whereas most of the boys I know don't. (pc, Kim, 2008)

Pamela also describes the financial and physical difficulties and personal sacrifices she made as a semi-professional athlete and snow-sport migrant during the 1990s:

'Living the lifestyle' meant a small bag, not many possessions, all funds funnelled into travelling to the next competition. I used to come home and think I could have had a street lined with cars, but I'd spent all that money on snowboarding, and I guess, my 'life education' . . . I was riding up to 200 days a year; I had chill-blains, constant aches and pains, and colds and flu that would last for months. My body never got to recover or get strong between seasons . . . Doing back-to-back winters also puts a lot of strains on your relationships. It's hard to maintain a long-term relationship when you are constantly on the move. (pc, February 2008)

Interestingly, while Erin, Kim, Lisa and Pamela focused on broader social pressures, and particularly traditional expectations of femininity (such as wanting lots of pairs of shoes, long-term relationships), Belinda and Rose offered a different perspective when asked why women appeared to be transitioning out of the transnational lifestyle earlier than their male counterparts.

During my interviews with Belinda and Rose, they argued that, once they 'got over' these social expectations and pressures from others and themselves, they found the industry to be highly conducive to women in positions of leadership. Rose recalls 'an important switch' in her thinking about the transnational career and lifestyle:

For the first 5–6 years of doing this, I was like 'oh yeah, it's great', and then I carried on doing it, and this is when I started feeling the pressure to get what people term a 'real job'. I looked at my friends from university, and they were all in serious jobs or getting married and having kids.

I started wondering if this is what I wanted. Then at about year 10 or 11, I don't know what changed, but I suddenly thought, 'you know what, I don't want it to be any different. I love my life and I just want to enjoy it. From that switch, I have just been looking forward and it seems so much easier since I made that decision.

Belinda acknowledged the importance of her skiing ability and past competitive successes in gaining the respect necessary to manage other instructors: 'I had a head start because of my skiing. I know that sounds really weird, but in this industry you need to have something like that. It's really hard to get that respect and credibility without it.' Clearly, symbolic capital earned via demonstrations of physical prowess and commitment is highly valued in the snow-sport instructional field. When asked whether she believes it is harder for a woman to stay in this industry, Belinda replied: 'No. We've got more women in more senior positions here [at the New Zealand ski resorts she works at] than anywhere else.' Rose makes similar observations at her workplace:

[M]ost ski-towns, there are many more males than females, but our resort is quite balanced. There is something interesting going on in the top jobs, all of these are held by women at the moment. We have three male supervisors (of instructors), but everyone at the management level is female.

Interestingly, Belinda acknowledged the importance of economic success for men's sense of masculinity, which she believes may have led to a feminization of leadership at the ski resorts for whom she works: 'I actually think it's probably harder for men [to stay in the industry for a long time] because there's so much pressure on them to have a job that earns proper money. For women, it's almost acceptable' to be working a seasonal job without a high-paying salary. With almost 20 years working in the snow-sport industry, Belinda and Rose have both developed an intricate understanding of the hierarchies and politics within ski resorts and have negotiated space for themselves (and supported other women's participation) within these international and highly transient workplaces.

The transnationality of ski resort staff makes for a stimulating and culturally diverse workplace that offers each of the participants rich experiences on a daily basis. As the manager of the snow-sport school at a New Zealand ski resort, Cesar manages between 120 and 160 staff, 'we have Argentinians, Americans, Canadians, Japanese, Koreans, and people from all over Europe – Italians, French, Swiss, German, English, Welsh – and obviously Kiwis and Aussies', adding 'one of the beauties of working in an international resort such as [name of resort], is that you do get to experience a lot of other different cultures and it's really interesting to see how they deal with certain situations'. Connections made within such transnational workplaces, and across the global ski sport industry, were also integral to the careers of the participants. 'It's all about connections,' explained Stuart, offering the following example:

> The ski shop I've worked at in Wanaka employed an American boot-fitter who was from a shop in Mammoth [in California] and he set me up with the contacts there to get a job ski tuning . . . it's basically who you know, and who you meet along the way.

Similarly, Gary described the unexpected value of 'emails and addresses of people that I met when there was the whole Japanese crew going on over here [in New Zealand during the early 2000s and at the ski resort where he worked]' for his latter travels to Japan, adding 'I'm still in touch with some of them via email and Facebook'.

John Urry's concept of 'network capital' has relevance here. According to Larsen and Urry (2008), 'network capital is the capacity to engender and sustain social relations with individuals who are not necessarily proximate, which generates emotional, financial and practical benefit' (p. 93). The concept stresses that such social relations 'are not products of – but only afforded by – mobility', and thus require 'access to communication technologies, transport, meeting places and the social and technical skills of networking' (p. 93). Even though many snow-sport migrants are living on near-minimum wages with most of their savings being reinvested back into the lifestyle (flights, accommodation, visas), they typically have a middle-class habitus embodied since childhood and, often supported with a good education, they appear to embody high levels of confidence interacting and establishing relationships with others in the snow-sport industry who tend to share their class background. While new electronic communications enable snow-sport migrants to maintain connections with international friends and employers, it is the co-present encounters, social relations and shared experiences with international colleagues, as well as their clients and employers from similarly privileged backgrounds, that are integral to the establishment of (sometimes) enduring networks that create and enable future opportunities. Stuart identifies the migrant's relationship with their international employer as integral to enabling future mobilities: 'you've got to have an employer that is prepared to get visas for you in the States or wherever else. That is what makes it happen . . . otherwise you wouldn't be able to do back-to-back winters.' Thus, the snow-sport migrant becomes reliant on their international employer's willingness and ability to support their visa applications. However, international employers must work within national rulings and regulations that make such working arrangements possible.

Negotiating borders and barriers: the case of the diminishing H2B visa

Many action sport enthusiasts appear to 'have the freedom, legally, culturally and economically, to move across borders and between cultures' at their will (Duncan, 2012, p. 116). It is important to keep in mind, however, that the transnational mobilities of action sport migrants are facilitated and constrained by various factors, including work and travel visas, travel and accommodation costs, employment opportunities and wages, languages, and exchange rates. In contrast to the availability of short-term work and travel visas to tertiary education students, a recent quota on the number of H2B visas (which permit internationals with the support of a US sponsor to work temporarily in the US) has significantly impacted the seasonal migration of *skilled* snow-sport industry employees. In light of government concerns about US unemployment, the law was amended in 2008 such that only 66,000 visas would be available to 'alien' workers per year. Visas were spread out over 12 months and excluded from the cap workers who had been employed in the US during the previous three years. Prior to this law, the ski industry accounted for approximately one third of all H2B visas issued each year (H2B Visa Information, 2009). Recognizing the detrimental effects of this quota on the US snow-sport industry, the National Ski Areas Association (NSAA) actively lobbied Congress to reconsider this law. In 2013, Democratic Senator Michael Bennet supported the Senate immigration bill that included a provision that would enable US ski resorts to hire more foreign instructors, arguing 'snow sports in this country have a $66 billion economic impact and generate half-a-million jobs. It is hard to grow your business when you want to have people, for example, to come from Brazil to ski in Vail if you don't have ski instructors who speak Portuguese' (cited in Chebium, 2013, para. 8). If the bill is signed into law it could reopen opportunities for careerist action sport migrants. In the meantime, however, thousands of committed Australasian, European, South American and South African skiers and snowboarders – many of whom have invested heavily in their 'careers' in the sport and industry (as, for example, instructors, snow groomers, rental technicians) and the establishment of long-standing relationships with host resorts in the US – have been forced to reconsider their travel, employment and lifestyle options. The limit on H2B visas has had a major impact on the lives of snow-sport migrants, including each of the six participants introduced in the previous section.

Between 2008 and 2013, there was some variation across US states such that some ski resorts were able to continue their H2B visa program, though on a much smaller scale. For example, Cesar has witnessed the H2B visa program at Aspen shrink from 400 to 30 since 2003. In their efforts to understand these changes and the options available to them, some snow-sport migrants have developed an in-depth understanding of the US legal system. For example, Rose explained:

> . . . the legislation that oversees the H2B visas is obviously federal, so that the immigration status is nationwide, but it has been put into action differently across the states. What's happening now is it's closing down

even further, so really there are no loops for any of the states to actually get through now.

While some resorts, such as Mammoth in California, worked with lawyers to prolong their visa program, such legal 'loopholes' are continuing to close. For example, in 2013 the Steamboat Ski and Resort (Colorado) website featured the following notice:

> Attention H2B applicants: Due to changes in the policies set forth by the US Department of Labor and the current economic conditions that have impacted our industry and companies across the US, we regret to inform you that we cannot pursue any H2B work visas for the upcoming winter season. It is our hope that in the future H2B visa regulations will accommodate our industry to allow multi-cultural employees to obtain this important work visa.

Although most US ski resorts have cancelled their H2B visa programs, many continue to actively pursue J-1 worker programs, hiring tertiary students from Australia, New Zealand and South America to work in cafes, on chairlifts, in hospitality, and in ski schools. For example, Winter Park in Colorado hired approximately 60 J-1 workers from Argentina and Peru for the 2012–13 season because, in the worlds of Vail Resorts Director of Hiring, Becca Borden, 'we think it enhances the *cultural flavour* of our resorts' (cited in Blevins, 2012, para. 12; emphasis added). Students on J-1 visas do not bring the same level of skill and experience to the ski resort as those travelling on H2B visas, but they are valued by US employers not only because they are willing to do the poorly paid, low-skilled jobs that many Americans are not interested in, but also because, as the 'exotic other' (Said, 1979), they 'enhance the cultural flavour' of the resorts. In contrast to many other forms of tourism in which travellers have to go to foreign places to consume the 'exotic other' (Aitchison, 2001), in the American ski industry, the 'exotic others' are brought to the mostly white, privileged ski resort patrons.

Debates about the impacts of the H2B visa changes have focused on the effect of these changes on the US ski industry. However, this new legislation also has major consequences for ski resorts and other snow-sport-related businesses in the southern hemisphere, particularly Australia and New Zealand. Conversations with ski resort managers both in New Zealand and the US revealed different understandings of the H2B debacle. During an interview with an American snow-sport school manager in Colorado, she revealed her disappointment in losing the 'exotic other', but very little empathy for how this change impacts the lives of non-American snow-sport migrants:

> We have always had a lot of certified instructors from New Zealand, Australia and Argentina here. But, ya know, I think we're going to have

trouble getting them back next year with the visa problem. I think it's been a treat to have them here, they really give our resort a bit of flair. Everyone expects to hear people speaking a different language with a different tone, it makes your ski resort more international, which is kinda cool. We enjoy it. But now we are just going to have to get our American instructors certified so they can step up and take those spots next year. (pc, Rhonda, 2009)

As an American citizen, Keith can still continue his back-to-back career working between the US and New Zealand, but he is upset to be losing so many of his non-American friends who are no longer able to sustain their transnational careers due to visa changes. Whereas Rhonda was already working with her colleagues to retool in response to the lack of H2B visas, Keith was more personally affected by the changes. In his own candid words, the visa change is 'totally fucking the industry. [. . .] It's going to be rough for me too. It's like not having my friends around anymore, as well as that I am trying to sort out a different visa for my girlfriend because she's British, so that's stressful as well'.

The H2B visa has impacted the US ski industry, but it did not limit the mobilities of American snow-sport workers. In contrast, New Zealand ski resorts expressed deep concern about losing some of their most experienced instructors from both New Zealand and an array of other countries. As Belinda observes:

We're starting to see a younger drop out of our instructors because there's no way for them to make enough money anymore. The season in the US helps fund your season in New Zealand, so it throws an already fragile balance into disarray. This is really sad for the industry . . . the American visa situation is probably one of the worst things to happen to our industry in a long time. It's really sad for us because we're going to lose so many of our most experienced instructors, and just be left with one-season instructors who don't have the same skill set.

Each of the interviewees described the devastating effects such changes were having on the broader snow-sport industry, as well as their own lives and their peers. 'There are people who have been working in the US every winter for 20 years, they have houses and apartments there, and they aren't going to be able to get in [to the US] anymore. It's tragic . . .' proclaimed Rose.

Changes in H2B visa regulations have redirected the mobilities of many action sport migrants. Cesar observed the following changes in the direction of flows of his international ski and snowboard instructor employees:

A lot of Europeans are going back to Europe because they don't have restrictions as far as being able to work in different places. Canada is picking up quite a few of the top end, which is really good to see. Japan is still kind of in a holding pattern to see what's going to happen with their economy, so instructors aren't rushing over there. But places like South Korea, which recently won the 2018 Olympic Games, and Sochi Russia are also starting to open up. So, there are still opportunities out there, but you just have to be a bit more creative and willing to work your way up through the ranks all over again.

While some snow-sport migrants are looking elsewhere for opportunities for their northern hemisphere winter, many others have ceased to pursue their international careers in the snow-sport industry, either searching for summer jobs in their home country to tide them over until the following winter, or giving it up entirely. Belinda predicted such changes, noting differences based on migrants' position in the field: 'people who are fairly new to the industry are trying to go to Canada, despite there only being so many jobs there', adding, 'but many others who are later in their careers won't be willing to work from the bottom up again, and so will probably stop.' Rose offered similar observations:

> I think we're going to lose a certain population of our instructors that have been going back and forth for five to 10 years, because there are not many options for them. And once they don't do a season overseas, it becomes very hard to do a season here [New Zealand] not only because you have to find another job that fits with the seasons, but because your season overseas finances your season here.

Cesar is among the many highly committed and skilled snow-sport migrants who decided not to pursue another season in the US, at least for the time being. In so doing, he demonstrates an in-depth understanding of the broader political and economic context in his decision to stay in New Zealand for his first summer in many years:

> I was offered support in pursuing a professional visa, an athlete-type visa but it's cost prohibitive, and also now with the way the US economy is going, and it's an election year so everyone is making promises, the whole immigration is in a state of flux combined with a really weak US dollar . . . it just doesn't make sense right now to try to force your way though.

As an Australian citizen, Cesar has the opportunity to stay in New Zealand. In contrast, as a British citizen Rose has fewer options available to her:

> If you're a Kiwi or an Aussie instructor and you have been going back and forth, then your option of course is to stay here [in New Zealand]. Now, as a UK person, I don't have residency in New Zealand and for me to stay it

would be pretty tricky. It really kicks up a lot of issues as far as what your options are because not everybody has options to stay where they are.

With few options available, Rose is pursuing an athlete visa based on her skills and expertise, but such visas are very expensive and not guaranteed.

Mobility is often associated with freedom and flows of people, products and ideas. However, as this example illustrates, it is also about power and government (Bærenholdt, 2013). As Favell (2007) explains, while 'some people have rights to physically move over the border . . . others do not', and an 'even smaller number have a right to migrate' (p. 272). Continuing, he notes that, 'some movements are counted as immigration, others illegal migration, still others asylum seeking, and so on', but the key point is that 'all these distinctions are more or less arbitrary and defined wholly by conventions imposed by the nation-states in question' (Favell, 2007, p. 272). Drawing upon Foucault's concept of governmentality and his 1978 lectures on security, territory and population, Bærenholdt (2013) describes societies as 'increasingly governed through mobility' (p. 20). He offers the concept of 'governmobility' to reveal 'how mobility is infused with power': 'Mobility may be governed, but it is first and foremost a way of governing, a political technology' (p. 20). Foucault's (2007) understanding of 'circulation' also helps us 'problematize [sic] the mobility/immobility dichotomy' (Salter, 2013, p. 7). According to Foucault (2007), we should understand circulation as not only a 'material network [of roads, rivers, and canals, etc] that allows the circulation of goods and possibly of men [sic]', but also 'the circulation itself, that is to say, the set of regulations, constraints, and limits, or the facilities and encouragements that will allow the circulation of men [sic] and things in the kingdom and possibly beyond its borders' (cited in Salter, 2013, pp. 10–11). Foucault's understanding of circulation in both 'its repressive and its productive guise', is informed by his rich analysis of power (Salter, 2013, p. 11). Contemporary governments control and policing of the flows of (some groups of) people are intimately connected to 'the facilitation and regulation of trade' and 'the protection of the free market' (Salter, 2013, p. 11). Thinking with Foucault's notion of 'circulation' offers a unique perspective on how the corporeal mobilities of contemporary youth and action sport migrants are being enabled, controlled and constrained via accessibility to visas, which are processes of policing and governmental management.

In an insightful investigation of the formal regulatory framework of overseas work and travel, Haverig (2011) illustrates the ways in which 'the freedom to go away for an OE [overseas experience – see Chapter 4] is constructed through bureaucratic practices and regulations that govern many young adults' travel and work opportunities elsewhere' (p. 108). Drawing upon the work of Rose (1996), she explains that 'the freedom to go away for an OE is not unlimited' but rather 'tied to conditions that systematically limit the capacities of so many to shape their own destinies' (p. 108). For both youth travelling on their OE, and highly skilled action sport migrants who have developed transnational careers working between the US and countries in the southern hemisphere, governments' decisions about visas 'form the horizon of what is achievable in terms of work and travel' (Haverig, 2011, p. 108). The 'fields of possibilities' for youth on their OE and skilled action sport migrants are currently being 'set up by different authorities' in both the home and host nations. Far from free, their mobilities are highly vulnerable as they are always inextricably linked to the changing conditions of global capitalism, as well as the continuing power of nation-states.

Transnational subjectivities: redefining place, self and identity

According to Ghosh & Wang (2003), the transnational process is essentially individualistic as one composes a sense of multiple or hybrid selves through 'an abstract awareness of one's self, diaspora and multiple belonging' (p. 278). Indeed, for many action sport travellers and migrants, international travel can offer new cultural experiences, which can prompt new understandings of self. In the second part of this chapter I illustrate how individual action sport participants' transnational experiences influence their understandings of self, belonging and 'home', including their sense of national, gender and cultural identity (McKay, 2005; Knowles, 1999; Wiles, 2008). I reveal how these phases of travel influence action sport enthusiasts' experiences of, and future decisions regarding, a less mobile lifestyle, education, relationships, employment, residency, and sport and leisure participation and consumption. I conclude this part by explaining how for some (though certainly not all) action sport travellers and migrants, crossing local, regional and national 'fields' with different cultural, social and gender values, norms and rules, leads to moments of dissonance and tension, and thus a 'more reflexive account of one's location and habitus' (Kenway & McLeod, 2004, p. 525; Bourdieu, 1992; Bourdieu & Wacquant, 1992). I conclude by explaining how, for some action sport participants, international travel and migration experiences can prompt reflexivity regarding particular aspects of their own habitus (such as privilege, national identity) and/or social inequalities within and across local, regional or national social fields.

Transnational lives and place attachment(s)

Transnational action sport migration may stimulate 'new subjectivities', or a kind of 'diasporic consciousness' marked by multiple (or partial) identifications. For example, after many years of travelling and working as a surf instructor, Chris – a British citizen – proclaims to embody a more global identity:

I think you take a bit of every culture you travel within. I've got lots of Aussie slang in my lingo now, which is rather amusing and confuses lots of people. At the moment, I'm currently sporting [wearing] a Thai bamboo tattoo, a kiwi jade pendant and anklets from all over the world. I'm a mish mash. (Cited in Levitz, 2013, para. 13)

Some action sport migrants may believe themselves to have become 'global citizens' as a result of their travels, yet this does not mean that they are 'set completely loose from their social moorings'; 'the tether may be loosened, redirected, and perhaps frayed but not lost into an imaginary "third space"' (Mahler, 1999, p. 712). As Jackson et al. (2004) argue, while borders and boundaries are, in some places and for some people, becoming 'increasingly porous', we 'must not let the often elite ideology of transnationalism blind us to the practical and emotional importance of attachments to and in place' (p. 7).

For many action sport migrants, 'place plays a pivotal role in constructing transnational identities' as their 'total attachment to a single place loosens, so dividing their attention and presence between two places or more' (Duncan, 2012, p. 116; Hannerz, 2002; Jackson et al., 2004). Rose describes feeling deep connections to the two places she divides her working year between:

I love being here in New Zealand . . . I love the culture. I've been coming here for 19 years . . . so the people that I work with now are a lot of people who I started with 19 years ago, so we've sort of all grown up together. And now I'm in a position where I have an input into that, so that's exciting. But I also love being in the States. Here [in Wanaka] it's a real community and I love that. But when I'm in the States, I get on a plane and I'll fly to Seattle for the weekend, or get in my car and drive to Vegas . . . The scale of things in the States is just so much bigger. I love the adventures I have in the States. I rarely go back to the UK these days. New Zealand and the US are my two homes now.

After spending many seasons working in Japan, New Zealand snow-sport migrant Belinda waxes lyrical: 'I attached myself to Japan. I absolutely love everything about Japan. It's so foreign. It's the most foreign country . . . it's like being on Mars sometimes, and I love that. The skiing is great. It's really grass roots but then ultra-modern at the same time.' Continuing, Belinda expressed her excitement about the possibility of taking her children to Japan for a skiing trip in the future and sharing this 'special place' with them.

For many action sport participants, their connections to places are less about the physical environment or the unique cultural experiences, and more about the relationships with people in these places. Cesar describes his relationships with fellow action sport migrants as integral to his attachment to a particular resort destination in the US:

You're either living with them or you'll see them every single day so your relationships are very full on. The northern hemisphere season encompasses New Years which is probably one of the biggest celebrated holidays of the year and we always have dinners together and it is like a little family group, a family unit that we create for ourselves. But also, you're removed from close family for a lot of the time, so personal struggles and things like that, you tend to rely on those people for support, for advice, for whatever it is you need at the time. These people are definitely a big part of why I keep going back, and I think why many of them continue to go back year after year as well.

Similarly, Gary described the importance of relationships for his attachments to places and his decisions to return:

You definitely end up developing makeshift families all around the world. I guess that's probably why I went to America for so long. I started dating an American girl and then I came home. Basically we did the long distance relationship thing for about four years. She came out here for a while with her family, I kept going back . . . and her family basically took me in like the son they never had. I definitely felt very at home, and without that I probably wouldn't have gone back as much as I did. After the wheels fell off that, that's when I went to Japan. But a couple of years later I went back to California because I wanted to see all of my really good friends there again. It was like coming home again, and that was really nice. People definitely make places.

For many action sport migrants the formation and metamorphoses of their transnational consciousness, sense of belonging, and national and cultural identities are intimately connected with conceptualizations of 'home'.

Reimagining 'home' and 'mobile forms of belonging'

Far from a fixed and bounded location, 'home' – as symbolic meaning, as social relationship, as developed rhythms, and as physical place – is a 'multi-layered, interactive and productive process' (Wiles, 2008, p. 123). For some scholars, transnational flows and mobilities further complicate understandings of 'home' (for example, Morley, 2000; Vertovec, 1999). For some action sport migrants, understandings of 'home' become much more complex as their lives become increasingly transnational. After many years following the winter between the hemispheres, Brazilian-born Australian ski instructor Cesar is often asked 'where home is', and his common response has been that 'home is where you spend most of your year': for him 'It's been Aspen for a long time. I've been there for eight years which is more than any other place of my adult life'. In contrast to Cesar, who did not mention either Brazil or Australia during our discussion of 'home', Gary proclaimed that 'New Zealand is always going to be home, no matter where I go or how long I'm gone for'. Similarly, Stuart explained:

My sister is always asking me where I consider home. She studied anthropology, so she is always saying things like 'Your sense of place, your sense of being'. I definitely consider New Zealand home, but I love working in the US and don't want to give this up. To be honest, when I am there, I feel really comfortable. It's very familiar now, and so I feel quite at home there too.

American snowboard instructor Keith also experiences a sense of 'home' both in the US and New Zealand. Keith was one of many participants who described the importance of relationships with fellow snow-sport migrants for creating a sense of home:

The crew that travels back and forth together, they sort of become your family, so your family travels. Even though you're away somewhere else it still feels fairly homely because your family, your working family, is there as well. We do Christmas and those types of typically family occasions together, so you don't often feel homesick or lonely.

Continuing, he adds: 'I've just bought a house in the States so I definitely feel like that's home, but my girlfriend has a house here [in Wanaka, New Zealand] so we've been living in that for quite a while. I feel just as much at home in her house as I do in my house.' Interestingly, for Rose it was the realization that 'home is wherever I am' that ultimately freed her from the many social expectations to 'settle down', thus enabling her to fully embrace the highly mobile lifestyle that she loves without feelings of hesitation or regret.

Mobility is popularly understood as 'the antithesis of belonging', yet many of the action sport migrants interviewed for this project appear to have developed 'mobile forms of belonging' (Fallov et al., 2013, p. 1). Here I draw upon Fallov and colleagues' (2013) understanding of belonging as having 'both temporal and spatial dimensions': it is a 'continuing and contextual process . . . that maps out between the dimensions of people, place and mobility, and which is conditioned by the sub-dimensions of time, resources and structures of meaning' (p. 4). According to Hummon (1992), one's sense of place can be influenced in complex ways, 'by the frequency of mobility, the conditions of mobility (voluntary and constrained moves), the timing of mobility in terms of life stages (e.g., retirement), and the patterns of mobility (e.g., homecoming)' (p. 276). As various scholars have illustrated, people's understandings of place, mobility and belonging 'change during different life stages and depend on the particular biography of individuals' (Fallov et al., 2013, p. 3; Hummon, 1992; Gustafson, 2001; Lewicka, 2011). Indeed, action sport migrants' mobilities are voluntary and typically pursued between their late teens and early thirties, during a life stage that often has fewer responsibilities and social expectations of permanence than later phases. Yet, as revealed in my interviews with retired action sport migrants, for many their sense of belonging and attachment to place(s) continues to change during different phases of their lives.

In contrast to popular understandings, mobility does 'not necessarily serve to threaten an attachment to place' (Adey, 2010, p. 73). For a route well travelled may, over time, 'turn into a meaningful place, just like the places or the nodes at either end of the route. Repetition is key' (p. 73). Of course, there are many ways of experiencing action sport travel and migration. The action snow-sport migrants interviewed for this project, however, had been pursuing their transnational careers between the hemispheres for many years. In so doing, they developed a familiarity with seasonal time-space patterns, and comfort in the knowledge that they are part of a transnational community of others who are sharing this highly mobile lifestyle. Many described developing a sense of belonging in the familiarity and ease of their well-practised transnational migration patterns, particularly later in their careers. For example, Rose acknowledged the difficulties of a transnational lifestyle, 'the expense, and the constant packing up and moving does affect some people', but explained that 'you get into a routine about it':

> . . . the people who have been doing it for a long time, it might sound funny, but it's honestly like getting on a bus. You organise your ticket, you know the routine, you know your flight, you know what you're doing, and you know what to do when you get off at the other end. There is something comforting about the routine.

Continuing, Rose describes the pleasure she gains from the familiarity of her transnational migration rhythms:

> Once you've been back to a resort for 2–3 years, then it's much easier. You know exactly what you're going back to, you sort yourself out for accommodation, you already have friends there, so you have a life there. I feel like now, when I literally get off the plane in the States, I open up my American wallet and it has my American driving license and my bank accounts, and I just start living my life in America. Same thing when I come back over here [New Zealand]. It's brilliant . . . I get off the plane and just start living my other life.

Similarly, Gary acknowledges the 'comfort' in familiar patterns of migration in contrast to the excitement of travelling to new destinations:

> Going somewhere for the first time, there is a lot of nervous energy, it's like 'oh what's going to happen?' It's a new happiness. And when you go back lots of times, it's good to rekindle those relationships and friendships that you have with people. There's some form of comfort returning to familiar places.

Arguably, for many experienced action sport migrants, their hyper-mobile lifestyles do not necessarily weaken their attachment to place. Rather, some develop intimate connections to various places and what Fallov and colleagues (2013) refer to as 'mobile forms of belonging' (p. 1).

Affective homecomings

For many action sport migrants, coming or going 'home' – either temporarily or permanently – can prompt them to 'renegotiate their entwined understandings of place and subjectivity' (McNay, 2005, p. 75; Knowles, 1999; Wiles, 2008). As the following comments from Lisa suggest, for some seasoned migrants the familiarity of cultural norms, values and relationships within the transnational snow-sport culture offers a symbolic and social 'home' while 'away' from their physical or spatial 'home':

> I've done 15 winters in a row, between here [New Zealand], Australia, the US and Canada . . . all of them instructing. I usually go *home* for a week between winters. My parents kind of know the deal now. I arrive, unpack my bags, sleep for a couple of days, do my washing, get organized, see all my family, eat some good food, pack my bags, and then head off again . . . back to my *other home* in the mountains with my snowboarding family. (pc, 2008, emphasis added)

'Returning' home from an action sport-related journey can also be a highly affective experience, as one New Zealand snowboarding migrant and journalist writes:

> There's nothing quite like returning to New Zealand after a winter overseas, and on the plane home emotions can be mixed. You might be dreading coming back after living it up in North America or Europe and having what can only be described as the 'best time of your life'. On the other hand you're probably looking forward to getting back to good food, friends and family. [. . .] You may be returning home battered and bruised, dosed up on codeine with a broken wrist, tweaked shoulder or torn ACL, and facing the daunting task of rehab before the next season. Whatever the case . . . you can't help but feel some kinda 'butterflies in the stomach' when you look down and see the Southern Alps, Mt Ruapehu or Mt Taranaki. (Westcot, 2006, p. 18)

A Polish kite-surf instructor, Zuza, describes a visit home as highly emotional and leading to new understandings of belonging and attachment:

> After the whole nine-month-long Greece–Egypt–Asia chapter, I was more than happy to visit Poland for a while – see old friends, spend some time with my family, finally take care of things that needed to be taken care of.

It was all great and I'm glad I did it. But the one thing that I did realise while sitting in my old room, is that the feeling of this place being mine, being my home base, being the place which I can mark as the starting X on the map . . . is gone. It's gone, and it's both extremely scary and very exciting, because it means that from now on there is no turning back, no safe haven where I can return if everything screws up. (Czaplinska, 2013)

For core Canadian snowboarder, Aaron, temporarily returning 'home' can be a 'frustrating' experience:

I've spent 12 years riding in Whistler and five winters living there full-time . . . I've also travelled throughout most of Canada and the United States, as well as several countries in Europe, Japan, India and South America for snowboarding. For so long I've lived in the mountains, and I've dedicated a huge part of my life to snowboarding. But when I go home at Christmas to visit my family, I'll often run into old friends or seldom-seen relatives and it's like we live on different planets . . . Sometimes I am so relieved to get back to Whistler where people understand snowboarding, and my friends get me. (pc, 2008)

Other action sport migrants describe the 'home' visit as prompting some reflection on lifestyle choices:

Coming back from a winter overseas and going home to [small New Zealand town] on my way down south was always a weird reality check . . . Many of my mates from home hadn't been overseas; in fact they had gone straight from school to work. They had nice houses, long-term girlfriends and wives, and some had kids. There was always a little part of me that would briefly wonder if I was doing the wrong thing. I always thought that it must be nice to have some money. I was living on a couch, borrowing blankets, eating Weetbix for lunch, cutting my own hair. But many of my old friends, particularly the ones who still lived in [name of home town] and were married with kids, were really interested in my snowboarding stories . . . I even felt there was some jealousy there too. (pc, Nathan, 2008)

For some action sport migrants, coming 'home' from a season overseas can evoke affective and cognitive responses, and questions regarding national identity, lifestyle and career decisions, and social relationships with family and friends.

Transnational action sport retirement and (im)mobility
In contrast to temporary homecomings in which action sport migrants are still 'moving', retiring from a transnational career in the action sport

industry and adopting a less mobile lifestyle can raise different practical and emotional issues. Whatever the cause of 'retirement' (injury, social pressures to 'grow up and get a real job', or adoption of more social responsibilities such as marriage, children and a mortgage) from the transnational lifestyle, re-emplacement can be an emotional experience. Indeed, some action sport migrants describe experiencing physiological and socio-psychological difficulties transitioning out of the hyper-mobile transnational action sport lifestyle and into a more permanent and/or structured existence. For example, Gary revealed his fears of adopting a less mobile lifestyle:

> I don't know what made me do it [stop following the winter between the hemispheres]. Maybe it was turning 40, I'm not sure. But it really freaked me out. I felt really scared. Scared of having to find a summer job, I didn't know what I was going to do. I ended up doing some building, a bit of painting, some houses. Then I started mountain biking, and it helped me get my fix.

Later in our conversation, he came back to the topic without any prompting, obviously wanting to add to his previous comments:

> But dealing with it, I definitely went through . . . not so much post-travel blues, but I guess it was some form of depression of not being able to travel. I don't know how to describe it, not nervous but a little bit unsettled. Just knowing that come 20 November, when you're normally packing your bags to head away . . . well, you're planting your veggies in the garden and that sort of thing. Everyone you have spent the winter with is packing their bags and heading away, and you are kinda getting left behind. But I'm cool with it now . . .
>
> This year and last year I have been seeing a psychologist about a bunch of stuff, just about travelling and all that sort of stuff. I came to the realization that I wasn't running away from anything, it was what I was searching for, so the whole thing has come together now and it makes a lot of sense to me personally, which I can totally accept.

Continuing, he describes eventually finding satisfaction upon buying a house and settling into a local lifestyle:

> I've definitely embraced [name of New Zealand town] because it's home for me now. I actually have a pretty good sense of belonging here. I never thought I'd be one for growing my own vegetables, landscaping, planting tussocks and mountain grasses. I don't know where it came from, but it's something that I have come to really enjoy.

Despite enjoying a less mobile lifestyle, he continues to live in a transnational action sport community and his relationships continue to be affected by the ongoing flows of tourists and migrants. With the winter season coming to an end, he was preparing for his Italian snowboarder girlfriend to leave: 'She rips [demonstrates prowess on her snowboard] and is a really strong woman, but she's only here for another couple of weeks, then she's back home.' Probing a little further, I asked 'will that be difficult?' to which he replied: 'Yeah, for sure. But I am definitely trying to entice her to come back so hopefully it all works out. It is what it is, that's the whole seasonal relationship thing . . . As they say, "a reason, a season, a lifetime".' As these comments suggest, this retired action sport migrant is very familiar with the rhythms of seasonal relationships.

Although not as emotional as the narrative above, other participants' accounts described similar struggles. For example, Phillipa explained:

> When I stopped snowboarding it was really hard, but it was less the snowboarding and more the people I missed the most. [. . .] Going back to university after snowboarding more than 200 days per year for seven years was incredibly difficult. I was always looking for a window to open. I couldn't handle being inside all day, everyday . . . I had horrendous headaches. (pc, February 2005)

Others, however, embrace their less mobile lifestyles. Upon returning to Poland after working in Egypt as a kite-surfing instructor, Zuza wrote on her blog:

> After a year of travelling, the time has come to finally say 'that's enough for a while'. It's amazing to see the places I've always been dreaming of, it's even more incredible to meet the amazing people I've stumbled upon on the way. But, for some unknown reasons to me, during the year that has just passed, the further I went the more I missed the one place that has always been right under my nose. Maybe I will never be a 'true' traveller. Maybe I will never really become the 'wanderer' that people started to call me . . .
>
> I used to say that 'I don't feel rooted in any place, I'm fine wherever I go', but I suppose the only way to discover it's not true was to go away for a long while. I do feel rooted. And my home is exactly where I am right now, on this little Polish campsite, in an old caravan shared with two other people, surrounded by sun, water, green trees and that particular loud beep noise the trains make when they stop at the station 100m away. (Czaplinska, 2013)

For Zuza and many other action sport enthusiasts, returning 'home' does not mean they give up their sporting participation or the action sport lifestyle. While older or injured migrants may no longer be able, or willing, to organize their whole lives around the 'transnational' action sport lifestyle, many continue to pursue action sport-related careers and enjoy regular participation within local, regional and national contexts. Many also plan international trips to visit new and familiar places for action sport participation with family and/or groups of friends.

Even when action sport migration patterns come to a close, those retired from the transnational lifestyle continue to possess network capital that enables them to sustain social relations across distances (Fallov et al., 2013). As Duncan (2012) observes, transnational peoples (migrants, backpackers, tourists) have been shown to 'construct an intricate, multi-webbed network of ongoing social relations that span their country of origin and their country (or countries) of settlement/visitation' (p. 116). For many action sport migrants, the transnational networks established during their travels continue to inform their connections with people across places even once they have settled into a more permanent lifestyle. Many of the participants in this study discussed the importance of email, Facebook and Skype for maintaining their relationships with friends and colleagues met overseas. Some regularly host their international friends, and others have travelled (or are making plans) to visit their peers living overseas. Many current and ex-action sport migrants also use various cultural artefacts (such as magazines, websites and films) to maintain – real, virtual and imaginary – connections with local and global action sport cultures. As Cohen (1996) explains, transnational identities 'no longer have to be cemented by migration or by exclusive territorial claims': 'in the age of cyberspace, a diaspora can, to some degree, be held together or re-created through the mind, through cultural artefacts and through a shared imagination' (p. 516, cited in Vertovec, 1999, p. 450; also see Chapter 3).

With many youth (particularly those from the world's wealthier societies) travelling for work and/or leisure and communicating across borders on a regular basis, some researchers are seeking to understand the longer-term consequences for mobility at the individual and population levels: What role do such moves play in the dynamics of 'life geographies' (Daniels & Nash, 2004, p. 450)? 'To what extent do they lead to transnational lives of some kind?' asks Frändberg (2013, p. 1). Even for those long retired from the transnational action sport lifestyle, memories and stories of places travelled and experiences shared with close friends often remain in heavy – verbal, virtual and cognitive – circulation (for example, 'I will spend much of the day at work dreaming of the snow and thinking back to the old days . . .'), and continue to influence their sense of identity and personal history for many years (see Robertson et al., 1994). According to Appadurai & Breckenridge (1989), diasporas always leave a trail of 'fractured memories' about 'another place and time' which can 'create new maps of desire and of attachment' (p. i). Moreover, when combined with an awareness of multi-locality, such memories can result in 'a refusal of fixity often serving as a valuable resource for resisting repressive local or global situations' (Vertovec, 1999, p. 451). For example, after more than a decade 'following winter from mountain to mountain around the world', Ste'en no-longer organizes his life around snowboarding, yet he believes

> snowboarding will always be part of who I am . . . The freedom of the lifestyle and individual expression in snowboarding is residual and it remains a defining feature in the way I live my life. I won't ever settle for the 9-to-5 lifestyle because I know there are other ways of doing it, if you can be creative and flexible. (pc, July 2008)

Despite adopting a more permanent lifestyle, he has reorganized his life around surfing and frequently travels overseas for surfing trips. Indeed, it is common for retired migrants to redirect their passion towards another action sport that is more accessible and sustainable within their local or regional communities.

As these enduring transnational emotional, social, virtual and imaginative connections suggest, for action sport migrants 'movement and attachment is not linear or sequential but capable of rotating back and forth and changing direction over time . . . and depending on context' (Levitt & Glick Schiller, 2004, p. 1011). In addition to personal transformations of national, gender and/or cultural identity, memory, and other modes of consciousness, for some participants collective meanings and perspectives of action sport migration results in a 'transnational imaginary' (Wilson & Dissanayake, 1996) that 'criss-crosses [sic] societal borders in new temporal-spatial patterns' (Urry, 2000a, p. 186). Indeed, many action sport migrants share similar experiences of transnational mobility (such as creative entrepreneurial and frugal practices, pressures to 'get a real job', time-space-seasonal rhythms) which produce a 'common consciousness' or an 'imaginary coherence' (Vertovec, 1999, p. 450), such that many committed action sport enthusiasts proclaim to belong to 'a planet-wide culture' that 'transcends borders and language barriers' (Sherowski, 2004, p. 106).

Narratives of adventure and transformation

Not dissimilar from the adventure tourists in Kane & Tucker's (2004) research, action sport migrants 'play with the reality of their experience through stories of freedom, identity and status' (p. 217). The act of telling travel stories within action sport cultures not only provides status to the teller, but also contributes to the production of a transnational imaginary across local action sport cultures. Action sport migrants frequently recount dramatic and exciting stories of their journeys abroad. These travel narratives take various forms, including verbal storytelling, written and photographic blogs, poems and short stories on action sport websites or in magazines, and home-made videos posted on YouTube and Facebook. Many of these travel stories refer to the geography of the location (terrain, weather conditions and so on) and psychological experiences of the individual or group (feelings of fear, anxiety, excitement, flow and the like), as well as socio-cultural dynamics (such as interactions and relationships with local residents or fellow travellers). Interestingly, many action sport migrants' narratives of transnational work, leisure and travel also reveal complex and fluid temporal-spatial patterns. For example, comments from snow-sport migrants included: 'one year turned into seven pretty fast', 'those winters seemed to blur', 'summer disappeared off my radar and life just became one long wonderful winter', 'I was so focused on the next storm that I stopped structuring my year in terms of weeks and months . . . the weather maps were much more important than the calendar' (field notes and pcs, 2008). As transnational action sport migrants become embedded in the global processes and flows of the action sport culture and/or industry, many experience similar 'time-space rhythms' (Burawoy, 2000, p. 4). Action sport migrants often become highly attuned to weather and seasonal patterns, such that they narrate their journeys in terms of winters, summers, storms and the total number of 'on snow' or 'on the water' days per season or year. As previously mentioned, the number of 'back-to-back' or consecutive winters or summers, and the places travelled for their sports, are important symbols of cultural commitment, and thus a regular topic of conversation among core action sport participants.

Not dissimilarly to other young budget travellers, many action sport migrants appear to have developed 'specific, well-stylized forms of narrating their travel experiences' (Noy, 2004, p. 79). In recounting their travel narratives, many action sport tourists and migrants gloss over less-than-savoury aspects of their journeys, such as homesickness, experiencing injuries without adequate insurance, poor living conditions, low pay rates, or tensions between colleagues, housemates or local residents, and zealously endorse popular discourses of travel that emphasize its facilitation of self growth, identity transformation and personal empowerment. This is perhaps not surprising given the lengthy tradition in popular literature and everyday discourse that characterizes travel as providing opportunities to 'search for self'. Tourism scholarship reflects similar sentiments (Cohen, 2010). Various scholars have found self-actualization to be a common travel motive (Cohen, 1996), with many backpackers travelling to 'find themselves' (Richards & King, 2003), and journeys seen as providing 'the opportunity to acquire experiences that become the basis for discovering and transforming one's self' (Neumann, 1992, cited in Cohen, 2010, p. 117). Although the importance of self to tourism studies has long been theorized, 'self' is, of course, a highly contested concept within the social sciences. Adopting a postmodern understanding of selves as 'relational, fluid and performed' (Cohen, 2010, p. 122), I am cautious of scholarship and cultural narratives that reproduce 'essentializing concepts such as self-actualization, self-realization, self-fulfilment, discovering one's self' (Cohen, 2010, p. 118). The majority of the participants in this study, however, appear to have internalized more Romantic understandings of travel as leading to positive self-transformation and the finding of one's 'true' self.

Many action sport tourists and migrants believe that travel can lead to better understandings of self and personal development (Noy, 2004). Action sport travellers often narrate journeys of self-growth and personal transformation. For example, reflecting upon his previous action sport migration experiences, one New Zealand snowboarder proclaims:

> Looking back, the years when I was immersed in snowboarding had a huge impact on me. I think I gained a lot of confidence out of my experiences, and self-belief. There is something about moving to a ski-town without a job or a place to live. If you can sort all that out, survive and have a great time, then you can do anything. It puts a lot of stuff in perspective. It made me think 'if I can do this, what else can I do?' It changed the future I saw for myself. (pc, June 2008)

Many other participants also waxed lyrical about the opportunities for personal growth offered through their travel experiences – for example, Gary:

> For me, looking back now, it was a personal journey more than a physical journey around the world. There's something about travelling that makes you realize more about yourself than you probably would have if you stayed home. Just travelling in a foreign country where you don't speak the language and no one knows you. You're at the airport and you don't know where you're going, or at the train station and it's all a foreign language. And this was all before iPhones and stuff that makes all of this so much easier now. I didn't even have a Lonely Planet. You've got no one to rely on but yourself, so it's like 'right, gotta sort this out otherwise I'm going to be here for weeks'. It's all about personal growth. Sometimes what you learn can be really surprising. You learn things about yourself that you wouldn't expect.

As these comments suggest, action sport migrants have internalized dominant discourses about the potential of travel for self-discovery and personal growth. While I am critical of suggestions that travel helps one find their 'true' self, action sport tourism and migration do 'afford increased contact with an array of cultural praxes and ways of life that can challenge notions of self' (Cohen, 2010, p. 118) and facilitate the development of new skills and competences.

Action sport migration and transnational competence

Many of the long-time action sport migrants I spoke with described their mobile lifestyles as leading to a sense of global citizenship and a unique set of attributes and competences. For example, Belinda believes her experiences of travelling and working abroad have helped her become 'more open-minded':

> Sometimes when talking to people, even my mom, I realise that I've had so many more life experiences . . . I feel like I've grown up and learnt how to really look after myself and deal with different cultures, and deal with things out of the ordinary. I'm really proud of who I've become because I feel like I can handle a lot and cope with lots of different things. I know how to go up to a Japanese person and have a conversation and respect their culture, understand where they've come from. I can talk to people and know what it's like for them. I think travel does that to people. It makes you really open-minded. [. . .] You can see that a lot in the ski community too because everyone travels so much.

The attributes of 'openness toward difference and otherness' referred to by Belinda (and many other action sport migrants) are often associated with 'cosmopolitanism' (Vertovec & Cohen, 2003). Interest in cosmopolitanism has grown considerably over the past two decades, with an array of scholars suggesting that processes of globalization are contributing to a 'new kind of tolerance based on pluralism, dialogue and a recognition of difference' (Savage et al. 2005, p. 181; also see Beck, 2002; Hannerz, 1996; Turner, 2002; Vertovec & Cohen, 2003). For the purposes of this chapter, however, it is important to note that the presence of a 'cosmopolitan outlook' is 'conceptually distinct from the transnational experience' (Roudometof, 2005, p. 121). Indeed, with global flows of media, products and other people, one does not need (as Belinda implies) to travel internationally to be exposed to other cultures on a regular basis. Similarly, experiences of international travel and migration do not necessarily promise a cosmopolitan orientation, and 'a willingness to engage with the other' (Hannerz, 1996, p. 103).

According to Vertovec (2009), attributes of 'openness toward difference and otherness' is just one of the features of 'cosmopolitan competence' that may develop through transnational lives. Of course, such competences depend on individuals and their willingness and/or ability to open themselves to new experiences, and to appreciate and respect other ways of living. Engaging with Bourdieu's conceptual schema, Guarnizo (1997) suggests that we may think of a transnational habitus as arising from experiences of migration and the practices and relationships across borders. He describes transnational habitus as entailing

> a particular set of dualistic dispositions that inclines migrants to act and react to specific situations in a matter that can be, but is not always, calculated . . . The transnational habitus incorporates the social position of the migrant and the context in which transmigration occurs. (1997, p. 311)

Such an approach may help explain the similarity in the transnational habitus of action sport migrants, many of who grew up in different countries but share similar social groupings (of, for example, class and generation) and rhythms of migration. Vertovec (2009) sees much value in conceptualizing transnational experience through the idea of habitus, arguing that the notion 'shines light upon the ways in which transnational life experience may give rise not only to dual orientations but also to a personal repertoire comprising varied values and potential action-sets from diverse cultural configurations' (p. 69). Continuing, he describes the kinds of attributes that might entail from a transnational habitus, including, but not limited to, the rise of 'cosmopolitan competence' (p. 25). Drawing upon the work of Koehn and Rosenau (2002), he lists an array of other skills and attributes that can be acquired through transnational experiences, including:

1. *Analytic competence*, that is, understanding of the central beliefs, values, practices, and paradoxes of country and/or culture of residence, and ability to make connections and comparisons between current conditions and one's past circumstances and vica versa;
2. *Emotional competence*, which includes motivation and ability to open oneself up to divergent cultural influences and experiences, maintain respect for different values, traditions, experiences and challenges, and the ability to manage multiple identities within and across different spaces;
3. *Creative/imaginative competence*, including the ability to tap into diverse cultural sources for inspiration, and/or collaborate with others to articulate novel and shared transnational synthesis; and
4. *Behavioural competence*, which includes the ability to communicate with others using verbal and/or nonverbal cues and codes, relate to counterparts and to develop and maintain positive interpersonal relationships, and to overcome problems/conflicts and accomplish goals when dealing with transnational challenges and globalization/localization pressures. (adapted from Vertovec, 2009, p. 71)

As Vertovec (2009) is careful to note, not all of these attributes are developed or utilized at once, with some actors possessing 'components of the several skills in varying degrees and in different mixes' (Koehn & Rosenau, 2002, p. 114). It was not the purpose of this project to assess the skills and competences developed by action sport migrants, yet many participants spoke passionately about the 'life skills' they believe had been acquired through their transnational experiences. My conversations with, and sustained observations of, an array of long-time action sport migrants confirm that many do appear to develop at least some of the attributes listed above, which some go on to apply to their subsequent careers with much success.

Vertovec (2009) does not explicitly refer to the development of reflexivity in his list of transnational competences. However, in their examination of cosmopolitanism among English migrants, Savage and colleagues (2005) reveal that *some* of their participants (13 per cent) exhibited 'developed forms of global reflexivity', that is 'an ability to look at their lives, thoughts and values from a perspective that did not take English referents as the implicit frame of reference, but which was able to place them in some kind of broader global comparative framework' (p. 191). My research also reveals that, for some action sport migrants, their transnational careers can prompt greater cultural understanding and, in some cases, lead to greater personal and social reflexivity, which, in some cases, contributes to transnational competences utilized both during and following their corporeal mobilities.

Field-crossing and the potential for reflexivity

As various tourism scholars have illustrated, holiday escapism 'may well tempt ignorance of unethical practices' (Gibson, 2012, p. 60). Some travellers are oblivious to local, regional and national differences, and others are aware of differences but are more concerned about their personal and group pleasure-seeking experiences and overlook unique cultural praxes within and across fields. The following comments from the autobiography of professional US snowboarder Todd Richards (2003) offer just one of many examples of action sport travellers disrespecting local peoples and cultures:

> Japanese skiers and snowboarders made their way down [the slopes of a ski resort in Hokkaido, Japan] in an orderly fashion, staying inside the ropes like cattle. [. . .] The visiting snowboarders, on the other hand, ducked under (or aired over) the ropes and rode the amazing powder between the runs. It was paradise. The ski patrol tried to stand between us and the closed powder fields. They'd blow whistles, wave their arms, and point at the rope saying, 'No!' We'd just dodge them, yelling, 'I'm American!' (p. 142)

An older, and somewhat more reflective, Richards (2003) concludes adding: 'We were blatant assholes, and I feel bad about it now, but that's how we were. It was mob mentality. One person did it, and everybody followed. These days, I have a greater respect for the Japanese people and their culture; if I have to break the rules, I do it very discreetly' (p. 142). But Gibson (2012) prompts us to consider whether travel might also have the potential to encourage greater awareness and alternative practices:

> What moral gateways are opened (or closed) by the 'embodied knowledge deriving from travelling, witnessing, climbing, walking, touching and being touched' (Waitt et al., 2007, p. 248) – given the possibility to interrupt dominance is ever-present?

In the remainder of this chapter I build upon Gibson's (2012) questions about the potential of encounters with 'other places, landscapes and peoples possessing varying geographical resources and spatial literacies' (p. 59) to reveal action sport travel and migration as 'full of contradictory possibilities and potentials' (Watson & Kopachevsky, 1994, p. 660). In so doing, I engage and extend the latter work of French sociologist Pierre Bourdieu.

Many have critiqued Bourdieu's work for invoking determinism. There appears to be little potential for personal or social change within his conceptual schema. Yet some of Bourdieu's texts provide more space for agency and reflexivity than others. In particular, in some of his later work, especially *The State Nobility* (1998), Bourdieu suggests that moments of disalignment and tension between habitus and field may give rise to increased reflexive awareness. For Bourdieu, habitus typically operates at an unconscious level unless individuals with a well-developed habitus find themselves moving across new, unfamiliar fields. It is in such moments that an individual's habitus may become 'divided against itself, in constant negotiation with itself and its ambivalences' resulting in 'a kind a duplication, to a double perception of the self' (Bourdieu, 1999, cited in Reay, 2004, p. 436). This becomes what Bourdieu (2003) has termed a *habitus clivé*, or a 'split habitus' (cited in Krais, 2006, p. 130). For Bourdieu, reflexive awareness arises from the 'negotiation of discrepancies by individuals in their movement within and across fields of social action' (McNay, 1999, p. 110; see also Powell, 2008). Bourdieu was careful to emphasize, however, that despite a proliferation of fields and an increasingly mobile population, such disjunctions between habitus and field are not common occurrences. Chambers (2005) notes that 'most people tend to remain within compatible fields most of the time', and thus there is usually a fit between field and habitus (p. 340). In such circumstances, the habitus tends to be reinforced rather than challenged. Therefore, Bourdieu shows how reflexivity is not an inherently universal capacity of subjects; rather, it is a 'piecemeal, discontinuous affair' (McNay, 1999, p. 110), uneven in its application, emerging only with its experience of dissonance. In the following discussion I draw upon Bourdieu's understanding of the 'destabilizing and potentially subversive effects that might arise from movement across fields' (McNay, 1999, p. 107) to consider how action sport travel and migration prompts heightened reflexivity among some travellers.

For action sport migrants, crossing local, regional and national 'fields' with different cultural, social and gender values, norms and rules has the potential to lead to moments of dissonance and tension, and thus a 'more reflexive account of one's location and habitus' (Kenway & McLeod, 2004, p. 525; Bourdieu, 1992; Bourdieu & Wacquant, 1992). International travel and interactions with locals and action sport enthusiasts from different nationalities prompts some participants to reflect upon various aspects of their own habitus, including national identity, social privilege, and gender and race relations within their host and home countries. For Gary, working

and travelling overseas prompted him to reflect upon his national identity and his understandings of New Zealand as 'home'. He also describes
using his travel experiences as an opportunity to educate others about New
Zealand:

> A lot of people in America didn't know where New Zealand was. They
> thought it was in Norway or Finland or somewhere. But I always used
> to rock [wear proudly] a New Zealand sticker on my helmet and on my
> boards and stuff. So I always had a bit of national pride while I was away.
> Sometimes it's not until you step away that you realize what is so special
> about New Zealand and that you are actually proud to be a Kiwi.

Committed New Zealand snowboarder and surfer, Mel, attributes her
action sport travel experiences with helping her reflect upon her privileged
upbringing and position in society:

> [Snowboarding] helped me push myself to places there's no way I would've
> gone otherwise, and I'm not just talking about cliff drops, rails and
> booters [terrain features upon which snowboarding manoeuvres are
> performed]. I'm talking about people, places and major attitude adjust-
> ments. I grew up on the Northshore, sheltered as, basically, a snob. But
> through the places snowboarding's taken me, here and overseas, the
> people I've met, it's made me a much more open and accepting person.
> It made me think differently about where I've come from and how I came
> to be the person I am today. (pc, February 2005)

During her transnational snowboarding experiences, Pamela witnessed a
'really strong Japan–Canada–New Zealand triangle', which prompted her to
reflect upon national and cultural differences in group dynamics and social
support, and gender expectations and opportunities:

> I spent a lot of time hiking the half-pipe at Cardrona [New Zealand ski
> resort] when it was just me – a little white-European girl – and the rest
> were Japanese. I really noticed how positive and supportive they were
> of each other. If one of them falls they would just say good stuff. I used
> to think how different this was to western culture, where we seem to be
> pretty good at tearing each other down. Trying new things is much more
> difficult if you think people are going to laugh [at] and criticize you.
>   I always loved talking to the Japanese snowboarding girls hiking the
> pipe. At that time, it was a huge thing for them to be travelling alone
> and to 'be snowboarders'. A lot of them were a bit older too. It was so less
> expected for Japanese girls to travel than Kiwi girls, which kind of showed
> a lot more spirit for them to pursue the snowboarding lifestyle around
> the world. (pc, September 2005)

During his second season working at a ski resort in America, core New Zealand snowboarder and skateboarder Adam became aware of class and ethnic inequalities in his workplace that encouraged him to question race relations in his home country:

> Working in the Food and Beverages department [. . .] gave me an interest-ing insight into all the stuff that goes on 'behind the scenes' of ski resorts. It was pretty much me and all the Mexican guys, which was awesome. They weren't there for the same reasons as me, you know, the free season pass and to snowboard as much as possible, but we had lots of fun work-ing together. Those guys really get treated like crap though . . . they get all the worst jobs and get paid the least. [. . .] When I went home I saw similar things happening for Maori people in our country, which I hadn't really noticed before. (pc, 2006)

As these comments illustrate, action sport migration can 'involve exposure to an array of cultural praxes as individuals encounter the Other' (Cohen, 2010, p. 122) in various work and leisure contexts, which prompts some to critically reflect upon some of their own assumptions and embodied ways of knowing the world.

For a few action sport participants, reflexivity regarding particular aspects of their habitus embodied from a young age (for example, privilege) and/ or social inequalities within local, regional or national social fields, gained via their international travel and migration experiences, can prompt empa-thetic, altruistic and/or political responses. For example, later in her career Pamela organized inclusive, supportive, inter-cultural snowboard camps and clinics in New Zealand and Canada; upon returning to New Zealand, Adam enrolled in a Te Reo Māori language course in an effort to enhance his cul-tural sensitivity and understanding. As will be illustrated in Chapter 9, some travelling action sport enthusiasts are so deeply moved by the injustices and inequalities observed or experienced across fields that they become inspired to develop non-profit organizations in their attempts to create change in local contexts.

Conclusion

In sum, this chapter has examined the lived transnationalism of action sport migrants, focusing particularly on how practices of migration influence understandings of self, identity and 'translocal subjectivities' (Conradson & McKay, 2007). I also revealed how the transnational life-style of action sport migrants impacts their attachment to place, particu-larly 'home', with some experiencing a sense of belonging in movement and familiarity with the rhythms and routines of seasonal migration. In the latter parts of this chapter, I drew upon the work of Pierre Bourdieu to suggest that action sport travel is a form of field crossing that can prompt some travellers to critically reflect upon aspects of their habitus and/or inequalities within and across local fields. Yet, it is important to keep in mind that such opportunities for voluntary field-crossing are only available to a select few privileged action sport enthusiasts. Thus, in the third and final part of this book I examine the experiences of less-privileged youth who engage in action sports as a response to immobilities caused by earthquakes and war.

Part III
Action Sport (Im)mobilities in Disrupted and Conflicted Spaces

7
Action Sports and Natural Disaster Immobilities: Arrhythmic Experiences in Christchurch, New Zealand

At 12.51pm on February 22, 2011, a violent 6.3 magnitude earthquake struck the city of Christchurch – New Zealand's second most populous city, and the largest city in the South Island. Centered two kilometres (1.2 miles) west of the town of Lyttleton and ten kilometres (6 miles) south east of the centre of Christchurch, the earthquake followed nearly six months after a 7.1 magnitude earthquake that caused significant damage across the Canterbury region, but no direct fatalities. Striking closer to the city centre at midday, the February 2011 earthquake killed 185 people and injured another 2164. Although lower on the moment magnitude scale (MMS, now used to measure the size of earthquakes in terms of energy released instead of the Richter scale) than the September 2010 earthquake, the intensity and violence of the ground shaking during the February 2011 quake was measured on the Modified Mercalli Scale (used to measure the intensity and effects of an earthquake rather than just energy released) to be MM IX – among the strongest ever recorded globally in an urban area (Davidson, 2011). The earthquake flattened the downtown district, and damaged or destroyed over 180,000 homes. The earthquakes severely damaged 80 per cent of the water and sewerage systems, with repairs continuing for many months. Moreover, extensive liquefaction (the conversion of soil into a fluid-like mass during an earthquake or other seismic event) caused ongoing ground movement leading to the undermining of many more foundations and the destruction of further infrastructure. For weeks following the September 2010 and February 2011 earthquakes, communities rallied together to remove over 535,000 tons of silt from roads, footpaths, houses and parks. However, with the rebuild estimated to cost the nation NZ$15 billion, the event is New Zealand's costliest disaster. Global insurance research also estimated the event to be the third most expensive insured natural disaster worldwide after the March 2011 Tohoku earthquakes and the floods in Thailand the same year (Booker & Greig, 2012). Between September 2010 and February 2011, the region experienced 10,000 earthquakes and associated aftershocks, which further exacerbated the high levels of post-traumatic stress being reported across the city. Statistics New Zealand recently revealed that more than 13,500 people have migrated from Christchurch since the earthquake, with predictions suggesting slow population growth over the next decade (Christchurch population, 2012).

In this chapter I draw upon interviews with 14 residents who were living in Christchurch before, during and after the 2010–11 earthquakes to explain how the February event (and ongoing earthquakes in the region) affected the everyday sporting mobilities and lifestyles of residents (see Thorpe, 2013a).[1] Recognizing theoretical limitations in disaster studies scholarship, however, I engage French sociologist and philosopher Henri Lefebvre's spatial theory to explain how some residents came to know, construct, negotiate and understand Christchurch as a post-disaster space through their sporting practices. More specifically, I draw upon Lefebvre's notion of 'rhythmanalysis', and particularly the concept of 'arrhythmia', to describe how some committed action sport participants adopted highly creative practices to continue their participation in sports such as surfing, skateboarding, mountain biking and climbing. In so doing, the familiar rhythms of sporting bodies and lifestyles helped some cope with the many stresses of daily life and contribute to the rebuilding of personal and collective identities, and a sense of belonging in a new Christchurch.

When the earth moves: rethinking the mobilities turn

Concerned to understand both the 'large-scale movements of people, objects, capital and information across the world' and 'local processes of daily transformation, movement through public space' (Hannan et al., 2006, p. 1), some mobilities scholars are examining the (im)mobilities and migration patterns of those directly and indirectly affected by natural disasters. For example, *Mobilities* journal featured a special section on the disruptions to air travel triggered by Iceland's Eyjafjallajökull's eruptions in April and May 2010 (see Birtchnell & Büscher, 2011). Others have illustrated how catastrophes such as hurricanes, tsunamis and floods also 'engender their own unique mobilities as people seek to flee the onset of an impending disaster' (Hannan et al., 2006, p. 8). As various scholars have revealed, the mobilities within, and migration from, disaster areas can be deeply embodied and affective experiences for individuals' and communities (Hannan et al., 2006, p. 8; Cresswell, 2008; Grieco & Hine, 2008; Litman, 2006). In *Hurricane Katrina and the Redefinition of Landscape*, for example, Miller & Rivera (2008) vividly illustrate how the destruction of the physical landscape altered community residents' 'sense of place' and thus, personal and collective identities.

Typically adopting interdisciplinary approaches and asking different sets of questions to those working in disaster studies and environmental sociology, scholars working within the mobilities paradigm offer a fresh approach to understanding the politics of disaster-related mobilities and migration practices, and the changing definitions of space and place. Most of these studies have, however, focused on the macro-mobilities of poor or marginalized citizens, and/or the migration of residents away from, and sometimes back to, their homes and communities following major disasters. Less consideration has been given to the effects of natural disasters on the *everyday* micro-mobilities of those who choose (or are forced) to continue living in cities and towns damaged by natural disaster. Even less attention has been given to the movement and mobilities of the natural and built environment in natural disaster spaces.

Mobilities scholars have tended to focus predominantly on the movement of people, objects and ideas within and across places that are presumed 'relatively fixed' (Hannan et al. 2006, p. 13). Only recently have some come to recognize places as dynamic, with their own unique mobilities (for example, Kabachnik, 2012). 'Places of movement' (Hetherington, 1997) themselves can be seen as 'becoming or travelling, slowly or quickly' (Hannan et al., 2006, p. 13). The subtle, and sometimes violent, movements of the earth's crust, however, have yet to gain critical scholarly attention within the mobilities paradigm: how do earthquakes affect the 'spatial, infrastructural and institutional moorings' (Hannan et al, 2006, p. 3) that (re)configure and (dis)enable everyday mobilities? In the following section I briefly outline the theoretical and methodological approach employed in this chapter to examine how the vigorous and unpredictable movements of the earth's crust affected residents sporting (im)mobilities and rhythms of everyday life.

Rhythmanalysis and mobile methods

Seeking to understand movements within and across spaces and places, scholars in the social sciences and humanities are increasingly drawing upon the work of French sociologist and philosopher Henri Lefebvre. In particular, geographers have engaged his urban theory and ideas about spatial justice presented in *The Right to the City* (1968/1996), *The Production of Space* (1974/1991), and his three volume *Critique of Everyday Life* (1947/2008, 1961/2002, 1981/2005), to examine the power and politics involved in the production and use of contemporary urban geographies. In the field of sport sociology, Michael Friedman & David Andrews (2011) and Cathy van Ingen (2003, 2004) have advocated the value of Lefebvre's spatial theory for examining the connections between social space, power, identity, and the body in sport and physical culture. Applying Lefebvrean spatial theory to the leisure practices of running groups, van Ingen (2003) claims his work offers valuable theoretical tools to 'explore the production of space, place the body at the centre of inquiry and explore the ways in which socially constructed differences are materialized in social space' (p. 207). Others have applied a Lefebvrean approach to examine the production of sporting spaces, such as

Washington Nationals Park (Friedman, 2008) and the spatial experiences of skateboarders (Borden, 2003), parkour practitioners (Atkinson, 2009; Kidder, 2012) and bike messengers (Kidder, 2009, 2011). Following Friedman & van Ingen (2011), I see much value in Lefebvre's spatial theory for building upon the foundational work of sports geographers (for example, Bale, 1996, 2003), and further examining the connections between social space, power, identity and the body in sport and physical culture. In this chapter, however, I draw inspiration from Lefebvre's (1992/2004) lesser-known investigation of the distinct rhythms permeating everyday life.

Published posthumously in France in 1992, *Rhythmanalysis: Space, Time and Everyday Life* is a collection of essays about the temporal and cyclical rhythms of social life and nature. It begins with a seemingly straightforward question: 'what is rhythm? What do we understand by it, be it in everyday life, or in the established sectors of knowledge and creation?' (Lefebvre, 1992/2004, p. 3). As with many of my favourite French theorists, Lefebvre refused to give a clear definition, instead starting with the premise that 'everywhere where there is interaction between a place, a time, and an expenditure of energy, there is rhythm' (p. 26). Broadly conceived as 'repetition of movements and action' (Edensor, 2012, p. 3), Lefebvre's analysis of rhythms ranges from biological and internal bodily processes, to the flows within an urban metropolis, to the ocean tides. In his own words,

> Everyday life remains shot through and traversed by great cosmic and vital rhythms: day and night, the months and the seasons, and still more precisely biological rhythms. In the everyday, this results in the perpetual interaction of these rhythms with repetitive processes linked to . . . time. (Lefebvre, 1992/2004, p. 73)

Focusing on the intersection of time and space in rhythm, it is here, in his final work, that Lefebvre's lifelong interest in time is most apparent:

> Concrete times have rhythms, or rather are rhythms – and all rhythms imply the relation of a time to a space, a localised time, or, if one prefers, a temporalised space. Rhythm is always linked to such and such a place, to its place, be that the heart, the fluttering of the eyelids, the movement of a street or the tempo of a waltz. (Lefebvre, 1992/2004, p. 89)

Insisting on the importance of 'thinking space and time together', *Rhythmanalysis* makes clear that Lefebvre was indeed a theorist of time as much of space (Horton, 2005, p. 157).

For Lefebvre, the relationships between time and place can be 'depicted, performed and sensed through its ensemble of normative and counter rhythms' (Edensor, 2010a, p. 4). Places are far from static in Lefebvre's work (Mels, 2004). Although he conceives of places as 'always in a process of becoming, seething with emergent properties', Lefebvre recognizes they are 'usually stabilized' by rhythms of varying qualities 'steady, intermittent, volatile or surging' (Edensor, 2010a, p. 3). For Lefebvre (2004), 'rhythms imply repetition' (p. 90) that lead to various forms of 'eurhythmia, arrhythmia, and polyrhythmia' (p. 26). Again avoiding clear definitions, Lefebvre refers to polyrhythmia as being the composition of diverse and multiple rhythms, eurhythmia as the 'harmony of rhythms' (20), and arrhythmia as 'the discordance of rhythms' (p. 16).

According to Lefebvre (1992/2004), 'rhythm enters into the lived; though that does not mean it enters into the known' (p. 77). Everyday habits, schedules and routines become 'sedimented' in our bodies through 'familiar bodily routines in local space' (Edensor, 2010a, p. 8). The repetitive rhythms of everyday life become 'part of the way things are', which can lend to an 'ontological predictability and security' (p. 8). For Lefebvre (1992/2004), we are 'only conscious of most of our rhythms when we begin to suffer from some irregularity' (p. 77). He uses the term arrhythmia to describe disruptions of everyday rhythms and routines, which can in some cases lead to discomfort, distress and suffering. In their attempts to minimize the discomfort caused by such arrhythmic disruptions, many people attempt to restore familiar spaces, routines and timings (Edensor, 2010a). But, as Lefebvre (1991/2004) suggests, such arrhythmic experiences can, in some cases, lead to heightened awareness and reflexivity of previously unquestioned dimensions of social space, the body and everyday life. Put simply, 'rhythms become clearer with their breakdown, the onset of arrhythmia' (Horton, 2005, p. 158). Lefebvre's notion of arrhythmia has interesting parallels with other key social theorists such as Karl Marx, who theorized different crises as potential transitions from one mode of production to another, and Pierre Bourdieu's discussion of field-crossing, which he believed could provoke tensions, and in some cases heightened reflexivity, when moving across social fields with different social rules and norms (see Chapter 6).

At just 100 pages, *Rhythmanalysis* is a brief yet wide-reaching project. Some are cautious of adopting Lefebvre's underdeveloped theory of rhythms, while others increasingly recognize the virtue in the open-ended and multifarious nature of this work. A strong voice among the latter, Edensor (2012) argues that, 'while a generalized science of the study of rhythms has not eventuated (though this was Lefebvre's dream)' (p. 92), rhythmanalysis 'introduces richly suggestive ways for thinking about rhythms' about the conjugation of spaces and time, and 'allows scope for wide interpretation and provides basis for further exploration' (p. 56). Scholars from varied disciplines are increasingly employing, and extending upon, Lefebvre's rhythmanalysis to examine how social and/or natural rhythms permeate an array of social spaces and spatial practices, including city life (Highmore, 2005; Amin & Thrift, 2002), tourist travel (Edensor & Holloway, 2008; Edensor,

2012), urban train travel (Wilken, 2011), dance (McCormack, 2008), walking (Edensor, 2010b), street performance (Simpson, 2008) and the urban experiences of youth enrolled in recreation music programs (Lashua & Kelly, 2008). Despite growing interest in the rhythms operating within and through various spaces, the notion of arrhythmia has gained little scholarly attention to date. Much of the research adopting a Lefebrevian approach has involved researchers describing the repetitive rhythms of bodies or objects observed within and across particular times and spaces. But rhythms are always relational, thus analyses should look to 'discern and compare' the familiar, embodied, often unconscious rhythms, with unsettling arrhythmic experiences (Lefebvre, 1991/2004, p. 77). Moreover, I see a need to give participants more agency and voice in contemporary rhythmanalyses. Individuals are not all oblivious to the rhythms of their everyday lives, and some recognize that operations of power can produce particular rhythms while limiting others.

Lefebvre's analysis of rhythms has political underpinnings. 'The Marxist roots of his analysis are rarely far from the surface,' explains Horton (2005, p. 159). Indeed, Lefebvre never loses sight of how everyday rhythms are produced 'by the structuring rhythms of the state and capital' (p. 159). In contrast to Lefebvre's earlier work, however, *Rhythmanalysis* does not offer a detailed examination of the spatial and rhythmic operations of power. Rather, examinations of power appear secondary to observations of the diverse rhythms operating within and across time-geography. Thus, many of the scholars cited above combine Lefebvre's concepts of rhythmanalysis with his earlier work on the social production of social space to go beyond descriptions of 'social' and 'natural' rhythms. Whether this was Lefebvre's intention or not, such syntheses have enabled an array of insightful critical analyses of the rhythms of social life in a variety of contemporary contexts. *Rhythmanalysis* may fail to offer a coherent conceptual schema, yet Lefebvre's work provides a 'richly suggestive' impetus for exploring the disruption to everyday sporting rhythms caused by earthquakes, as well as how alternative sporting mobilities contribute to the (re)imagining of earthquake-damaged spaces and places.

Acknowledging that the search for the 'exact theoretical fit' is futile (Slack, 1996, p. 112), I approach social theorizing as 'an adventure' in which I 'set out to see things differently' (Thorpe, 2011, p. 269). Rather than trying to neatly 'fit' my data into a theoretical framework, I prefer to 'work with our always inadequate theories' with the aim of moving understanding 'a little further down the road' (Slack, 1996, p. 112). Arguably, 'pushing, pulling and stretching theories and concepts in relation to our empirical evidence' can help us 'identify their strengths and limitations for explaining particular aspects of contemporary society and/or the physically active body' (Thorpe, 2011, p. 269). Thus, in this chapter, I do not strictly pursue the kind of rhythmanalysis suggested by Lefebvre. Rather, I draw inspiration from his thinking because it encourages a particular sensitivity to the 'diverse, multiple rhythms of everyday life' (Horton, 2005, p. 158). In particular, I see value in this approach for encouraging new questions about the rhythmic and arrhythmic experiences of sporting bodies in spaces of movement. Recognizing the limits of Lefebvre's work, however, I engage the notion of arrhythmia in conversation with literature from mobilities studies and cultural and emotional geography. In so doing, I hope to point to the potential of theoretical synthesis for each of these strands of thought. Adopting an interdisciplinary approach and a rhythmanalysis sensitivity, this chapter reveals some of the social, psychological and physical affects of earthquakes on the bodies of committed action sport participants.

As well as destroying vital infrastructure, such as roads, water and power, natural disasters also destroy built sporting facilities (gyms, playing fields, swimming pools, club rooms, stadiums and so on). Understandably, the rebuilding of these facilities is not of immediate concern to councils and residents during a state of emergency. In the weeks and months following a natural disaster, however, the damage to such facilities is often keenly felt by residents as they seek to re-establish post-earthquake lifestyles. Damage to such facilities seriously affects participation in organized recreational and competitive team or individual sports, and exercise practices, as well as the hosting of major sporting events. The rebuilding of such facilities is highly political and often controversial: whose sporting and physical activity pursuits are prioritized in the rebuild process? In Christchurch, for example, the suggestion of including a covered 35,000-seat rugby stadium in the city rebuild plan was hotly contested (Gorman, 2012).

Here my focus is on the experiences of participants in recreational, non-competitive, non-traditional, action or 'lifestyle sports' (Wheaton, 2009, 2010) for whom regular participation is an integral part of their everyday lives and sense of identity and community. As a number of researchers have revealed, action sport participants often develop intimate relationships with natural and urban geographies (Atkinson, 2009; Booth & Thorpe, 2007; Borden, 2003; Ford & Brown, 2006; Stoddart, 2012; Thorpe, 2011; Kidder, 2012). According to Thorpe and Rinehart (2010), action sports often involve a special relationship with the environment and the reconceptualization of space and time: 'These relationships can be quite different to those in established sport where the body acts on artificial, formally constituted spaces (e.g., courts, arenas, fields, ovals, tracks, pistes) in formally recognized time trajectories (e.g., start, finish; time pauses, time-outs)' (p. 1273; also see Booth & Thorpe, 2007; Wheaton, 2010). A skateboarder in Borden's (2003) research, for example, explains that 'being a skateboarder means . . . you don't just walk through space, without learning anything about it, or without having a kind of relationship with where you are'; rather, 'through the medium of a skateboard . . . you can actually interact with the world around you' (p. 200). Similarly, James, a highly committed surfer living in

Christchurch, identifies differences between action sports and more traditional organized sports:

> if you're a surfer, it's always on the back of your mind – what's the surf like? A surfer always knows if it's offshore or onshore, what the swell conditions are. It just plays on your mind, I think more than other sports because we need the right conditions to go out. You can go down and kick a soccer ball or rugby ball at any time, at any park.

As this chapter illustrates, the disruption and destruction of places of action sport participation – beaches, trails, rock walls and streets – by natural disaster can evoke highly affective and emotional responses among enthusiasts (such as surfers, mountain bikers, climbers and skateboarders) who have often developed intimate relationships with these geographies.[2]

Interested to understand how committed 'lifestyle sport' enthusiasts adapted their action sport participation in the changing socio-cultural-economic-physical geography and made meaning of new sportscapes, I conducted interviews with 14 (11 male and three female) surfers, skateboarders, climbers and mountain bikers who were living in Christchurch before, during and after the February 2011 earthquake. Interviewees included eight surfers (aged 24–49 years old), four climbers (aged 19–35 years old) and two skateboarders (18 and 22 years old).[3] Six of the participants were also active mountain bikers (aged 30–44 years old). Participants varied considerably in socio-economic status; at the time of interviews, participants' occupations included unemployed, skateboard shop employee, surf shop manager, builder, undergraduate and postgraduate students, professional photographer, environmental manager and university lecturer. Participants were accessed via existing social networks, as well as visits to local surf, skateboard and climbing shops, and snowball sampling.[4] Interviews ranged from 45 minutes to two hours, and took place in an array of locations selected by the participants (such as participant's house, surf shop and university offices, cafeteria, at the airport). The aim of this project was not to offer findings representative of all Christchurch residents, but rather to reveal rich insights into the lived experiences of an array of action sport participants.

Participants' experiences during and after the earthquake also varied considerably, with some involved in life-threatening scenarios, dramatic rescues or trapped a long way from family, while others were in relatively safe environments. Despite varying earthquake experiences and socio-economic status, all participants described daily and chronic stresses and frustrations associated with living in a severely damaged city with continuous aftershocks. Concerns regarding roads, employment insecurity, family health and wellbeing, housing and insurance featured strongly in all interviews; one participant lost a close friend, another lost his family home during the earthquake, another was forced to relocate due to damage to his rental property, and others had to make costly repairs to their houses. As with most Christchurch residents at this time, all interviewees were actively involved in their local communities' recovery response, and three were members of the much-praised Student Volunteer Army.[5] Some also belonged to sport-related clubs that 'got together to lend a practical hand whenever we could to members in need of help' (pc, Peter Mannix, President of Sumner Longboarders Surf Club, 2013,).[6]

While the focus in this chapter is the influence of the earthquake on individuals' sporting rhythms and mobilities, it is important to note that such experiences are intimately connected to all other aspects of their post-disaster lives (such as family, work, accommodation, community). Of the 14 participants, three continued to live at home with their parents, four had children of their own, and seven were either married or living with their partner. Ten were New Zealand residents – seven of whom were 'born and bred' in Christchurch – and four had migrated to Christchurch from the US, England, Germany and Japan, for work, postgraduate studies and in pursuit of new sporting opportunities. The personal information offered here is relevant to this chapter because the sporting experiences of interviewees before, during and after the earthquake cannot be separated from the life stresses experienced by participants and their families.

As disaster studies researchers are well aware, conducting interviews and fieldwork in disaster spaces requires a heightened sensitivity to the psychological trauma experienced by some participants (Collogan et al., 2004). To further enhance my understanding of the everyday stresses within the households of Christchurch residents, I stayed with my aunt and uncle in their family home of more than 30 years that had recently been 'red zoned' (declared no longer habitable). Driving to and from interviews, I came to understand the daily frustrations of driving in a city ravaged by potholes and construction. I also experienced two small aftershocks during my visit, including one during an interview. Adopting a methodological approach sensitive to the (im)mobilities of the post-disaster environment helped me gain a greater understanding of the ongoing psychological, emotional and logistical stresses of Christchurch residents more than a year after the devastating February earthquake; this embodied knowledge facilitated my rapport with participants and analysis of interview transcripts.

Disrupted sporting mobilities: the effects of earthquake arrhythmia

Every place used for action sport participation is a unique 'polyrhythmic ensemble' (Crang, 2000). Through regular practice, committed action sport participants often develop an implicit and embodied understanding of the multiple social and natural rhythms operating within and across these places. For committed action sport participants, everyday routines and rituals are then organized around such movements and mobilities (for example, tides, wind, flows of people) (Wheaton, 2003b). The February 2011 earthquake seriously damaged and destroyed many of the spaces used for recreational sports such as skateboarding, surfing, climbing and mountain biking and, in so doing, evoked experiences of arrhythmia among participants.

The downtown district of Christchurch experienced the most extreme damage from the February 2011 earthquake, such that the central city was cordoned off from the public for more than a year. Inside the chain-linked fences of the 'red zone', more than 130 buildings have been, or are in the process of being, demolished; many of these are high-rise and heritage buildings (Lynch, 2011). The closure of the city centre affected all Christchurch residents in various ways. But for local skateboarders, this meant the loss of one of their favourite urban playgrounds. As one local skateboarder laments:

> It's hard for anyone who's not in Christchurch to imagine 'no city' . . . whole blocks are just written off. There used to be so much to do in that area – you could skate down High Street to go and meet some people, and you could just carve up the roads and ollie the little gutters. Even the Cathedral, there were some really good stair sets there, and you could just roll between them all. It was just such a big part of the city to be shut off, there's no way you couldn't lose a bunch of cool [skateboarding] stuff in it, no matter what. (Trent)

In comparison to many other Christchurch residents who miss their favourite shops or seeing beautiful heritage buildings, Trent's relationship with the downtown urban spaces – the roads, stairs and gutters – was intimate and sensual based on his physical engagement with the urban space. As with many local skateboarders, Trent's body recalls the familiar sound of his wheels on the pavement in particular parts of the city, the vibration that passed through his feet and up his legs as he travelled with speed across sections of rough seal, the smoothness of the concrete near the Cathedral. When he recalled the skateboarding spaces lost in the downtown district, he remembered through his body so clearly that his face was animated and his words vivid.

Damage to major sewer pressure mains also forced the Christchurch City Council (CCC) to release untreated wastewater into the rivers. On March 1 the council released the following statement:

> Please stay away from beaches. The public are urgently being asked to stay away from all Christchurch beaches, as seawater is currently contaminated with sewage. Contaminated water poses a serious health threat, with risk of disease. (Please stay away, 2011)

It took over nine months to replace 12 kilometres of major sewer pressure mains during which time more than 7.8 billion litres of untreated wastewater had flowed into the waterways. To the relief of local residents, and particularly surfers, the beaches officially reopened for recreational use in November, just in time for summer. As the following comment suggests, the redistribution of earthquake waste also affected the use of other recreational areas: 'they dumped a lot of rubble up there by the New Brighton mountain bike trails . . . I also heard, informally, that there was a lot of asbestos in the rubble up there' (Nathan).

The Port Hills – a range of hills between Christchurch city and the port at Lyttelton – suffered considerable damage from the February earthquake. Prior to the earthquake, the area was a popular recreational site offering more than 46 maintained walking and mountain bike tracks, many with spectacular coastal views. The Port Hills were also a world-renowned climbing destination, offering approximately 1400 known climbing lines within a short 20 to 25-minute drive of the city. According to local climbers, the February 2011 earthquake destroyed an estimated 80 per cent of these climbing routes. Although most of the climbs were unrecoverable, the council went to great lengths to reopen some of the walking and biking trails. Ongoing rock fall hazards, however, continued to cause delays. In October 2012, only 18 of the 46 walking and biking tracks (less than 40 per cent) had reopened for public use. The closure of trails and routes in the Port Hills, the 'red zoning' of the city centre and the prolonged closure of the beaches seriously affected the everyday sporting experiences of mountain bikers, climbers, skateboarders and surfers.[7]

For committed action sport participants, the closure, destruction and pollution of their 'local' spaces of participation evoked highly affective arrhythmic experiences. Prior to the earthquake, the surfers, climbers, mountain bikers and skateboarders interviewed for this project enjoyed regular participation, often organizing their daily routines around their sporting activities in contradistinction to modernist pastimes. As one highly committed surfer proudly proclaimed: 'I surfed everyday; regardless of conditions, or if I was well or not, just go straight down and jump in.' A Japanese climber who moved to Christchurch for the climbing explained, 'I'm just working for climbing, living for climbing. Everything in my life is for climbing' (Yukimi). Few of these individuals participate in competitions or consider themselves 'athletes', yet their regular sporting participation, and relationships with fellow participants, are integral parts of their everyday lives.

Despite extensive damage and destruction across the city, the February earthquake did not cease all action sport participation. Rather, for some committed individuals, participation intensified in the immediate post-disaster period:

> . . . when February happened there was a three-day period when the surf was pumping and you couldn't get out of the area, so we just surfed heaps. Then about three days afterwards, Bob Parker [Mayor of Christchurch] jumped on the box [television] and said 'we're going to start discharging

into the ocean'. I had access to the data at work, so I looked at the times and dates of when they were starting to release the sewage. As soon as I did that I grabbed my surfboard went down and surfed for the full day . . . until the moment they turned on the drains. (Ruben)

Some skateboarders had a similar sense of urgency in their use of the post-disaster space:

. . . the period straight after the quake, it was quite good, all these new spots appeared and the cops had other things to be worrying about than getting us. So everyone was out skating all these new, crazy spots. But they [the council] got onto it pretty fast and just started blocking sections or ripping up concrete. So you had to make the most of those first few weeks. As soon as they started fixing it up, the opportunities for skating all the new terrain quickly disappeared. (Trent)

Speaking specifically of his peer group, Trent continued to explain: 'Everyone for that first week, if not six weeks, had nothing to do. I think a lot of people thought "man I'm just going to skate all day, coz I'm not doing anything else"'. For another highly committed skater, however, immediate participation raised moral issues:

I actually did skate the day after it happened, but just to get place to place because I couldn't use my car at the time because it was under liquefaction, and we had to dig it out and fix it. While I was rolling around [skateboarding] from one place to another, I found a whole bunch of new spots. But we really couldn't do them for at least a week because we kind of felt real bad if we did it. Some of my buddies were tempted, but I felt a bit guilty that people had probably died in these spots we were skating, so we just thought we'd wait a while. (Brad)

Despite some desperate bids to surf or skateboard amid the ruins of an earthquake-ravaged city, most action sport participants were otherwise pre-occupied for the first few weeks following the event.

The majority of participants in this project described their sporting activities being sidelined in the wake of the earthquake by the health and well-being of family and friends. For example, Will was preoccupied with 'trying to find somewhere to live' and then 'getting the kids into new schools' so that 'surfing was gone from my mind', and James found himself 'taking care of others' and in so doing 'realized surfing was no longer the priority in life'. Similarly, a female surfer recalls, 'earlier on after the February quake we all had shit to deal with anyway, we had no power, no water, then we were busy at work, so life was kind of busy' (Emma). As such, the closure of the beaches seemed relatively insigificant during the period of emergency.

A few weeks after the earthquake, however, as participants had more time and energy, and sought to re-establish some familiar everyday practices and routines, many realized that their sporting activities were no longer accessible. As Emma explains, 'once we got most of the chores done, we started to realize that something huge was missing from our lives and it was going to be gone for a long, long time'. The closure of the beaches, climbing routes and mountain bike tracks took on much greater significance for these individuals following the emergency period and as residents attempted to negotiate new post-disaster lifestyles and work and leisure routines. All of the action sport participants interviewed for this study described experiencing strong emotional and psychological responses to their disrupted sporting routines. A committed female surfer observed high anxiety among her surfing friends and admits to tensions within her relationship with another passionate surfer: 'we were both a bit more grumpy . . . going through surfing withdrawals. [Tim] was definitely grumpy . . . I probably would have been more grumpy if I didn't have to calm him down all the time.' James made similar observations: 'I don't know what surfing does for me, but if I don't do it, the wife will soon tell you that I'm not a very nice person to be around. Without surfing, I got pretty stressed.' As well as increased anxiety and tension, James also described experiencing a loss of motivation in a weekly routine sans surfing:

> [Not being able to surf] really took some of the passion out of my life. Sure, there were a lot of other things to get on and do, recovery sort of stuff, but there wasn't a lot of reward. It feels like, surfing is always the 'cherry' you're looking for in life; get your jobs done and go surfing, it's your reward. Then it became, get your jobs done and get a beer. Some days you were just 'oh, I'm so over this', and we found ourselves drinking a lot more. (James)

Others also admitted to 'partying way too hard because we couldn't go surfing' (Mark). Although drinking and socializing with friends 'was fun and exciting at the time', during our interview Aaron reflected critically upon the post-disaster response adopted by his surfing peer group: 'you kind of look back and think "shit, we were a bit out of hand there a few times".'

In *Rhythmanalysis*, Lefebvre (1992/2004) explores the intersections of bodies, rhythms, space and time, evocatively describing bodies as 'bundles of rhythms' (p. 20). Continuing, he argues that it is necessary to listen to these 'bundles' or 'braiding of rhythms' in order to 'grasp the natural or produced ensembles' (p. 20) that result from them (see also Edensor & Holloway, 2008; Stuartsen, 2005). For many Christchurch residents, the earthquake prompted them to reflect upon the importance of social and bodily sporting rhythms in their everyday lives. The earthquake arrhythmia was certainly felt by the bodies of committed action sport participants. Nathan was alarmed to notice that he 'put on about 4 kg' following the earthquake, and Will attributed his weight gain to an '80 per cent reduction in surfing' combined with stress and increased alcohol consumption. Importantly, at the time of the interviews, most participants had recommenced their physically active lifestyles and thus mostly regained their pre-earthquake physiques. Emma recognized her weight gain as a temporary bodily response to beach closure caused by the earthquake: 'we substituted surfing for drinking shitloads of wine. I put on five kilos at least, six if I'm honest. Life was just quite depressing, so you'd get home from work and have a wine. [. . .] When we went surfing again, I actually noticed that my mal [surfboard] was sitting lower in the water. I swear to god, I was paddling out and my board was sinking, I was so fat! (laughing)'. This comment highlights the temporality of bodily and socio-psychological responses to the earthquake; both bodies and places were in a constant state of flux for more than a year following the earthquake.

Alternative sporting rhythms and (re)imagining disaster spaces

Extending the work of Lefebvre, Edensor (2010) explains that it is common for individuals to attempt to minimize the affects of an arrhythmic experience by trying to 'restore familiar spaces, routines and timings' (p. 5). This was certainly true for many action sport participants living in Christchurch after the February earthquake. Attempting to regain some sense of familiarity in the rhythms of everyday life, passionate skateboarders, surfers and climbers adopted creative practices and alternative sporting mobilities. In so doing, they contributed to redefining 'traumascapes' (Tumarkin, 2005) into 'therapeutic spaces' (Williams, 1999) of physical play and performance.

Skateboarders

In *Skateboarding, Space and the City: Architecture and the Body*, Iain Borden (2003) describes skateboarders as 'dismissive of authority and convention'. For skateboarders, the 'city is not just a place for working and shopping but a true pleasure-ground, a place where the body, emotions and energy can be expressed to the full' (Borden, 2003, back cover). This was certainly true for many Christchurch skateboarders for whom the earthquake-damaged streets and buildings offered exciting new obstacles and spaces for play. As one committed skateboarder writes, 'All our historic town spots are gone, there's dust everywhere . . . still it's kinda cool that every street can be re-explored'. Less than a month after the earthquake, a video produced by local skateboarders titled 'Quaked: Skateboarding in Christchurch after Earthquake' was posted on YouTube.[8] The short video shows a group of young male skateboarders creatively adapting to earthquake-damaged streets and sidewalks. With over 360,000 views, the YouTube video not only appealed to skateboarders around the world, but also to residents in

Christchurch and across New Zealand who celebrated the playful, youthful, creative use of space. Online responses were almost entirely positive: 'Wow guys, this really blew my mind, and I am a 34-year-old mum, really made me smile'; 'This is one of the most creative things I've seen to come out of the quake'; 'At first I thought, "bloody disrespectful vandals", then I thought, "nah, just young kids making the best of a bad situation", a well put together vid' (Skateboarders take to quake, 2011, para. 9). Brad, one of the skateboarders featured in the film, admits to the difficulties of skateboarding in post-disaster spaces: 'to be honest, most of the spots were an absolute mission to skate, they were pretty haggard, your board got really chipped and you got the dirtiest grip tape in the world'. Continuing, he admits, 'I suppose it was worth it. Mom and Dad were pretty impressed that I got on the news, and my sponsors were stoked on the coverage too' (Brad).

Despite the public celebration of the video, skateboarders in Christchurch continued to struggle to find places to practice due to heightened security and the highly regulative uses of public space. Skateboarders had to draw upon their intimate understandings of the social dynamics of this urban geography to access new spaces of play and performance:

[After the quake] there are a few awesome skate spots that are desolate, but they are behind fences. We usually try to sneak into them when we know the workers and security guards aren't around. The first time you get busted, you're usually asked to leave, but if it happens again you'll get a trespass notice, or worse. [. . .] There was one spot on Moorhouse Ave, where the bus depot was, so it was easy for us to get to. But you could only go there for fifteen, twenty minutes before someone would kick you out. It was just too visible. (Trent)

I was skating a bridge on Fitzgerald Ave and there was a bunch of the Australian police. One of them walks up and . . . says, 'you're pretty good at your skating are you . . . go on then, entertain me'. So I did a whole bunch of tricks . . . then he was like, 'after all that, maybe just chill out a bit, it's pretty soon to start skating these sorts of things, and I'm supposed to be doing my job so I'll ask you guys to go do it somewhere else'. At least the guy was good about it, he even had a little roll around on the [skate]board himself, so that was pretty funny. (Brad)

In response to the heightened regulation and 'red zoning' of the down-town cityscape, many skateboarders ventured out into the suburbs to explore new spaces. As the following comment suggests, however, some found these new mobilities less than satisfying:

With street skating downtown, we used to skate from spot to spot, but when there's no town, we have to drive. It takes a lot of the fun away. [. . .] You

Figure 7.1 A skateboarder creatively appropriating earthquake-damaged streets in Christchurch. Image used with permission of *The Press*

can't just go down all the back alleys to find something cool like we used to. You've got to go in the car to a spot in Hornby or wherever, session the spot, then put everyone's boards away, hop in, go to the next spot. There's just no flow. (Trent)

Engaging Lefebvre's rhythmanalysis here, it might be argued that skateboarding mobilities were 'erased and reborn' in skateboarders' encounters with post-earthquake Christchurch spaces (Borden, 2003, p. 2).

Another example of skateboarders' creative exploration and appropriation of the possibilities of the earthquake-damaged cityscape was the development of indoor skate parks. Embracing the do-it-yourself, anti-authoritarian attitude at the core of the culture, skateboarders (re)appropriated earthquake-damaged architecture:

> We started exploring all those abandoned buildings. There's this abandoned warehouse where the doors been jimmied open . . . now it's full of ramps, rails and boxes. There's also a really cool theatre warehouse on the cusp of the city border. Basically someone reached around, unlocked the door and jimmied the door open. Skateboarders just started building all sorts of fun stuff in there – boxes, manual pads, ramps. There was a massive stage that people had built ramps all down the centre of so you could skate off the stage. It was so rad, it was probably like Tony Hawk's or something. Ramps built out of everything. (Trent)

According to Borden (2003), 'skaters create [sic] spatial enclaves . . . adopting and exploiting a given physical terrain in order to present skaters with new and distinctive uses other than the original function of that terrain' (p. 29). Expressing a similar sentiment, Trent proclaimed the appropriation of damaged buildings as a 'salute to all the people that look down their noses at us and think we're just nuisance, good-for-nothing skaters'; rather than 'sitting around and moaning about all the damage', skateboarding was a way of saying, 'look what we can do with all the broken stuff'. Brad also experienced pleasure in skateboarders' alternative responses to the post-earthquake environment:

> Other people in my family don't really do much at all anymore, they just kind of hang around, waiting for the city to be rebuilt, whereas I'll just go skating, and I'll be happy. Most people don't understand us, but skateboarding is a more productive way of dealing with your emotions than sitting around and getting depressed.

Through the creative use of earthquake-damaged spaces, skateboarders constructed different spatial re-imaginings of a post-earthquake city. Skateboarders' creative use of 'found' and 'built' spaces in Christchurch enabled participants to reconstruct new meanings of the cityscape. In so doing, their practices worked to subtly disrupt dominant readings of earthquake spaces as dead, damaged and only fit for demolition.

Surfers

Committed surfers living in Christchurch were understandably distraught by news that the beaches would be closed indefinitely due to the health risks posed by the release of untreated sewage in the waterways. Surfers debated amongst themselves as to whether to accept or reject council warnings. The majority of surfers interviewed for this project made highly calculated decisions not to surf: 'I don't want to bring any illness into the house, we have enough to deal with right now. I'm also a plasma donor and I take that really seriously' (Will); 'My health is important to me and I can't have a week off work sick because I went surfing for an hour' (James); 'the thought of catching hepatitis from poo water was enough to put me off' (Emma). Official warnings, combined with personal observations, and the circulation of rumours within the surfing community, kept most from entering the water.

Yet surfing culture has long celebrated hedonistic, irreverent and anti-authoritarian behaviour (Booth, 1995; Ford & Brown, 2006; Stranger, 2011), thus it is perhaps not surprisingly that a few Christchurch surfers refused to heed official warnings. Some opted to make decisions based on their own research:

> I was able to see the water quality results at work, so the moment it dropped under the acceptable levels of e-coli in the water, I let the boys know, and we went surfing. We also used satellite data to find out where we could probably surf. (Ruben)

Others adopted less scientific approaches. For example, after giving in to the temptation to go for a surf in front of his house when the 'waves were pumping', James and his surfing buddy employed the unique strategy of 'drinking lots of whiskey at 10.30 in the morning just in case there were any bugs' (James). Whereas James and his friend got lucky on this occasion, a few local surfers were hospitalized for various water-related illnesses and infections. While the surfing community was divided as to whether it was socially acceptable to surf during this period, 'most people outside of surfing just thought they were complete idiots' (Shaun).

For highly committed lifestyle surfers not willing to risk their health by surfing the local beaches, the best alternative was travelling to unpolluted beaches north (Waikuku) and south (Banks Peninsula) of Christchurch. Travelling to unpolluted beaches was an expensive and time-consuming activity requiring considerable resources and organization which caused problems for even the most committed surfers: 'If you want to continue surfing every day, we're looking at $20 a day, $100 a week, which puts a massive drain on your resources . . . especially with house repairs and other extra costs of living' (Ruben). Similarly, Aaron complained: 'there was so much preparation and planning involved just to go for a surf. [. . .] I would spend half the night texting everyone to get a group together, and then have to take the whole morning off work'. In contrast to older surfers for whom family and work commitments made accessing the time and resources for such trips difficult, young surfers with flexible employment arrangements continued to prioritize surfing. For example, Mark travelled frequently with a group of friends, all tradesmen, for whom 'surfing comes before work' and were thus willing to 'drop the tools and go' whenever the conditions were right. According to travelling surfers, the additional effort and resources required to surf post-earthquakes 'sorted out people that are really committed to surfing as a way of life' (Ruben), and distinguished the 'hard core surfers' from the 'weekend warriors' (James).

New social dynamics also developed as a result of alternative post-earthquake surfing mobilities. Previously quiet surfing spots became crowded and, with highly stressed surfers competing for limited resources, altercations were not uncommon. Ruben recalled arriving at Waikuku to find 'more than three hundred people in the water'. With limitied resources and some people 'so stressed . . . just right on the edge', he observed 'one guy who just wouldn't stop swearing at people', and another get 'into fisticuffs with another dude in the water' (Ruben). Despite overcrowding and the additional resources required, those who were able to travel for surfing strongly advocated the socio-psychological value of their experiences.

Those surfers with the opportunity and motivation to travel embraced the escapism and excitement offered by these new surfing spaces and mobilities. Aaron, for example, enjoyed the new sense of 'adventure and exploration' that came with 'finding new waves and testing out different boards'. Continuing, Aaron described the importance of surf trips for social interaction and fun with his peers, which had a lingering positive effect:

> There is such a strong presence of community and fulfilment in relationships within surfing. So when we go for a roadtrip up the coast – even if it's shit when you get there, that drive up the coast talking crap, having fun the whole way up, that's part of the whole day as well. I think just getting away from it all, just for a few hours, is so important. If you went away for a day's surf, you'd come back and be in a calm place for at least a few days. But, because it was so continuous, earthquakes and more shit happening, as soon as you get immersed back into Christchurch, you slowly go downhill again and you're just waiting for another day to get away.

Similarly, Will appreciated the short-term escapism and 'endorphin rush' that helped 'take my mind off everything for a while'. He also enjoyed the opportunities to 'connect with my friends and surfing colleagues from Christchurch': 'If you saw someone you knew in the waves, suddenly it's "how are you doing, how's your house, what's happening?" It was great to catch up with mates that you hadn't seen for a while.' Despite the socio-psychological and physical benefits, travelling at least an hour from 'home' to surf was not ideal and was perceived as a temporary substitute.

Climbers

In a scenario not dissimilar to the debates among surfers, the climbing community was divided as to whether to accept the closure of the Port Hills or to continue climbing despite the risks. Caitlin, a highly committed and proficient climber, adopted a cautious approach:

> I just didn't really feel like you should go climbing when there is a potential of rock fall coming down on you. They say it's dangerous, and I know a lot of people that really pushed it and went anyway even when it wasn't recommended. For me, I don't think it's really worth the risk. I'd rather climb indoors, or do some bouldering at Castle Hill.

As in the surfing community, local climbers shared information about the risks associated with various climbs via everyday conversations and new media such as Facebook. Interestingly, Caitlin expressed hesitation in returning to the Port Hills even to witness the damage: 'I hear all the rumours and have seen the photos on other climbers' Facebook pages, but I haven't seen it physically myself. I'll wait a little bit longer before I go back up there again. I'm quite nervous to see how bad it really is'. Yukimi puts it simply, 'I feel scared to go to the dangerous places. I don't want to go there'. Sam, the only climber in this study who continued to climb in the Port Hills following the earthquakes, held a different perspective:

> . . . technically I think [all the climbs are] closed, and so for the vast majority of people, no one is going climbing because there are big blunt signs up at Godley Head and Redcliffs saying you will be fined $2,000 or $5,000 if you're caught in the area. But a few of us are like, 'well it's a bit of a dodgy place anyway and the bits of the climbs that are left, they stood up so far, so they'll probably be alright'. It all depends on how you look at risk.

With frequent rock falls, the Port Hills are in a constant state of movement. For some, such as Sam, this offers a new sense of adventure and added risk, thrill and excitement; for others, the Port Hills are no longer a place of play and pleasure, instead evoking feelings of fear and anxiety.

For committed climbers not willing to return to the dangerous Port Hills, the next best alternative was to drive 100 kilometres west of the city to Castle Hill – an area offering over 250 climbs and 1000 boulder problems. As it is a world-class bouldering site, many Christchurch climbers redirected their energies toward bouldering post-earthquake. As the following quote illustrates, climbers experienced some of the same financial limitations as travelling surfers: 'being a poor student . . . unless you can fill up your car with other climbers, none of us can really afford to go' (Sam).[9]

Despite the additional effort required, all climbers in this study proclaimed the psycho-social and physical benefits of participation after the earthquake:

> A lot of people go to climb to seek to de-stress from their family, and it's also a good way to vent some anger. I'm very much an active relaxer, so for me, climbing was especially important after the earthquake. (Sam)

When we go to Castle Hill, it's an escape. It's like in this really nice pro-tected space. When you're there, you *finally* stop thinking 'what if there's another earthquake?' (Caitlin)

Caitlin also describes the importance of her relationships within the climb-ing community: 'some of us talked about what happened' and agreed that going climbing together was a good way to 'move on from it [the earth-quake]'. For Caitlin, the climbing community and the re-establishment of familiar sport and work rhythms aided her recovery from the arrhythmic experience of the February earthquake: 'Once I got back into it, I found climbing is a way just to carry on, move forward. [. . .] For me, it was really good just to be back doing something I enjoy, and now that work and uni have started again, it finally feels like everything is how it should be.'

Due to long-term changes in the physical environment, and the difficul-ties of accessing alternative climbing spaces on a regular basis, many climb-ers set about establishing new sporting rhythms. Sam and friends went from 'climbing outdoors four times' a week prior to the earthquake to 'just once a week outdoors, a few times indoors, and then mountain biking two or three times a week'. Others took up running, swimming and visits to the gym to maintain their physical fitness. Some climbers, however, were less willing to substitute alternative activities for climbing. Yukimi, for example, travels regularly to Wanaka where she stays with climbing friends who moved from Christchurch following the earthquake. She notes that, 'if the Port Hills do close' permanently, she will likely follow her peers to Wanaka.[10]

Re-imagining sporting spaces: fears, anxieties and resistance

Tuan (1974, 1990) and other cultural, urban and sport geographers (González, 2005; Bale, 1996) have used the terms 'topophilia' and 'topopho-bia' to describe the positive and negative affective relations people develop with places. Following the earthquakes, previously topophilic sporting places became topophobic sites, evoking new fears and anxieties from some participants (Tuan, 1979). Many interviewees admitted to looking at the urban architecture differently after the earthquakes, and constantly plan-ning 'escape' routes in case of another earthquake. Shaun, for example, noted that, when walking in particular places 'sometimes I think, OK, if I sense things about to hit the fan, which way do I go?' Similarly, Nathan revealed that he finds himself constantly assessing his environment: 'when I'm between the shadows of a number of buildings, I'll look and see where do I run if it happens?' He admits to new spatial anxieties:

> We probably didn't think of consequences so much before, now I do look around me and think, what could happen here? It's a weird thing... what-ever I do, it's different, because I have this new caution. I'll ask myself questions now that I never used to ask. (Nathan)

234

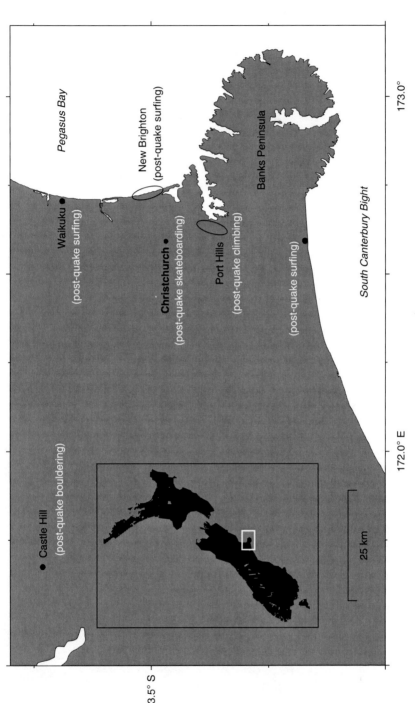

Figure 7.2 Map of Christchurch and action sport-related areas disrupted or destroyed by the February 22, 2011 earthquake, and alternative spaces used by committed participants during the weeks and months after the earthquake. The epicentre of the February 2011 earthquake is marked with a star (Map created by José Borrero)

Caitlin observed 'a lot more cautious behaviour' among patrons of the indoor climbing facility at which she works:

> We had a lot of corporate groups coming into the YMCA wanting to rebuild team morale. They came in for the whole trust thing, but they would ask so many questions, like 'was this building OK in the earthquake? What happens if there's an earthquake when I'm halfway up the wall? Is it safe to be up there?'.

Some surfers also found themselves asking new questions following the Christchurch earthquake. For example, out surfing during a few aftershocks, Ruben found himself worrying 'what if there's going to be a tsunami that really does get us?'.

With a heightened awareness of the potential risks in the natural environment, participants described investing considerable energies to imagining emergency routes:

> When we went skiing in the winter, my wife and I had in our minds that there is the Alpine fault, there are things that happen, we could be blocked out of coming back into Christchurch, and to getting home. (Shaun)

> You're out in the water, and we're still getting the aftershocks, so you're always planning routes to get home. [. . .] so you always had a map in the back of your head, a 'what if' plan. (James)

> When I went snowboarding, I found myself thinking, what happens if I'm up on the lift and there's a quake, and it stopped – how are they going to get me down? Never in 15 years of snowboarding had I had these kinds of fears before. (Nathan)

In comparison to their more carefree pre-earthquake sporting mobilities, many participants described carrying their cell phones to contact family, as well as emergency supplies (clean water, warm clothing, food and the like) in their vehicles in the case of another event.

The earthquake also evoked new anxieties regarding the separation from families, which encouraged some to develop more socially sensitive approaches to their sporting participation:

> Being in the water means you don't have a cell phone . . . you're going to be at least an hour and a half away from your family. So you're inherenly worried about your family. We put plans in place in case of an event, and when I go out now, no matter how good the surf is, if I say I'm going to be forty minutes, I'm forty minutes. (Ruben)

I used to be the guy that would have a family dinner at six o'clock and I'd get there at quarter to seven because I just had to have a surf first after work. Now I can look at that surf and think, next time. [. . .] I guess for me, it's about probably trying to be a little bit nicer, especially to my family. (James)

To minimize separation anxieties, some action sport enthusiasts took to travelling with their families:

Before the earthquakes, it typically would have been me just jetting off down [to the beach] for a while by myself then cruising back. But since Christmas, when we go to the beach, we've tended to all go together . . . and we will all be in the water doing stuff together. My wife and daughters are really into it now and it's so cool that we can all be out surfing and paddling together. (Shaun)

A lot of the times I took them [my family] with me [when I went for a surf up the coast]. [. . .] I would go for a paddle while my wife was with the kids, and then she'd go for a paddle and I would be with the kids . . . we'd all go together . . . that was fun. (Will)

As these comments suggest, for some family-oriented action sport enthusiasts, post-earthquake sporting mobilities offered new social pleasures.

In contrast to the heightened spatial anxieties and new familial considerations experienced by some action sport participants, others used their sporting participation to resist dominant discourses of fear and experiences of depression and social expectation following the earthquake:

Different friends, parents and stuff like that, were thinking, 'what are you doing going surfing, leaving the missus at home, how can you be going half a day away when there could be another quake anytime?' But you kind of get to the stage where you think, 'I can't live my life worrying about when the next earthquake is going be'. You do have times like that, but then you actually get annoyed with the earthquakes, you get angry and think 'I'm not going to let you ruin my life. I'm going to do the things I enjoy'. I just can't live here to work a 40-hour week and sit around at home waiting and thinking, what if? (Brad)

When the September quake hit, it was just the most beautiful day, there was no wind, not a cloud in the sky. I was out surfing when the earthquake hit. The parents were ringing up going 'where are you? What are you doing?' But it was actually really nice just sitting out there on my own, surfing and relaxing. Mum was going crazy over it, you know 'get out, go somewhere high, there could be a tsunami'. But I just didn't really care; I just wanted to chill out. (Mark)

Clearly, as a form of arrhythmia, the earthquakes had varying socio-psychological, bodily and embodied effects on individual action sport participants. For many, action sports were an 'in-between' space of both destruction and disruption, and recovery, resilience and the reimagining of life beyond the earthquakes. Although the alternative sporting mobilities pursued by many following the earthquakes were not the same as previously – often in new locations, and with different people – the rhythmic practices of ollying a skateboard and surfing a wave, or the flow of oxygenated blood and endorphins following a good climb or mountain bike ride, helped some return to familiar bodily experiences, regain a sense of identity and belonging to their sporting communities, and (re)develop a physical connection to the natural or built environment.

Lost and (re)found: sporting places of attachment

Working at the intersection of the spatial and affective turns in the social sciences and humanities, emotional geographers understand 'place attachment' as an 'emotional link to a physical site given meaning through social interaction' (Milligan, 2003, p. 382). Relationships to place can significantly influence identity, particularly when an individual has had memorable experiences in the built or social environment. 'Repeated interactions in specific sites or types of site will typically result in place attachment, or the bonding of people to place,' explains Milligan (p. 382). Many of the participants in this study revealed a strong sense of place attachment intimately connected to their sporting experiences: 'Surfing is a big part of why we live here,' explained Emma, 'we have all these amazing experiences just 100 metres from our house.' According to emotional geographers, disruption of place attachment caused by events such as war, natural disaster and rezoning can result in 'identity discontinuity' (Milligan, 2003, p. 382), and feelings of loss and mourning (Connerton, 2011; Manzo, 2003; Read, 1996; Winter, 1998). Morrice (2013) makes a valuable contribution to geographic literature on trauma, disasters and the concept of 'home' in her exploration of the influence of loss and nostalgia experienced by Hurricane Katrina evacuees' decisions to return or relocate following displacement. Recognizing such decisions as 'complex, multidimensional and individual', she reveals the 'powerful emotional quality associated with how people relate to place' (Morrice, 2013, p. 1).

Mourning and (temporarily) forgetting sporting places

Through their regular action sport experiences on rock walls, in the waves, on mountain bike trails, or in the city streets, action sport participants develop intimate relationships with the natural and built environment. As this chapter reveals, the Christchurch earthquakes caused substantial disruption to both people and places, disturbing 'not only the physical structures of localities [sic], but also the emotional attachments people feel to places'

(Morrice, 2013, p. 2; see also Blunt & Dowling, 2006; Farrar, 2009). Climbers and mountain bikers, in particular, mourned the loss of so many world-class climbing and biking routes in the Port Hills. 'I feel so sad for the places we lost,' proclaimed Japanese climber, Yukimi, 'my favourite climbs [routes] were there, my projects were there. I miss them.' Similarly, Shaun waxes lyrical about the mountain bike trails destroyed in the earthquake:

> Those trails *were* pretty amazing. They were pretty world-class, single-track trails that are up on a ridgeline above the ocean coastline, it was pretty remarkable really. Having those trails just outside my door, I always had a sense all along that it was almost too good to have the trails and the beach four blocks away . . . And now they're gone.

For Shaun, the activities of mountain biking and surfing were so intimately connected to this particular place that he did not seek out alternative sporting spaces following the earthquake:

> I had this great thing right outside my door, and now it's gone, and I don't really care to try to replicate it by putting my bike in a car and going somewhere. [. . .] It was almost painful to go somewhere else to do it. It wasn't the hassle; it just didn't feel like the same activity to me.

Whereas most participants focused on the loss of physical places (such as favourite climbing routes, or a set of stairs used for skateboarding), others mourned the loss of the social interactions offered through participation in these sporting geographies. Aaron, for example, missed seeing his 'regulars': many of them 'you know only through the water, you mightn't even know their names, but you still talk to them three or four days a week . . . having a chat in the waves, or just getting changed back at the car. Then you just don't see them for months . . . it was a major loss of social interaction'. As Milligan (2003) explains, nostalgia is a common experience as individuals seek to establish new identity categories and negotiate new relationships with places and people following natural disaster.

According to archaeologist Tim Ingold (1993), 'to perceive the landscape is therefore to carry out an act of remembrance, and remembering is not so much a matter of calling up an internal image, stored in the mind, as of engaging perceptually with an environment that is itself pregnant with the past' (pp. 152–3). For action sport participants, memories of place are stored in the mind and the body. Bodily memories of place are intimately connected with 'rhythmic interrelations' (Ingold, 1993) of the body and its extensions – surfboard, skateboard, mountain bike, rope – in dialogue with the earth's surfaces (waves, rock walls, dirt trails, concrete footpaths) and forces (gravity, wind), and with fellow participants (paddling for the same wave, taking turns to perform skateboard manoeuvres on a kerb, belaying a climbing partner). Through their regular sporting participation in these places, however, action sport participants are intimately aware of the 'temporality of the landscape' (Ingold, 1993) – local surfers know that a sandbar forming a good wave could be gone with the next storm; climbers understand rock walls as constantly being eroded by the sun, wind and rain. Interestingly, understandings of landscape as 'fundamentally temporal' (Ingold, 1993) facilitated optimistic visions of post-disaster places for some participants. For example, Brad was 'gutted to see so many of my favourite downtown [skateboard] spots disappear forever', adding 'it was depressing to see the demolition team taking apart so many of the best spots in town', yet he remained positive: 'I know that when they rebuild there will be so many other amazing things to skate.'

Of course, individuals mourn people and places differently. To aid the mourning and recovery process, some participants opted to (temporarily) 'forget' the places they had lost or were temporarily unable to access. Caitlin has yet to return to the Port Hills, admitting that it has 'become a place that I've forgotten I can climb'. Similarly, Nathan 'stopped going to look at the surf. It was like there was the Great Wall of China around it . . . you forget it's even there'. For participants such as Nathan, the routines and rituals associated with their sporting activities were integral to their sense of place attachment, and subsequent feelings of loss:

> I enjoyed just jumping on my skateboard and bombing the block and a half to the beach just to have a look at the waves, just to have a little chill out, see if there was a wave, then skating back, but the earthquake stopped that.

Mark also felt dislocated by the loss of his surfing routines, and was relieved when the beaches reopened: 'it was really good to get back into the routine of going and checking the waves. It just felt like being home again. Without the beach and the surf, it's just not home.' In contrast to research on the experiences of natural disaster evacuees who experience loss through displacement, and for whom 'home' becomes defined as 'something that must be returned to; a place of both familiarity and safety' (Morrice, 2013, p. 3), for action sport enthusiasts 'home' is directly connected to familiar sporting places, rhythms and routines.

According to emotional geographers, the 'most direct way to assess the degree of an individual's place attachment is to examine the perceived degree of substitutability of other sites for the one in question' (Milligan, 2003, p. 383). The attachment to place among participants in this study became apparent as they discussed their decisions to stay in Christchurch rather than joining the 13,500 others who migrated to other New Zealand cities or to Australia. Sam, a graduate student from the UK, plans to stay: 'Earthquakes aside, I really like it here. Christchurch is brilliant. There's still some [climbing] crags that are open, there's still surf at my doorstep, I can snowboard and surf in the same day. There are maybe only two places in the world where you can do that.' For Sam, the unique sporting opportunities offered by the coastal and mountain environments of Christchurch have developed a strong sense of place attachment. For others, the social relationships forged in these places were equally or more important in their decisions to stay: 'We did have other options presented to us, but yet we've decided to stay because we live in a nice surfing community where people really care about each other and we live where we can walk down to the ocean' (Shaun). For committed action sport participants, decisions regarding residence and migration are intimately connected to the social and physical experiences offered by particular natural and built sporting spaces.

Given the significant relationships action sport participants develop with sporting places, it is not surprising that the reopening of beaches and some mountain biking trails were momentous occasions. As Will recalls, 'when the all clear came through for the water, surfers, kayakers, windsurfers, kiteboarders, surf lifesavers across Christchurch were jumping for joy'. Many participants embraced their sporting activities with new levels of vigour:

> Now it's amazing. There is a full increase in appreciation for what we have right here. I've probably been surfing more now than I was before it all happened; I just thought, shit, make the most of it, get out every morning before work, try for twice a day. (Aaron)

> Now we, as a family, are really making the most of the ocean as a resource. We're using the beach more so than we were prior to the earthquakes because we value it more, but also it helps us justify why we've decided to stay in a place that so many others have chosen to leave. (Shaun)

As the comments from Aaron and Shaun suggest, some action sport participants became more conscious of the importance of their everyday sporting practices for their place attachment, identity and belonging (Milligan, 1998; Chamlee-Wright & Storr, 2009), and ultimately their decisions not to migrate from Christchurch.

For Lefebvre (1992/2004), we are 'only conscious of most of our rhythms when we begin to suffer from some irregularity' (p. 77). As this chapter has illustrated, the earthquake arrhythmia certainly heightened action sport participants' awareness of their everyday sporting rhythms. For some, the earthquakes also prompted broader reflections:

> For a lot of people who've stayed here, who've lived through the major ones . . . there's a different sensibility about taking things for granted. Be they natural resources or people that are around us. [. . .] It's almost like you want to take things on a bit more because you know they're temporary, nothing is permanent. (Shaun)

Lefebvre (1992/2004) recognized war and disease as arrhythmic experiences, with the potential to prompt reflection upon previously taken-for-granted rhythms of the daily life and the body. Here I have examined earthquakes as similarly arrhythmic experiences that can lead to heightened awareness and reflexivity of social places, moving bodies and everyday life.

Summary

Sport – and particularly action sports – may seem trivial pursuits in the wake of a natural disaster. However, in the weeks and months following a natural disaster, as individuals and communities attempt to re-establish some sense of normalcy in their everyday lives, sport and physical activity can play an important role in (re)creating familiar rhythms and routines, (re)imagining spaces beyond disaster and renewing relationships with places of attachment. This is particularly the case for those whose sporting activities were an integral part of their everyday life, sense of identity and community before the event. As illustrated in this chapter, the February 2011 earthquake was an arrhythmic experience for action sport enthusiasts living in Christchurch. The disruption and destruction of sporting places, as well as everyday routines, prompted some committed participants to adopt highly creative practices in order to access familiar rhythms of surfing, skateboarding, climbing and mountain biking. Despite some lingering fears and anxieties, such alternative sporting mobilities offered participants new social and physical pleasures.

Surveying New Orleans residents about their use of neighbourhood parks following Hurricane Katrina, Rung et al. (2011) revealed the 'psychological, physical and social benefits' of these recreational spaces for escapism, social experiences and physical activity (p. 384). Similarly, for the Christchurch residents in this project, beaches, indoor skate parks, bouldering routes and mountain bike trails became 'therapeutic landscapes' – their sporting participation in these spaces contributed to perceived health and wellness (Gesler & Kearns, 2002; van Ingen, 2004; Williams, 1999). Building upon the work of Rung et al. (2011), it may be argued that local governments would do well to also consider the role of non-traditional sporting and recreational spaces for residents' recovery and resilience. Moreover, if one accepts Lefebvre's premise that stepping outside our familiar rhythms can offer new understandings of the significance of such familiar patterns, flows and practices in our everyday lives, then it might be suggested that asking individuals and groups to reflect upon experiences of arrhythmia is an important avenue for future mobilities scholarship. Arguably, interdisciplinary research that examines individuals' and groups lived experiences of the disruption of everyday rhythms could make a valuable contribution to this literature.

8
The Emergence of Action Sports in the Middle East: Imagining New Mobilities with Parkour in Gaza[1]

> When I was young, I could not imagine that anything would dominate our consciousness more than our isolation or the occupation. All of Gaza was a series of obstacles – closures and checkpoints. Today, all and any obstacles are my point of departure. With free running, I overcome. (Al-Jakhbeer, co-founder of Parkour Gaza, cited in Shahin, 2012, para. 9)

> Many young people in Gaza are angry because they have very few opportunities and are locked in. An art and sports form such as free running gives them an important method to express their desire for freedom and allows them to overcome the barriers that society and politics have imposed on them. It literally sets them free. (Gazan psychologist, Eyad Al Sarraj, MD, cited in Shahin, 2012, para. 17)

To date, action sports have been a predominantly western phenomenon. Despite increasing diversity, many action sports (such as BMX, surfing, skateboarding, snowboarding, windsurfing) have been dominated by young, white, heterosexual, privileged men in North America, Europe, Australia and New Zealand, as well as some Asian countries (particularly Japan) (Beal, 1995; Booth, 2011; Thorpe, 2011; Wheaton & Tomlinson, 1999). Moreover, with many action sports having roots in North America, and the majority of transnational action sport-related media and companies based in the United States, action sports have become closely interconnected with American popular culture, fashion and music, and particularly the 'cool' California youth culture aesthetic. For some – though certainly not all – this is part of the appeal. With the development of highly mediated action sport events such as the X Games, Gravity Games, and the inclusion of action sports into the Olympics, highly evocative images of (predominantly North American and European) action sport athletes riding waves, carving down snowy mountains, leaping across buildings and grinding empty swimming pools are reaching even the remotest of destinations. With the rapid expansion of the Internet and the global reach of transnational action sport companies, media and events, combined with the increasingly 'exotic' travel patterns of action sport athletes and enthusiasts, children and youth throughout the Eastern world are also exposed to action sports. While some reject them as 'crazy American sports', others adopt and reappropriate these activities in relation to their local physical and social environments. In the Arab world, for example, surfing is gaining popularity in Iran and Bangladesh; Pakistani youth are taking up skateboarding in growing numbers; and sand-boarding is a popular activity among privileged youth (and ex-pats) in Saudi Arabia. The (re)appropriation of the predominantly western phenomenon of action sports by local groups in the Eastern world raises interesting questions about the complex and multi-faceted nature of global flows of sport and physical culture in the 21st century.

As various researchers and social commentators have suggested, global media cultures and patterns of consumption are changing contemporary youth cultural formations. According to youth cultural scholars Nayak & Kehily (2008), everyday cultural flows and mobilities of objects, images and information are 'transforming young people's identities in complex ways as they come to interact with and reconfigure processes of globalization' (p. 32). Attempting to understand and explain these changes, researchers are increasingly offering insightful theoretical and discursive analyses of the transnational flows of youth cultural discourses, products and images across and within local, national and virtual spaces (for example, Barker et al., 2009; Henseler, 2012; Horak, 2003; Huq, 2003; Nayak, 2003; Nayak & Kehily, 2008; Pilkington & Johnson, 2003). In this chapter I build upon recent scholarship on the globalization of youth culture and sport (Giulianotti, 2004; Giulianotti & Robertson, 2004; Henseler, 2012; Wheaton, 2004b) to shed light on the development of action sports in the Middle East and, in so doing, reveal the agency of youth to negotiate space for themselves within complex networks of power in global, local and virtual geographies. Here we see how youth in local contexts are adapting and redefining action sports to 'suit their particular needs, beliefs and customs' (Giulianotti & Robertson, 2004, p. 546; Robertson, 1992, 1995; Robertson & White, 2003). More importantly, I reveal how youth in Gaza are using action sport and new social media to call for political change and solidarity for their cause.

This chapter begins by contextualizing the growing popularity of action sports among groups of Middle Eastern youth within broader social, cultural, political and economic trends. In the remainder of this chapter I focus on the development of the urban physical practice of parkour (also known as free running) – the act of running, jumping, leaping through an urban environment as fluidly, efficiently and creatively as possible – among youth living in the Middle East. Drawing upon personal communication and media analysis of various print, digital and social media, I reveal how youth (particularly young men) in Gaza developed their own unique parkour group, despite various social, cultural, economic, physical and psychological obstacles. I explain the proactive approaches adopted by these young men to find appropriate training spaces, to develop the skills of local children and youth, and to support their peer groups. In particular, I describe how these young men are creatively engaging social media (YouTube, Facebook, Twitter) to gain inspiration from the transnational parkour community, and to open new dialogue and establish informal cultural exchanges with parkour enthusiasts around the world. Here I am interested to explore the ways underprivileged youth are using digital technologies to communicate with the transnational action sport community, and to assert their agency and organize resistance amidst oppression, inequality and severely constrained mobilities. As I illustrate via the case of parkour in Gaza, practising this urban sport in the local community and communicating with other enthusiasts via the transnational parkour network offers both physical and virtual forms of (temporary) escapism, political activism and inspiration for alternative ways of living. Moreover, we see how action sport participants are using their participation and engagement with social and digital media to imagine connections between individuals, groups and sites around the world. As Wilding (2007) reminds us, 'imagining links with other people, places and perspectives is important in the construction of local places and relationships' (p. 341).

Ultimately, this chapter suggests that action sports are no longer solely the interest of white, privileged youth living in western countries. More importantly, however, this chapter also challenges assumptions (particularly by western audiences) that youth in the Middle East are victims, ideologues or fundamentalists (Barber, 2001; Bayat, 2010; Gregory, 2004; McEvoy-Levy, 2001; Spaaij, 2011). Through my analysis of young parkour participants practices of resilience and resistance, I contribute to resisting the 'orientalist' tendencies among westerners to presume knowledge of youth in Gaza (and the Middle East) in ways that fit with, or confirm to, western goals, narratives and ideologies, but often overlook the actual experiences and voices of everyday people. Moreover, I reveal the agency of youth via their embrace of transnational networks to facilitate action sport mobilities in local contexts, which in some cases is helping them imagine new futures beyond the constraints of war and poverty.

Grassroots action sports in new contexts: the case of parkour

It is beyond the scope of this chapter to examine the multiple and varied ways children and youth are engaging in action sports across the Middle East. Thus, in this chapter I focus on the practice of parkour, which is arguably one of the most accessible action sports. In contrast to skateboarding, surfing or sand-boarding, which require (often expensive) equipment (such as skate-, surf- and sand-boards) and access to specific types of environments (smooth concrete, waves, sand dunes), parkour requires little more than a pair of shoes fit for moving efficiently within the urban environment, and when training in the sand dunes – as is common in many Arab countries – the activity can be performed barefoot. Simply defined, parkour (also known as 'the art of displacement' or free-running) is the practice of moving fluidly and efficiently across an urban environment, and often involves spectacular manoeuvres (inspired by gymnastics, breakdancing, climbing and/or skateboarding) on obstacles found in city spaces. Although the terms are often used interchangeably, free-running refers to a slightly different version of the activity that encourages greater individual expression and creative interpretation of the urban environment. Both parkour and free-running have roots in military obstacle-course training and martial arts; they are non-competitive and encourage a unique philosophy towards the self and bodily movement in space. Parkour participants or 'traceurs' train both their bodies and minds to creatively and safely navigate their way through the urban environment. Well-trained traceurs run, jump, roll and leap over, across and from rooftops, staircases, raised surfaces and walls, efficiently and with a fluid style. Despite a long tradition, parkour as we know the activity today was developed in France during the 1980s and 1990s by a group of young men, including Raymond Belle, his son David Belle and Sebastien Foucan. During the late 1990s and early 2000s, however, parkour rapidly gained popularity among urban youth around the western world, in part due to the highly evocative media coverage of Belle, Belle, Foucan and others, performing spectacular feats in films, advertisements and documentaries.

Scholars in an array of disciplines (including cultural geography, architecture, urban studies and sport sociology) have examined the rapid growth and popularity of parkour in urban metropolises such as London, Toronto and Chicago. In so doing, they have described the unique spatial politics practised by parkour enthusiasts (Atkinson, 2009), the highly affective experiences of participants (Saville, 2008), and the value of parkour for 'encouraging youth engagement, physical health and well-being' (Gilchrist & Wheaton, 2011, p. 109). As well as recognizing traceurs' intimate engagement with their immediate physical and social environments, some scholars have also examined the 'dialectical connection' between parkour practices and the Internet (Kidder, 2012, p. 2). Indeed, the Internet and new social media have played an important role in the global dissemination of parkour, and the production of a transnational imaginary in which participants in local contexts feel part of a broader movement. Based on his study of traceurs in Chicago, Kidder (2012) illustrates how 'globalized ideas and images available through the Internet and other media can be put into practice within specific locals' (p. 1). Describing practitioners of parkour as simultaneously 'engag[ing] their immediate, physical world' and 'draw[ing] upon an imagination enabled by their on-screen lives' (p. 2), he argues that urban researchers need to 'consider the ways that virtual worlds can change and enhance how individuals understand and utilize the material spaces of the city' (p. 1). Similarly, Gilchrist & Wheaton (2013) draw upon original research into the emergence and institutionalization of parkour in the UK to analyse the 'impact of networked communications in parkour'. They describe digital media as 'an important means of communication, connecting participants trans-locally, and for some transnationally', allowing participants to learn about the activity and its culture, 'as a creative form of performance and self-expression, and a route to possible entrepreneurial activity' (Gilchrist & Wheaton, 2013). In this chapter I draw inspiration from the work of Kidder (2012) and Gilchrist & Wheaton (2013) to examine the use of electronic media by youth in Middle East countries for sporting inspiration and connecting with fellow enthusiasts around the world.

Some may be surprised to learn that youth living in such poverty have access to such technologies. Of course, there are ongoing inequalities in access to computers and mobile communication or recording devices (for example, cellphones, iPads, GoPro). Recent research, however, reveals that Internet and social media consumers are increasingly from lower socio-economic backgrounds, and while they might not own iPhones or the latest technologies, less privileged youth are using whatever technologies are available to them for entertainment, communication and access to information (Duggan & Brenner, 2013; Kreutzer, 2009; Rideout, 2011). For example, observing new-media trends among children and youth in low-income areas in Cape Town, South Africa, Kreutzer (2009) recognized cheap mobile phones as introducing 'a range of new possibilities for the use and production of media, as well as for personal networking and communication, political activism, and economic development' (no page). Here I build upon this research to illustrate how young men in the war-torn region of Gaza are creatively utilizing cheap mobile phones and computers to connect to and communicate with the transnational parkour community, and to use action sport for political change and solidarity for their cause.

In the remainder of this chapter I explore the grassroots development of parkour in the Middle East at a unique historical conjuncture in which youth have (to varying degrees) gained greater access to global information and opportunities to virtually communicate beyond their local environments, yet continue to live with the everyday realities (or threats) of war, poverty and political upheaval. To understand the development of parkour in the Middle East, I conducted electronic interviews with key members of parkour groups in Kuwait, Egypt and Gaza. I engaged the electronic interviews in dialogue with media analysis of various print (such as magazine articles), digital (YouTube clips, parkour websites) and social media (Twitter postings by group leaders, Facebook), to identify themes across the data. In so doing, I gained a better understanding of how youth are engaging social media for inspiration, and also for sharing their experiences with parkour enthusiasts around the world. Despite many similarities in the development of parkour across Middle Eastern countries, there are also unique differences based on the particular socio-cultural and political contexts. Unfortunately, it is beyond the scope of this chapter to offer in-depth insights into parkour in the various contexts; therefore, in the final part of this chapter I focus on parkour in the Gaza Strip.

Youth, parkour and political agency in the Middle East

The Middle East has been a site of much discussion and debate over the past three decades. Despite massive oil reserves, Arab countries are faced with 'declining productivity . . . decreasing school enrolment, and high illiteracy, and with health conditions lagging behind comparable nations' such that they seem 'richer than they are developed' (Bayat, 2010, p. 1). The delays in social development in the region cannot be separated from poor political governance. Providing a valuable overview of recent events in the region, Bayat (2010) describes 'authoritarian regimes ranging from Iran, Syria, Egypt, Jordan and Morocco to the sheikhdoms of the Persian Gulf, and chiefly Saudi Arabia (incidentally, most with close ties to the West)' continuing to 'frustrate demands for democracy and the rule of law, prompting (religious) opposition movements that espouse equally undemocratic, exclusive, and often violent measures' (p. 1).

Following long histories of war, conflict and political unrest, the Arab Spring uprisings in 2010 saw radical political and social changes in many Middle Eastern countries (Tunisia, Libya, Egypt, Syria, Yemen, Kuwait, Saudi Arabia, Morocco and Bahrain), which have seriously impacted their internal, regional and international relations. The Arab Spring started in Tunisia with its citizens protesting against oppression by their government and calling for enhanced civil rights. Assisted by the use of new media and communication technologies, protest spread across the region and affected many countries. The use of cell-phones and social media such as email, Facebook, YouTube and Twitter were vital vehicles in both 'sustaining [the] reform movement within countries and spreading the wave of demonstrations across the region' (Mohammad, 2011, p. 159). In many cases, civil protests in these countries led to the dissolution of governments. Consequently, democratic elections were held, new constitutions were drafted and there was a general shift of power away from the status quo ante. With the Middle East purportedly 'falling into disarray', it is not surprising that the western world became highly concerned about the 'international destabilizing ramifications of this seeming social and political stagnation' (Bayat, 2010, p. 1).

In the past three decades, there have been major societal changes in many of the Arab states, and sporting values, policies and politics have been transformed within the Arab world. According to Amara (2012), many of those in power understood well the 'multiple uses of sport as an element of political, social and cultural recognition' and thus the 'western dominant model of sport' was 'accepted by the newly independent countries with little criticism or adaptation to local particularism' (p. 7). Many Middle Eastern countries are increasingly embracing the 'strategy of development through sport in the bidding for, and staging [of], mega-sport events' as a 'scheme for urban regeneration, for strengthening internal and external political legitimacy and for integrating the commercial values of sport' (Amara, 2012, p.14). Through relationships with FIFA and the IOC, sport in the Arab world 'came to be regarded in general as an effective arena for future international treaties and conventions between North and South, East and West' (p. 7). But, as Slisli (2009) is careful to point out, 'the adoption of democratic or popular practices' in the Arabic world 'are always fragmentary and deceiving' (p. 1). Indeed, despite recognition among the Arabic elite of the potential of sport, some cultural and religious differences between the west and the Arab world continue to pose difficulties, particularly regarding women's participation in sport, and youths' participation in unorganized, non-competitive sports that celebrate fun, creativity and self-expression.

Parkour in the Middle East: reclaiming youthfulness and the everyday politics of fun

Many countries in the Middle East face their largest youth cohort in modern history. Young men and women in these countries are, according to Chaaban (2008), encountering 'increased social exclusion and marginalization . . . rising unemployment rates, higher exposure to health issues, and a precarious education system' (p. 6). Many social commentators and researchers have identified the large number of unemployed youth in Arab nations as a major cause of recent political unrest. According to Mohammad (2011), unemployed youths' political frustrations were 'aggravated by their inability to express themselves in tightly controlled police state', combined with 'political corruption and the incapability of the state to deal with social and economic problems' (p. 159). At the same time, youth were also gaining access to new media, which not only exposed them to other ways of knowing the world, but also facilitated greater communication and organization across groups. According to Amara (2012), the new type of politics practised by this younger generation was 'the product of "societies of knowledge" (*sociétés du savoir*), new technology, globalization, open media and web-based social networks, against the interventionist and coercive model of politics of state (be it a party or a monarchy)' (p. 19; also see Levine, 2012).

In his book, *Life as Politics: How Ordinary People Change the Middle East*, Asef Bayat (2010) describes a 'deep distrust' of the state developing among Muslim youth such that the young increasingly 'took solace in non-state spaces that infringed only marginally on political and moral authorities. They resorted to the cultural politics of everyday life, where they could reassert their youthful claims' (p. 131). Here 'youthful claims' refers to Muslim youths' collective efforts to defend and extend the conditions that allow them to embrace expressions of fun and play in everyday life, and 'free them from anxiety over the prospect of the future' (Bayat, 2010, p. 18). Although rarely acknowledged in discussions and debates about youth movements, or the political mobilization of youth in the Middle East, such 'claims of youthfulness' are, according to Bayat, at the core of ongoing youth discontent in the Muslim Middle East (p. 18).

For Bayat, puritan Islamists' apprehension, even hostility, toward the expression of fun and joy is part of the problem. During the 1980s and 1990s, conservative Islamists 'battled against those who desired to demonstrate public joy. Fun, playfulness, lightness, and laughter were seen as instances of immorality, laxity, and waste' (Bayat, 2010, p. 140). But 'young mullahs also need to have fun' (Bayat, 2010, p. 137), and as youth were increasingly exposed to global media they became more and more 'informed by western technologies of fun' (music, fashion, sport, dancing, drinking, dating). Such 'spontaneous, erotically charged, and commodified pleasures' were framed in terms of 'western cultural import' (pp. 138–9), and deemed 'alien to Islamic culture' (p. 139). The morality of youth became a matter of serious concern among many Islamists, the conservative media and what Bayat refers to as 'anti-fun adversaries', such that bans and strict codes of conduct were imposed upon youth in many Islamic states. Of course, the intensity of youthful challenges to such authoritarian restrictions 'depends on the capacity of the adversaries, the moral and political authorities, to accommodate and contain youthful claims' (p. 116), as well as the numbers and networks of disaffected youth.

For many frustrated, angry and 'fun'-deprived youth, the streets served as the 'key theatre of contentions' (Bayat, 2010, p. 11) and the 'ultimate arena to communicate discontent' (p. 12). According to Bayat, the active use of the urban environment for purposes other than those dictated by the state (for example, walking, driving, watching) has become a form of 'street politics' that 'infuriate officials who see themselves as the sole authority to establish and control public order' (p. 12). In this chapter I identify parkour as a form of 'everyday politics' being expressed by Arab youth in their attempts to 'reclaim youthfulness' through physical play, self-expression and public performance amidst ongoing authoritarian rule. Parkour is a subtly anti-authoritarian gesture in that youth seek to negotiate physical and symbolic space in local and global (virtual) communities as the Middle East continues the messy process of integration into the global economic system.

Drawing upon research with parkour participants from the USA, the UK and Australia, Bavinton (2007) explains that the 'spontaneous fun and creativity characteristic of parkour' is closely associated with the 'reinterpretation and utilisation of constraints'; participants are empowered by their ability 'to wrest (admittedly partial and momentary) control of the power relations embedded within public urban spaces' (p. 391). As I illustrate in this chapter, however, the creative uses of the urban environment by parkour practitioners in Middle Eastern countries – where the streets have been key sites of social unrest (and thus remain under close surveillance) – carry different meanings for participants. Parkour is not only a symbolic form of 'street politics', but it is also an alternative to the top-down, state-defined forms of sport that are emerging in the Middle East (Amara, 2012).

Parkour had been popular among western youth for almost a decade before it reached the Middle East in the new millennium. In contrast to the historical movement of sports across countries – in which colonizers often imposed their sports on the local peoples who adopted, appropriated or rejected the activities – young men in the Middle East were first exposed to the activity via cable television and the Internet in the early 2000s. According to photojournalist David Denger, parkour 'migrated to Egypt without direct contact but through iconic movies such as *District 13* and homemade YouTube videos' (pc, January 2013). Inspired by the athleticism and novelty of parkour, some young Middle Eastern men quickly adopted active roles in learning the sport, finding and creating their own spaces for participation, training others, and establishing their own media (such as videos, websites, newsletters).

Youth in the Middle East are some of the world's most active users of the Internet and new social media. Youth make up around 70 per cent of the 45 million Facebook users in the Arab world, and Arabic is the fastest growing language in Twitter history (Facebook in the Arab region, 2012; More than half, 2012; Richards, 2012). It is perhaps not surprising then that the Internet and social media have been integral to the development of parkour in Middle Eastern countries. For example, in 2003, a small group of young Egyptian men became inspired after watching parkour online. Nasser Al-Refaei – a physical education graduate – was among the first to start practising parkour in Egypt. In his own words, he had 'always been in love with extreme sports', and was quickly impressed by the manoeuvres he saw on YouTube: 'I started to analyse the moves based on my background studies and then applied that to myself. Then I shot a small clip of my trainings and posted it on YouTube' (cited in Against gravity, 2012). Al-Refaei then went on to become the primary trainer for Parkour Egypt, the first official parkour group in the Middle East. Since its establishment in 2005, Parkour Egypt has grown to include more than 200 members. Virtual media continue to play an integral role in the daily organization, and local and international communications, of the group. As Mahmoud explained,

> the social networking websites are helping us to spread the art and keep all our fans and students updated with anything we do. [The] Internet has an essential role making the parkour spread in Egypt, and for communication with many groups from different Arabic states (pc, January 2013).

Shortly after the development of parkour in Egypt, the activity also drew the attention of young men in Kuwait who went on to found PK Jaguars in 2006. The primary goal of this group is to 'spread Parkour's way of life to Middle East any way possible and make the youth and community realize how important Parkour and movement is to our daily lives' (PK Jaguars Facebook page). As with Parkour Egypt, the PK Jaguars are very active in their use of online media.

Many of the early participants tended to be young men in their late teens and early twenties, and often university graduates unable to find full-time employment. As coaching sessions have been made available, however, the groups are becoming more diverse, with younger boys increasingly taking up the activity. Of course, these groups are not free from hierarchical and patriarchal practices that continue to proliferate in many Arab countries. According to one young Kuwaiti interviewee, 'a lot of women want to join, but our religion doesn't allow it. In Islamic [tradition], man can't touch the woman, so captains [trainers] can't catch them during training' (pc, 2013). Similarly, a coach at Parkour Egypt explained:

> We don't train girls due to religious and traditional reasons. In Islam it is not allowed to touch women at certain sensitive body parts, as parkour training requires the trainer to hold and catch the student in specific positions, this makes training impossible. Also … for a girl it will be dangerous and more risky than a boy to have an injury. In Egypt people criticize boys who do parkour and always mock them in streets, imagine a girl doing parkour in the streets, she would get negative feedback. (pc, Mahmoud, 2013)

While women are not allowed to participate with most parkour groups in the Middle East, differences in the gender regimes across and within countries are such that a few women are practising parkour with groups in Egypt (Egyflow) and Iran (Hitall). Yet, for girls and women in some Muslim countries, the street can be a particularly dangerous space if one's behaviour is not deemed to be culturally and socially appropriate.[2]

Today, groups of (mostly young male) traceurs and free-runners can be found in Bahrain, Doha, Egypt, Israel, Kuwait, Libya, Morocco, Oman, Palestine, Saudi Arabia and UAE. Almost all have Facebook pages with the number of followers ranging from 300 (Parkour Libya Free) to 42,000 (Parkour Egypt). These pages feature short edited videos with group members performing parkour or free-running in various environments, news of upcoming training sessions and performances, or reviews of events, mostly written in Arabic. Some parkour groups are relatively small, informal groups of young men who train together, whereas others have grown into highly organized, hierarchical and commercial organizations with hired training facilities and coaches. Key members of some groups travel internationally to compete and perform, and make regular appearances in movies and commercials (for example, Chevrolet, Vodafone, Pepsi). For example, members of the PK Kuwait and Bahrain Parkour teams performed together on the beach at the Qatar National Day celebration in December 2011. Both Parkour Egypt and PK Jaguars have featured in the *Arabs Got Talent* television program, and in 2011 Kuwait hosted the Red Bull Art of Motion international competition, which included some of the top free-runners and parkour athletes from Kuwait and around the world. In contrast, the development of parkour in Gaza has been considerably more difficult.

PK Gaza: overcoming obstacles

The Gaza Strip is a territory on the eastern coast of the Mediterranean Sea that borders Egypt on the southwest and Israel on the east and north. With approximately 1.7 million residents and refugees occupying an area of 365 square kilometres (40 kilometres long and 10 kilometres wide), the Gaza Strip is among the most densely populated regions in the world. Originally administered by Egypt (which retains control of Gaza's southern border), the area was captured by the Israelis in 1967 during the Six Day War (Oren, 2001). Israeli settlements in the region were a constant source of tension, such that in 2005 Israel withdrew its troops and settlers. Research shows that youth held significant roles in the Intifada (Arabic for uprising or shaking off); 80 per cent of male children and 50 per cent of female children, and 85 per cent of male adolescents and 65 per cent of female adolescents, were involved in demonstrations against the occupation (Barber, 2001). Interviews with Palestinian youth revealed that their involvement was 'driven by informed and advanced levels of awareness and commitment to the broader social goal of relief from the occupation' (Barber, 2001, p. 259). In an excellent historical and geographical analysis of the Palestine–Israel conflict, Gregory (2004) identifies the heightened militarization of the al-Aqsa Intifada as the 'product of a profound, desperate anger born out of the sustained and asymmetric violence of Israel's continuing military occupation of Gaza and the West Bank' (p. 105). He describes the Palestinian 'youth culture from which many suicide bombers have emerged' as 'both communal and competitive' (p. 105), and draws upon the work of Hage (2003) to suggest 'a sort of jockeying for symbolic capital among those for whom most other opportunities for recognition and worth have been systematically withdrawn' (p. 105).

A year after the Israeli withdrawal, the Islamist militant group Hamas won elections in Gaza. In June 2007, Hamas took complete control of the strip, ousting the more moderate rival Fatah, the faction of Palestinian leader Mahmoud Abbas, who continues to run parts of the West Bank. The Israelis responded by tightening a blockade on Gaza, seriously limiting the transit of goods and people into and out of the territory. Such blockades restrict opportunities for trade, such that Gaza is largely dependent on external aid and the 'shadow tunnel economy' that is said to include hundreds of tunnels built under the border with Egypt, enabling the movement of goods, including weapons. The words of Palestinian author and poet Mahmoud Darwish provide insight into the difficulties and atrocities faced by Palestinians living in Israeli-occupied territories: 'the occupation does not content itself with depriving us of the primary conditions of freedom, but goes on to deprive us of the bare essentials of a *dignified human life*, by declaring constant war on our bodies, and our dreams, on the people and the homes and the trees, and by committing crimes of war . . .' (cited in Gregory 2004, p. 133). This is, according to Gregory (2004), a 'world wrenched upside down' (p. 129) where Israel continues to 'extend its illegal settlement of the occupied territories and asserts its monopoly of violence', and 'criminalizes any act of Palestinian resistances to its illegal operations and its state terrorism' (p. 129), all with the intent to 'paralyse Palestinian agency' (p. 126).

As a result of years of conflict and ongoing blockages, almost 80 per cent of the Gazan population is dependent on international assistance (UNRWA, 2013). Gaza suffers from high unemployment (approximately 40 per cent), with a particularly high rate (58 per cent) among those aged 20 to 24 years (Life in the Gaza Strip, 2012). With over 50 per cent of the population under the age of 15 years, the 'youth bulge' is the most severe of all the Middle Eastern countries. The infrastructure in Gaza is also very poor compared to the other Palestinian territories. It is thought that a lack of funding for infrastructure or investment is a strategic move by the Israeli government to limit satisfaction of basic human needs, in order to regain power over the region. In 2012, there were several rockets and airstrikes that were exchanged in retaliation against both Israelis and Palestinians being killed. While many NGOs, governments and peace activists have been involved (for decades) in trying to resolve the conflict, the violence continues, with no real peace strategy in sight. Various Sport for Development and Peace Building (SDP) organizations, such as Right to Play, Peace Players International and Kicking the Ball and Taking Care, are also actively working in the region in efforts to enhance the health, well-being and resilience of Palestine residents living in refugee camps and conflict zones, and to facilitate cultural exchanges between groups of different religious and cultural backgrounds (Bellotti, 2012; Sugden, 2006, 2008). Several local football teams also participate in the Gaza Strip League. In the context of such hardship, however, organized sport seems to offer little more than a short-term escape from the harsh realities of life in Gaza.

Parkour reached Gaza in 2005, when recent university graduate Abdullah Anshasi watched the documentary *Jump London* on the Al Jazeera documentary channel. He promptly followed this up by searching the Internet for video clips of parkour, before recruiting Mohammed Aljkhbayr to join him in learning the new sport. Mohammed recalls the day fondly:

> Abdullah, my best friend, told me he had just seen a video clip online about 'free-running' which is about overcoming obstacles. It just sounded

like a sport that I would love to practice. We started to practice every day, and our liking of this sport increased. We kept looking at the video clips online, whenever the electricity worked. We toned our bodies and practiced jumps, rolls and runs daily. (cited in Shahin, 2012, paras. 6–7)

As with parkour practitioners in Kuwait and Egypt, the Internet and online videos were their initial inspiration for practising the sport, and integral to their skill development over the following years. Abdullah and Mohammed 'never had any formal training' and took it upon themselves to 'learn from the videos we saw on the net' (Enshasi, cited in Shahin, 2012). Continuing to develop their skills, they soon found parkour to be so much more than a sport, 'it is a life philosophy' that encourages each individual to 'overcome barriers in their own way' (cited in Shahin, 2012). In a world surrounded by obstacles and blockades, the symbolism is not lost on these young men:

I dream of travelling abroad to compete in international competitions, but we can't leave this place. We're caged in on all sides. [. . .] When I had nothing to do I would go to the border with Abdallah. We'd sit at the Rafah border which is our border with Egypt. We would ask ourselves, what is beyond this border and how do people live on the other side? We would dream that one day our sport will help us get past this obstacle . . . crossing this border is a big dream. (cited in Shahin, 2012)

Such goals inspired the young men to continue in their physically demanding training despite physical and social risks.

Reappropriating dangerous spaces

The young men experienced resistance from their parents and many in the local community who did not understand their quest for physical expression, creativity and pleasure in the urban environment surrounding the Khan Younes refugee camps: 'We practice every day in isolated areas. When I come home there are always questions: where have you been? What are you doing? We face a lot of resistance from family, neighbours, and the police' (cited in Shahin, 2012). The parents of another parkour recruit, Abu Sulton, also 'forbade it': 'they tried to stop me, especially after I was injured, but they couldn't. It's in my blood' (cited in Hussein, 2012). As Abdullah and Mohammad recruited other young men to join their training sessions, groups of children and youths often gathered in the streets to watch with fascination. Yet many older local residents were unsure what to make of these young men running up walls, jumping off roofs, and performing spectacular flips and rolls in the streets. 'At first people didn't accept us. People would say, "you jump like monkeys and you climb buildings like thieves. What are you doing?",' explained Abdullah (pc, January 2013). Similarly, another PK Gaza recruit, Jakhibir, recalled: 'people would complain and the police would come. It became a game, we'd practice until they arrived and then run away' (cited in Hussein, 2012).

To avoid conflicts with family members, local residents and police, members of PK Gaza (the name chosen by the group) sought out unpopulated spaces where they could train without interruption. Popular training areas included cemeteries, the ruined houses from the Dhraha occupation, UNRWA (United Nations Relief and Works Agency) schools, and on the sandy hills in Nusseirat, formerly an Israeli settlement now deserted in the centre of Gaza City. The latter is particularly meaningful for the youth who proclaim that by practising parkour in the space, 'we demonstrate that this land is our right and we do what we like in a place that we want, even if you have to kill us or bomb us . . . we will continue to practise our sport in any place and at any time' (pc, Mohammed, January 2013). Despite ongoing resistance from family members and local authorities, Mohammed is a strong advocate for the potential of parkour for raising awareness about the conditions of those living in Gaza: 'I want people to change their ideas about sports, all sports. They need to understand that sport is something very important. Athletes can raise Palestine's name throughout the world' (cited in Hussein, 2012). Indeed, Mohammed, Abdullah and other members of PK Gaza are very proactive at using the Internet to share their unique skills and experiences with the transnational parkour community, and in so doing, are advancing an informal form of cultural diplomacy.

YouTube, Twitter and Facebook: tapping into transnational networks

Despite such poverty, Gazan residents have remarkably high levels of access to the Internet and telecommunications. In 2011, 95 per cent of households in Palestinian territories owned a mobile phone, compared with 72.8 per cent in 2004, and 93.9 per cent of households had satellite dishes. Over the same period, the number of households connected to the Internet more than tripled from 9.2 per cent to 30.4 per cent (More than half, 2012). The increasing youth engagement with the Internet is the most noteworthy, with the number of young Palestinians with access to the Internet and with email accounts growing five-fold (to 46.5 per cent) between 2004 and 2011 (More than half, 2012). Their usage of the Internet, however, is intermittent, with regular electricity outages and blackouts, and threats of Internet surveillance, censorship and control of information. But with support from international groups such as Telecomix, an organization that believes in freedom of information, Gazan residents are finding alternative means to maintain their broadband services (McGuire, 2012).[3]

As part of the younger generation of increasingly technologically savvy Gazan residents, the founders of PK Gaza are explicitly aware of the potential of the Internet for their parkour practices, and also for broader political purposes: 'YouTube, Facebook and Twitter are very important for us because we use it to show our skills and deliver a message to the world that Palestine exists and stems of [sic] life and love and peace' (pc, Mohammad, January 2013). 'We started filming ourselves with mobile phones and putting the videos on YouTube,' explains Mohammed, and they continued to develop more advanced filming techniques using borrowed cameras and editing the footage on a cheap computer. The PK Gaza and Freerunning Facebook page has almost 4000 followers from around the world, and provides space for PK Gaza members to chat (mostly in Arabic) with parkour enthusiasts across the Middle East and around the world (Farrell, 2011). The group also post regular YouTube videos that can receive upwards of tens of thousands of views. As the following comment from Mohammed suggests, both Facebook and YouTube are key spaces for interaction and dialogue with youth beyond the confines of the Gaza Strip:

> [social media] contribute very significantly to raising international awareness of what is happening in Gaza. We offer video clips, photographs and writings related to the situation in which we live in the Gaza strip and deliver the message to all the people's that's watching online that there are oppressed people . . . we were able to take advantage of parkour . . . to deliver the right message of what is happening in the Gaza Strip . . . we won the world's sympathy with our cause. (pc, Mohammed, January 2013)

A particularly evocative video reveals the everyday risks facing the PK Gaza participants. Training in the sand dunes on the outskirts of the Khan Younis refugee camp on the first day of the Israeli assault on the Gaza Strip on November 14, 2012, 'the occupation forces bombed a site very close to the place of our training with a group of children, some of whom panicked because they fear the Israeli army. We documented the event on camera, so we can not forget' (pc, January 2013). Indeed, the short video of the bombing that interrupted the training mentioned above, titled 'Despite the pain there is hope', was re-posted, linked and 'liked' on news sites around the world. The original YouTube video has been viewed more than 150,000 times. As Mohammed explained: 'We did this video to convey [the] message to the world that we, despite all what is happening in the Gaza Strip – killing and bombing and destruction of facilities – there is hope in life' (cited in Gaza parkour team, 2012, para. 2).[4]

Interestingly, these virtual spaces also enable dialogue that may contribute to building respect between participants of varying socio-cultural, religious and/or national backgrounds based on parkour participation. For example, YouTube videos created by the PK Gaza group receive support in Arabic and English from fellow parkour enthusiasts around the world, including the following comment from an Israeli parkour practitioner: 'Amazing guys! You got so much better than last year. I hope there will be peace between us one day'; the message was signed 'Peace from Israel!' In some cases, it seems the virtual communications between parkour participants from different countries may also facilitate cultural understanding that has the potential to contribute to future peace-building.

As well as posting their own media on universal providers such as YouTube, the founders of PK Gaza have also reached out to the international parkour community by contributing to existing online platforms. Abdullah recalls his initial efforts to negotiate legitimate space within the transnational parkour community:

> When I tried to register [PK Gaza] on the [international parkour] website, I looked for the Palestinian flag in the country section. I wrote them several letters . . . for a month I kept writing. In the end they wrote back . . . I was so happy when I saw it. Before this they only had the Israeli flag. We wanted the world to know we were here – we were free runners. It took a while, but eventually they reached out to us. (pc, 2013)

Indeed, after successfully registering on an international parkour online network, their video 'Free running Gaza' was posted on the website and thus shared with parkour participants around the world. With such global exposure, the PK Gaza group began to receive offers of support from individuals and groups from an array of countries. For example, an Australian viewer offered to design their logo – this now features on the team websites and team t-shirts. They also received invitations from around the world to compete in international events and competitions. Due to the blockages, they were regrettably unable to accept such invitations. In February 2012, with sponsorship from the Unione Italiana Sport per Tutti ('Sport for All'), however, Mohammed, Abdullah and Jihad were able to travel outside of Gaza for the first time to attend the Italian Free Running and Parkour Federation's annual event in Milan. On this trip, they also performed in Rome, Bologna and Palermo, and met free runners from across the world, including practitioners from Egypt, Lebanon and Morocco: 'those were the most memorable 17 days of our lives. [. . .] The other free runners were kind and helpful, and they wanted to hear what we had to say about Gaza,' recalled Mohammed (cited in Shahin, 2012). Continuing to wax lyrical about the generosity of their Italian hosts, he proclaimed: 'they were able to make our biggest dream come true . . . [overcoming] the biggest obstacle of all – the Israeli checkpoint – and travel abroad' (Mohammed, cited in Hussein, 2012). The young men used this trip as an opportunity for cultural diplomacy and raising awareness of the plight of those living in Gaza: 'we talked to people about our lives in Gaza, that we're living under siege, and in a continually tense situation. We face financial, social and political obstacles' (cited in Hussein, 2012). As Figures 8.1 and 8.2 illustrate, the young men received much support from various parkour groups and sports teams whom they met during their Italian trip.[5]

Figure 8.1 A group of Italian parkour practitioners (Parkour Wave) makes a public statement following their interactions with the PK Gaza team in November 2012 (Image used with permission of photographer, Luca Colombo, and UISP Milano, Unione Italiana Sport per Tutti)

Figure 8.2 The Stella Rosa rugby team in Milan offers their support of Gaza after meeting the PK Gaza team (Image used with permission of photographer, Luca Colombo, and UISP Milano, Unione Italiana Sport per Tutti)

Parkour for resilience and coping

As well as raising awareness of the conditions in Gaza and offering a temporary escape from the harsh realities of everyday life, the PK Gaza team also emphasize the socio-psychological benefits of their everyday parkour experiences. They proclaim the value of parkour for their resilience and coping with the frustrations, fears, anxieties and pains of living in the Khan Younes refugee camp. As Anshasi explains, 'I have witnessed war, invasion and killing. When I was a kid and I saw these things, blood and injuries, I didn't know what it all meant . . . this game [parkour] makes me forget all these things' (cited in Sorcher, 2010). With a background in kickboxing, Jihad joined the PK Gaza team after seeing a clip of Mohammed on YouTube, and he enjoys the physicality and psychology of the activity: 'It uses physical strength more than any other sport . . . parkour teaches us to overcome obstacles. It makes me feel free, it makes my body feel strong, that I can overcome anything' (cited in Hussein, 2012). Similarly, Mohammed describes a dire situation: 'the sanctions have created enormous obstacles. It's been five years and things keep getting worse. We have wars regularly and the sanctions make our lives miserable'; but, he continues, 'this sport has given me the ability to overcome many obstacles. It's made me steadfast and has given me the strength to face the pressures of the occupation' (cited in Shahin, 2012). Although Mohammed has become well-practised in answering questions from journalists about the socio-psychological benefits of parkour, he remains adamant that parkour helps him untangle the 'anger and depression' that comes with living in the narrow, politically and militarily confined Gaza Strip (cited in Shahin, 2012). He explains, 'There is always a problem here of one sort or another. If it's not the war or the sanctions, then it's an internal issue. It's depressing but we try to practise self-help. We try to be our own doctors' (cited in Shahin, 2012). As the quote at the head of this chapter from Gazan psychologist, Eyad Al Sarraj, MD, suggests, some medical and health professionals also acknowledge the value of activities such as parkour for young men trapped in such a stressful environment. Such observations are supported by a plethora of research that has illustrated the value of physical play and games for resilience in contexts of high risk and/or ongoing physical and psychological stress (such as refugee camps), and the restorative value for children and youth who have experienced traumatic events (such as natural disaster, war, forced migration) (Berinstein & Magalhaes, 2009; Evers, 2010b; Kunz, 2009; Rung, et al., 2011; Samara, 2005).

Looking forward: mentoring the next generation

The pioneers of parkour in Gaza, Mohammed and Abdullah, are now working with a group of peers to support the next generation of parkour enthusiasts. According to Mohammed, 'Palestinian society requires us to . . . dedicate our lives to work and found a family'. Thus, recognizing that he will soon be 'forced to leave the sport' that he has dedicated almost a decade of his young life toward developing, he is now investing his energies into 'training larger groups' and expanding to various provinces in the Gaza Strip. He does so with the hope of the 'formation of a large academy to train new generations . . . and disseminate [parkour] among young men and women all over Palestine' (pc, January 2013). As Enshasi, one of the trainers for a group of eight to 16-year-old male parkour enthusiasts, explains:

> My main focus as I grow older is to make sure that PK Gaza continues as an art and sports form in Gaza. I do not want it to die with us. I want it to continue and grow. This is why now I feel our main focus should be on training the next generation. They are young minds and bodies who want to be set free. (Enshasi, cited in Shahin, 2012)

The regular training sessions and informal peer mentoring provided by the PK Gaza leaders offer boys and young men growing up in Gaza valuable social networks beyond the family, and support structures that facilitate coping and resilience through everyday physical pleasures. Perhaps most importantly, the social and physical experiences offered through parkour offer youth a sense of hope for a future with surmountable obstacles.

Concluding thoughts

This chapter examined how youth living in the Middle East are actively reconfiguring global (or rather, western) action sport commodities, images and texts, and creatively re-embedding them within local contexts and cultures to suit their particular needs, beliefs and customs. In so doing, we gain fresh insights in the processes of 'glocalization' operating within and across contemporary action sport cultures. More specifically, this chapter offers insight into the meanings and practices of sport in Gaza, and particularly how youth in Gaza are using parkour to enhance the quality of their everyday lives, and also to make people aware of their sporting practices, politics and everyday living conditions. In a place of conflict and poverty, many Gazan children and youth face 'apathy, low self-esteem and a sense of powerlessness' (McEvoy-Levy, 2001, p. 24). Yet, as this case illustrates, we should not overlook their agency, nor should we assume them to be victims, ideologues or fundamentalists. Some youth are demonstrating remarkable agency in creating sporting opportunities that cater to their own and other local children's and youths' physical, social and psychological needs. Acknowledging the agency and privileging the voices of youth involved in grassroots sporting groups seems particularly important in regions, such as the Middle East, where the huge and growing population of young people has the potential to 'shake present regimes from within more devastatingly than even the forces of international politics' (Fuller, 2004, p. 4).

As I have argued in this chapter and the previous one, we cannot understand the mobilities within contemporary action sport cultures without also considering various immobilities. Yet even in places where corporeal mobilities are limited by war, poverty or natural disaster, local residents are using electronic media to connect with transnational networks and to imagine new possibilities for themselves through action sport participation. In so doing, some are using the physicality of action sports and existing networks to connect with local and global communities, and ultimately to expand their opportunities for movement within local spaces and across borders.

Conclusion

9
Transnational Connections and Transformation: Action Sport for Development and Peace Building

This book has offered a multidimensional examination of the macro and micro processes of transnationalism operating within and across global and local action sport cultures. It has examined the various forms of power working within transnational action sport cultures, ranging from corporate, media and governmental institutions, to the everyday politics within action sport communities. In so doing, it has revealed how corporeal, virtual and imaginative (im)mobilities are informing contemporary youth's participation in, and consumption of, sport and physical culture, as well as their understandings of place, space, identity and belonging. However, some might question the broader social significance of such trends, particularly if they continue to be experienced primarily (though not exclusively, see Chapter 8) by privileged youth. Thus, in this concluding chapter I consider the transformative potential of transnational action sport connections, networks and mobilities.

A common concern in studies of transnationalism has been how the scope and scale of networks and connections across borders are contributing to broader social transformation. In *Global Transformations*, for example, David Held and colleagues (1999) suggest that long-term changes are coming about as a result of the intensification of cross-border networks and connections. They suggest that the stretching of social relationships is such that events, decisions and activities in one region of the world are increasingly coming to have significance for individuals and communities in distant regions of the globe. Building upon this 'transformationalist' thesis, scholars across an array of disciplines are examining how transnational networks, modes of communication and mobilities are contributing to new forms of emancipatory politics and social engagement (Smith et al., 1997). Such research ranges from immigrants transnational political engagement with their polities of origin (Guarnizo et al., 2003) to the efforts of transnational activist groups such as Greenpeace and Amnesty International (Wapner, 1995). In *The New Transnational Activism*, for example, Sidney Tarrow (2005) illustrates how 'ordinary people gain new perspectives, experiment with new forms of action, and sometimes emerge with new identities through their contacts across borders'. In previous chapters I have examined how transnationalism is informing the identity politics of action sport migrants, how some action sport participants have responded to and resisted some processes of globalization, and the micro politics within transnational action sport destinations. Here, however, I am particularly interested in how transnational social formations and mobilities are contributing to the efforts by some action sport enthusiasts to create social change within and across local contexts. Thus, in this final chapter I draw together strands from various chapters to examine the potential for the transnational imagination to lead to transformation via the rise of action sports for development and peace building (ASDP) organizations, many of which are established by highly mobile action sport participants who then set about tapping into global networks and engaging the support of transnational corporations to initiate change in local communities.

Acknowledging the complex relationships between action sports, identity, consumption, politics and new forms of media, Wheaton (2007) describes lifestyle sport participants as 'individualistic *and* part of a collectivity: they are hedonistic *and* reflexive consumers, often politically disengaged yet environmentally aware and/or active' (p. 298; emphasis in original). Building upon Wheaton's thesis, I argue that contemporary action sport-related politics and social activism are being informed by the transnational imaginary, or participants' sense of belonging to a transnational community, and thus taking different shapes, and occurring in different spaces and places, than in previous generations. As Norris (2002) suggests, relying on traditional conceptions and 'conventional indicators' of what constitutes politics, we risk being 'blind' to some of the highly nuanced and variegated forms of political agency being expressed by youth in the early 21st century (p. 222). Youth involvement in politics and the significance of new technologies and social media for civic engagement has garnered considerable public and academic attention (Bennett, 2008; Harris, 2008; Maira, 2004; Schilt & Zobl, 2008; Wilson, 2002; Wilson & Hayhurst, 2009), this is particularly true following the so-called 'Arab Spring' uprising which revealed how youth across many Arab Middle Eastern countries were using social media to organize and communicate within and across borders (Comunello & Anzera, 2012). In the remainder of this chapter I illustrate how transnational social formations and corporeal, virtual and imagined mobilities are also contributing to new forms of politics in action sport cultures via a discussion of the recent growth of ASDP organizations.

Action Sports for Development and Peace Building (ASDP)

In 2001, Kofi Annan founded the United Nations Office on Sport for Development and Peace (SDP), advocating sport as having 'an almost unmatched role to play in promoting understanding, healing wounds, mobilising support for social causes, and breaking down barriers' (Annan, 2010). More recently, the United Nations defined April 6, 2013, as the inaugural International Day of Sport for Development and Peace. The Sport for Development and Peace (SDP) movement has proliferated in the current neoliberal context with groups and organizations using sport and physical activity to help improve the health and well-being of individuals and communities around the world (Beutler, 2008; Black, 2010; Darnell, 2012; Donnelly et al., 2011; Giulianotti, 2011a, 2011b; Kidd, 2008, 2011; Levermore, 2008; Levermore & Beacom, 2009; Thorpe & Rinehart, 2012). Of the 700 organizations working under the SDP umbrella, the lion's share involves traditional sports such as football, basketball, volleyball and hockey. Organizations such as Football for Peace, Right to Play, Hoops 4 Hope and Peace Players International have been acclaimed for making valuable contributions to the quality of many individuals' lives. It is only recently that the growth of ASDP has gained the attention of those working within the broader SDP movement (see Thorpe, 2013b; Thorpe & Ahmad, 2013; Thorpe & Rinehart, 2012).

For many years, action sports were thought to be the exclusive domain of privileged, white, narcissistic western youth. Stereotypes of surfers, skateboarders, snowboarders and climbers as hedonistic, thrill-seeking, anti-authoritarian, individualistic youth continue to proliferate in the mass media and popular cultural sentiment. Since the late 1990s, however, some action sport participants have established non-profit organizations and movements relating to an array of social issues, including *health* (for example, Boarding for Breast Cancer; Surf Aid International), *education* (for example, Chill – providing underprivileged youth with opportunities to learn to snowboard, skate and surf; Skateistan – co-educational skateboarding schooling in Afghanistan), *environment* (for example, Protect Our Winters [POW]; Surfers Environmental Alliance [SEA]; Surfers against Sewage [SAS]; see Heywood & Montgomery, 2008; Laviolette, 2006; Wheaton, 2007, 2008), and *anti-violence* (for example, Surfers for Peace – an informal organization aimed at bridging cultural and political barriers between surfers in the Middle East). In a broader social context in which acts of social activism and philanthropy are increasingly celebrated, many action sport athletes, corporations and enthusiasts are utilizing the networks and resources available within their sporting cultures and industries to create change within local and international communities.

There is considerable variation within contemporary action sport-related non-profit organizations and social campaigns. Some ASDP organizations can be broadly categorized within the SDP sector. Action sport organizations, such as Skateistan, Surfers for Peace and Chill, for example, employ action sports, such as skateboarding, surfing or snowboarding, as an 'intervention-ist tool to promote peace, reconciliation, and development in different locations across the world' (Giulianotti, 2011a, p. 50). For many other ASDP organizations, while the physical act of surfing, snowboarding or skiing plays an important role in uniting members of these groups and inspiring potential donors, the action sport is not *directly* used as an 'interventionist tool'. Rather, these organizations are founded by action sport participants who utilize pre-existing structures and connections within and across local, national and global sporting cultures and industries to raise awareness and funds for issues they deem to be socially significant. While some of these action sport-related social justice organizations remain at the grassroots level and are relatively unknown beyond the local community or outside the action sport culture, others are gaining recognition from mainstream social justice and humanitarian organizations for their innovative efforts and creative strategies to create change and bring about social justice in local and global contexts. For example, Surf Aid International received the World Association of Non-Governmental Organizations (WANGO) Humanitarian Award in 2007 for their 'unique cutting edge solutions to alleviate human suffering in the Mentawai Islands', and for the organization's ability to 'tap into the inherent values in the surfing community – individualism, courage, dynamism, and adaptability' (Hamad, 2007); and Skateistan won the 2009 Peace and Sport Non-Governmental Organization Award for its efforts in educating urban and internally displaced children in Kabul (Afghanistan), as well as the 2012 Innovation through Sport Award at the Beyond Sport Forum. Skateistan was also selected as a Top 100 NGO for 2013 by *The Global Journal*, making it the highest-ranking sport-related NGO.

To date, the founders of most ASDP organizations have typically been action sport enthusiasts (rather than experienced humanitarian or aid workers) who became inspired to create change when they observed poverty, inequalities and injustices during their sport-related travel (see Thorpe & Rinehart, 2012). Here I build upon the Bourdieusian-inspired argument offered in Chapter 6 that movement across fields with different social rules, norms and values can prompt some travellers to experience moments of dissonance and tension that may prompt some to critically reflect upon some of their own assumptions and embodied ways of knowing the world. Interestingly, Kaufman & Wolff (2010) made similar observations among athletes in traditional sports, including basketball, football, baseball and track-and-field. Although not adopting a Bourdieusian perspective, they reveal how, for some athletes, travelling around the world for competitions and sharing experiences with athletes from different countries in foreign contexts can broaden their perspectives and contribute to the 'development of the sociological imagination through understanding one's biography and history' (p. 161). Building upon Kaufman & Wolff's (2010) observations of athlete activism, I am not suggesting that all action sport participants will 'automatically develop such a social consciousness' through their mobilities across fields, 'but the potential is certainly there' (p. 161). My argument here is that, for a few action sport participants, reflexivity regarding particular aspects of their habitus (for example, privilege) and/or social inequalities within local, regional or national social fields, gained via their international travel and migration experiences, can prompt empathetic, altruistic and/or humanitarian responses.

Field-crossing, reflexivity and action sport activism

For some action sport athletes, their movement across fields has inspired them to utilize their symbolic and network capital in attempts to create social change. For professional US snowboarder Jeremy Jones, his observations of the effects of global warming on mountains, and in mountain communities, around the world provided the initial motivation for founding Protect Our Winters – a non-profit organization dedicated to educating and activating snow-sport participants on issues relating to global warming:

> It's shocking to look through some of my own photos taken over the last two decades from snowfields all over the world, and to see the clear recession of these glaciated regions. (Jeremy Jones, 2007, para. 4)

> Hiking up a grassy ski hill in Northern BC, a local skier is explaining to me how he had grown up skiing on this very hill as a kid. Unfortunately, due to rising snow levels, the town was forced to close the mountain. The local was only 30 years old, so if he has seen such a drastic change in the last 30 years, then what was in store for the next 30? It [was] experiences like this that motivated me to start Protect Our Winters. (About POW, no date, para. 1)

Importantly, Jones's 'network capital', accumulated over many years working in the global action sport industry, was integral to his success in accessing useful resources (social, cultural and financial) that could be fruitfully utilized to raise the awareness of snow-sport enthusiasts:

> Through snowboarding I started to see more and more the mountains were changing. Something needed to be done; I had built some great relationships in the snowboard and ski industry; and, I felt like our culture needed to come together and slow down climate change. I went back and forth on the idea for a while, because I had a lot of thoughts of, 'Who am I to start this foundation? I'm not an environmental saint'. But it was something that just wouldn't go away. So I went full on into it, because I felt our industry really needed it . . . (cited in McDermott, 2009, para. 2)

As well as establishing Protect Our Winters, Jones is 'practising what he preaches' by embracing a 'greener' alternative to big mountain snowboarding travel. He has rejected high-polluting helicopters and snowmobiles for accessing the remote backcountry terrain in which he films the video segments that ultimately pay his salary, instead embracing human-powered backcountry expeditions, such as using a snow-plane and then hiking, climbing and camping to access terrain. In an article published in *Transworld Snowboarding* magazine, Jones highlights the high carbon footprints of some of the sport's most respected athletes:

> Let's be honest, pro snowboarders are fundamentally at odds with the environment. Their globetrotting ways are pretty damn detrimental to the globe and its increasingly fragile climate. (Variables, 2008, p. 62)

Jones embraces both magazine and film as media for communicating his message to the broader snow culture, providing space for him to discuss and illustrate some of the joys (and challenges) of pursuing personal and professional snowboard travel with a 'different mindset', that is, with the aim of minimizing his carbon footprint rather than 'run, after run, after run' provided by heavily polluting helicopters and snowmobiles. In April 2013, Jones was among the recipients of a 'Champions of Change' award at the White House in recognition of 'ordinary Americans doing extraordinary things in their communities to out-innovate, out-educate, and out-build the rest of the world' (Gross, 2013, para. 1).

Another example of an action sport participant becoming inspired to act in response to environmental issues can be seen in the political work of New Zealand-born and Australian-raised professional surfer and environmentalist Dave Rastovich. In an attempt to raise awareness about the detrimental effects of seabed mining off the West Coast of New Zealand, Rastovich paddled 350 kilometres (217 miles) along the West Coast of the North Island of New Zealand. In an interview published on an international action sport website, Rastovich explains how his travels as a professional surfer helped draw his attention to issues regarding environmental degradation:

> When I started traveling . . . I actually got sick in a few places; I got really sick surfing South Mission Beach in San Diego after a big rain. I got really sick surfing a river mouth in Japan, and in Bali. Those experiences really opened my eyes, especially coming from Australia, where the beaches are really clean. It really blew me out that there were places in the world where you couldn't surf after it had been raining and that animals were dying because of the water quality. I just figured if we are going to be traveling to these places and we have cameras, photographers and writers, then we might as well get the word out about these issues. (Vanatta, 2013, para. 7)

For Rastovich, the awareness gained from his corporeal mobilities as a professional surfer ultimately led to his political activism surrounding the protection of the ocean and coastal environments. Interestingly, both Jones and Rastovich are using their celebrity profile within the global snow and surf communities, and adopting alternative action sport mobilities, to draw attention to environmental issues that are related specifically to their sports.

In contrast to the experiences and actions of Jones and Rastovich, the final two examples illustrate how some travelling action sport enthusiasts are so deeply moved by the injustices and inequalities observed across fields that they become inspired to develop non-profit organizations in their attempts to create change in local contexts. The first example of action sport-related mobilities contributing to heightened empathy and a desire to create change is that of Australian skateboarder Oliver Percovich. In 2006 Percovich went to Kabul, Afghanistan, with his girlfriend Sharna Nolan. With a Masters degree in International Development and Environmental Analysis, Nolan had taken a position with the Afghanistan Reconstruction and Evaluation Unit; despite a background in emergency management and a social science degree, Percovich's original aim was simply to 'follow' Nolan, and upon arriving in Kabul, thought 'it'd be really cool if we could build a miniramp somewhere' (cited in Brooks, 2009, para. 4). However, as soon as Percovich started skateboarding in the streets of Kabul, he was 'surrounded by eager children begging to learn how to skate' (Ramp it up, 2010). Deeply moved by the poverty-ridden and high-risk environments in which many of these children lived and their enthusiasm for the simple act of skateboarding, he felt inspired to work to improve the quality their lives in some small way. Thus, using the three boards he and Nolan had brought with them, Percovich 'developed a small school giving free skate lessons to street children' (Ramp it up, 2010). This was the humble beginning of Skateistan, an 'independent, neutral, Afghan NGO' that has grown to provide skateboarding tuition, and art and language education, to 'urban and internally-displaced youth in Afghanistan', and more recently, in Cambodia (What we do, 2011).

In 2009, with US$1 million in local and international donations and land gifted by Afghanistan's Olympic Committee, Skateistan built a 1800 square metre indoor skateboard park – Kabul's largest indoor sports facility. Since the opening of this skate park, Skateistan has registered more than 500 Afghan boys and girls, and currently has more than 350 regular students. But skateboarding is just 'the carrot' to 'connect with kids and build trust,' says Percovich (pc, 2011). As well as teaching key interpersonal skills and respect across cultural and gender divides, the aim underpinning the skateboarding instructional and educational programs offered at Skateistan is to prepare Afghan children and youth to become future leaders. As the executive director of Skateistan, Percovich continues to live in Kabul where he manages more than 20 international and local volunteers and staff including teachers, skateboard coaches, media and marketing advisers, and educational, art and sport coordinators.

Another example of action sport-related travel inspiring humanitarian action can be seen in the work of Dr Dave Jenkins, MD, and colleagues at

SurfAid International. In 1999, New Zealander Jenkins took a break from his job as educational director of a multinational health organization in Singapore and, with a group of friends, chartered a luxury yacht in the surf Mecca of the Mentawai Islands (an archipelago 150 kilometres to the west of Sumatra, Indonesia) with the sole purpose 'to find perfect waves' (SA FAQ, no date, para. 2). However, Jenkins found more than perfect waves. After a surf-filled day he ventured beyond the 'palm-fringed shores of this so-called surf paradise' and, to his horror, discovered 'dreadful misery, poverty, and death' (AR, 2005/06, p. 4). Jenkins recalls:

> I was a career-focused doctor working out of Singapore taking a break from a stressful corporate directorship and arrived in the islands with the aim of feeding myself upon the buffet of tropical waves on offer. I wasn't disappointed. However, late one afternoon, on what I thought would be a harmless tourist venture inland to one of the villages, my beliefs in what is important in life were changed forever. (Founders story, 2011, para. 1)

On his walk into the village, Jenkins had taken his medical kit as an after-thought, but within minutes of his walk he had stumbled across many requiring urgent medical treatment. Upon entering the local village he approached the chief and offered his medical services. A makeshift clinic was quickly established in a nearby hut and, as the word filtered through the jungle, Jenkins was inundated with Mentawai Islanders, many delivered to him in wheelbarrows, suffering and dying from malaria and other prevent-able diseases.

The radical disjuncture between the hedonistic pursuit of surfing and the extreme poverty of the local peoples had a profound impact on Jenkins: 'My experience vividly demonstrated the disparity between our lives as rich Western surfers visiting and playing on the Mentawai reefs, and those of the reef owners who so often suffer and die just meters from our luxury charter yachts' (cited in Barilotti, 2002, p. 4). Deeply troubled by the 'inequity of lifestyles', Jenkins left the Mentawai Islands inspired to do something to help the local peoples, but he admits some initial doubts:

> The scene haunted me for the rest of the trip, and followed me back to Singapore where I began questioning my life. Did it have meaning? Were my skills wasted chasing some corporate carrot? What if I could make a real difference to these people? The thought of more children dying drove me mad with frustration and helplessness yet, at the same time and in some strange way, the potential solutions inspired me. (Founders story, 2011, para. 4)

'After wrestling with my voices of self-interest', Jenkins left his six-figure sal-ary, sold his house and, with a small group of like-minded surfing friends, established SurfAid International. The SurfAid Malaria Control Project officially began in 2000 with a small group of surfing volunteers providing insecticide-treated mosquito nets to a handful of villages near surfing locations in the Mentawai Islands. Today, SurfAid is an internationally recognized non-profit humanitarian organization with the mission 'to improve the health, well-being and self-reliance of people living in isolated regions connected to us through surfing' (SurfAid website [www.surfaidinternational.org], 2013). The organization has grown to consist of six separate projects – the Mother and Child Health program, Malaria Free Mentawai program, Community-based Health, Emergency Preparedness, Emergency Response, and a Schools Program. The stated goals underpinning these projects are threefold: 1) 'To improve the health of community members using a sustainable, community-based approach'; 2) 'To assist vulnerable communities in preparation for future disasters'; and 3) 'To support, fund and advise local organizations committed to improving the quality of life of community members' (SurfAid Annual Report, 2006, p. 3).

Some interesting commonalities can be observed between Skateistan and SurfAid International. In my work with Robert Rinehart, we note that both of these ASDP organizations were 'established by highly educated, white Western male action sport participants who experienced a dissonance when they were confronted by the poverty of local residents encountered while pursuing individualistic (and hedonistic) leisure pursuits – skateboarding and surfing – in exotic and foreign destinations' (Thorpe & Rinehart, 2012, p. 15). Indeed, we found it interesting that Percovich and Jenkins decided to establish their NGOs in foreign countries, despite there being identifiable social needs in their own. There are, for example, many underprivileged Australian youth who may have benefited from an educational skateboarding-related program (Robinson et al., 2011), and ongoing health inequalities in New Zealand, particularly among Maori, Pacific Island and low socio-economic groups, requiring further medical attention and investment (Blakely & Simmers, 2011). We concluded by suggesting that for many ASDP founders and volunteers there seems to be a particular appeal in 'helping' the exotic "Other" (Said, 1979) (Thorpe & Rinehart, 2012, p. 15).

Here I argue that such initiatives are inspired by action sport-related travel across fields that can prompt heightened awareness about one's own habitus (including one's position of privilege) and inequalities and injustices in local fields. As Bourdieu reminds us, it can be difficult to critically reflect upon one's habitus when immersed in habituated practices and surrounded by those who are similar to us. As Bottero (2010) explains, habitus is rarely challenged or threatened because most people tend to associate with others much like themselves, seeking out the familiar and similar. Chambers (2005) also asserts that, while some fields prompt us to reflect critically upon some aspects of our habitus, they may also reinforce other dimensions. Indeed, when action sport participants travel to destinations where they are surrounded by like-minded peers from similar socio-economic backgrounds, it is unlikely that they will experience what Bourdieu (2004) has termed '*habitus clivé*' (p. 127; see Bennett, 2007). For Bourdieu, reflexivity tends to emerge 'from moments of "crisis", from mismatches between habitus and field' (Bottero, 2010, p. 11). So, in contrast to those who travel to action sport destinations heavily populated by privileged youth, it tends to be travel to more remote destinations such as Afghanistan, or leaving the luxury charter boat and visiting the local peoples of the Mentawai Islands, that highlights discrepancies within and across different fields and prompts emotional responses and critical reflection by *some* action sport travellers.

For some action sport enthusiasts, field-crossing can encourage greater empathy and prompt new forms of agency, which has led to inspired humanitarianism and political activism in local, national and global sport and social fields. However, as SurfAid International Chairman Dr Steve Hathaway recognizes, there are often differences in action sport participants' reflexivity and empathetic responses based on age. He proclaimed that core surfing culture is 'not exactly peppered with humanitarian values':

> In the early days we tried to raise money from surfers on boats with promo pamphlets, and we would talk to them, but all they really wanted to do was go surfing. [. . .] A 22-year-old surf-rat doesn't really care about global issues. [But] we get a lot of support from older surfers . . . As they get a bit more affluent . . . and they start seeing things beyond the surf break . . . they start wanting to give something back. (pc, October 2008)

Indeed, while some action sport migrants experience perceptions of self-change, identity transformation and enhanced reflexivity via their corporeal mobilities, I am wary of romanticizing the effects of such transnational mobilities. Reflexivity is not an inherently universal capacity. Put simply, there is 'nothing inherently transgressive or emancipatory about transnationalism. Rather, the effects are contradictory and complex, and must be assessed within specific times and places' (Pratt & Yeoh, 2003, p. 159), and during different life stages.

Not all action sport travellers are inspired to action, despite some experiencing similar discrepancies across fields. The select few who do pursue such activism tend to be those who have acquired considerable social and network capital from their past travel, educational and/or work experiences, and thus the ability to imagine and realize strategies for change. In other words, the habitus of the young, white, able-bodied, educated men who have been inspired to respond to such 'moments of crisis' and attempt to improve the lives of locals through health, educational, or peace-building initiatives is important. Those who respond to their experiences of dissonance and tension, and engage in action, tend to already have the embodied confidence and courage to imagine social change by drawing upon combinations of their social, cultural, symbolic, network, and perhaps economic, capital. Arguably, their strategies for change are intimately informed by, and connected to, the transnational networks and structures discussed throughout this book.

Utilizing transnational networks

The founders and staff of ASDP organizations are tapping into the existing transnational imaginary and established corporate, media and social networks within the transnational action culture, sport and industry to create greater awareness and raise funds from companies and enthusiasts around the world. For example, Protect Our Winters has gained the support of various transnational action sport-related corporations (including The North Face, Burton, Rossignol, Volcom, O'Neill, Dakine, Vans, Clif), media agents (*Onboard Snowboarding, Backcountry Magazine, Transworld Snowboarding,* Cruxco.tv) and professional snow-sport athletes from around the world, to help 'unite and mobilize the winter sports community to have a direct and positive impact on climate change' (About POW, no date, para. 6). Skateistan and SurfAid International have also both developed highly creative, collaborative relationships with transnational action sport companies. For example, Blackbox Distribution and TSG have provided Skateistan with skateboarding equipment (skateboards, wheels, trucks and bearings) and safety gear (helmets and wrist-guards), and host various awareness- and fund-raising events in an array of countries (including Australia, Germany and the United States). According to the 2012 Annual Report, donations-in-kind (such as equipment donations and sponsorships) made up 31 per cent of Skateistan's income. Similarly, global surf conglomerates Billabong and Quiksilver fund separate SurfAid projects, donating more than US$100,000 and US$50,000, respectively, each year.

Various scholars have examined how the Internet enables sport-related NGOs and social movements by enhancing their campaign tactics (Lenskyj, 2002), attracting funding and donor support (Wilson & Hayhurst, 2009) and supporting collaboration amongst organizations (Hayhurst et al., 2011). As these studies reveal, many new sport-related social movements – including nongovernmental organizations, not-for-profit organizations and commercial organizations – are drawing on an array of new technologies to produce political demonstrations quickly, with very little infrastructure, and often from a distance (Wilson, 2007). The Internet also plays an integral role in the development, communication and fundraising efforts of action sport-related NGOs (see Thorpe & Rinehart, 2012). Many ASDP organizations are particularly effective in their use of an array of social media (Youtube videos, blogs, Twitter, Facebook) to connect and communicate with action sport enthusiasts around the world. The Protect Our Winters Facebook page, for example, hosts more than 13,000 'fans' (many of whom consume, produce and respond to regular blogs), links to recent news items regarding POW and relevant environmental policies, as well as videos, photos, personal stories, comments and responses, and calls to action within local, national, global and virtual communities. Similarly, the Facebook pages for Skateistan and SurfAid have more than 37,000 and 19,000 supporters, respectively.

For Percovich, the Skateistan website has always been an important tool for garnering global support and recognition: 'We're very active on Facebook and Twitter . . . even when the organization was very very basic . . . there was the Skateistan website that had photos on there that connected with people' (pc, September 8, 2011). Continuing, he describes the ability to 'document and share' their work in Kabul with a global audience via the website and other visual media as 'just as important as the activities . . . because not everybody can come and see with their own two eyes what we were doing' (pc, September 8, 2011). For Percovich, the value of the Skateistan website is more than its 'ability to win awards and bring money in'; but also for its 'connecting effect' between 'Afghan youth and youth around the world':

> . . . if they can share stories with each other and they can share experiences . . . I think that breaks down a lot of barriers, a lot of misunderstanding. I do believe that's a really important tool in the interaction between the Muslim world and non-Muslim world. (pc, September 8, 2011)

It is important to note, however, that although the Skateistan website offers western consumers an unlimited flow of information – stories, photos, videos, and art (and commodities) – featuring and/or produced by Skateistan participants, the media consumption by Afghan youth is carefully controlled so as not to over-expose them to western influences. Indeed, Percovich and his team take particular care not to impose western skateboarding styles of practice and consumption upon Skateistan participants. Similarly, SurfAid International also describes the importance of developing culturally appropriate forms of communication and practice specific to the locations in which they work. For example, recognizing the value of story-telling and cultural performance within the Mentawai Islands, SurfAid staff worked with local children to produce short skits to communicate key health messages.

Humanitarian organizations have long employed marketing and communication styles that seek to evoke affective responses, or more specifically the 'registers of pity' (guilt and indignation, empathy and gratitude), as a 'motivation for action' (Chouliaraki, 2010, p. 114). As revealed in my previous work with Robert Rinehart, action sport-related NGOs are creatively engaging an array of affective technologies to evoke affective responses (guilt, empathy) from audiences and potential donors (Thorpe & Rinehart, 2010). To help garner 'support' from global action sport cultures and industries, POW, Skateistan and SurfAid marketing and media personnel have employed various strategies, including highly affective origination stories, the use of personalities and various new social media (see Thorpe, 2011; Thorpe & Rinehart, 2010). A particularly strong theme across such online and print marketing materials is the notion of the imagined transnational action sport community. Common affective discourses identified in the various SurfAid documents and texts, for example, include guilt, cultural debt and imagined community responsibility. For example, during an interview in a surfing magazine, Dave Jenkins called upon the transnational surfing community:

> Despite the soulful image of the sport, surfers are too often 'takers'. In places like the Mentawais they go and 'take' the surfing experience but don't give back to the locals – locals who have nothing and urgently need help. *The surfing world owes a debt of gratitude to these people.* (Dave Jenkins, cited in Barilotti, 2002; emphasis added)

This comment is illustrative of the media and marketing materials from various ASDP organizations that are strategically working with the transnational imaginary to encourage action sport participants and enthusiasts around the world to feel empathy and responsibility to help those 'connected' to them through shared participation in action sports.

The financial and symbolic response from transnational action sport cultures and industries to such ASDP organizations suggests that many do feel connections to people in foreign places as a result of their participation in, and sense of belonging to, these global physical cultures. SurfAid, for example, has the support of 34 professional surfers and surf-related musicians, including Kelly Slater, Mark Occhilupo, Laird Hamilton and Ben Harper, who act as 'ambassadors' for the organization and draw upon their celebrity profile and symbolic capital to raise awareness among the global surfing culture. The 2012 SurfAid Annual Report also acknowledges the 'hard-working affiliate teams in Australia, New Zealand and the US' who 'push on with fundraising' events within surfing communities in these countries. As a result of such marketing and fundraising initiatives, SurfAid received 16 per cent (US$556,528) of its annual income from individual supporters, and another 14 per cent from fundraising events. In 2012, Skateistan hosted fundraising events in 14 countries, many of which were organized by passionate action sport enthusiasts who volunteered their time and energy towards hosting events ranging from art exhibitions to skateboarding contests to film premieres. According to its 2012 Annual Report, Skateistan raised more than US$223,700 from individuals, corporations and events, and thanked its many supporters and volunteers by stating 'we are very happy that you share our vision of bringing children together through skateboarding' (p. 24).

As I have suggested elsewhere, 'for many action sport-related NGO officials, winning the resources required to continue their day-to-day operations as well as plan for future developments, while maintaining a sense of autonomy and integrity, is a complex business that requires careful negotiation with an array of actors with different political motives' (Thorpe & Rinehart, 2012, p. 13). It is not my intention here to reveal the various politics, strategies, negotiations and compromises being experienced by those working within such transnational organizations in their efforts to initiate local change. Rather, my key point here is that action sport-related NGOs are a product of the transnational imaginary and economic, social and cultural networks that are continuously being produced and consumed within and across local action sport communities around the world. Thus, to paraphrase Beck (1998), there is a new dialectic of global and local questions about the social engagement of contemporary youth that do not fit into national politics, and 'only in a transnational framework can they be properly posed, debated and resolved' (p. 29).

Concluding thoughts

Scholarship in the fields of transnational studies and the mobilities paradigm has proliferated over the past two decades as a response to social, economic, cultural and political formations and new modes of communication that are producing an array of networks and corporeal, virtual and imagined movement across borders. Yet concerns have been raised as to a series of binary divisions that are limiting our understandings of the complexities of such social formations. In particular these include: divisions between macro and micro scales of analysis; the role of economic structures versus agency within everyday contexts; and tensions between theoretical and empirical analyses. Another concern expressed by youth cultural scholars is that 'much work on globalization and transnationalism has tended to focus largely or explicitly only on adults' and youth are too often 'assumed to be less fully formed social actors or subjects less able to exert the[ir] agency in the face of globalization' (Maira, 2004, p. 206). This project was a response to such concerns.

In this book I adopted a global ethnographic and multi-theoretical approach to offer a valuable contribution to transnational studies and the mobilities paradigm by presenting a multidimensional analysis of the various forms of power operating within and through youth-dominated transnational action sport cultures. With this aim in mind, the book was structured into three main parts. It began with a macro, structural focus on the global economic, cultural and media institutions that continue to play an integral role in the production of a transnational imaginary in action sport cultures via transnational corporations, media conglomerates and events, as well as global action sport celebrities. In the second part of the book I focused on the corporeal and imagined mobilities within action sport cultures, examining the various travel patterns adopted by athletes, tourists and migrants, their interactions within transnational action sport destinations, and then finally how such mobile lifestyles contribute to new subjectivities and understandings of place, space, identity and belonging. In the third and final part of this book, I examined the various forms of agency being practised by predominantly young action sport participants when confronted with immobilities caused by natural disaster and war. While various forms of embodied and/or local micro politics were discussed in the preceding chapters, in this final, concluding chapter I considered the potential of the transnational imaginary to lead to new forms of politics and efforts by action sport participants to create or support social justice and humanitarian projects in local contexts.

The three parts and eight chapters of this book are broadly organized from macro to micro levels of analysis. However, globalization is 'not a linear process but is inherently and deeply uneven', and thus the 'processes of both globalization and youth, and the conjunctures and disjunctures between them, must be considered together' (Maira, 2004, p. 207). Thus, each chapter seeks to reveal the complexities of the global and local intersections, and the power of both social structures and everyday agency, via an array of empirically grounded case studies from various action sport cultures within particular historical moments. While the various chapters draw upon a range of theoretical perspectives and ethnographic methods to examine different features of transnationalism, key sociological themes, such as power, structure, agency, politics, the body and space, are woven throughout the book. In so doing, the book reveals how new social formations and transnational flows of capital, culture, media and labour are impacting the everyday lives and imagined futures of youth in both the developed and developing world.

Notes

2 Producing Transnational Networks: Action Sport Companies, Media and Events

1. Although his full name is Jake Burton Carpenter, Jake changed it to Jake Burton to avoid confusion. From hereafter I will refer to him as Burton, except where he has published under either Jake Burton or Jake Burton Carpenter.
2. Some of the responses to Evers' post reveal intimate understandings of surfing politics, and broader global politics, while others illustrate the divisions within the surfing culture as to understandings of cultural imperialism. For example, Tim wrote: 'I think Clifton's article is well written and informed, but agree with [another poster] that 'pro surfing isn't even a pimple on the arse of a Chinese baby when it comes to problems in China. The problems with China are profound and institutional, and need to be confronted and managed by the highest level of leadership in America. They've been cleaning our clock for years in economic chess and someone needs to stand up to them and say "enough" of the currency manipulation and intellectual property theft'. Jeff responded: 'The most certain way to influence/affect China's human rights positions is to expose the Chinese people to western culture to the maximum extent possible. The sport of surfing would seem especially appropriate to achieve this objective due to the inherent values the sport promotes: freedom, individualism, a sense of adventure and daring, free-spirit, etc. All seem antithetical to the Chinese Communist core beliefs. The more we expose the Chinese to the sport and the most accessible we make it to them, the more likely they will experience the stoke for themselves – and that can only lead to good things.' Al replies: '[I'm] not so sure. Once the power elite get hip to the high of surfing I'm willing to bet they'll privatize the experience and close spots to all but those who they deem fit ($$$) to have access to them.' Also in response to Jeff's statement 'The most certain way to influence/affect China's human rights positions is to expose the Chinese people to western culture...', Bert wrote: 'I don't think so. First, because it would mean that the 'western culture' (what's that? US culture?) should be adopted everywhere in the world, and I can't see why. Second, because the Chinese are already exposed to 'western culture' and especially the rulers. They have already swallowed our western way of making money and politics. There is no difference between a greedy businessman in China and another in Europe or the US. Ethics and social issues are present in Chinese culture as much as in western culture, it's a question of people, not a question of culture' (retrieved from Evers, 2012).

3 Digital Media and the Transnational Imaginary: Virtual Memorialization of Global Action Sport Stars

1. As will be discussed in Chapter 6, mobile media also offers 'different ways to experience and record journeys' for immediate and future reference, and to continue communication upon returning 'home' (cited in Watkins et al., 2012, p. 667).

2. For this section, I am grateful to the University of Illinois Press for permission to republish parts of my chapter entitled 'Death, mourning and cultural memory on the Internet: The virtual memorialization of fallen sports heroes' originally published in *Sport History in the Digital Era* (2014), edited by Gary Osmond & Murray Phillips.

3. Memory has both individual and collective dimensions. In this chapter the focus is on collective, or cultural memory. Barbara Misztal (2003) describes cultural memory as 'the representation of the past, both that shared by a group and that which is collectively commemorated, that enacts and gives substance to the group's identity, its present conditions and its vision of the future' (p. 7). Collective memory is passed on to us in various cultural practices, routines, institutions and artifacts, and is always contested (see Thorpe, 2010).

4. According to Vealey (2011), 'After the nation viewed literal bodies falling from the World Trade Center – an image branded onto the national consciousness despite the post facto censoring of media coverage – the urge to interchange one object with another expanded from 9/11 memorials and acts of remembrance to the preemptive preservation of our bodies into digitized forms' (para. 2).

4 Corporeal Mobilities in Action Sport Cultures: Tourists, Professionals and Seasonal Migrants

1. International travel is less central to urban action sport cultures such as skateboarding, parkour and BMX (see Chapters 7 and 8).

2. Interestingly, some action sport athletes are also using their cultural positions and adopting alternative mobilities to draw attention to broader social issues such as environmental warming and seabed mining (see Chapter 9).

5 Pleasure, Play and Everyday Politics in Transnational Action Sport Destinations

1. I am grateful to Taylor and Francis for permission to reprint parts of my article titled '"Sex, drugs and snowboarding": (il)legitimate definitions of taste and lifestyle' (Thorpe 2012a) in this section.

7 Action Sports and Natural Disaster Immobilities: Arrhythmic Experiences in Christchurch, New Zealand

1. Here I am grateful to Sage Publications for permission to republish parts of my article entitled 'Natural disaster arrhythmia and action sports: The case of the Christchurch earthquake' originally published in *International Review for the Sociology of Sport* (see Thorpe, 2013a).

2. This is not to suggest, however, that participants in other forms of sport and exercise will not experience affective responses to the closure of facilities. Indeed, a gym member may feel saddened when the gym at which he has been a long-time member is destroyed, and a soccer player may be equally upset when her favourite field is covered in liquefaction.

3. As per my university ethics requirements, pseudonyms have been used for all interviewees.

4. My research assistant, Nick Maitland, was integral to this operation. As a Christchurch resident, Nick helped me establish contact with participants prior to my visit. Moreover, our conversations throughout the data-gathering phase helped me develop a greater sensitivity to some of the everyday lived experiences of residents.

5. The Student Volunteer Army (SVA) – a 15,000-strong group of university and high school students organized primarily through social media (such as Facebook, text messaging) – has been widely praised for its collective efforts during the immediate and long-term rebuild process. In particular, the SVA cleared over 65,000 and 360,000 tonnes of silt following the September 2010 and February 2011 earthquakes, respectively; the latter was a result of 75,000 volunteer hours (see www.sva.org).

6. Although sporting clubs are not the focus of this chapter, it is worth noting that most of the surfers and climbers in this project were members of surfing and climbing clubs. Although most of these clubs 'went into recession for a few months' after the February earthquake, many members continued to reach out to their colleagues (either via surf or climbing trips, visits to their homes or electronic communication), some of whom had been forced to leave Christchurch following the earthquakes. According to Peter, surfing was 'extremely important' for rebuilding a sense of community among local surfers in the Sumner area. In his own words: 'the reason our membership stayed so stable, despite the closure of our beach and damage to our clubrooms, was because the club is part of a small and active community, and keeping in touch – especially for those forced to relocate – was important because they virtually all have relocated, or intend to relocate, back to the area when they can' (pc, Peter, 2013).

7. The closure of other sporting facilities, such as climbing walls, sporting equipment stores, and the cancellation of events, also caused disruption to sporting participation and consumption.

8. See www.youtube.com/watch?v=i2bvozq-KK8

9. Interestingly, Sam also observes the potential environmental impact of post-quake climbing mobilities: 'Castle Hill is seeing a huge increase in climbers. And unfortunately for Castle Hill, it's a very soft sandstone, so we're probably going to see in the next 10 years, it's going to have a huge impact on the quality of the rock there.'

10. Importantly, while this project focuses on the micro-mobilities of those who continued to live in Christchurch following the earthquake, many lifestyle sport participants left the city. According to participants interviewed, the mobilities of some of their peers were informed by the opportunities to participate in their sports. For example, some skateboarders opted to move to Melbourne because 'that's where the skating scene is happening right now' (Brad), and climbers moved to Wanaka were the opportunities for climbing are 'amazing' (Yukimi). Participants also observed that the mobilities of lifestyle sport tourists to Christchurch have also been affected.

8 The Emergence of Action Sports in the Middle East: Imagining New Mobilities with Parkour in Gaza

1. This chapter is based on work conducted with the help of Nida Ahmad (see Thorpe & Ahmad, 2013). I am grateful to both Nida and Sage Publications for permission to republish parts of our article entitled 'Youth, action sports and political agency

in the Middle East: Lessons from a grassroots parkour group in Gaza' in this chapter.

2. It is important to note, however, that while girls and young women do participate in parkour in western cities, the activity remains dominated by young men who perform for their peers and thrive on attention obtained through spontaneous public performances in urban spaces.

3. Palestinian hackers are responding by forcing temporary shutdowns and defacements of hundreds of Israeli websites, such that some describe the 'cyber war' as the 'second front' in 21st-century Israeli–Palestinian conflicts. As military conflict develops in the Gaza Strip, the complex efforts by hackers and the governments to control the flow of information are only expected to increase (McGuire, 2012).

4. The video recording of the PK Gaza training day that was disrupted by Israeli bombing nearby: see www.youtube.com/watch?v=qE2eWlHEPwI

5. The following Youtube video further illustrates the experiences of PK Gaza in Italy in November 2012: www.youtube.com/watch?v=Y77uuTcpe00

Bibliography

About POW. (no date). Retrieved March 8, 2010, from http://protectourwinters.org/about

Abudheen, S.K. (2013). Facebook claims 71M active users in India. *TechCircle. In*, February 6. Retrieved October 25, 2013, from http://techcircle.vccircle.com/2013/02/06/facebook-claims-71m-active-users-in-india-or-around-half-of-netizens-in-the-country

Adam, B. (2006). Time. *Theory, Culture and Society, 23*(2/3), 124–125.

Adey, P. (2010). *Mobility.* London: Routledge.

Against gravity. (2012). *Al-Ahram Weekly*, 26 December. Retrieved 22 December 2013 from http://weekly.ahram.org.eg/News/698/26/Against-gravity.aspx

Agger, B. (2011). iTime: Labor and life in a smartphone era. *Time and Society, 20*(1), 119–136.

Aguerre, F. (2013). ISA President's message. International Surfing Association. Retrieved September 10, 2013, from www.isasurf.org/isa-info/presidents-message

Air China. (2008). *Transworld Snowboarding*, February 10. Retrieved December 10 2010, from http://snowboarding.transworld.net/1000026579/featuresobf/air-china-2/

Aitchison, C.C. (2001). Theorising Other discourses of tourism, gender and culture: Can the subaltern speak (in tourism)? *Tourist Studies, 1*(2), 133–147.

Allon, F., Anderson, K. & Bushell, R. (2008). Mutant mobilities: Backpacker tourism in 'global' Sydney. *Mobilities, 3*(1), 73–94.

Altsurfing.org history. (no date). Retrieved from www.hisurfadvisory.com/ashub/as_history.htm

Always, J., Belgrave, L. & Smith, K. (1998). Back to normal: Gender and disaster. *Symbolic Interaction, 21*(2), 175–195.

Amara, M. (2012). *Sport, Politics and Society in the Arab World.* London: Palgrave Macmillan.

America's top 10 colleges for mountain biking. (2013). *Mountain Bike Action,* retrieved November 2, 2013, from www.mbaction.com/Main/News/VOLUME-28-NUMBER-2-FEBRUARY-2013-6169.aspx

AMG. (2007). Action sports: The action sports market. Active Marketing Group. Retrieved January 10, 2013, from www.activenetworkrewards.com/Assets/AMG+2009/Action+Sports.pdf

Amin, A. & Cohendet, P. (1999). Learning and adaptation in decentralised business networks. *Environment and Planning D: Society and Space, 17*(1), 87–104.

Amin, A. &, Thrift, N. *Cities: Reimagining the Urban.* Cambridge: Polity Press.

Amit, V. (2000) 'Introduction: Constructing the field. In V. Amit (Ed.), *Constructing the Field: Ethnographic Fieldwork in the Contemporary World.* Florence: Routledge.

Andy Irons memorial paddle out. (2010). *Transworld Surf*, November 3. Retrieved from http://surf.transworld.net/1000118573/photos/andy-irons-memorial-paddle-out/

Annan K. (2010). We must use the power of sport as an agent of social change. *The Kofi Annan Foundation*, 2010. Retrieved March 18, 2013, from http://kofi-annanfoundation.org/newsroom/press/2010/04/kofi-annan-we-must-use-power-sport-agent-social-change

Andersen, H. (2010). An Olympic-sized rant. *Method Magazine*, February 19. Retrieved September 18, 2013, from www.methodmag.com/node/6525

Anderson, B. (1983). *Imagined Communities: Reflections on the Origin and Spread of Nationalism*. London: Verso.

Anderson, K. (1999). Snowboarding: The construction of gender in an emerging sport. *Journal of Sport and Social Issues, 23*(1), 55–79.

Andrews, D.L., (1991). Welsh Indigenous! and British Imperial? Welsh rugby, culture and society 1890–1914. *Journal of Sport History, 18*(3), 335–349.

Andy Irons passes away. (2010). *Surfer Magazine*, November 2. Retrieved July 3, 2012, from www.surfermag.com/features/breaking-news-andy-irons-passes-away

Aouragh, M. (2008). Everyday resistance on the Internet: The Palestinian context. *Journal of Arab and Muslim Media Research, 1*(2), 109–130.

Appadurai, A. (1995). The production of locality. In R. Fardon (Ed.), *Counterworks: Managing the Diversity of Knowledge*. London: Routledge, 205–225.

Appadurai, A. (1996). *Modernity at Large: Cultural Dimensions of Globalization*. Minneapolis: University of Minnesota Press.

Appadurai, A. & Breckenridge, C. (1989). On moving targets. *Public Culture, 2*, i–iv.

Arthur, P. (2008). Pixelated memory: Online commemoration of trauma and crisis. *Interactive Media, 4*, 1–19.

Atencio, M. & Beal, B. (2011). Beautiful losers: the symbolic exhibition and legitimization of outsider masculinity. *Sport in Society: Cultures, Commerce, Media, Politics. 14*(1), 1–16.

Atencio, M., Beal, B. & Wilson, C. (2009). The distinction of risk: Urban skateboarding, street habitus and the construction of hierarchical gender relations. *Qualitative Research in Sport and Exercise, 1*(1), 3–20.

Atkinson, M. (2009). Parkour, anarcho-environmentalism and poiesis. *Journal of Sport and Social Issues, 33*(2), 169–194.

Atkinson, M. and K. Young (Eds.) (2008). *Tribal Play: Subcultural Journeys through Sport* (Volume IV, Research in the Sociology of Sport). Bingley: JAI.

Azzarito, L. (2010). Ways of seeing the body in kinesiology: A case for visual methodologies. *Quest, 62*(2), 155–170.

Bærenholdt, J.O. (2013). Governmobility: The powers of mobility. *Mobilities, 8*(1), 20–34.

Bærenholdt, J., Haldrup, M., Larsen, J. & Urry, J. (2004). *Performing Tourist Places*. Aldershot: Ashgate.

Baccigaluppi, J., Mayugba, S. & Carnel, C. (2001). *Declaration of Independents: Snowboarding, Skateboarding and Music: An Intersection of Cultures*. San Francisco: Chronicle Books.

Bailey, R. (1998). Jake Burton: King of the hill. *Ski, 62*(6), 60–66.

Bairner, A. (2001). *Sport, Nationalism and Globalization: European and North American Perspectives*. Albany: State University of New York Press.

Bakesale. (2009). December 9. Retrieved April 12, 2010, from www.snowboardingforum. com/snowboarding-general-chat/20572-resort-one-night-stand.html

Baldwin, S. (2006). Riding high? Skiing, snowboarding and drugs. *Snowsphere.com*. Retrieved March 12, 2010, from www.snowsphere.com/special-features/riding-high-skiing-snowboarding-and-drugs

Bale, J. (1986). Sport and national identity: A geographical view. *The British Journal of Sports History, 3*(1), 18–41.

Bale, J. (1996). *Kenyan Running: Movement Culture, Geography and Global Change*. London: Frank Cass.

Bale, J. (2003). *Sports Geography*. 2nd edition. London: Routledge.

Bale, J. & Krogh-Christensen, M. (Eds.) (2004). *Post-Olympism? Questioning Sport in the Twenty-First Century*. Oxford: Berg Publishers.

Bang, K., Brooks, G., Alberto Delaroca, J. & Jiménez, M. (2010). *The Multiculturals in Action Sports Report: 2010 Hispanic Snow Summary*. Retrieved from www.masreport. com/wp-content/uploads/2010/11/2010_MAS-Report_HispanicSnow-FULL.pdf

Barber, B. (2001). Political violence, social integration, and youth functioning: Palestinian youth from the Intifada. *Journal of Community Psychology, 29*(3), 259–280.

Barilotti, S. (2002). The jungle is looking back. *Surfer magazine*, November 5. Retrieved from http://surfermag.com/magazine/archivedissues/jungle

Barker, J., Kraftl, P., Horton, J. & Tucker, F. (2009). Editorial introduction: The road less travelled? New directions in children's mobility. *Mobilities, 4*(1), 1–10.

Barr, M., Moran, C. & Wallace, E. (2006). *Snowboarding the world*. Bath: Footprint.

Bavinton, N. (2007). From obstacle to opportunity: Parkour, leisure and the reinterpretation of constraints. *Annals of Leisure Research, 10*(3-4), 391–412.

Bayat, A. (2010). *Life as Politics: How Ordinary People Change the Middle East*. Stanford: Stanford University Press.

Beal, B. (1995). Disqualifying the official: An exploration of social resistance through the subculture of skateboarding. *Sociology of Sport Journal, 12*(3), 252–267.

Beal, B. (1996). Alternative masculinity and its effects on gender relations in the subculture of skateboarding. *Journal of Sport Behavior, 19*(3), 204–221.

Beal, B., & Weidman, L. (2003). Authenticity in the skateboarding world. In R. E. Rinehart & S. Sydnor (Eds.), *To the Extreme: Alternative Sports, Inside and Out*. Albany: SUNY Press, 337–352.

Beal, B. and Wilson, C. (2004). Chicks dig scars: Commercialisation and the transformations of skateboarders' identities. In B. Wheaton (Ed.), *Understanding Lifestyle Sports: Consumption, Identity and Difference*. London: Routledge, 31–54.

Beamish, R. (2002). Karl Marx's enduring legacy for the sociology of sport. In J. Maguire & K. Young (Eds.), *Theory, Sport and Society*. London: Elsevier Science, 25–39.

Beck, U. (1998). The cosmopolitan manifesto. *New Statesman*, March 20, 28–30.

Beck, U. (2002). The cosmopolitan society and its enemies. *Theory, Culture and Society, 19*(1–2), 17–44.

Becker, S. & Knudson, R. (2003). Visions of the dead: Imagination and mourning. *Death Studies, 27*(8), 691–716.

Beddall-Hill, N. L., Jabbar, A. & Al Shehri, S. (2011). Social mobile devices as tools for qualitative research in education: iPhones and iPads in ethnography, interviewing and design-based research. *Journal of the Research Center for Educational Technology, 7*(1), 67–89.

Beer, D. & Burrows, R. (2013). Popular culture, digital archives and the new social life of data. *Theory, Culture and Society, 30*(4), 47–71.

Belcher, J. & Bates, F. (1983). Aftermath of natural disasters: Coping through residential mobility. *Disasters, 7*(2), 118–128.

Belgrave, L., & Smith, K. (1994). Experiencing Hurricane Andrew: Environment and everyday life. In N. Denzin (Ed.), *Studies in Symbolic Interaction*. Greenwich: JAI Press, 251–273.

Bellotti, J.A. (2012). Peace and sport: Challenging limitations across the sport for development and peace sector. Unpublished Masters thesis, Indiana University. Retrieved January 28, 2013, from scholarworks.iupui.edu/bitstream/handle/1805/3009/FINAL%20Thesis%20PDF%20(F).pdf?sequence=1

Bennett, J. (2010). Michael Jackson: Celebrity death, mourning and media events. *Celebrity Studies, 1*(2), 231–232.

Bennett, S. (2012). The numbers just keep on getting bigger: Social media and the Internet. *MediaBistro*. Retrieved May 28, 2012, from www.mediabistro.com/alltwitter/social-media-internet-2011_b17881

Bennett, T. (2007). *Habitus clivé*: Aesthetics and politics in the work of Pierre Bourdieu. *New Literary History*, *38*(1), 201–228.

Bennett, W.L. (2008). *Civic Life Online: Learning How Digital Media can Engage Youth*. Cambridge, MA: Massachusetts Institute of Technology.

Berinstein, S. & Magalhaes, L. (2009). A study of the essence of play experience to children living in Zanzibar, Tanzania. *Occupational Therapy International*, *16*(2), 89–106.

Best of the best: The top 5 iPhone apps for surfers (no date). *Surfers Village*. Retrieved October 25, 2013, from www.surfersvillage.com/surfing-news/48123#.UmnDaY5x63A

Beutler, I. (2008). Sport serving development and peace: Achieving the goals of the United Nations through sport. *Sport in Society*, *11*(4), 359–369.

Bianchi, R. V. (2012). A radical departure: A critique of the critical turn in Tourism Studies. In J. Wilson (Ed.), *The Routledge Handbook of Tourism Geographies*. London: Routledge, 46–54.

Billig, M. (1995). *Banal Nationalism*. Sage: London.

Billing, A. C. & Ruihley, B. J. (2013). Why we watch, why we play: The relationship between Fantasy Sport and fanship motivations. *Mass Communication and Society*, *16*(1), 5–25.

Bird, D.K., Chagué-Goff, C. & Gero, A. (2011). Human response to extreme events: A review of three post-tsunami disaster case studies. *Australian Geographer*, *42*(3), 225–239.

Birtchnell, T. & Büscher, M. (2011). An eruption of disruption. *Mobilities*, *6*(1), 1–9.

Black, D. (2010). The ambiguities of development: Implications for 'development through sport'. *Sport in Society*, *13*(1), 121–129.

Blakely, T. & Simmers, D. (2011). *Fact and Action Sheets on Health Inequalities*. June. Retrieved from www.otago.ac.nz/wellington/otago023745.pdf

Blevins, J. (2012). Colorado ski resorts keep staff levels steady. *The Denver Post*. Retrieved September 12, 2013, from www.denverpost.com/ci_22056298/colorado-ski-resorts-keep-staff-levels-steady

Blunt, A. (2007). Cultural geographies of migration: Mobility, transnationality and diaspora. *Progress in Human Geography*, *31*(5), 1–11.

Blunt, A. & Dowling, R. (2006) *Home*. London: Routledge.

Bodnar, J. (1992). *Remaking America: Public Memory, Commemoration, and Patriotism in the Twentieth Century*. Princeton: Princeton University Press.

Bolin, H. (2009). Skateboarding out of the shadows. *China Daily*. Retrieved May 10, 2013, from www.chinadaily.com.cn/business/2009-06/22/content_8308648.htm

Bolter, J.D. & Grusin, R. (2000). *Remediation: Understanding New Media*. Cambridge: Cambridge University Press.

Bondi, L., Smith, M. & Davidson, J. (2005). (Eds.). *Emotional Geographies*. Aldershot: Ashgate.

Booker, J. & Greig, S. (2012,). Christchurch earthquake third most expensive disaster. *The New Zealand Herald*, March 29. Retrieved September 14, 2012, from www.nzherald.co.nz/nz/news/article.cfm?c_id=1&objectid=10795342

Boon, B. (2006). When leisure and work are allies: The case of skiers and tourist resort hotels. *Career Development International*, *11*(7), 594–608.

Booth, D. (1994). Surfing '60s: A case study in the history of pleasure and discipline. *Australian Historical Studies*, *26*(103), 262–279.

Booth, D. (1995). Ambiguities in pleasure and discipline: The development of competitive surfing. *Journal of Sport History, 22*(3), 189–206.

Booth, D. (2001). *Australian Beach Cultures: The History of Sun, Sand and Surf.* London: Frank Cass.

Booth, D. (2002). From bikinis to boardshorts: Wahines and the paradoxes of the surfing culture. *Journal of Sport History, 28*(1), 3–22.

Booth, D. (2005). Paradoxes of material culture: The political economy of surfing. In J. Nauright and K. Schimmel (Eds.), *The Political Economy of Sport.* International Political Economy Series. New York: Palgrave Macmillan, 310–343.

Booth, D. (2008). (Re)reading the surfers' bible: The affects of *Tracks. Continuum: Journal of Media and Cultural Studies, 22*(1), 17–35.

Booth, D. (2011). *Surfing: The Ultimate Guide.* Santa Barbara: Greenwood Publishing.

Booth, D. & Thorpe, H. (2007). The meaning of extreme. In D. Booth & H. Thorpe (Eds.), *The Berkshire Encyclopedia of Extreme Sports.* Great Barrington: Berkshire, 181–197.

Borden, I. (2003). *Skateboarding, Space and the City: Architecture and the Body.* London: Berg.

Borenstein, S. (2012, July 3). Climate change: US heat waves, wildfires and flooding are 'what global warming looks like'. *Huffington Post.* Retrieved October 25, 2012, from www.huffingtonpost.com/2012/07/03/climate-change-us-heat-wave-wildfire-flooding_n_1645616.html

Bottero, W. (2010). Intersubjectivity and Bourdieusian approaches to 'identity'. *Cultural Sociology, 4*(1), 3–22.

Bourdieu, P. (1984). *Distinction: A Social Critique of the Judgement of Taste.* London: Routledge.

Bourdieu, P. (1985). The social space and the genesis of groups. *Theory and Society, 14*(6), 723–744.

Bourdieu, P. (1992). *The Logic of Practice* (translated by Richard Nice). Cambridge: Polity Press.

Bourdieu, P. (1998) *The State Nobility: Elite Schools in the Field of Power* (Cambridge: Polity Press).

Bourdieu, P. (2004). *Esquisse Pour Une Auto-Analyse.* Paris: Éditions Raisons D'Agir.

Bourdieu, P. & Wacquant, L.J.D. (1992). The purpose of reflexive sociology. In P. Bourdieu & L.J.D. Wacquant (Eds.), *An Invitation to Reflexive Sociology.* Cambridge: Polity Press, 61–215.

Bowman, N. D., McCabe, J. & Isaacson, T. (2012). Fantasy sports and sports fandom: Implications for mass media research. In A. Earnheardt., P. Haridakis & B. Hugenberg (Eds.), *Sports Fans, Identity, and Socialization: Exploring the Fandemonium.* Plymouth: Lexington Books, 255–274.

Bradley, S. (2010). Campaign targets boozy Brits on the piste. *Swissinfo.ch,* January 28. Retrieved March 12, 2010, from www.swissinfo.ch/eng/culture/Campaign_targets_boozy_Brits_on_the_piste.ht...

Brayton, S. (2005). 'Black-lash': Revisiting the 'white negro' through skateboarding. *Sociology of Sport Journal, 22*(3), 356–372.

Brockmeier, J. (2002). Remembering and forgetting: Narrative as cultural memory. *Culture and Psychology, 8*(1), 15–43.

Brockmeier, J. (2010). After the archive: Remapping memory. *Culture and Psychology, 16*(1), 5–35.

Brooks, J. (2009). Skateistan: A rebirth of skateboarding in Afghanistan. August 8. Retrieved September 20, 2013, from http://xgames.espn.go.com/skateboarding/article/4384172/rebirth-skateboarding-afghanistan

Brooks, R. (2010). Success stories: Jake Burton charts a new course in snowboarding. *Success Magazine*. Retrieved January 7, 2010, from www.successmagazine.com

Bruce, T. & Wheaton, B. (2009). Rethinking global sports migration and forms of transnational, cosmopolitan and diasporic belonging: A case study of international yachtsman Sir Peter Blake. *Social Identities, 15*(5), 585–608.

Bryant, G. (2013). Skyline Queenstown announces new bike trail. *The Southland Times*. Retrieved October 19, 2013, from www.stuff.co.nz/southland-times/business/9048699/More-bike-trails-mean-more-thrills

Burawoy, M. (2000). Introduction: Reaching for the global. In M. Burawoy, J.A. Blum, S. George, Z. Gille, T. Gowan, L. Haney, M. Klawiter, S. Lopez, S. Riain & M. Thayer (Eds.), *Global Ethnography: Forces, Connection, and Imaginations in a Postmodern World*. Berkeley: University of California Press.

Burgess, J.E. (2012). YouTube and the formalisation of amateur media. In D. Hunter, R. Lobato, M. Richardson & J. Thomas (Eds.), *Amateur Media: Social, Cultural and Legal Perspectives*. London: Routledge, 53–58.

Burgess, J. & Green, J. (2009). *YouTube: Online Video and Participatory Culture*. Cambridge: Polity Press.

Burns, P. & Novelli, M. (2008). Introduction. In P. Burns & M. Novelli (Eds.), *Tourism and Mobilities: Local-Global Connections*. Wallingford: CABI, xvii–xxvi.

Burton Carpenter, J. & Dumaine, B. (2002). My half-pipe dream come true. *Fortune Small Business, 12*(8), 64.

Burton goes global. (2005). Retrieved July 15, 2006, from www.burton.com/Company/Companyresearch.aspx

Burton history. (2005). Retrieved July 15, 2006, from www.burton.com/Company/Companyresearch.aspx

Burton snowboards announces new leadership structure for product and sales. (2013). *Snowboarder Magazine*, May 3. Retrieved June 11, 2013, from www.snowboardermag.com/industry-news/burton-snowboards-announces-new-leadership-structure-for-product-sales

Burton snowboards closes Vermont plant. (2010). *Vermont Energy Partnership, 6*(Spring/Summer). Retrieved May 12, 2013, from www.vtep.org/newsletters/vtspringsummer2010_2/pdf/vtspringsummer2010.pdf

Burton sponsors national Snowboard Team of China. (2005). 14 October. Retrieved from www.twsbiz.com/twbiz/print/0,21538,1119465,00.html

Burton, J. (2003). Snowboarding: The essence is fun. In R. Rinehart & S. Sydnor (Eds.), *To the Extreme: Alternative Sports, Inside and Out*. Albany: State University of New York Press, 401–406.

Burton, J. (2008). Jake and Donna share some LOVE. November 26. Retrieved December 12, 2009, from www.burton.com

Büscher, M. & Urry, J. (2009). Mobile methods and the empirical. *European Journal of Social Theory, 12*(1), 99–116.

Büscher, M., Urry, J. & Witchger, K. (Eds) (2011). *Mobile Methods*. Oxford: Routledge.

Business Week. (2009). The Burton corporation. Retrieved January 6, 2010, from http://investing.businessweek.com/research/stocks/private/snapshot.asp

Butcher, J. & Smith, P. (2010). 'Making a difference': Volunteer tourism and development. *Tourism Recreation Research, 35*(1), 27–36.

Butt, D. (2005). Pros and cons. *New Zealand Snowboarder*. July/August. 88–92.

Butt, D. (2006). Abby Lockhart interview. *New Zealand Snowboarder*, September/October, 34–39.

Byrant, G. (2013). Mountainbikers to get new season challenge. *The Southland Times*, July 6. Retrieved August 10, 2013, from www.stuff.co.nz/southland-times/news/8885510/Mountainbikers-to-get-new-season-challenge

Campbell, L. (2010). Woodward Beijing announces grand opening celebrations on May 15, 2010. April 23. Retrieved May 11, 2013, from www.campwoodward.com/component/content/article/262-news/latest-news/588-official-woodward-beijing-press-release.html

Canniford, R. (2005). Moving shadows: Suggestions for ethnography in globalized cultures. *Qualitative Market Research*, 8(2), 204–218.

Carter, T. (2011). *In Foreign Fields: The Politics and Experiences of Transnational Sport Migration*. London: Pluto Press.

Casalegno, F. (2004). Thought on the convergence of digital media, memory and social and urban spaces. *Space and Culture*, 7(3) 313–326.

Castells, M. (1996). *The Rise of the Network Society*. Oxford: Blackwell.

Castells, M. (1997). *The Power of Identity*. Oxford: Blackwell.

Castells, M. (1998). *End of Millennium*. Oxford: Blackwell.

Castells, M. (2000). *The Rise of the Network Society* (2nd edition). Oxford: Blackwell.

Cava, G. et al. (2010). Investing in youth in the MENA region: Lessons learned and the way forward. *MENA Knowledge and Learning: Quick Notes Series*. Retrieved February 9, 2013, from www. siteresources.worldbank.org/INTMENA/Resources/QuickNoteYouth31.pdf

Celebrate Sarah Burke, 1982–2012. (2012). *Freeskier Magazine*. Retrieved August 1, 2012, from http://freeskier.com/sarah

Chaaban, J. (2008). The costs of youth exclusion in the Middle East. Middle East Youth Initiative Working Paper No. 7. Wolfensohn Center for Development and Dubai School of Government. Retrieved February 9, 2013, from ssrn.com/abstract=1139172 or dx.doi.org/10.2139/ssrn.1139172

Chambers, C. (2005). Masculine domination, radical feminism and change. *Feminist Theory*, 6(3), 325–346.

Chamlee-Wright, E. & Storr, V. (2009). 'There's no place like New Orleans': Sense of place and community recovery in the Ninth Ward after Hurricane Katrina. *Journal of Urban Affairs*, 31(5), 615–634.

Chang, T.C. (2012). Making and unmaking places in tourism geographies. In J. Wilson (Ed.), *The Routledge Handbook of Tourism Geographies*. London: Routledge, 133–138.

Chayko, M. (2002). *Connection: How We Form Social Bonds and Communities in the Internet Age*. Albany: State University of New York Press.

Chebium, R. (2013). Senate immigration bill could open more doors for foreign ski, snowboard instructors. *The Coloradan*. Retrieved September 10, 2013, from www.coloradoan.com/article/20130616/NEWS11/306160047/Senate-immigration-bill-could-open-more-doors-foreign-ski-snowboard-instructors?nclick_check=1

Cheong, S-M. & Miller, M.L. (2000). Power and tourism: A Foucauldian observation. *Annals of Tourism Research*, 27(2), 371–390.

China X Game in Shanghai sponsored by KIA Motors matches news sports moves to attract youth culture and cool factor, however 1-child rule backlash disses skate, moto, BMX as too 'extreme'. (2007). *Label Networks*. Retrieved January 10, 2010, from www.labelnetworks.com/sports/xgames_china_07.html

Chiu, C. (2009). Street and park skateboarding in New York City public space. *Space and Culture*, 12(1), 25–42.

Chouliaraki, L. (2010). Post-humanitarianism: Humanitarian communication beyond a politics of pity. *International Journal of Cultural Studies, 13*(2), 107–126.

Chovet, B. (no date). Why the digital space is so powerful for surf, board and action sports brands. *Interbrand.* Retrieved from www.interbrand.com/Libraries/Articles/boarding_paper_12-5-2011.sflb.ashx

Christchurch population continues to decline. (2012). *Radio New Zealand,* October 23. Retrieved October 25, 2012, from www.radionz.co.nz/news/canterbury-earthquake/118903/christchurch-population-continues-to-decline

Clancy, R. (2012). Red Bull 'worth £5bn' after Felix Baumgartner skydive. *The Daily Telegraph,* October 15. Retrieved May 19, 2013, from www.telegraph.co.uk/finance/newsbysector/retailandconsumer/leisure/9609231/Red-Bull-worth-5bn-after-Felix-Baumgartner-skydive.html

Clark, A. (2003). *Natural-born Cyborgs: Minds, Technologies, and the Future of Human Intelligence.* New York: Oxford University Press.

Clifford, H. (2002). *Downhill Slide: Why the Corporate Ski Industry Is Bad for Skiing, Ski Towns and the Environment.* San Fransisco: Sierra Club Books.

Cloke, P. & Perkins, H. (1998). 'Cracking the canyon with the awesome foursome': Representations of adventure tourists in New Zealand. *Society and Space, 16*(2), 185–218.

Cohen, R. (1996). Diasporas and the nation-state: From victims to challengers. *International Affairs, 72*(3), 507–520.

Cohen, S. (2010). Chasing a myth? Searching for 'self' through lifestyle travel. *Tourist Studies, 10*(2), 117–133.

Collins, F.L. (2008). Bridges to learning: international student mobilities, education agencies and social networks. *Global Networks, 8*(4), 398–417.

Collogan, L., Tuma, F., Dolan-Sewell, R., Borja, S. & Fleishman, A. (2004). Ethical issues pertaining to research in the aftermath of disaster. *Journal of Traumatic Stress, 17*(5), 363–372.

Comer, K. (2010). *Surfer Girls in the New World Order.* Durham: Duke University Press.

Comunello, F. & Anzera, G. (2012). Will the revolution be tweeted? A conceptual framework for understanding the social media and the Arab Spring. *Islam and Christian-Muslim Relations, 23*(4), 453–470.

Connerton, P. (2011). *The Spirit of Mourning: History, Memory and the Body.* Cambridge: Cambridge University Press.

Conradson, D. & Latham, A. (2007). The affective possibilities of London: Antipodean transnationals and the Overseas Experience. *Mobilities, 2*(2), 231–254.

Conradson, D. & McKay, D. (2007). Translocal subjectivities: Mobility, connection, emotion. *Mobilities, 2*(2), 167–174.

Cooper, H. (2010). On Liberia's shore, catching a new wave. *The New York Times,* retrieved October 2, 2013, from www.nytimes.com/2010/01/24/travel/24explorer.html?pagewanted=all&_r=0

Corkill, C. & Moore, R. (2012). 'The Island of Blood': Death and commemoration of the Isle of Man TT Races. *World Archaeology, 44*(2), 248–262.

Corner, S. (2008). An ethnographic exploration of gender experiences of a New Zealand surf culture. Unpublished Masters dissertation, University of Waikato.

Cover, R. (2006). Audience inter/active: Interactive media, narrative control and reconceiving audience history. *New Media and Society, 8*(1), 139–158.

Crang, P., Dwyer, C. & Jackson, P. (2003). Transnationalism and the spaces of commodity culture. *Progress in Human Geography, 27*(4), 438–456.

Cresswell, T. (2004). *Place: A Short Introduction.* Malden: Blackwell Publishing.

Crocket, H. (2009). Rethinking resistance: Technologies of the self and ethical action. Paper presented at Australian Society for Sport History Conference, Wellington, New Zealand, July 2.

Crocket, H. (2012). This is *Men's* ultimate: (Re)creating multiple masculinities in elite open ultimate Frisbee. *International Review for the Sociology of Sport* DOI: 10.1177/1012690211435185.

Crosbie, C. (2012). Fed-up judge to tourists: 'Wish I could deport you'. *Mountain Scene*, September 24. Retrieved August 11, 2013, from www.scene.co.nz/fedup-judge-to-tourists-wish-i-could-deport-you/303332a1.page

Crouch, D. (2000). Places around us: Embodied lay geographies in leisure and tourism. *Leisure Studies, 19*(2), 63–76.

Czaplinska, Z. (2013). I kite it [personal blog]. Retreived August 20, 2013, from http://ikiteit.wordpress.com

D'Andrea, A., Gray, B. & Ciolfi, L. (2011). Methodological challenges and innovations in mobilities research. *Mobilities, 6*(2), 149–160.

Daniels J. D. (2012). Surfing the quakes. *KiwiSurf,* 60-65.

Daniels, S. & Nash, C. (2004). Lifepaths: Geography and biography. *Journal of Historical Geography, 30*(3), 449–458.

Darnell, S. (2012). *Sport for Development and Peace: A Critical Sociology.* London: Bloomsbury Academic.

Daskalaki, M., Stara, A. & Imas, M. (2008). The 'parkour organization': Inhabitation of corporate spaces. *Culture and Organization, 14*(1), 49–64.

David. (2011a). Action sports and sport participation in China. *China Sports Review,* June 20. Retrieved May 9, 2013, from www.chinasportsreview.com/2011/06/20/action-sports-and-sport-participation-in-china

David. (2011b). At 2011 X Games Asia, China's best talents were missing: Part 1. *China Sports Review,* May 11. Retrieved May 9, 2013, from www.chinasportsreview.com/2011/05/11/at-2011-x-games-asia-china's-best-talents-were-missing-pt12

David. (2011c). At 2011 X Games Asia, China's best talents were missing: Part 2. *China Sports Review,* May 13. Retrieved May 9, 2013, from www.chinasportsreview.com/2011/05/13/at-2011-x-games-asia-china's-best-talents-were-missing-pt22

Davidson, I. (2011). Christchurch earthquake: Deadly tremors rebounded in city. *The New Zealand Herald,* February 25. Retrieved October 15, 2012, from www.nzherald.co.nz/science/news/article.cfm?c_id=82&objectid=10708579

Davies, L. (2009). Drinking on a ski holiday can be a recipe for disaster, Britons warned. *The Guardian,* December 9. Retrieved August 11, 2013, from www.theguardian.com/travel/2009/dec/09/ski-holiday-drinking-risk-warning

Davis, N.W. & Duncan, M.C. (2006). Sport knowledge is power: Reinforcing masculine privilege through Fantasy Sport league participation. *Journal of Sport and Social Issues, 30*(3), 244–264.

Dayan, D. & Katz, E. (1992). *Media Events: The Live Broadcasting of History.* Cambridge, MA: Harvard University Press.

Dean, B. (2012). No X Games for Whistler, apparently $750,000 isn't enough. *Unofficialnetworks.com,* May 1. Retrieved June 12, 2013, from http://unofficialnetworks.com/xgames-whistler-apparently-750000-94484

Deemer, S. (2000). Snow business is booming in sunny Orange County. *Los Angeles Business Journal,* January 24. Retrieved from www.findarticles.com/cf_dIs/m5072/4_22/59634968/p...

Deforges, L. (1997). Checking out the planet: global representations/local identities and youth travel. In T. Skelton and G. Valentine (Eds.), *Cool Places: A Geography of Youth Culture.* London: Routledge.

Degner, D. (no date). Growth of parkour in Egypt. Retrieved January 28, 2013, from www.incendiaryimage.com/projects/parkour-in-egypt

deGroot, J. (2009). Reconnecting with the dead via Facebook: Examining transcorporeal communication as a way to maintain relationships. Unpublished dissertation. Retrieved from https://etd.ohiolink.edu/ap:10:0::NO:10:P10_ETD_SUBID:61095

Dijck, J. van (2007). *Mediated Memories: In the Digital Age*. Stanford: Stanford University Press.

Donnelly, P. (1996). The local and the global: Globalization in the sociology of sport. *Journal of Sport and Social Issues, 20*(3), 239–257.

Donnelly, P., Atkinson, M., Boyle, S. & Szto, C. (2011). Sport for development and peace: A public sociology perspective. *Third World Quarterly, 32*(3), 589–601.

DPM. (2012). Alex Johnson: Pro climber. *DPM Climbing*. Retrieved from www.dpmclimbing.com/articles/view/alex-johnson-pro-climber

Du Gay, P., Hall, S., Janes, L., Mackay, H. & Negus, K. (1997). *Doing Cultural Studies: The Story of the Sony Walkman*. London: Sage.

Duffy, M., Waitt, G., Gorman-Murray, A. & Gibson, C. (2011). Bodily rhythms: Corporeal capacities to engage with festival spaces. *Emotion, Space and Society, 4*(11), 17–24.

Duggan, M. & Brenner, J. (2013). The demographics of social media users—2012. Pew Internet. Retrieved April 24, 2013, from http://pewinternet.org/Reports/2013/Social-media-users/Social-Networking-Site-Users/Overview.aspx

Duncan, T. (2008). The internationalisation of tourism labour markets: Working and playing in a ski resort. In C.M. Hall and T. Coles (Eds.), *International Business and Tourism*. London: Routledge, 181–194.

Duncan, T. (2009). Transient workers in Queenstown and Whistler: Case study 9.1. In J. Higham and T. Hinch (Eds.), *Sport and tourism: Globalisation, mobility and authenticity*. Oxford: Butterworth Heinemann, 173–174.

Duncan, T. (2012). The 'mobilities turn' and the geography of tourism. In J. Wilson (Ed.), *The Routledge Handbook of Tourism Geographies*. London: Routledge, 113–119.

Duncan, T., Scott, D. & Baum, T.D. (2013). The mobilities of hospitality work: An exploration of issues and debates. *Annals of Tourism Research, 41*(April), 1–19.

Durkheim, E. (1915/2012). *Elementary Forms of the Religious Life*. Translated by J.W. Swain. London: George Allen and Unwin Ltd.

Ebner, D. (2009). US snowboarder at top of fame mountain. *Globe and Mail*, February 11. Retrieved January 5, 2010, from http://license.icopyright.net/user/viewfreeuse.act?fuid=NjM5MTQ1MQ%3D%BD

Edensor, T. (2002). *National Identity, Popular Culture and Everyday Life*. Oxford: Berg.

Edensor, T. (Ed.) (2010a). *Geographies of Rhythm: Nature, Place, Mobilities and Bodies*. Wey Court East: Ashgate.

Edensor, T. (2010b). Walking in rhythms: Place, regulation, style and the flow of experience. *Visual Studies, 25*(1), 69–79.

Edensor, T. (2012). The rhythms of tourism. In C. Minca & T. Oakes (Eds.), *Real Tourism: Practice, Care and Politics in Contemporary Travel Culture*. Abingdon: Routledge, 54–71.

Edensor, T. & Holloway, J. (2008). Rhythmanalysing the coach tour: The Ring of Kerry, Ireland. *Transactions of the Institute of British Geographers, 33*(40), 483–501.

Ellison, K. (2011). Do you travel more than a pro surfer? *Gadling*. Retrieved from www.gadling.com/2011/11/03/do-you-travel-more-than-a-pro-surfer

Ess, C. (2009). *Digital Media Ethics*. Cambridge: Polity Press.

Ettema, D. & Schwanen, T. (2012). A relational approach to analysing leisure travel. *Journal of Transport Geography, 24*(Sept), 173–191.

Evers, C. (2004). Men-who-surf. *Cultural Studies Review, 10*(1), 27-41.

Evers, C (2006). How to surf. *Journal of Sport and Social Issues, 30*(3), 229–243.

Evers, C. (2009). 'The Point': Surfing, geography and a sensual life of men and masculinity on the Gold Coast, Australia. *Social and Cultural Geography, 10*(8), 893–908.

Evers, C. (2010a). *Notes for a Young Surfer.* Melbourne: Melbourne University Press.

Evers, C. (2010b). Intimacy, sport and young refugee men. *Emotion, Space and Society, 3*(1), 56–61.

Evers, C. (2012). Growth of surfing in China: At what cost? *The Inertia,* February 24. Retrieved May 10, 2013, from www.theinertia.com/business-media/growth-of-surfing-in-china-at-what-cost

Facebook in the Arab region. (2012). *Arab Social Media Report.* Retrieved February 9, 2013, from www.arabsocialmediareport.com/Facebook/LineChart.aspx?&PriMenuID=18&CatID=24&mnu=Cat

Fact sheet: Burton Snowboards (2003). Retrieved from www.burton.com

Fallov, M.A., Jørgensen, A. & Knudsen, L. (2013). Mobile forms of belonging. *Mobilities,* DOE: 10.1080/17450101.2013.769722

Faron, L. (1967). Death and fertility rites of the Mapuche (Araucanian) Indians of Central Chile. In J. Middleton (Ed.), *In Gods and Rituals.* Garden City: The Natural History Press, 227–254.

Farrar, M.E. (2009). Home/sick: Memory, place and loss in New Orleans. *Theory and Event, 12*(4).

Farrell, S. (2011). The graveyard shift. *The New York Times Style Magazine.* Retrieved January 26, 2013, from http://tmagazine.blogs.nytimes.com/2011/12/02/the-graveyard-shift/?pagewanted=print

Fast, A. (2005). *Transworld Snowboarding Resort Guide,* 24.

Favell, A. (2001). Migration, mobility and globalony: Metaphors and rhetoric in the sociology of globalisation. *Global Networks, 1* (4), 389–398.

Favell, A. (2007). Rebooting migration theory: Interdisciplinarity, globality and postdisciplinarity in migration studies. In C. Brettell & J. Hollifield (Eds.), *Migration Theory: Talking across Disciplines.* 2nd edition. Abingdon: Routledge, 259–278.

Fincham, B., McGuinness, M. & Murray, L. (2010). *Mobile Methodologies.* Basingstoke: Palgrave Macmillan.

Findlay, A.M., King, R., Stam, A. & Ruiz-Gelices, E. (2006). Ever-reluctant Europeans: the changing geographies of UK students studying and working abroad, *European Urban and Regional Studies, 13*(4), 291–318.

Fine, G. (1996). Reputational entrepreneurs and the memory of incompetence: Melting, supporters, partisan warriors and images of President Harding. *American Journal of Sociology, 101*(5), 1159–1193.

Foot, K., Warnick, B. & Schneider, S. (2006). Web-based memorializing after September 11: Toward a conceptual framework. *Journal of Computer-Mediated Communication, 11*(1), 72–96.

Ford, N. & Brown, D. (2006). *Surfing and Social Theory.* London: Routledge.

Founders story. (2011). *Surf Aid International.* Retrieved September 23, 2013, from www.surfaidinternational.org/foundersstory

Foss, J. (2013). New year-round X Games app launches. April 17. Retrieved from http://xgames.espn.go.com/article/8849915/new-mobile-tablet-apps-launch-x-games-2013

Foucault, M. (2007). *Security, Territory, Population.* Basingstoke: Palgrave Macmillan.

Frändberg, L. (2013). Temporary transnational youth migration and its mobility links. *Mobilities,* DOI: 10.1080/17450101.2013.769719

Franklin, A. & Crang, M. (2001). The trouble with tourism and travel theory? *Tourist Studies*, 1(5), 5–22.

Fried, M. (1963). Grieving for a lost home. In L.J. Duhl (Ed.), *The Urban Condition: People and Policy in the Metropolis*. New York: Basic Books, 124–152.

Fried, M. (2000). Continuities and discontinuities of place. *Journal of Environmental Psychology, 20*, 193–205.

Friedman, M.T (2008). *The Transparency of Democracy: A Lefebvrean Analysis of Washington's Nationals Park*. PhD thesis, University of Maryland, College Park.

Friedman, M.T. & Andrews, D.L. (2011). The built sport spectacle and the opacity of democracy. *International Review for the Sociology of Sport, 46*(2), 181–204.

Friedman, M.T. & van Ingen, C. (2011). Bodies in space: Spatializing physical cultural studies. *Sociology of Sport Journal, 28*(1), 85–105.

Frohlick, S. (2005). 'That playfulness of white masculinity': Mediating masculinities and adventure at mountain film festivals. *Tourist Studies, 5*(2), 175–193.

Fuller, G. (2004). *The Youth Crisis in Middle Eastern Society: Brief paper*. The Institute for Social Policy and Understanding. Michigan.

Garde-Hansen, J. (2009). MyMemories? Personal digital archive fever and Facebook. In J. Garde-Hansen, A. Hoskins & A. Reading (Eds.), *Save As... Digital Memories*. Basingstoke: Palgrave Macmillan, 135–150.

Garde-Hansen, J. (2010). Measuring mourning with online media: Michael Jackson and real-time memories. *Celebrity Studies, 1*(2), 233–235.

Garde-Hansen, J., Hoskins, A. and Reading, A. (Eds.) (2009). *Save As... Digital Memories*. Basingstoke: Palgrave Macmillan.

Gardner, K. (2013). X Games names Chicago as host finalist. *DNAinfo Chicago*, April 30. Retrieved May 25, 2013, from www.dnainfo.com/chicago/20130430/chicago-citywide/x-games-names-chicago-as-host-finalist

Gavelda, B. (2010). Higher education: The lonesome, crowded West. *Transworld Snowboarding*, May 19. Retrieved November 2, 2013, from http://snowboarding.transworld.net/photos/higher-education-the-lonesome-crowed-west/#.Ux-xu45x7Rc

Gaza parkour team – 'there is hope in life' (2012). *War in Context*. Retrieved April 12, 2013, from http://warincontext.org/2012/11/21/gaza-parkour-team-there-is-hope-in-life

Gesler, W. & Kearns, R. (2002). *Culture/Place/Health*. London: Routledge.

Ghosh, S. & Wang, L. (2003). Transnationalism and identity: A tale of two faces and multiple lives. *The Canadian Geographer, 47*(3), 269–282.

Giacaman, R., Mataria, A., Nguyen-Gillham, V., Safieh, R. A., Stefanini, A. & Chatterji, S. (2007). Quality of life in the Palestinian context: An inquiry in war-like conditions. *Health Policy, 81*(1), 68–84.

Gibson, C. (2012). Space, ethics and encounter. In J. Wilson (Ed.), *The Routledge Handbook of Tourism Geographies*. London: Routledge, 55–60.

Gibson, M. (2007a). Death and mourning in technologically mediated culture. *Health Sociology Review, 16*(5), 415–424.

Gibson, M. (2007b). Some thoughts on celebrity deaths: Steve Irwin and the issue of public mourning. *Mortality, 12*(1), 1–3.

Gieryn, T. (2000). A space for place in sociology. *Annual Review of Sociology, 26*, 463–496.

Gilchrist, P. and Wheaton, B. (2011). Lifestyle sport, public policy and youth engagement: Examining the emergence of parkour. *International Journal of Sport Policy and Politics, 3*(1), 109–131.

Gilchrist, P. and Wheaton, B. (2013). New media technologies in lifestyle sport. In B. Hutchins and D. Rowe (Eds.), *Digital Media Sport: Technology, Power and Culture in the Network Society*. New York: Routledge.

Gill, R. (2008). Empowerment/sexism: Figuring female sexual agency in contemporary advertising. *Feminism and Psychology, 18*(1), 35–60.

Giulianotti, R. (2004). Celtic, cultural identities and the globalization of football. *Scottish Affairs, 48*, 1–23.

Giulianotti, R. (2011a) Sport, transnational peacemaking, and global civil society: Exploring the reflective discourses of 'Sport, Development and Peace' project officials. *Journal of Sport and Social Issues, 35*(1), 50–71.

Giulianotti, R. (2011b). The sport, development and peace sector: A model of four social policy domains. *Journal of Social Policy, 40*(4), 757–776.

Giulianotti, R. & Brownell, S. (2012). Olympic and world sport: Making transnational society? *The British Journal of Sociology, 63*(2), 199–215.

Giulianotti, R. & Robertson, R. (2004). The globalization of football: A study in the glocalization of the 'serious life'. *The British Journal of Sociology, 55*(4), 545–568.

Giulianotti, R. & Robertson, R. (2012). Mapping the global football field: A sociological model of transnational forces within the world game. *The British Journal of Sociology, 63*(2), 216–240.

Global Boardsports. (2011). Global boardsports market to reach $20.5 billion by 2017, according to new report by Global Industry Analysts, Inc. April. Retrieved September 14, 2013, from www.prweb.com/releases/summer_boardsports/snowboarding/prweb8286170.htm

Goggin, G. & Hjorth, L. (2009). *Mobile Technologies*. New York: Routledge.

Gold, S.J. (2000). Transnational communities: Examining migration in a globally integrated world. In P. Aulakh & M. Schechter (Eds.), *Rethinking Globalization(s): From Corporate Transnationalism to Local Interventions*. Basingstoke: Palgrave Macmillan, 73–90.

González, B.M. (2005). Topophilia and topophobia: The home as an evocative place of contradictory emotions. *Space and* Culture, *8*(2), 193–213.

Gorman, P. (2012). City wants pools, sports fields first. *The Press*, May 30. Retrieved October 8, 2012, from www.stuff.co.nz/the-press/news/christchurch-earthquake-2011/our-rebuild-your-views/7011682/City-wants-pools-sports-fields-first

Greenblat, E. (2010). Quiksilver still riding the downturn. *The Sydney Morning Herald*, March 22. Retrieved May 21, 2013, from www.smh.com.au/business/quiksilver-still-riding-the-downturn-20100321-qo3z.html

Gregory, D. (2004). *The Colonial Present*. Malden: Blackwell.

Grider, S. (2001). Spontaneous shrines: A modern response to tragedy and disaster. *New Directions in Folklore, 5*. Retrieved from https://scholarworks.iu.edu/dspace/handle/2022/7196

Grieco, M. & Hine, J. (2008). Stranded mobilities, human disasters: The interaction of mobility and social exclusion in crisis circumstances. In S. Bergmann and T. Sager (Eds.), *The Ethics of Mobilities: Rethinking Place, Exclusion, Freedom and Environment* Farnham: Ashgate.

Griffiths, M., Light, B. & Lincoln, S. (2012). Connect and create: Young people, YouTube and graffiti communities. *Continuum Journal of Media and Cultural Studies, 26*(3), 343–341.

Groom, A. (2010). China travel interview: Waiting for the wind with Xiamen kitesurf instructor David Zhai. *China Travel*. Retrieved September 12, 2013, from http://blog.chinatravel.net/sports-adventure/china-travel-interview-waiting-for-the-wind-with-kitesurf-instructor-david-zhai.html

Gross, G. (2013). Jeremy Jones receives White House 'Champions of Change' award. *Transworld Snowboarding*, April 12. Retrieved September 20, 2013, from http://snowboarding.transworld.net/1000200633/news/jeremy-jones-receives-white-house-champions-of-change-award/

Gruneau, R. & Whitson, D. (1993). *Hockey Night in Canada: Sport, Identities and Cultural Politics.* Toronto: Garamond Press.

Gschwandtner, G. (2004). The powerful sales strategy behind Red Bull. *Selling Power*, September. Retrieved May 12, 2013, from www.sellingpower.com/content/article/?i=1181&ia=9278

Guarnizo, L.E. (1997). The emergence of a transnational social formation and the mirage of return migration among Dominican transmigrants. *Identities, 4*(2), 281–322.

Guarnizo, L.E., Portes, A. & Haller, W. (2003). Determinants of transnational political action among contemporary migrants. *American Journal of Sociology, 108*(6). 1211–1248.

Gustafson, P. (2001). Meanings of place: Everyday experience and theoretical conceptualizations. *Journal of Environmental Psychology, 21*(1), 5–16.

Hafner, K. & Lyon, M. (1996). *Where Wizards Stay Up Late: The Origins of the Internet.* New York: Simon & Schuster.

Hage, G. (2003). *Against Paranoid Nationalism: Searching for Hope in a Shrinking Society.* Sydney: Pluto Press.

Haldrup, M. (2011). Choreographies of leisure mobilities. In M. Büscher, J. Urry & K. Witchger (Eds.). *Mobile Methods.* Abingdon: Routledge, 54–71.

Hall, S. (1981). Encoding/decoding. In S. Hall, D. Hobson, A. Lowe & P. Willis (Eds.), *Culture, Media, Language.* London: Hutchinson.

Hall, S. (1997). The centrality of culture: Notes on the cultural revolutions of our time. In K. Thompson (Ed.), *Media and Cultural Regulation.* London: Sage, 208–236.

Hallam, E. & Hockey, J. (2001). *Death, Memory and Material Culture.* Oxford: Berg.

Hamad, T. (2007). Humanitarian Award 2007: Surf Aid International. Retrieved from www.wango.org/awards.aspx?section=awards2007&sub=3

Hannam, K. & Knox, D. (2010). *Understanding Tourism: A Critical Introduction.* London: Sage.

Hannan, K., Sheller, M. & Urry, J. (2006). Editorial: Mobilities, immobilities and moorings. *Mobilities, 1*(1), 1–22.

Hannerz, U. (1992). *Cultural Complexity.* New York: Columbia University Press.

Hannerz, U. (1996). *Transnational Connections: Cultures, People, Places.* London: Routledge.

Hannerz, U. (2002). Where we are and who we want to be. In U. Hedetoft & M. Hjort (Eds.), *The Postnational Self: Belonging and Identity.* Minneapolis: University of Minnesota Press, 217–232.

Hargrove, K. (2012,). X Games 2012 ratings soar. *Transworld Business*, February 9. Retrieved March 25, 2013, from http://business.transworld.net/86566/news/x-games-2012-ratings-soar

Haridakis, P. & Hanson, G. (2009). Social interaction and co-viewing with YouTube: Blending mass communication reception and social connection. *Journal of Broadcasting and Electronic Media, 53*(2), 317–335.

Harney, N. & Baldassar, L. (2007). Tracking transnationalism: Migrancy and its futures. *Journal of Migration Studies, 33*(2), 189–198.

Harris, A. (2005). Discourses of desire as governmentality: Young women, sexuality and the significance of safe spaces. *Feminism and Psychology, 15*(1), 39–43.

Harris, A. (Ed.) (2008). *Next Wave Cultures: Feminism, Subcultures and Activism.* New York: Routledge.

Harvey, D. (1989). *The Condition of Postmodernity.* Oxford: Basil Blackwell.

Harvey, J., Rail, G. & Thibault, L. (1996). Globalization and sport: Sketching a theoretical model for empirical analysis. *Journal of Sport and Social Issues, 20*(3), 258–277.

Hassan, R. (2004). *Media, Politics and the Network Society.* Maidenhead: Open University Press.

Hauben, M., Hauben, R. & Truscott, T. *Netizens: On the History and Impact of Usenet and the Internet (Perspectives)*. New York: Wiley-IEEE Computer Society Press.

Haverig, A. (2011). Constructing global/local subjectivities: The New Zealand OE as governance through freedom. *Mobilities, 6*(2), 103–123.

Hayhurst, L., Wilson B. & Frisby W. (2011). Navigating neo-liberal networks. *International Review for the Sociology of Sport, 46*(1), 1–15.

Held, D., McGrew, A. G., Goldblatt, D. & Perraton, J. (1999). *Global Transformations: Politics, Economics and Culture*. Redwood City: Stanford University Press.

Helmich, P. (2000). Chairman of the board. August 8. Retrieved from www.vermontguides.com/2000/8-aug/aug1.html

Henderson, M. (2001). A shifting line up: Men, women, and *Tracks* surfing magazine. *Continuum: Journal of Media and Cultural Studies, 15*(3), 319–332.

Hendry, J. (2003). An ethnographer in the global arena: Globography perhaps? *Global Networks, 3*(4), 497–512.

Henseler, C. (Ed.) (2012). *Generation X Goes Global: Mapping a Youth Culture in Motion*. New York: Routledge.

Hetherington, K. (1997). *The Badlands of Modernity: Heterotopia and Social Ordering*. London and New York: Routledge.

Hewer, C. & Roberts, R. (2012). History, culture and cognition: Towards a dynamic model of social memory. *Culture and Psychology, 18*(2), 167–183

Heywood, L. (2007). Third wave feminism, the global economy, and women's surfing: Sport as stealth feminism in girls' surf culture. In A. Harris (Ed.), *Next Wave Cultures: Feminism, Subcultures, Activism*. London and New York: Routledge, 63–82.

Heywood, L. & Montgomery, M. (2008). Ambassadors of the last wilderness: Surfers, environmental ethics, and activism in America. In K. Young & M. Atkinson (Eds.), *Tribal Play: Sub-cultural Journeys through Sport*. Bingley: JAI Press, 153–172.

Higgins, M. (2011). Surfer Irons died of heart attack and drugs, autopsy says. *The New York Times*, June 8. Retrieved July 12, 2012, from www.nytimes.com/2011/06/09/sports/cause-released-in-surfer-andy-irons-death.html

Higher education: The lonesome, crowded west. (2010). *Transworld Snowboarding*. Retrieved August 10, 2013, from http://snowboarding.transworld.net/1000124526/featuresobf/higher-education-the-lonesome-crowed-west

Highmore, B. (2005). *Cityscapes: Cultural Readings in the Material and Symbolic City*. Basingstoke and New York: Palgrave Macmillan.

Hjorth, L., Burgess, J. & Richardson, I. (2012). *Studying Mobile Media: Cultural Technologies, Mobile Communication and the iPhone*. New York: Routledge.

Holden, A. & Fennell, D.A. (Eds.). (2013). *The Routledge Handbook of Tourism and the Environment*. Routledge: New York.

Holt, R. (1989). *Sport and the British : A Modern History*. Oxford : Oxford University Press.

Horak, R. (2003). Diaspora experience, music and hybrid cultures of young migrants in Vienna. In D. Muggleton and R. Weinzierl (Eds.), *The Post-Subcultures Reader*. Oxford: Berg.

Horne, J. & Manzenreiter, W. (2006). An introduction to the sociology of sports mega-events. *The Sociological Review, 54*(S2), 1–24.

Horton, D. & Wohl, R.R. (1956). Mass communication and para-social interaction: Observations on intimacy at a distance. *Psychiatry, 19*(3), 215–229.

Horton, D. (2005). Henri Lefebvre: Rhythmanalysis: Space, Time and Everyday Life. *Time and Society, 14*(1), 157–159.

Houlihan, B. (1994). Homogenization, Americanization and creolization of sport: Varieties of globalization, *Sociology of Sport Journal, 11*(4), 356–375.

How surf travel will make you a better surfer (no date). *Surf Science.* Retrieved from www.surfscience.com/topics/travel/excursions-and-tours/surf-travel-benefits

Howe, S. (1998). *(SICK) A Cultural History of Snowboarding.* New York: St Martin's Griffin.

Huffington Post (2012). Sarah Burke tribute: X Games remember freestyle skier after her tragic death, January 26. Retrieved from www.huffingtonpost.com/2012/01/26/burke-honored-skier-death-memorial-winter-x-games-video_n_1235534.html

H2B visa information. (2009). Retrieved August 17, 2009, from www.outbreak-adventure.co.uk/recruitment/visa.php

Huggins, M. (2011). Reading the funeral rite: A cultural analysis of the funeral ceremonials and burial of selected leading sportsmen in Victorian England, 1864–1888. *Journal of Sport History, 38*(3), 407–424.

Hummon, D.M. (1992). Community attachment: Local sentiment and sense of place. In I. Altman & S.M. Low (Eds.), *Place Attachment.* New York: Plenum Press, 253–277.

Humphreys, C. (2011). Who cares where I play? Linking reputation with golfing capital and the implications for gold destinations. *Journal of Sport and Tourism, 16*(2), 105–128.

Humphreys, D. (1996). Snowboarders: Bodies out of control and in conflict. *Sporting Traditions, 13*(1), 3–23.

Humphreys, D. (1997). Shredheads go mainstream? Snowboarding an alternative youth. *International Review for the Sociology of Sport, 32*(2), 147–160.

Humphreys, D. (2003). Selling out snowboarding. In R. Rinehart and S. Sydnor (Eds.), *To the Extreme: Alternative Sports, Inside and Out.* Albany: State University of New York Press, 407–428.

Hunter, J. (2003). Flying the flag: Identities, the nation and sport. *Identities: Global Studies in Culture and Power, 10*(4), 409–425.

Huppatz, K. (2009). Reworking Bourdieu's 'capital': Feminine and female capitals in the field of paid caring work. *Sociology, 43*(1), 45–66.

Huq, R. (2003). Global youth cultures in localized spaces. In D. Muggleton and R. Weinzierl (Eds.), *The Post-Subcultures Reader.* Oxford: Berg.

Hussein, S. (2012). Daredevil Gazans run free with parkour. Retrieved from www.google.com/hostednews/afp/article/ALeqM5hZ-metg1krfDx-vvd1MldV_HpFgQ?docId=CNG.dbfb8c0eb97949bc88eb3f2f9c92bda3.371

Hutchings, T. (2012). Wiring death: Dying, grieving and remembering on the Internet. In D. J. Davies & C. W. Park (Eds.), *Emotion, Identity and Death: Mortality across Disciplines,* Aldershot: Ashgate, 43–58.

Hutchins, B. (2011). The acceleration of media sport culture: Twitter, telepresence and online messaging. *Information, Communication and Society, 14*(2), 237–257.

Hutchins, B. & Rowe, D. (2009). From broadcast scarcity to digital plenitude: The changing dynamics of the media sport content economy. *Television and New Media, 10*(4), 354–370.

Hutchins, B. & Rowe, D. (2012). *Sport Beyond Television: The Internet, Digital Media and the Rise of Networked Media Sport.* London and New York: Routledge.

Hutton, F. (2004). Up for it, mad for it? Women, drug use and participation in club scenes. *Health, Risk and Society, 6*(3), 223–237.

In the Arab world, social media has developed into a medium for the masses. (2012). *Knowledge@Wharton.* Retrieved February 9, 2013, from knowledge.wharton.upenn.edu/arabic/article.cfm?articleid=2837&language_id=1

Ingold, T. (1993). The temporality of landscape. *World Archaeology, 25*(2), 152–174.

Interview with a professional mountain bike racer. (no date). *Job Shadow.* Retrieved from www.jobshadow.com/interview-with-a-professional-mountain-bike-racer/

Jackson, P., Crang, P. & Dwyer, C. (2004). Introduction. In P. Jackson, P. Crang & C. Dwyer (Eds.), *Transnational Spaces.* London: Routledge, 1–23.

Jaimangal-Jones, D., Pritchard, A. & Morgan, N. (2009). Going the distance: Locating journey, liminality and rites of passage in dance music experiences. *Leisure Studies, 29*(3), 253–268.

Jansson, A. (2007). A sense of tourism: New media and the dialectic of encapsulation/decapsulation. *Tourist Studies, 7*(1), 5–24.

Jarrett, K. (2010). YouTube: Online video and participatory culture. Book review. *Continuum: Journal of Media and Cultural Studies, 24* (2), 327–330.

Jarvie, G. (1993). Sport, nationalism and cultural identity. In L. Allison (Ed.), *The Changing Politics of Sport.* Manchester: Manchester University Press.

Jarvie, G. (2006). *Sport, Culture and Society: An Introduction.* Oxford: Routledge.

Jayne, M., Gibson, C., Waitt, G. & Valentine, G. (2013). Drunken mobilities: Backpackers, alcohol and 'doing place'. *Tourist Studies, 12*(3), 211–231.

Jeffery, K. (2000). Karleen Jeffery and Craig Kelly interview. *Transworld Snowboarding.* Retrieved August 2, 2013, from http://snowboarding.transworld.net/1000030576/photos/backcountry/karleen-jeffery-and-craig-kelly-interview

Jeremy Jones establishes Protect Our Winters (POW) in fight against global warming crisis. (2007). March 28. Retrieved March 10, 2010, from www.snowboard-mag.com/node/19938

Jessop, A. (2012). The secret behind Red Bull's rise as an action sports leader. *Forbes Magazine,* retrieved May 10, 2013, from www.forbes.com/sites/aliciajessop/2012/12/07/the-secret-behind-red-bulls-action-sports-success

Johnson, S. (2012). The energy drink market world outlook for 2013. July 31. Retrieved June 30, 2013, from www.liefinternational.com/blog/market-research/consumer-trends/world/energy-drink-market-world-outlook-for-2013

Johnston, L. (2013). Queering skiing and camping up nature in Queenstown: Aotearoa New Zealand's Gay Ski Week. In J. Caudwell and K. Browne (Eds.), *Sexualities, Spaces and Leisure Studies.* London: Routledge, 43–58.

Kabachnik, P. (2012). Nomads and mobile places: Disentangling place, space and mobility. *Identities: Global Studies in Culture and Power, 19*(2), 210–228.

Kane, M.J. (2010). Adventure as a cultural foundation: Sport and tourism in New Zealand. *Journal of Sport and Tourism, 15*(1), 27–44.

Kane, M.J. & Tucker, H. (2004). Adventure tourism: The freedom to play with reality. *Tourist Studies, 4*(3), 217–234.

Kansteiner, W. (2002). Finding meaning in memory: A methodological critique of collective memory studies. *History and Theory, 41*(2), 179–197.

Karim, K. H. (2004). *The Media of Diaspora: Mapping the Globe.* Routledge.

Katzenstein, J. (2013). Detroit organizers have bold bid to host Summer X Games. *The Detroit News,* May 1. Retrieved June 10, 2013, from www.detroitnews.com/article/20130501/SPORTS07/305010325

Kaufman, P. & Wolff, E.A. (2010). Playing and protesting: Sport as a vehicle for social change. *Journal of Sport and Social Issues, 34*(2), 154–175.

Kay, J. & Laberge, S. (2002). The 'new' corporate habitus in adventure racing. *International Review of the Sociology of Sport, 37*(1), 17–36.

Kear, A. & Steinberg, D.L. (1999). Ghost writing. In A. Kear & D.L. Steinberg (Eds.), *Mourning Diana: Nation, Culture and the Performance of Grief.* London and New York: Routledge, 1–14.

Kennett-Hensel, P.A., J. Sneath. & Lacey, R. (2012). Liminality and consumption in the aftermath of a natural disaster. *Journal of Consumer Marketing, 29*(1). 52–63.

Kenway, J. & McLeod, J. (2004). Bourdieu's reflexive sociology and 'spaces of points of view': Whose reflexivity, which perspective? *British Journal of Sociology of Education, 25*(4), 525–544.

Kern, R., Forman, A. & Gil-Egui, G. (2013). R.I.P: Remain in Perpetuity: Facebook memorial pages. *Telematics and Informatics, 30*(1), 2–10.

Kidd, B. (2008). A new social movement: Sport for development and peace. *Sport in Society, 11*(4), 370–380.

Kidd, B. (2011). Cautions, questions and opportunities in sport for development and peace. *Third World Quarterly, 32*(3), 603–609.

Kidder, J. (2009). Appropriating the city: Space, theory and bike messengers. *Theory and Society, 38*(3), 307–328.

Kidder, J. (2011). *Urban Flow: Bike Messengers and the City.* Ithaca: ILR Press.

Kidder, J. (2012). Parkour, the affective appropriation of urban space, and the real/virtual dialectic. *City and Community, 11*(3), 229–253.

Kien, G. (2009). *Global Technography: Ethnography in the Age of Mobility.* New York: Peter Lang.

Klein, K.L. (2000). On the emergence of memory in historical discourse. *Representations, 69*(Winter), 127–150.

Kling, J. (2012). Review: The rise of the global imaginary. *New Political Science, 34*(1), 101–106.

Knowles, C. (1999). Here and there: Doing transnational fieldwork. In V. Amit (Ed.), *Constructing the Field: Ethnographic Fieldwork in the Contemporary World.* Florence: Routledge.

Knowles, C. (2005). Making whiteness: British lifestyle migrants in Hong Kong. In C. Alexander & C. Knowles (Eds.), *Making Race Matter: Bodies, Space and Identity.* Basingstoke: Palgrave Macmillan, 90–110.

Koblin, J. (2013). ESPN X Games memo asks staffers to work for free and not make fun of Brazilian people. *Deadspin.* Retrieved May 12, 2013, from http://deadspin.com/espn-x-games-memo-asks-staffers-to-work-for-free-and-no-471205365

Koehn, P.H. & Rosenau, J.N. (2002). Transnational competence in an emerging epoch. *International Studies Perspectives, 3*(2), 105–127.

Kong, L. (2012). No place, new places: Death and its rituals in urban Asia. *Urban Studies, 49*(2), 415–433.

Korpela, M., (2009). When a trip to adulthood becomes a lifestyle: Western lifestyle migrants in Varanasi, India. In M. Benson and K. O'Reilly (Eds.), *Lifestyle Migration: Expectations, Aspirations and Experiences.* Farnham: Ashgate, 15–30.

Krais, B. (1993). Gender and symbolic violence: Female oppression in the light of Pierre Bourdieu's theory of social practice. In C. Calhohn, E. LiPuma & M. Postone (Eds.), *Bourdieu: Critical Perspectives.* Cambridge: Polity Press, 156–177.

Krais, B. (2006). Gender, sociological theory and Bourdieu's sociology of practice. *Theory, Culture and Society, 23*(6), 119–134.

Krakauer, J. (1997). *Eiger Dreams: Ventures among Men and Mountains.* New York: Anchor Books.

Krapp, P. (2004). *Déjà vu: Aberrations of Cultural Memory.* Minneapolis: University of Minnesota Press.

Kreutzer, T. (2009). Generation mobile: Online and digital media usage on mobile phones among low-income urban youth in South Africa. Retrieved April 25, 2013, from www.tinokreutzer.org/mobile/MobileOnlineMedia-SurveyResults-2009.pdf

Kübler-Ross, E. (1969). *On Death and Dying.* New York: Routledge.

Kunz, V. (2009). Sport as a post-disaster psycho-social intervention in Bam, Iran. *Sport in Society, 12*(9), 1147–1157.

Kusz, K. (2007a). *Revolt of the White Athlete: Race, Media and the Emergence of Extreme Athletes in America.* New York: Peter Lang.

Kusz, K. (2007b). Whiteness and extreme sports. In D. Booth and H. Thorpe (Eds.), *Berkshire Encyclopedia of Extreme Sport.* Great Barrington: Berkshire Publishing, 357–361.

Lashua, B.D. & Kelly, J. (2008). Rhythms in the concrete: Re-imagining relationships between space, race, and mediated urban youth cultures. *Leisure/Loisir, 32*(2), 461–487.

Latham, A. (2003). Research, performance and doing human geography: Some reflections on the diary-photograph, diary-interview method. *Environment and Planning A, 35*(11), 1993–2018.

Laurendeau, J. (2004). The 'crack choir' and the 'cock chorus': The intersection of gender and sexuality in skydiving texts. *Sociology of Sport Journal, 21*(4), 397–417.

Laurendeau, J. (2006). 'He didn't go in doing a skydive': Sustaining the illusion of control in an edgework activity. *Sociological Perspectives, 49*(4). 583–605.

Laviolette, P. (2006). Green and extreme: Free-flowing through seascape and sewer. *Worldviews, 10*(2), 178–204.

Law, J. & Urry, J. (2004). Enacting the social. *Economy and Society, 33*(3), 390–410.

Lawrence, S., De Silva, M. & Henley, R. (2010). Sports and games for post-traumatic stress disorder. *The Cochrane Library,* retrieved from http://www.thecochranelibrary.com/userfiles/ccoch/file/PTSD/CD007171.pdf

Lefebvre, H. (1947/2008). *Critique of Everyday Life, vol. 1: Introduction.* Translated by J. Moore. New York: Verso. Originally published as *Critique de la vie quotidienne, vol 1: Introduction* (Paris: Grasset, 1947).

Lefebvre, H. (1961/2002). *Critique of Everyday Life, vol. 2: Foundations for a Sociology of the Everyday.* Translated by J. Moore. New York: Verso. Originally published as *Critique de la vie quotidienne, vol 2: Fondements d'une sociologie de la quotidienneté* (Paris: L'Arche, 1961).

Lefebvre, H. (1968/1996). The right to the city: In *Henri Lefebvre: Writings on Cities.* Translated by E. Lebas and E. Kofman. Oxford: Blackwell, 1996, 63–182. Originally published as *Le droit à la ville* (Paris: Anthropos, 1968).

Lefebvre, H. (1974/1991). *The Production of Space.* Translated by D. Nicholson-Smith. Oxford: Blackwell. Originally published as *La Production de l'espace* (Paris: Anthropos, 1974).

Lefebvre, H. (1981/2005). *Critique of Everyday Life, vol. 3: From Modernity to Modernism: Towards a Metaphilosophy of Daily Life.* Translated by J. Moore. New York: Verso. Originally published as *Critique de la vie quotidienne, vol 3: De la modernité au modernisme: Pour une métaphilosophie du quotidien* (Paris: l'Arche, 1981).

Lefebvre, H. (1992/2004). *Rhythmanalysis: Space, Time and Everyday Life.* Translated by S. Elden & G. Moore. London: Continuum. Originally published as *Éléments de rhythmanalyse: Introduction á la connaissance des rythmes* (Paris: Éditions Syllepse, 1992).

Lenskyj, H. (2002). *The Best Olympics Ever? Social Impacts of Sydney 2000.* Albany: State University of New York Press.

Leonard, D. (2009). New media and global sport cultures: Moving beyond clichés and binaries. *Sociology of Sport Journal, 26*(1), 1–16.

Levermore, R. (2008). Sport: A new engine of development? *Progress in Development Studies, 8*(2), 183–190.

Levermore, R. & Beacom, A. (2009). *Sport and International Development.* London: Palgrave Macmillan.

Levin, D. (2011). Chinese athletes say no to the system. *The New York Times,* August 18. Retrieved May 21, 2013, from www.nytimes.com/2011/08/19/sports/chinese-athletes-begin-to-challenge-governments-tight-grip.html?pagewanted=all

Levine, M. (2012). Generation G comes of age: Youth and the revolution in the Middle East and North Africa. In C. Henseler (Ed.), *Generation X Goes Global.* New York: Routledge, 293–314.

Levitt, P. & Glick Schiller, N. (2004). Conceptualizing simultaneity: A transnational social field perspective on society. *International Migration Review, 38*(3), 1002–1039.

Levitz, D. (2013). How to travel and surf the globe for a living: Interview with Chris Stevens. *The Trip Tribe,* June 28. Retrieved August 19, 2013, from http://blog.thetriptribe.com/how-to-travel-and-surf-the-globe-for-a-living-interview-with-chris-stevens/

Lewicka, M. (2011). Place attachment: How far have we come in the last 40 years? *Journal of Environmental Psychology, 31*(3), 207–230.

Lewis, M. (2010a). Finding opportunities in an aging action sports demographic. *Transworld Business.* Retrieved September 14, 2013, from http://business.transworld.net/49555/features/finding-opportunities-in-an-aging-action-sports-demographic

Lewis, M. (2010b). How to grow your business in the Hispanic community. *Transworld Business.* Retrieved November 23, 2010, from http://business.transworld.net/51577/features/how-to-grow-your-business-in-the-hispanic-community

Lewis, M. (2011a). Snowboarding participation increases 10%. *Transworld Business.* Retrieved December 6, 2013, from http://business.transworld.net/66828/news/snowboarding-participation-increases-10

Lewis, M. (2011b). Vans Triple Crown webcast sets record 10.4 million streams. *Transworld Business.* Retrieved October 25, 2013, from http://business.transworld.net/80440/news/vans-triple-crown-webcast-sets-record-10-4-million-streams

Lewis, M. (2012). Sunday Biz: The rise and stall of snowboarding. *Transworld Snowboarding.* Retrieved December 6, 2013, from http://business.transworld.net/110863/features/sunday-biz-the-rise-and-stall-of-snowboarding/3

Li, W. (2005). Speedy skateboarding. Retrieved May 13, 2013, from www.btmbeijing.com/contents/en/btm/2005-06/coverstory/skateboarding

Lidz, F. (1997). Lord of the board. *Sports Illustrated, 87* (December), 114–119.

Life in the Gaza Strip. (2012). *BBC News.* Retrieved on February 10, 2013, from www.bbc.co.uk/news/world-middle-east-20415675

Light, B., Griffiths, M. & Lincoln, S. (2012). 'Connect and create': Young people, YouTube and graffiti communities. *Continuum: Journal of Media and Cultural Studies, 26*(3), 343–355.

Little, S. (2006). Twin towers and Amoy Gardens: Mobilities, risks and choices. In M. Sheller & J. Urry (Eds.), *Mobile Technologies of the City.* London: Routledge.

Longman, J. (2010). China grooms team to become a powerhouse. *The New York Times,* February 15. Retrieved March 1, 2010, from www.nytimes.com/2010/02/15/sports/olympics/15longman.html

Lynch, K. (2011). More than 128 Christchurch buildings face demolition. *The Press,* April 1. Retrieved October 12, 2012, from www.stuff.co.nz/the-press/news/christchurch-earthquake-2011/4838607/More-than-128-Christchurch-buildings-face-demolition

Lyons, G. (2012). Facebook to hit a billion users in the summer. January 11. Retrieved March 12, 2012 from http://connect.icrossing.co.uk/facebook-hit-billion-users-summer_7709

Lyons, K., Hanley, J., Wearing, S. & Neil, J. (2012). Gap year volunteer tourism: Myths of global citizenship? *Annals of Tourism Research, 39*(1), 361–378.

Maguire, J. (1994). Sport, identity politics and globalization: Diminishing contrasts and increasing varieties. *Sociology of Sport Journal, 11*(4), 398–427.

Maguire, J. (1996). Blade runners: Canadian migrants, ice hockey, and the global sports process. *Journal of Sport and Social Issues, 23*(3), 335–360.

Maguire, J. & Bale, J. (1994). Introduction: Sports labour migration in the global arena. In J. Bale & J. Maguire (Eds.), *The Global Sports Arena: Athletic Talent Migration in an Independent World*. London: Frank Cass, 1–21.

Maguire, J. & Falcous, M. (2010). *Sport and Migration: Borders, Boundaries and Crossings*. London: Routledge.

Mahler, S. (1999). Engendering transnational migration: A case study of Salvaldorans. *American Behavioral Scientist, 42*(4), 690–719.

Maira, S. (2004). Imperial feelings: Youth culture, citizenship and globalization. In M.M. Suárez-Orozco & D.B. Qin-Hilliard (Eds.), *Globalization: Culture and Education in the New Millennium*. Berkeley: University of California Press, 203–234.

Manago, A., Taylor, T. & Greenfield, P. (2012). Me and my 400 friends: The anatomy of college students' Facebook networks, their communication patterns, and well-being. *Developmental Psychology, 48*(2), 369–380.

Mandelbaum, D. (1959). Social uses of funeral rites. In H. Feifel (Ed.), *The Meaning of Death*. New York: McGraw Hill, 189–217.

Mann, C. (2011). Estuary, rivers, beaches reopen: Christchurch waterways open for summer. *The Press*, November 10. Retrieved from http://www.stuff.co.nz/the-press/news/christchurch-earthquake-2011/5944379/Estuary-rivers-beaches-reopen

Mann, M. (2012). *The Sources of Social Power: Volume 3, Global Empires and Revolution, 1890–1945*. Cambridge: Cambridge University Press.

Manzo, L.C. (2003). Beyond house and haven: toward a revisioning of emotional relationships with places. *Journal of Environmental Psychology, 23*(1), 47–61.

Manzo, L.C. (2005). For better or worse: exploring multiple dimensions of place meaning. *Journal of Environmental Psychology, 25*(1), 67–86.

Maoz, D. (2006). The mutual gaze. *Annals of Tourism Research, 33*(1), 221–239.

Marcus, G. (1995). Ethnography in/of the world system: The emergence of multi-site ethnography. *Annual Review of Anthropology, 24*, 95–117.

Marshall, P. (2004). *New Media Cultures*. London: Hodder Headline.

Mason, P. (2002). The Big OE: New Zealanders' overseas experience in Britain. In C.M. Hall and A.M. Wiliams (Eds.), *Tourism and Migration: New Relationships between Production and Consumption*. Dordrecht: Kluwer Academic, 87–101.

Massey, D. (1994). *Space, Place and Gender*. Minneapolis: University of Minnesota Press.

McCormack, D.P. (2008). Geographies for moving bodies: Thinking, dancing spaces. *Geography Compass, 2*(6), 1822–1836.

McDermott, M. (2009). Interview with Jeremy Jones: Founder of Protect Our Winters. *Tree Hugger*, November 24. Retrieved April 5, 2010, from www.treehugger.com/files/2009/11/the-th-interview-jeremy-jones-protect-our-winters.php

McEvoy-Levy, S. (2001). Youth as social and political agents: Issues in post-settlement peace building. Kroc Institute Occasional Paper #21:OP:2. Retrieved February 12, 2013, from www.unoy.org/downloads/resources/YandP/2001_McEnvoy-Levy.pdf

McGuigan, C. (2012). Red Bull: Masterminds of new age marketing. *Creative Guerrilla Marketing*, October 16. Retrieved May 2, 2013, from www.creativeguerrillamarket-ing.com/viral-marketing/red-bull-masterminds-of-new-age-marketing

McGuire, P. (2012). The Gaza Strip cyber war. *VICE magazine*. Retrieved February 9, 2013, from www.vice.com/read/the-gaza-strip-cyber-war

McKay, D. (2005). Migration and the sensuous geographies of re-emplacement in the Philippines. *Journal of Intercultural Studies, 26*(1–2), 75–91.

McKay, J., Lawrence, G., Rowe, D. & Miller, T. (2001). *Globalization and Sport: Playing the World*. London: Sage.

McNay, L. (1999). Gender, habitus and the field: Pierre Bourdieu and the limits of reflexivity. *Theory, Culture and Society, 16*(1), 95–117.

Media Man Australian Extreme Directory (no date). Retrieved November 19, 2009, from www.mediaman.com.au_profiles_snowboard.pdf

Melekian, B. (2010). Last Drop. *Outside*, November 2. Retrieved March 13, 2012, from www.outsideonline.com/outdoor-adventure/athletes/Last-Drop.html

Melekian, B. (2011, August 1). Crashing down. *Outside*. Retrieved March 12, 2012, from www.outsideonline.com/outdoor-adventure/athletes/andy-irons/Crashing-Down.html?page=all

Mels, T. (Ed.). (2004). *Reanimating Places: A Geography of Rhythms*. Aldershot: Ashgate.

Messner, M. (2002). *Taking the Field*. Minneapolis: University of Minnesota Press.

Mick, H. (2010). Formulaic approach paying off for Chinese athletes. *Globe and Mail*, January 22. Retrieved March 17, 2010, from www.militaryphotos.net/forums/showthreat.php?172972-Chinese-Olympic-Snowboarders

Mickle, T. (2008,). China: Action's next frontier. *Street and Smith's Sports Business Journal*, April 14. Retrieved October 20, 2013, from www.sportsbusinessdaily.com/Journal/Issues/2008/04/20080414/This-Weeks-News/China-Actions-Next-Frontier.aspx?hl=This%20Weeks%20Issue&sc=0

Mickle, T. (2011, July 25). Global expansion plans, Red Bull partnership boost X Games sponsorship revenue. *Street and Smith's Sports Business Journal*, retrieved April 20, 2013, from http://www.sportsbusinessdaily.com/Journal/Issues/2011/07/25/Marketing-and-Sponsorship/X-Games.aspx

Miegel, F. & Olsson, T. (2012). A generational thing? The internet and new forms of social intercourse. *Continuum: Journal of Media and Cultural Studies, 26*(3), 487–499.

Miller, D.S. & Rivera, J.D. (2009). *Hurricane Katrina and the Redefinition of Landscape*. Lanham: Lexington Books.

Milligan, M. (2003). Displacement and identity discontinuity: the role of nostalgia in establishing new identity categories. *Symbolic Interaction, 26*(3), 381–403.

Minsberg, T. (2013). To all surfing enthusiasts, there are online fantasy leagues for you, too. *The New York Times*, August 4, Retrieved October 25, 2013, from www.nytimes.com/2013/08/04/sports/to-all-surfing-enthusiasts-there-are-online-fantasy-leagues-for-you-too.html?_r=0

Mishra, S., Mazumdar, S. & Suar, D. (2010). Place attachment and flood preparedness. *Journal of Environmental Psychology, 30*(2), 187–197.

Misztal, B. (2003). *Theories of Social Remembering*. Philadelphia: Open University.

Mohammad, A.M. (2011). The Arab 'youth quake': Implications on democratization and stability. *Middle East Law and Governance, 3*(1–2), 159–170.

More than half of Palestinian youth own computers, have access to internet. (2012). *The Technologist Magazine*, July 5. Retrieved February 9, 2013, from http://technologist.ps/2012/07/05/more-than-half-of-palestinian-youth-own-computers-have-access-to-internet/?lang=en

Morley, D. (2000). *Home Territories: Media, Mobility and Identity*. London: Routledge.

Morrice, S. (2013). Heartache and Hurricane Katrina: Recognising the influ-ence of emotion in post-disaster return decisions. *Area*, *45*(1), doi: 10.1111/j.1475-4762.2012.01121.x

Morris, J. (2008). Research on the slopes: Being your own customer can be essential to success. *Change Agent: The Global Market Research Business Magazine*, June. Retrieved January 1, 2010, from http://synovate.com/changeagent.index.php

Muggleton, D. & Weinzierl, R. (Eds.). (2003). *The Post-Subcultures Reader*. Oxford: Berg.

Munster, A. (2006). *Materializing New Media: Embodiment in Information Aesthetics*. Hanover: Dartmouth College Press/University Press of New England.

Murphy, C. (2006). Sloping off to Mont Blanc. *The Post IE*, January 22. Retrieved December 2, 2009, from http://archives.tcm.ie/businesspost/2006/01/22/story11123.asp

Murthy, D. (2008). Digital ethnography: An examination of the use of new technolo-gies for social research, *Sociology*, *42*(5), 837–855.

Murthy, D. (2013). Ethnographic research 2.0. *Journal of Organizational Ethnography*, *2*(1), 23–36.

Nathan, D. (2004). *Saying It's So: A Cultural History of the Black Sox Scandal*. Urbana: University of Illinois Press.

Nayak, A. (2003). *Race, Place and Globalization: Youth Cultures in a Changing World*. Oxford: Berg.

Nayak, A. & Kehily, M. (2008). *Gender, Youth and Culture: Young Masculinities and Femininities*. Basingstoke and New York: Palgrave Macmillan.

Nayar, P. (2010). Introduction. In P. Nayar (Ed.), *The New Media and Cybercultures Anthology*. Oxford: Wiley-Blackwell, 1–16.

Neumann, M. (1992). The trail through experience: Finding self in the recollection of travel. In C. Ellis & M.G. Flaherty (Eds.), *Investigating Subjectivity: Research on Lived Experience*. Newbury Park: Sage Publications, 176–201.

Nicaragua: Pacific Side Introduction. (no date). *Surfline*. Retrieved from www.surfline.com/travel/index.cfm?id=3235

Nicholls, S. (2009). On the backs of peer educators: Using theory to interrogate the role of young people in the field of sport-in-development. In R. Levermore and A. Beacom (Eds.), *Sport and International Development*. London: Palgrave Macmillan, 156–175.

Nichols, S., Giles, A. & Sethna, C. (2011). Perpetuating the 'lack of evidence' discourse in sport for development: Privileged voices, unheard stories and subjugated knowl-edge. *International Review for the Sociology of Sport*, *46*(3), 249–264.

Nine cities advance to final phase of X Games global expansion bid process. (2012). *Supercross.com*, January 26. Retrieved May 15, 2013, from http://supercross.com/nine-cities-advance-to-final-phase-of-x-games-global-expansion-bid-process

Nonini, D. & Ong, A. (Eds.). (1997). *Ungrounded Empires: The Cultural Politics of Modern Chinese Nationalism*. Routledge: New York.

Norris, P. (2002). *Democratic Phoenix: Reinventing Political Activism*. Cambridge: Cambridge University Press.

Noy, C. (2004). 'This trip really changed me': Backpackers' narratives of self-change. *Annals of Tourism Research*, *31*(1), 78–102.

NSGA. (2008). Skateboarding 10-year winner in sports participation growth. *National Sporting Goods Association*. Retrieved September 12, 2013, from www.nsga.org/i4a/pages/index.cfm?pageid=3966

NSGA 2001-2004 participation by median age. (2005a). Retrieved October 12, 2006, from www.nsga.org/public/pages/index.cfm?pageid=1358

NSGA 2003 women's participation ranked by percent change. (2005b). Retrieved October 12, 2006, from from www.nsga.org/public/pages/index.cfm?pageid=155

NSGA Newsletter. (2001). Skiers/snowboarder profile continues to change. November 12, *3*(21).

O'Brien, J. (2012). How Red Bull takes content marketing to the extreme. December 20. Retrieved June 19, 2013, from http://mashable.com/2012/12/19/red-bull-content-marketing

O'Neil, D. (2012). X Games expands globally. *ESPN.com*, December 10. Retrieved April 20, 2013, from http://xgames.espn.go.com/xgames/cities/article/7862758/x-games-grow-three-six-events-2013

Oakley and Shaun White present Air & Style 2010. (2010). Retrieved June 19, 2013, from www.prnewswire.com/news-releases/oakley-and-shaun-white-present-air--style-2010-105468308.html

Olive, R. and Thorpe, H. (2011). Negotiating the F-word in the field: Doing feminist ethnography in action sport cultures. *Sociology of Sport Journal*, *28*(4), 421–440.

Olivier, S. (2010). 'Your wave, bro!': Virtue ethics and surfing. *Sport in Society, 13*(7/8), 1223–1233.

O'Malley, M. & Rosenzweig, R. (1997). Brave new world or blind alley? American history on the world wide web. *Journal of American History*, *84*(1), 132–155.

Onboard Media Pack. (2012). Retrieved April 12, 2013, from http://cdn4.coresites.mpora.com/factorymedia/wp-content/uploads/2010/05/Onboard-Media-Kit-2012-13.pdf

Orayb, S. (2005). The forgotten children of Albaqa'a: Children's play in a Palestinian refugee camp. Unpublished Masters thesis, University of British Columbia. Retrieved February 13, 2013, from http://circle.ubc.ca/bitstream/handle/2429/16203/ubc_2005-0109.pdf?sequence=1

Oren, M. (2002). *Six Days of War: June 1967 and the Making of the Modern Middle East*. Oxford: Oxford University Press.

Osgerby, B. (2004) *Youth Media*. Routledge: London.

Packard, S. (2006). French ski resort's lure leaves locals bruised. *The New York Times*, March 15. Retrieved June 20, 2009, from www.nytimes.com/2006/03/15/business/worldbusiness/15iht-chamonix.html?_r=0

Pantti, M, & Sumiala, J. (2009). Till death do us join: Media, mourning rituals and the sacred centre of the society. *Media, Culture and Society, 31*(1), 119–135.

Parsons, N.L. & Stern, M. (2012). 'There's no dying in baseball': Cultural valorization, collective memory, and induction into the Baseball Hall of Fame. *Sociology of Sport Journal, 29*(1), 62–88.

Pawle, F. (2011, June 11). Hidden truths about surfing's wild boy Andy Irons. *The Australian*. Retrieved from www.theaustralian.com.au/news/features/hidden-truths-about-surfings-wild-boy-andy-irons/story-e6frg6z6-1226073140036

Perlmutter, H.V. (1972). The development of nations, unions and firms as world-wide institutions. In H. Gunter (Ed.), *Transnational Industrial Relations*. New York: St Martin's Press.

Pickering, C. & Barros, A. (2013). Mountain environments and tourism. In A. Holden & D. Fennell (Eds.), *The Routledge Handbook of Tourism and the Environment*. New York: Routledge, 183–191.

Picou, S. (2009). Review essay: The shifting sands of post-Katrina disaster sociology. *Sociological Spectrum, 29*(3), 431–438.

Pilkington, H. & Johnson, R. (2003). Peripheral youth: Relations of identity and power in global/local context. *European Journal of Cultural Studies, 6*(3), 259–283.

Please stay away from beaches. (2011). Retrieved from http://canterburyearthquake.
org.nz/2011/03/01/please-stay-away-from-beaches

Ponting, J. (2007). The endless bummer: The past, present and future of surfing tourism in the Pacific. Paper presented at CAUTHE Conference, Sydney, Australia.

Ponting, J. (2009). *Consuming Nirvana? The Social Contructon of Surfing Tourist Space.*
Saarbrücken: VDM Publishing.

Ponting, J., McDonald, M.G. & Wearing, S.L. (2005). De-constructing wonderland:
surfing tourism in the Mentawai Islands, Indonesia. *Loisir et Société/Society and
Leisure, 28*(1), 141–162.

Pope, S.W. (2007). *Patriotic Games: Sporting Traditions in the American Imagination,
1876–1926.* Knoxville: University of Tennessee Press.

Porter, D. & Smith A. (Eds). (2004). *Sport and National Identity in the Post-war World.*
London: Routledge.

Portes, A. (1997). Globalization from below: The rise of transnational communities.
Working paper, retrieved September 18, 2013, from http://maxweber.hunter.cuny.
edu/pub/eres/SOC217_PIMENTEL/portes.pdf

Powell, A. (2008). Amor fati? Gender habitus and young people's negotiation of (hetero)sexual consent. *Journal of Sociology, 44*(2), 167–184.

Pratt, G. & Yeoh, B. (2003). Transnational (counter) topographies. *Gender, Place and
Culture, 10*(2), 159–166.

Press release. (2004). Burton teams with Mandalay Entertainment. October 17.
Retrieved November 12, 2006, from www.transworldsnowboarding.com/snow/
snowbiz/article/0,13009,710987,00.html

Prestholdt, J. (2012). Resurrecting Che: Radicalism, the transnational imagination,
and the politics of heroes. *Journal of Global History, 7*(3), 506–526.

Preston-Whyte, R. (2004). The beach as a liminal space. In A. Lew, M. Hall &
A. Williams (Eds.), *A Companion to Tourism.* Oxford: Blackwell, 173–183.

Pries, L. (Ed.). (2001). *New Transnational Social Spaces: International Migration and
Transnational Companies in the Early Twenty-first Century.* London: Routledge.

Pritchard, A. & Morgan, N. (2010). Wild on the beach: Discourses of desire, sexuality and liminality. In E. Waterson & S. Watson (Eds.), *Culture, Heritage and
Representation: Perspectives on Visuality and the Past.* Farnham: Ashgate, 127–144.

Pritchard, A. Ateljevic, I., Morgan, N. & Harris, C. (2007). *Tourism and Gender:
Embodiment, Sensuality and Experience.* Wallingford: CABI.

Queenstown New Zealand. (2013). Retrieved July 20, 2013, from www.queenstownnz.
co.nz

Queenstown's growing problem: Misbehaving drunk tourists. (2010). March 24.
Retrieved August 9, 2013, from www.eturbonews.com/15079/queenstowns-
growing-problem-misbehaving-drunk-tourists

Quiksilver to enter Chinese market. (2003). *Transworld Surf.* Retrieved April 3, 2013, from
http://surf.transworld.net/1000003533/features/quiksilver-to-enter-chinese-market

Radford, S.K. & Bloch, P.H. (2012). Grief, commiseration, and consumption following
the death of a celebrity. *Journal of Consumer Culture, 12*(2), 137–155.

Raid, J. & Norris, F. (1996). The influence of relocation on the environmental, social
and psychological stress experienced by disaster victims. *Environment and Behavior,
28*(2), 163–182.

Ramp it up. (2010). *Monash Magazine,* 25. Retrieved December 27, 2010, from www.
monash.edu.au/pubs/monmag/issue25-2010/alumni-news/ramp-it-up.html

Randall, L. (1995). The culture that Jake built. *Forbes, 155*(7), 45–46.

Raymond, E.M. & Hall, C.M. (2008). The development of cross-cultural (mis)understanding through volunteer tourism. *Journal of Sustainable Tourism, 16*(5), 530–543.

Re.Public (I. Ang, R. Barcan, et. al.) (Eds.). (1997). *Princess Diana: Cultural Studies and Global Mourning*. Kingswood: University of Western Sydney.

Read, P. (1996). *Returning to Nothing: The Meaning of Lost Places*. Cambridge: Press Syndicate of the University of Cambridge.

Reay, D. (2004). 'It's all becoming habitus': Beyond the habitual use of habitus in educational research. *British Journal of Sociology of Education, 25*(4), 431–444.

Reed, R. (2005). *The Way of the Snowboarder*. New York: Harry N. Abrams, Inc.

Reilly, M.P.J. (2012). Grief, loss and violence in Ancient Mangaia, Aotearoa and Te Waipounamu. *The Journal of Pacific History, 47*(2), 145–161.

Reilly, P. (2010). Fantasy Surfer: Slater primed for South Africa. *Bleacher Report*, retrieved October 25, 2013, from http://bleacherreport.com/articles/402224-fanatsy-surfer-slater-primed-for-south-africa

Reuters. (2009). Britain tells alpine enthusiasts don't drink and ski. December 9. Retrieved from www.reuters.com/article/idUSTRE5B84D020091209

Richards, G. & King, B. (2003). Youth travel and backpacking. *Travel and Tourism Analyst, 6*(December), 1–23.

Richards, L. (2012). Stats: Social media growth and impact across the Middle East. *Econsultancy*. Retrieved February 9, 2013, from http://econsultancy.com/nz/blog/10491-stats-social-media-growth-and-impact-across-the-middle-east

Richards, T. with Blehm, E. (2003). *P3: Pipes, Parks, and Powder*. New York: HarperCollins.

Rideout, V. (2011). Zero to eight: Children's media use in America. Retrieved April 25, 2013, from www.commonsensemedia.org/sites/default/files/research/zerotoeightfinal2011.pdf

Riding with your spouse – A Whistler survival guide. (2012). *The Whistler Insider*. Retrieved August 12, 2013, from www.whistler.com/blog/post/2013/03/13/Whistler-couples-ski-board.aspx

Rigauer, B. (1981/1969). *Sport and Work*. New York: Columbia University Press.

Rinehart, R. (2000). Emerging arriving sport: Alternatives to formal sports. In J. Coakley & E. Dunning (Eds.), *Handbook of Sports Studies*. London: Sage, 504–519.

Rinehart, R. (2008). ESPN's X games, contests of opposition, resistance, co-option, and negotiation. In M. Atkinson & K. Young (Eds.), *Tribal Play: Subcultural Journeys through Sport* (Volume IV 'Research in the Sociology of Sport'). Bingley: JAI, 175–196.

Rinehart, R. & Sydnor, S. (Eds.). (2003). *To the Extreme. Alternative Sports, Inside and Out*. Albany: State University of New York Press.

Ritzer, G. & Jurgenson, N. (2010). Production, consumption, prosumption: The nature of capitalism in the age of the digital 'prosumer'. *Journal of Consumer Culture, 10*(1), 13–36.

Roberts, P. (2004). The living and the dead: Community in the virtual cemetery. *Omega, 49*(1), 57–76.

Roberts, P. (2006). From my space to our space: The functions of web memorials in bereavement. *The Forum, 32*, retrieved from www.adec.org/AM/Template.cfm?Section=The_Forum&Template=/CM/ContentDisplay.cfm&ContentID=1554

Robertson, G., Mash, M., Tickner, L., Bird, J., Curtis, B. & Putnam, T. (1994). *Travellers' Tales: Narratives of Home and Displacement*. London and New York: Routledge.

Robertson, R. (1992). *Globalization: Social Theory and Global Culture*. London: Sage.

Robertson, R. (1995). Glocalization: Time-space and homogeneity-heterogeneity. In M. Featherstone, S. Lash & R. Robertson (Eds.), *Global Modernities*. London: Sage.

R. Robertson & K.E. White (Eds.). (2003). *Globalization: Critical Concepts in Sociology* (six volumes). London: Routledge.

Robinson, L., Long, M. & Lamb, S. (2011). How young people are faring. *Foundation for Young Australians*. Retrieved from www.fya.org.au/wp-content/uploads/2011/11/FYA_HYPAF_AtAGlance_PDF1.pdf

Rodgers, A.L. (2001). It's a (Red) Bull market after all. *Fast Company*, September 30. Retrieved May 14, 2013, from www.fastcompany.com/64658/its-red-bull-market-after-all

Rojek, C. & Urry, J. (1997). Transformations of travel and theory. In C. Rojek & J. Urry (Eds.), *Touring Cultures: Transformations of Travel and Theory*. London: Routledge, 1–19.

Romm, J. (2012). Seminal study finds 'climate change footprint' in North America 'contingent with the largest increases in disasters'. *Climate Progress*, October 21. Retrieved October 25, 2012, from http://thinkprogress.org/climate/2012/10/21/1054571/seminal-study-climate-change-footprint-in-north-america-the-continent-with-the-largest-increases-in-disasters

Roudometof, V. (2005). Transnationalism, cosmopolitanism and glocalization. *Current Sociology, 53*(1), 113–135.

Rung, A.L., Broyles, S.T., Mowen A.J., Gustat, J. & Sothern, M.S. (2011). Escaping to and being active in neighbourhood: Parks use in a post-disaster setting. *Disasters, 35*(2), 383–403.

Russell, D. (2006). 'We all agree, name the stand after Shankly': Cultures of commemoration in late twentieth century English football cultures. *Journal of Sport History, 26*(1), 1–25.

Ryan, C. (2002). Motives, behaviours, body and mind. In C. Ryan (Ed.), *The Tourist Experience*. London: Continuum.

SA FAQ (SurfAid Frequently Asked Questions). (no date). SurfAid International. www.surfaidinternational.org.

Said, E. (1979). *Orientalism*. New York: Vintage.

Sakr, N. (2001). *Satellite Realms: Transnational Television, Globalization and the Middle East*. London: I.B. Tauris & Co.

Salter, M. (2013). To make move and let stop: Mobility and the assemblage of circulation. *Mobilities, 8*(1), 7–19.

Samuel, R. (1994). *Theatres of Memory*. London: Verso.

Sanderson, J. & Hope Cheong, P. (2010). Tweeting prayers and communicating grief over Michael Jackson online. *Bulletin of Science, Technology and Society, 30*(5), 328–340.

Sarah Burke seriously injured. (2012, January). *FIS Freestyle Ski World Cup*, retrieved from http://www.fisfreestyle.com/uk/mobile/sarah-burke-seriously-injured,346.html?actu_page_42=2?sectorcode=&sector=

Saslow, E. (2012). One light will not go out. *ESPN: The Magazine*, June 1. Retrieved from http://espn.go.com/espnw/more-sports/7984690/freeskier-sarah-burke-leaves-lasting-legacy-women-sports-espn-magazine

Savage, M., Bagnall, M. & Longhurst, B. (2005). *Globalization and Belonging*. London: Sage.

Saville, S. (2008). Playing with fear: Parkour and the mobility of emotion. *Social and Cultural Geography, 9*(8), 891–914.

Scannell, L. & Gifford, R. (2010). Defining place attachment: A tripartite organizing framework. *Journal of Environmental Psychology, 30*(1), 1–10.

Scherer, J. & Jackson, S. (2012). *Globalization, Sport and Corporate Nationalism: The New Cultural Economy of the New Zealand All Blacks*. Oxford: Peter Lang.

Schilt, K. & Zobl, E. (2004). Connecting the dots: Riot grrrls, Ladyfests, and the International Grrrl Zine Network. In A. Harris (Ed.), *Next Wave Cultures: Feminism, Subcultures and Activism*. New York: Routledge, 171–192.

Schumacher, C. (2011). Why I'm boycotting. *The Inertia*, April 5. Retrieved May 15, 2013, from www.theinertia.com/politics/why-im-boycotting-cori-schumacher-longboarding-china

Seamon, D. (1980). Body-subject, time-space routines, and place-ballets. In A. Buttimer & D. Seamon (Eds.), *The Human Experience of Space and Place*. New York: St Martin's Press, 148–165.

SFIA. (2013). Skateboarding participation report 2013. *Sports and Fitness Industry Association*. Retrieved September 20, 2013, from www.sfia.org/reports/87_Skateboarding-Participation-Report-2013

Shahin, M. (2012). Free running Gaza. *Saudi Aramco World*, November/December. Retrieved February 12, 2013, from www.saudiaramcoworld.com/issue/201206/free.running.gaza.htm

Sheller, M. & Urry, J. (2004). Places to play, places in play. In M. Sheller & J. Urry (Eds.), *Tourism Mobilities: Places to Play, Places in Play*. London: Routledge, 1–10.

Sherker, S., Finch, C., Kehoe, E.J. & Doverty, M. (2006). Drunk, drowsy, doped: Skiers' and snowboarders' injury risk perceptions regarding alcohol, fatigue and recreational drug use. *International Journal of Injury Control and Safety Promotion*, *13*(3), 151–157.

Sherowski, J. (2004). Notes from down-under. *Transworld Snowboarding*, April, 104–117.

Sherowski, J. (2005). What it means to be a snowboarder. *Transworld Snowboarding*, January, 160–169.

Silk, M. (2005). Sporting ethnography: Philosophy, methodology and reflection. In D. Andrews, D. Mason & M. Silk (Eds.), *Qualitative Methods in Sports Studies*. Oxford: Berg.

Stuartsen, K. (2004). Spatiality, temporality, and the construction of the city. In J. Ole Bærenholdt & K. Stuartsen (Eds.), *Space Odysseys: Spatiality and Social Relations in the 21st Century*. Aldershot: Ashgate, 43–62.

Stuartsen, K. (2005). Bodies, sensations, space and time: The contribution from Henri Lefebvre. *Geografiska Annaler. Series B. Human Geography*, *87*(1), 1–14.

Simpson, K. (2004). 'Doing development': The gap year, volunteer-tourists and a popular practice of development. *Journal of International Development*, *16*(5), 681–692.

Simpson, P. (2008). Chronic everyday life: Rhythmanalysing street performance. *Social and Cultural Geography*, *9*(7), 807–829.

Sin, H.L. (2009). Volunteer tourism – 'Involve me and I will learn'? *Annals of Tourism Research*, *36*(3), 480–501.

Skateboarder Danny Way to leap Great Wall. (2005, July 9). *Asia Times*. Retrieved January 15, 2007, from www.atimes.com/atimes/China/GG09Ad02.html

Skateboarders take to quake-hit streets on YouTube (2011). *The New Zealand Herald*, April 7. Retrieved April 12, 2011, from www.nzherald.co.nz/news/print.cfm?objectid=10717755

Skateistan Annual Report. (2012). Retrieved September 12, 2013, from http://skateistan.org/annual-report-2012

Skeggs, B. (1997). *Formations of Class and Gender*. London: Sage.

Skelton, T. & Valentine, G. (Eds.). (1998). *Cool places: Geographies of Youth Cultures*. London: Routledge.

Slack, J. D. (1996). The theory and method of articulation in cultural studies. In D. Morley & K.H. Chen (Eds.), *Stuart Hall: Critical Dialogues in Cultural Studies*. London: Routledge, 112–127.

Slater, K. (2011). How I remember Andy. *The Inertia*, November 11. Retrieved from http://www.theinertia.com/surf/kelly-slater-remembers-andy-irons

Smart, B. (2007). Not playing around: Global capitalism, modern sport and consumer culture. *Global Networks, 7*(2), 113–134.

Smith, J., Chatfield, C. & Pagnucco, R. (1997). *Transnational Social Movements and Global Politics: Solidarity beyond the State.* New York: Syracuse University Press.

SnoDragon. (2011). Anyone live in Whistler? Retrieved August 13, 2013, from www. bcsportbikes.com/forum/archive/index.php/t-133375.html?s=d2a238d4941ae3dc4 8acf19bfa55c139

Snowboard shocker! Burton announces big layoffs. (2002). April 12. Retrieved July 12, 2006, from www.skipressworld.com/us/en/daily_news/2002/04/snowboard_ shocker_burton_announces_big_layoffs.html?cat=

Solomon, C. (2013). Has snowboarding lost its edge? *The New York Times,* January 16. Retrieved September 12, 2013, from http://travel.nytimes.com/2013/01/20/travel/ has-snowboarding-lost-its-edge.html?pagewanted=all

Song, F.W. (2010). Theorizing Web 2.0: A cultural perspective. *Information, Communication and Society, 13*(2), 249–275.

Sorcher, S. (2010). Palestinian parkour. *The New York Times.* Retrieved December 9, 2012, from www.nytimes. com/video/2010/10/13/world/middleeast/1248069141234/ palestinian-parkour.html

Spaaij, R. (2011). *Sport and Social Mobility.* New York: Routledge.

Stableford, D. (2005). Snow-mag renegades. *Folio Magazine: The Magazine for Magazine Management,* January 31. Retrieved July 20, 2006, from www.foliomag.com/ viewmedia.asp?prmMID=4469&prmID=249

Statement regarding Sarah Burke's halfpipe accident in Park City. (2012). *Canadian Freestyle Ski Association,* retrieved January 18, 2013, from http://freestyleski. com/2012/01/sarah-burkes-halfpipe-accident

Steger, M. (2008). *The Rise of the Global Imaginary: Political Ideologies from the French Revolution to the Global War on Terror.* Oxford: Oxford University Press.

Stoddart, M. (2010). Constructing masculinized sportscapes: Skiing, gender and nature in British Columbia, Canada. *International Review for the Sociology of Sport, 46*(1), 108–124.

Stoddart, M. (2012). *Making Meaning of Mountains: The Political Ecology of Skiing.* Vancouver: UBC Press.

Stoller, P. (1997). *Sensuous Scholarship.* Philadelphia: University of Pennsylvania Press.

Stranger, M. (2011). *Surfing Life: Surface, Substructure and the Commodification of the Sublime.* Farnham: Ashgate.

Sugden, J. (2006). Teaching and playing sport for conflict resolution and co-existence in Israel. *International Review for the Sociology of Sport, 41*(2), 221–240.

Sugden, J. (2008). Anyone for football for peace? The challenges of using sport in the service of co-existence in Israel. *Soccer & Society, 9*(3), 405–415.

Sugden, J. & Tomlinson, A. (1998). *FIFA and the Contest for World Football: Who Rules the People's Game?* Cambridge: Polity.

SurfAid Annual Report 2005/2006. (2006). *SurfAid International.* Retrieved from www. surfaidinternational.org/governance

SurfAid Annual Report. (2012). Retrieved September 12, 2013, from http://www. surfaidinternational.org/governance

Surfer remembers Andy Irons. (2010). *Surfer Magazine,* November 3. Retrieved from www.surfermag.com/features/surfer-remembers-andy-irons

Tarrow, S. (2005). *The New Transnational Activism.* Cambridge: Cambridge University Press.

Taylor, B., Demont-Heinrich, C., Broadfoot, K., Dodge, J. & Guowei, J. (2002). New media and the circuit of cyber-culture: Conceptualizing Napster. *Journal of Broadcasting and Electronic Media, 46*(4), 607–629.

Taylor, P. (2012). Deport bad Queenstown tourists. *Mountain Scene*, September 20. Retrieved August 8, 2013, from www.scene.co.nz/deport-bad-queenstown-tourists-/303286a1.page

The Aussies take over Whistler. (2009). February. Retrieved December 8, 2009, from http://tysonclarke.spaces.live.com/blog/cns!9EDF684300D9B683!318.entry?sa=122810826

The big Burton restructure. (2012). *YoBeat.com*. October 23. Retrieved May 2, 2013, from www.yobeat.com/2012/10/23/the-big-burton-restructure

The power of youth, passion and action sports: The X Games brand. (2013). Retrieved May 12, 2013, from www.bidxgames.com/the-x-games

Thomas, J. (2008). From people power to mass hysteria: Media and popular reactions to the death of Princess Diana. *International Journal of Cultural Studies, 11*(3), 362–376.

Thompson, J. (2006). Boys (and girls) from the white stuff. *The Independent*, February 5. Retrieved March 3, 2010, from http://license.icopyright.net/user/viewFreeUse.act?fuid=NzMxMTc1Nw%3D%3D

Thornton, P. (2011). Boosting the X factor in the X Games. *The New Zealand Herald*, May 28. Retrieved May 29, 2011, from www.nzherald.co.nz/sport/news/article.cfm?c_id=4&objectid=10728655

Thornton, S. (1996). *Club Cultures: Music, Media and Subcultural Capital*. London: Wesleyan University Press.

Thorpe, H. (2007). Gender and extreme sports. In D. Booth & H. Thorpe (Eds.), *Berkshire Encyclopedia of Extreme Sports*. Great Barrington: Berkshire, 103–111.

Thorpe, H. (2008a). Extreme sports in China. In F. Hong (Ed.) with D. Mackay & K. Christensen, *China Gold: China's Quest for Global Power and Olympic Glory*. Great Barrington: Berkshire.

Thorpe, H. (2008b). Foucault, technologies of self, and the media: Discourses of femininity in snowboarding culture. *Journal of Sport and Social Issues, 32*(2), 199–229.

Thorpe, H. (2009). Bourdieu, feminism and female physical culture: Gender reflexivity and the habitus-field complex. *Sociology of Sport Journal, 26*, 491–516.

Thorpe, H. (2010a). Bourdieu, gender reflexivity and physical culture: A case of masculinities in the snowboarding field. *Journal of Sport and Social Issues, 34*(2), 176–214.

Thorpe, H. (2010b). The politics of remembering: An interdisciplinary approach to physical cultural memory. *Sporting Traditions, 27*(2), 113–125.

Thorpe, H. (2011a). *Snowboarding Bodies in Theory and Practice*. Basingstoke: Palgrave Macmillan.

Thorpe, H. (2011b). 'Have board, will travel': Global physical youth cultures and transnational mobility. In J. Maguire and M. Falcous (Eds.), *Sport and Migration: Borders, Boundaries and Crossings*. London: Routledge, 112–126.

Thorpe, H. (2012a). 'Sex, drugs and snowboarding': (il)legitimate definitions of taste and lifestyle. *Leisure Studies, 31*(1), 33–51.

Thorpe, H. (2012b). *Snowboarding: The Ultimate Guide*. Santa Barbara: Greenwood.

Thorpe, H. (2013a). Natural disaster arrhythmia and action sports: The case of the Christchurch earthquake. *International Review for the Sociology of Sport*, DOI: 10.1177/1012690213485951

Thorpe, H. (2013b). Maximizing the potential of action sports. Report commissioned by the Commonwealth Secretariat for Sport and Development Meeting.

Thorpe, H. (2014). Death, mourning and cultural memory on the Internet: The virtual memorialization of fallen sports heroes. In G. Osmond and M. Phillips (Eds.), *Sport History in the Digital Age*. Chicago: University of Illinois Press.

Thorpe, H. & Ahmad, N. (2013). Youth, action sports and political agency in the Middle East: Lessons from a grassroots parkour group in Gaza. *International Review for the Sociology of Sport*. DOI: 10.1177/1012690213490521

Thorpe, H., Barbour, K. & Bruce, T. (2011). Wandering and wondering: Theory and representation in feminist physical cultural studies. *Sociology of Sport Journal*, 28(1), 106–134.

Thorpe, H. & Rinehart, R. (2010). Alternative sport and affect: Non-representational theory examined. *Sport in Society,* special issue: Consumption and representation of lifestyle sport, *13*(7&8), 1268–1291.

Thorpe, H. & Rinehart, R. (2012). Action sport NGOs in a neo-liberal context: The cases of Skateistan and Surf Aid International. *Journal of Sport and Social Issues*. DOI: 10.1177/0193723512455923

Thorpe, H. & Wheaton, B. (2011a). 'Generation X Games', action sports and the Olympic Movement: Understanding the cultural politics of incorporation. *Sociology*, *45*(5), 830–847.

Thorpe, H. & Wheaton, B. (2011b). The Olympic movement, action sports, and the search for generation Y. In J. Sugden & A. Tomlinson (Eds.), *Watching the Olympics: Politics, Power and Representation*. London: Routledge, 182–200.

Thorpe, H. & Wheaton, B. (2013). Dissecting action sports studies: Past, present and beyond. In D. Andrews & B. Carrington (Eds.), *A Companion to Sport*. Oxford: Blackwell, 341–358.

Thulemark, M. (2011). A new life in the mountains: Changing lifestyles among in-migrants to Wanaka, New Zealand. *Recreation and Society in Africa, Asia and Latin America*, *2*(1), 35–50.

Tobias, R. (2013). X Games VP Tori Stevens discusses global 'X'pansion, challenges and successes. *ESPN Front Row*, March 21. Retrieved May 9, 2013, from http://frontrow.espn.go.com/2013/03/x-games-vp-tori-stevens-discusses-global-xpansion-challenges-and-successes

Tolman, D. (2002). *Dilemmas of Desire: Teenage Girls Talk about Sexuality.* Cambridge, MA: Harvard University Press.

Tomlinson, J. (2007). *The Culture of Speed: The Coming of Immediacy*. London: Sage.

Tomlinson, A. & Young, C. (2006) *National Identity and Global Sports Events: Culture, Politics and Spectacle in the Olympics and the Football World Cup*. Albany: State University of New York Press.

Top 5 of the month (2013). Kingpin. Retrieved from http://kingpin.mpora.com/featured-content/top-5-of-the-month-march.html

Top online brands and sports websites. (2012). *Nielsen Wire*, April 26. Retrieved from http://blog.nielsen.com/nielsenwire/online_mobile/march-2012-top-us-online-brands

Track status. (2012 October). Christchurch City Council. Retrieved October 8 from www.ccc.govt.nz/cityleisure/gettingaround/cycling/trackstatus.aspx

Tuan, Y-F. (1974). *Topophilia: A Study of Environmental Perception and Values*. Englewood Cliffs: Prentice Hall.

Tuan, Y-F. (1979). *Landscapes of Fear*. Oxford: Blackwell.

Tumarkin, M. (2005). *Traumascapes: The Power and Fate of Places Transformed by Tragedy*. Melbourne: Melbourne University Press.

Turner. (2012). Get an adventure job as a surfing instructor. *Around the World in 80 Jobs*, November 3. Retrieved October 1, 2013, from www.aroundtheworldin80jobs.com/adventure-job-surfing-instructor

Turner, B.S. (2002). Cosmopolitanism virtue, globalization and patriotism. *Theory, Culture and Society*, *19*(1–2), 45–65.

Tuttle, B. (2013). Snowboarding may have reached its peak. *Time*, January 18. Retrieved September 12, 2013, from http://business.time.com/2013/01/18/snowboarding-may-have-reached-its-peak

Tweed, T. (1999). *Our Lady of Exile*. New York: Oxford University Press.

UNRWA (United Nations Relief and Works Agency for Palestine Refugees in the Near East). (2013) Gaza. Retrieved February 14, 2013, from www.unrwa.org/etemplate.php?id=6

Urry, J. (1990a). The consumption of tourism. *Sociology, 24*(1), 22–35.

Urry, J. (1990b). *The Tourist Gaze: Leisure and Travel in Contemporary Society*. London: Sage.

Urry, J. (1996). How societies remember the past. In S. Macdonald & G. Fyfe (Eds.), *Theorizing Museums*. Cambridge: Blackwell, 45–65.

Urry, J. (2000a). Mobile sociology. *British Journal of Sociology, 51*(1), 185–203.

Urry, J. (2000b). *Sociology Beyond Societies: Mobilities for the Twenty-First Century*. Routledge: London.

Urry, J. (2002). *The Tourist Gaze*. 2nd Edition. London: Sage.

Urry, J. (2003). *Global Complexity*. Cambridge: Polity Press.

Urry, J. (2007). *Mobilities*. Cambridge: Polity Press.

Urry, J. (2008). Foreword. In P. Burns & M. Novelli (Eds.), *Tourism and Mobilities: Local-Global Connections*. London: CABI, xiv–xv.

Urry, J. & Larsen, J. (2012). *The Tourist Gaze 3.0*. 3rd Edition. London: Sage.

Ussher, J. (2005). The meaning of sexual desire: Experiences of heterosexual and lesbian girls. *Feminism and Psychology, 15*(1), 27–32.

Valenti, M., Vinciguerra, M. G., Masedu, F., Tiberti, S. & Sconci, V. (2012). A before and after study on personality assessment in adolescents exposed to the 2009 earthquake in L'Aquila, Italy: Influence of sports practice. *British Medical Journal*, doi:10.1136/bmjopen-2012-000824

Vamplew, W. & Stoddart, B. (2008). *Sport in Australia: A Social History*. Cambridge: Cambridge University Press.

van Ingen, C. (2003). Geographies of gender, sexuality and race. *International Review for the Sociology of Sport, 38*(2), 201–216.

van Ingen, C. (2004). Therapeutic landscapes and the regulated body in the Toronto Front Runners. *Sociology of Sport Journal, 21*(3), 253–269.

Vanatta, M. (2013). Paddling in protest. January 4. Retrieved September 18, 2013, from http://xgames.espn.go.com/article/8797653/dave-rastovich-completes-paddle-mission-protect-new-zealand-seabed-mining

Variables: Protect Our Winters. (2008). *Transworld Snowboarding*, April, 62.

Vealey, K. (2011). Making dead bodies legible: Facebook's ghosts, public bodies and networked grief. *Journal of Communication, Culture and Technology*. Retrieved from http://gnovisjournal.org/2011/04/03/making-dead-bodies-legible

Vertovec, S. (1999). Conceiving and researching transnationalism. *Ethnic and Racial Studies, 22*(2), 447–462.

Vertovec, S. (2009). *Transnationalism*. London: Routledge.

Vertovec, S. & Cohen, R. (Eds.). (2003). *Conceiving Cosmopolitanism*. Oxford: Oxford University Press.

Vogt, J. (1976). Wandering: Youth and travel behavior. *Annals of Tourism Research, 4*(1), 25–41.

Waitt, G., Markwell, K. & Gorman-Murray, A. (2008). Challenging heteronormativity in tourism studies: Locating progress. *Progress in Human Geography, 32*(6), 781–800.

Wapner, P. (1995). Politics beyond the State: Environmental activism and world civic politics. *World Politics, 47*(3), 311–340.

Wark, M. (1999). *Celebrities, Culture and Cyberspace: The Light on the Hill of a Postmodern World*. Sydney: Pluto Press.

Wark, P. (2009). Skiing: Fun on the slopes or a risky business? *The Times*, March 19. Retrieved August 10, 2010, from http://women.timesonline.co.uk/tol/life_and_style/women/the_way_we_live/article5934246.ece

Watkins, J., Hjorth, L. & Koskinen, I. (2012). Wising up: Revising mobile media in an age of smartphones. *Continuum, 26*(5), 665–668.

Watson, H. & Kopachevsky, J. (1994). Interpretations of tourism as commodity. *Annals of Tourism Research, 21*(3), 643–660.

Wearing, S., Stevenson, D. & Young, T. (2010). *Tourist Cultures: Identity, Place and the Traveller*. London: Sage.

Weisberg, Z. (2011). For female surfers, challenges out of the water. *The New York Times*, March 26. Retrieved May 12, 2013, from www.nytimes.com/2011/03/27/sports/27surfing.html?pagewanted=all&_r=0

Wellman, B. & Gulia, M. (1999). Virtual communities as communities: New surfers don't ride alone. In M. Smith & P. Kollock (Eds.), *Communities in Cyberspace*. Routledge: London, 167–194.

Westcot, J. (2006). Onset. *New Zealand Snowboarding*, July/August, 18.

What is Transworld all about? (2008). *Transworld Business*, retrieved December 12, 2010, from www.transworldmediakit.com/2007GenMediaKitLR.pdf

What we do. (2011). Retrieved from http://skateistan.org/content/afghanistan

Wheaton, B. (2000). Just do it: Consumption, commitment, and identity in the windsurfing subculture. *Sociology of Sport Journal, 17*(3), 254–274.

Wheaton, B. (2002). Babes on the beach, women in the surf: Researching gender, power and difference in the windsurfing culture. In J. Sugden & A. Tomlinson (Eds.) *Power Games: A Critical Sociology of Sport*. London and New York: Routledge.

Wheaton, B. (2003a). Lifestyle sport magazines and the discourses of sporting masculinity. In B. Benwell (Ed.), *Masculinity and Men's Lifestyle Magazines*. Oxford: Blackwell Publishing, 193–221.

Wheaton, B. (2003b). Windsurfing: A subculture of commitment. In R. Rinehart & S. Sydnor (Eds.), *To the Extreme: Alternative Sports, Inside and Out*. Albany: State University of New York Press, 75–101.

Wheaton, B. (2004a). *Understanding Lifestyle Sports: Consumption, Identity and Difference*. Oxford: Routledge.

Wheaton, B. (2004b). Selling out? The globalization and commercialization of lifestyle sports. In L. Allison (Ed.), *The Global Politics of Sport: The Role of Global Institutions in Sport*. London: Routledge, 140–185.

Wheaton, B. (2007). Identity, politics, and the beach: Environmental activism in 'Surfers against Sewage'. *Leisure Studies, 26*(3), 279–302.

Wheaton, B. (2008). From the pavement to the beach: Politics and identity in surfing against sewage. In M. Atkinson & K. Young (Eds.), *Tribal Play: Subcultural Journeys through Sport*. Bingley: JAI, 113–134.

Wheaton, B. (2009). The cultural politics of lifestyle sport (re)visited: Beyond white male lifestyles. In J. Ormond & B. Wheaton (Eds.), *On the Edge: Leisure, Consumption and the Representation of Adventure Sport*. Eastbourne: Leisure Studies Association, 131–60.

Wheaton, B. (2010). Introducing the consumption and representation of lifestyle sports. *Sport in Society, 13*(7/8), 1057–1081.

Wheaton, B. (2013). *The Cultural Politics of Lifestyle Sports*. London: Routledge.

Wheaton, B. & Beal, B. (2003). 'Keeping it real': Sub-cultural media and discourses of authenticity in alternative sport. *International Review for the Sociology of Sport, 38*(2), 155–176.

Wheaton, B. & Tomlinson, A. (1998). The changing gender order in sport? The case of windsurfing subcultures. *Journal of Sport and Social Issues, 22*(3), 251–272.

Whistler2020. (2009). Retrieved July 9, 2012, from www.whistler2020.ca/whistler/site/genericPage.acds?instanceid=2986150&context=2985223

Whittle, R., Walker, M., Medd, W. & Mort, M. (2012). Flood of emotions: emotional work and long-term disaster recovery. *Emotion, Space and Society, 5*(1), 60–69.

Wilding, R. (2007). Transnational ethnographies and anthropological imaginings of migrancy. *Journal of Ethnic and Migration Studies, 33*(2), 331–348.

Wiles, J. (2005). Conceptualizing place in the care of older people: The contributions of geographical gerontology. *Journal of Clinical Nursing, 14*(s2), 100–108.

Wiles, J. (2008). Sense of home in a transnational social space: New Zealanders in London. *Global Networks, 8*(1), 116–137.

Wilken, R. (2011). Seen from a carriage: A rhythmanalytic study of train travel and mediation. In B. Fraser & S. Spalding (Eds.), *Trains, Culture and Mobility*. Lanham: Lexington Books, 91–113.

Williams, A. (2012). Skateboarding past a midlife crisis. *The New York Times*, May 9. Retrieved September 14, 2013, from www.nytimes.com/2012/05/10/fashion/skateboarding-past-a-midlife-crisis.html?pagewanted=all&_r=0

Williams, A. (Ed.). (1999). *Therapeutic Landscapes: The Dynamic between Place and Wellness*. New York: University Press of America.

Williams, J.P. & Copes, H. (2005). 'How edge are you?' Constructing authentic identities and subcultural boundaries in straightedge internet forums. *Symbolic Interaction, 28*(1), 67–89.

Williams, A.M. & Hall, C.M. (2000). Tourism and migration: New relationships between production and consumption. *Tourism Geographies, 2(1)*, 5–27.

Wilson, B. (2002). The 'anti-jock' movement: Reconsidering youth resistance, masculinity, and sport culture in the age of the Internet. *Sociology of Sport Journal, 19*(2), 206–233.

Wilson, B. (2007). New media, social movements, and global sports studies: A revolutionary moment and the sociology of sport. *Sociology of Sport Journal, 24*(4), 457–477.

Wilson, B. & Hayhurst, L. (2009). Digital activism: Neoliberalism, the internet, and sport for youth development. *Sociology of Sport Journal, 26*(1), 155–181.

Wilson, J., M. Fisher & K. Moore. (2009). The OE goes 'home': Cultural aspects of a working holiday experience. *Tourist Studies, 9*(3), 3–21.

Wilson, R. & Dissanayake, W. (1996). Introduction: Tracking the global/local. In R. Wilson & W. Dissanayake (Eds.), *Global/Local: Cultural Production and the Transnational Imaginary*. Durham: Duke University Press, 1–18.

Winter Games 2011. (2011). 100% Pure New Zealand Winter Games 2011, Games Report. Unpublished document received from Winter Games 2011 CEO Arthur Klap.

Winter, J. (1998). *Sites of Memory, Sites of Mourning: The Great War in European Cultural History*. Cambridge University Press.

Wixon, B. (2013). Think globally, skate locally. August 4. Retrieved September 20, 2013, from www.skatepark.org/park-development/management/2013/08/iasc-conference-2013

Woermann, N. (2012). On the slope is on the screen: Prosumption, social media practices, and scopic systems in the freeskiing subculture. *American Behavioral Scientist, 56*(4), 618–640.

World Congress of NGOs. (2007). Humanitarian award 2007: Surf Aid international. Retrieved from www.wango.org/congress2007/awards.aspx?p=4

World's largest skatepark opens in Shanghai, China. (2006). *Boardsport Source.* Retrieved June 12, 2013, from www.boardsportsource.com/#!/article/world-s-largest-skatepark-opens-in-shanghai-china

World ski and snowboard festival. (2013). Retrieved October 25, 2013, from www.wssf.com

Wright, B. (2012). Parkour: The art of obstacles. *Cairo West Magazine.* Retrieved January 12, 2013, from www.cairowestmag.com/?p=442

Yochim, E.C. (2010). *Skate Life: Re-imagining White Masculinity.* Ann Arbor: University of Michigan Press and Library.

Young, A. and Dallaire, C. (2008). Beware *#! Sk8 at your own risk: The discourses of young female skateboarders. In M. Atkinson & K. Young (Eds.), *Tribal Play: Subcultural Journeys through Sport.* Bingley: JAI, 235–254.

Yu, L. (2002). Extreme sports dazzle. *China Daily.* Retrieved January 18, 2011, from http://app1.chinadaily.com.cn/star/2002/0808/sp30-1.html

Index

Printed and bound in the United States of America